Adobe
InDesign CS6
Interactive

DIGITAL PUBLISHING FOR THE INTERNET & THE iPAD

Revealed

Adobe

InDesign CS6
Interactive

DIGITAL PUBLISHING FOR THE INTERNET & THE iPAD

Chris Botello

Dylan Dove

Revealed

DELMAR
CENGAGE Learning®

Australia • Brazil • Japan • Korea • Mexico • Singapore • Spain • United Kingdom • United States

DELMAR
CENGAGE Learning

Adobe InDesign CS6 Interactive: Digital Publishing for the Internet and the iPad
Chris Botello and Dylan Dove

Vice President, Career and Professional Editorial: Dave Garza

Director of Learning Solutions: Sandy Clark

Senior Acquisitions Editor: Jim Gish

Managing Editor: Larry Main

Product Managers: Meaghan Tomaso and Nicole Calisi

Editorial Assistant: Sarah Timm

Vice President Marketing, Career and Professional: Jennifer Baker

Executive Marketing Manager: Deborah S. Yarnell

Associate Marketing Manager: Erin DeAngelo

Senior Production Director: Wendy Troeger

Production Manager: Andrew Crouth

Senior Content Project Manager: Kathryn B. Kucharek

Developmental Editors: Sandra Kruse and Ann Fisher

Technical Editor: Tara Botelho

Director of Design: Bruce Bond

Cover Design: Riezebos Holzbaur/Tim Heraldo

Cover Photo: Riezebos Holzbaur/Andrei Pasternak

Text Designer: Liz Kingslein

Production House: Integra Software Services Pvt. Ltd.

Proofreader: Marj Hopper

Indexer: Alexandra Nickerson

Technology Project Manager: Jim Gilbert

For product information and technology assistance, contact us at **Cengage Learning Customer & Sales Support, 1-800-354-9706**

For permission to use material from this text or product, submit all requests online at **www.cengage.com/permissions**

Further permissions questions can be emailed to **permissionrequest@cengage.com**

Adobe® Photoshop®, Adobe® InDesign®, Adobe® Illustrator®, Adobe® Flash®, Adobe® Dreamweaver®, Adobe® Fireworks®, and Adobe® Creative Suite® are trademarks or registered trademarks of Adobe Systems, Inc. in the United States and/or other countries. Third party products, services, company names, logos, design, titles, words, or phrases within these materials may be trademarks of their respective owners.

Adobe product screenshot(s) reprinted with permission from Adobe Systems Incorporated.

The Adobe Approved Certification Courseware logo is a proprietary trademark of Adobe. All rights reserved. Cengage Learning and Adobe InDesign CS6 Interactive: Digital Publishing for the Internet and the iPad are independent from ProCert Labs, LLC and Adobe Systems Incorporated, and are not affiliated with ProCert Labs and Adobe in any manner. This publication may asssist students to prepare for an Adobe Certified Expert exam, however, neither ProCert Labs nor Adobe warrant that use of this material will ensure success in connection with any exam.

Library of Congress Control Number: 2011945480

ISBN-13: 978-1-133-69326-0
ISBN-10: 1-133-69326-1

Delmar
5 Maxwell Drive
Clifton Park, NY 12065-2919
USA

Cengage Learning is a leading provider of customized learning solutions with office locations around the globe, including Singapore, the United Kingdom, Australia, Mexico, Brazil, and Japan. Locate your local office at: **international.cengage.com/region**

Cengage Learning products are represented in Canada by Nelson Education, Ltd.

To learn more about Delmar, visit **www.cengage.com/delmar**

Purchase any of our products at your local college store or at our preferred online store **www.cengagebrain.com**

Notice to the Reader
Publisher does not warrant or guarantee any of the products described herein or perform any independent analysis in connection with any of the product information contained herein. Publisher does not assume, and expressly disclaims, any obligation to obtain and include information other than that provided to it by the manufacturer. The reader is expressly warned to consider and adopt all safety precautions that might be indicated by the activities described herein and to avoid all potential hazards. By following the instructions contained herein, the reader willingly assumes all risks in connection with such instructions. The publisher makes no representations or warranties of any kind, including but not limited to, the warranties of fitness for particular purpose or merchantability, nor are any such representations implied with respect to the material set forth herein, and the publisher takes no responsibility with respect to such material. The publisher shall not be liable for any special, consequential, or exemplary damages resulting, in whole or part, from the readers' use of, or reliance upon, this material.

Printed in the United States of America
1 2 3 4 5 6 7 16 15 14 13 12

Revealed Series Vision

The Revealed Series is your guide to today's hottest multimedia applications. For years, the Revealed Series has kept pace with the dynamic demands of the multimedia community, and continues to do so with the publication of 13 new titles covering the latest Adobe Creative Suite products. Each comprehensive book teaches not only the technical skills required for success in today's competitive multimedia market, but the design skills as well. From animation, to web design, to digital image-editing and interactive media skills, the Revealed Series has you covered.

We recognize the unique learning environment of the multimedia classroom, and we deliver textbooks that include:

- Comprehensive step-by-step instructions.
- In-depth explanations of the "Why" behind a skill.
- Creative projects for additional practice.
- Full-color visuals for a clear explanation of concepts.
- Comprehensive online material offering additional instruction and skills practice.

- Video tutorials for skills reinforcement as well as the presentation of additional features.
- NEW icons to highlight features that are new since the previous release of the software.

With the Revealed series, we've created books that speak directly to the multimedia and design community—one of the most rapidly growing computer fields today.

—The Revealed Series

CourseMate

Adobe InDesign CS6 Interactive: Digital Publishing for the Internet and the iPad includes a CourseMate, which helps you make the grade!

This CourseMate includes:

- An interactive eBook, with highlighting, note taking, and search capabilities
- Interactive learning tools including:
  - Chapter quizzes
  - Flashcards
  - Instructional video lessons from Total Training, the leading provider of video instruction for Adobe software. These video lessons are tightly integrated with the book, chapter by chapter and include assessment.
  - And more!

Go to login.cengagebrain.com to access these resources.

AUTHORS' VISION

A new publishing paradigm is upon us. It was a one-day revolution: when the first iPad was released, everything changed.

It's not going to take years for it to work; it already works. It's not going to take years for people to adopt it; they already have.

Tablet publishing is the Internet 2.0; it's a move away from the website as the sole venue; it's a move away from the personal computer as the sole device.

For the graphic designer, a new world has opened up, and InDesign is at its center. The same layout that you printed conventionally can now be uploaded to the web or published to the world on the iPad. All from InDesign. No coding. No scripting.

If you know how to use InDesign, congratulations. Your universe has expanded—big time.

If you teach InDesign, tell the administration you have a new class ready to go; you're now the iPad pro.

First and foremost, we want to thank the team at Cengage Learning: Senior Acquisitions Editor Jim Gish, thank you for believing in this book and backing it from concept to the day it was delivered. Thank you to Product Managers Meaghan Tomaso and Nicole Calisi for always being way out front and pulling the book through. Thank you to Editorial Assistant Sarah Timm for always being the can-do voice on the other end of the phone. Thank you to Copyeditor Marjorie Hopper and Technical Editor Tara Botelho for catching the subtle tricksters that snuck past both authors. Many thanks to Development Editors Sandy Kruse and Ann Fisher—Sandy for brainstorming the original idea with us two years ago, and Ann, as always, for the clear-eyed vision.

Thank you to the one-of-a-kind team at Tabor Academy. Thank you Jay Stroud and Andrew McCain for making the Tabor Academy components of the book available to us and for trusting us to get it done right. Thank you Taylor Washburn for patience and insight. Thank you Chris Cunningham and the student photo pool team for the incredible photography, without which, the book would be a mere shadow of itself.

Finally, to friends and family, as always.

—Chris Botello and Dylan Dove, June, 2012

Adobe InDesign CS6 Interactive: Digital Publishing for the Internet and the iPad

Welcome to *Adobe InDesign CS6 Interactive: Digital Publishing for the Internet and the iPad*. This book is an exploration of InDesign as an interactive software application, helping you to create websites, interactive forms and documents, and publications for the iPad and other tablet devices, all within InDesign.

This text is organized into eight chapters. The first three chapters focus on using InDesign to create beautifully designed and highly functional websites complete with hyperlinks, interactive buttons, video, and animation.

In Chapter 4, Creating a Website from an InDesign Layout, we give you step-by-step instructions for creating a website on GoDaddy.com and uploading your InDesign layout. You'll learn everything you need to know: how to register a domain name, what level of hosting service you need, how to set up your email, and how to make your site go live. When you're done with Chapter 4, you'll have your very own live website online.

Chapter 5, Creating Interactive Forms, gives you an in-depth exploration of creating interactive forms. Create a form in InDesign, then use text fields, check boxes, and radio buttons to make the form interactive. You can post the form online on a website or email it to your friends or clients for their input. Interactive forms open the door to a whole new level of communication and productivity through InDesign.

In Chapter 6, Publishing to the iPad, and Chapter 7, Creating Complex Interactivity in an iPad Presentation, you'll charge forward into the new frontier of tablet publishing on devices like the iPad and the Droid. Leverage all of your design and layout skills in InDesign and complement them with already-classic iPad interactivity like page rotation, finger swiping, scrollable text, slideshows, and interactive buttons. Sooner than you think, you'll be looking at your InDesign layout on your iPad!

In Chapter 8, Creating an App and Publishing It to the iPad, we take it to the limit and show you everything you need to know to create your very own app on Apple's App Store and publish your documents to the world. We don't just say you can do it, we show you how.

Image courtesy of Tabor Academy. Source Adobe® InDesign®, 2013.

What You'll Do

A What You'll Do figure begins every lesson. This figure gives you an at-a-glance look at what you'll do in the chapter, either by showing you a page or pages from the current project or a tool you'll be using.

Comprehensive Conceptual Lessons

Before jumping into instructions, in-depth conceptual information gives you a complete overview of what you'll be doing in the lessons. You'll understand the concepts that the lessons are based on and get specific information on how a given feature is set up and how it works.

Step-by-Step Instructions

This book combines conceptual information with concise steps to help you learn the interactive features of InDesign CS6. Each set of steps guides you through a lesson where you will create, modify, or enhance an InDesign CS6 file. Step references to large colorful images and quick step summaries round out the lessons. The Data Files for the steps are provided online at www.cengagebrain.com. For detailed instructions to access these files, please see page IX.

Images courtesy of Tabor Academy. Source Adobe® InDesign®, 2013.

Projects

When it's appropriate for a given chapter, this book contains a variety of end-of-chapter materials for additional practice and reinforcement. The Skills Review contains hands-on practice exercises that mirror the progressive nature of the lesson material. Project Builders and Design Projects ask you to apply the skills you've learned in the chapter to new challenges.

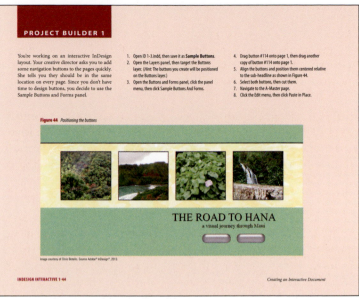

Images courtesy of Tabor Academy. Source Adobe® InDesign®, 2013.

What Instructor Resources Are Available with This Book?

The Instructor Resources are Delmar's way of putting the resources and information needed to teach and learn effectively into your hands. All the resources are available for both Macintosh and Windows operating systems. These resources can be found online at: **http://login.cengage.com**. Once you login or create an account, search for the title under 'My Dashboard' using the ISBN. Then select the instructor companion site resources and click 'Add to my Bookshelf.'

Instructor's Manual

The Instructor's Manual includes chapter overviews and detailed lecture topics for each chapter, with teaching tips.

Sample Syllabus

The Sample Syllabus includes a suggested syllabus for any course that uses this book.

PowerPoint Presentations

Each chapter has a corresponding PowerPoint presentation that you can use in lectures, distribute to your students, or customize to suit your course.

Data Files for Students

To complete most of the chapters in this book, your students will need Data Files which are available online. Instruct students to use the Data Files List at the end of this book. This list gives instructions on organizing files.

To access the Data Files for this book, take the following steps:

1. Open your browser and go to http://www.cengagebrain.com
2. Type the author, title, or ISBN of this book in the Search window. (The ISBN is listed on the back cover.)
3. Click the book title in the list of search results.
4. When the book's main page is displayed, click the Access button under Free Study Tools.
5. To download Data files, select a chapter number and then click on the Data Files tab on the left navigation bar to download the files.
6. To access additional materials, click the additional materials tab under Book Resources to download the files.

Solutions to Exercises

Solution Files are Data Files completed with comprehensive sample answers. Use these files to evaluate your students' work. Or distribute them electronically so students can verify their work. Sample solutions to lessons and end-of-chapter material are provided with the exception of some portfolio projects.

Test Bank and Test Engine

ExamView is a powerful testing software package that allows instructors to create and administer printed and computer (LAN-based) exams. ExamView includes hundreds of questions that correspond to the topics covered in this text, enabling students to generate detailed study guides that include page references for further review. The computer-based and LAN-based/online testing component allows students to take exams using the EV Player, and also saves the instructor time by grading each exam automatically.

BRIEF CONTENTS

Chapter 1   **Creating an Interactive Document**

Lesson 1   Explore Interactive Documents   1-4

2   Set Up An Interactive Document   1-8

3   Incorporate Hyperlinks and Buttons   1-14

4   Apply and View Page Transitions   1-30

Chapter 2   **Adding Animation to a Presentation**

Lesson 1   Apply Animation   2-4

2   Preview Animation   2-12

3   Use the Timing Panel to Control Animation   2-14

4   Use a Button to Trigger Animation   2-18

Chapter 3   **Working with Object States and Video**

Lesson 1   Work with Object States   3-4

2   Place Video in a Layout   3-12

3   Use Buttons as Video Controls   3-20

4   Control Video with Navigation Points   3-24

Chapter 4   **Creating a Website from an InDesign Layout**

Lesson 1   Register a Domain Name   4-4

2   Purchase Website Hosting   4-12

3   Upload an InDesign Layout to the Web   4-22

Chapter 5   **Creating Interactive Forms**

Lesson 1   Explore Strategies for Designing an Interactive Form   5-4

2   Create Text Input Fields   5-12

3   Create a Pull-Down List   5-18

4   Create Check Boxes and Radio Buttons   5-20

5   Create a Submit Form Button   5-30

6   Enter Information into an Interactive Form   5-34

Chapter 6   **Publishing to the iPad**

Lesson 1   Install Software for Working with the iPad   6-4

2   Set Up a Document for Upload to the iPad   6-12

3   Use Folio Overlays   6-18

4   Upload to the iPad with the Folio Builder   6-26

Chapter 7   **Creating Complex Interactivity in an iPad Presentation**

Lesson 1   Rotate Page Orientation on an iPad   7-4

2   Pan and Zoom Images   7-14

3   Use Object States for iPad Interactivity   7-18

4   Create a Scrollable Text Frame   7-24

5   Add an Image Sequence   7-32

6   Incorporate Web Content   7-36

Chapter 8   **Creating an App and Publishing to the ipad**

Lesson 1   Explore Apps and iPad Publishing   8-4

2   Explore the Digital Publishing Suite   8-8

3   Making the Leap from InDesign to the App Store   8-22

4   Submitting your App to the App Store   8-34

Data Files List   1

Glossary   8

Index   11

CONTENTS

CHAPTER 1: CREATING AN INTERACTIVE DOCUMENT

INTRODUCTION 1-2

LESSON 1
Explore Interactive Documents 1-4

Defining an Interactive InDesign Document 1-4
Identifying Destinations for an Interactive InDesign
    Document 1-5
Understanding the Relationship Between InDesign and
    Flash 1-5
Exporting InDesign Documents to Adobe Flash 1-6
Exporting a "Presentation-Ready" Interactive Document 1-6

LESSON 2
Set Up An Interactive Document 1-8

Creating an Interactive Document 1-8
Repurposing a Traditional Document as an Interactive
    Document 1-10
Tasks   Create a new interactive document for the Web 1-12
        Repurpose a print document as an interactive
            document 1-13

LESSON 3
Incorporate Hyperlinks and Buttons 1-14

Working with Hyperlinks 1-14
Creating Buttons 1-15
Changing Button Appearances for Rollover and Clicking 1-16
Adding Actions to Buttons 1-18
Using the Sample Buttons and Forms panel 1-20
Assigning a Sound to a Button 1-21
Tasks   Create hyperlinks between pages
            in a document 1-22
        Create a hyperlink to a web page 1-23
        Convert artwork to buttons 1-24
        Modify button appearances 1-25
        Apply actions to buttons 1-26
        Apply sounds to buttons 1-28

LESSON 4
Apply and View Page Transitions 1-30

Applying Page Transitions 1-30
Exporting an SWF File 1-31
Tasks   Add page transitions 1-34
        Export an SWF file 1-35
        Test interactive settings in an SWF file 1-37
        Remove page transitions and apply a page transition
            to all pages in a document 1-39

CHAPTER 2:   ADDING ANIMATION TO A PRESENTATION

INTRODUCTION 2-2

LESSON 1
Apply Animation 2-4

Using the Animation Panel 2-4
Tasks   Apply Fly-in animations 2-6
Apply a Fade animation 2-8
Apply a Shrink animation 2-9
Apply an Appear animation 2-11

LESSON 2
Preview Animation 2-12

Previewing Animations 2-12
Tasks   Use the SWF Preview panel 2-13

LESSON 3
Use the Timing Panel to Control Animation 2-14

Using the Timing Panel 2-14
Tasks   Use the Timing panel 2-16
Export an animated document as an SWF 2-17

LESSON 4
Use a Button to Trigger Animation 2-18

Using Buttons to Play Animations 2-18
Tasks   Use a button to trigger an animation 2-19

CHAPTER 3:   WORKING WITH OBJECT STATES AND VIDEO

INTRODUCTION 3-2

LESSON 1
Work with Object States 3-4

Understanding Object States 3-4
Assigning Buttons to Object States 3-4
Tasks   Create object states 3-7
Assign buttons to object states 3-10

LESSON 2
Place Video in a Layout 3-12

Placing Video Files 3-12
Choosing the Poster Image 3-13
Adding Preset Controls to a Placed Video 3-14
Saving Video for Use in InDesign 3-15
Tasks   Place a video file 3-16
Specify the poster image 3-17
Add a preset controller to a video 3-18

LESSON 3
Use Buttons as Video Controls 3-20

Using Buttons to Control a Video 3-20
Tasks   Use buttons as video controls 3-22

LESSON 4
Control Video with Navigation Points 3-24

Using Navigation Points to Play Video from a Specific
Frame 3-24
Tasks   Create navigation points 3-27
Link a button to a navigation point 3-28

CHAPTER 4: CREATING A WEBSITE FROM AN INDESIGN LAYOUT

INTRODUCTION 4-2

LESSON 1
Register a Domain Name 4-4

Registering a Domain Name 4-4
Receiving Email Through your Website 4-5
Creating a Website Using this Book 4-5
Tasks   Register a domain name 4-7

LESSON 2
Purchase Website Hosting 4-12

Purchasing Web Hosting 4-12
Setting up Your Web Hosting Account 4-13
Tasks   Purchase website hosting 4-14
            Set up website email 4-17
            Set up website hosting 4-20

LESSON 3
Upload an InDesign Layout to the Web 4-22

Packaging an InDesign Document for Upload to the Web 4-22
Uploading an exported InDesign document to your website 4-22
Uploading Video and Sound Files 4-23
Tasks   Package and export an InDesign layout for upload 4-25
            Upload an exported InDesign layout 4-28
            Create a directory and upload video and sound files 4-30
            View the live website 4-31

CHAPTER 5: CREATING INTERACTIVE FORMS

INTRODUCTION 5-2

LESSON 1
Explore Strategies for Designing an Interactive Form 5-4

Designing an Interactive Document 5-4
Tasks   Explore a layout for an interactive document 5-8

LESSON 2
Create Text Input Fields 5-12

Creating Interactive Fields for Forms 5-12
Tasks   Create text input fields 5-14

LESSON 3
Create a Pull-Down List 5-18

Formatting a Pull-down List 5-18
Tasks   Formatting a field as a pull-down list 5-19

LESSON 4
Create Check Boxes and Radio Buttons 5-20

Using Check Boxes and Radio Buttons 5-20
Using One Button to Trigger Another 5-21
Tasks   Formatting a field as a check box 5-22
            Create radio buttons 5-23
            Use radio buttons as triggers 5-24

LESSON 5
Create a Submit Form Button 5-30

Creating a Submit Form Button 5-30
Tasks   Create a button to submit a form to an email address 5-33

LESSON 6
Enter Information into an Interactive Form 5-34

Exporting an Interactive PDF 5-34
Tasks   Set the tab order for an interactive form 5-36
            Enter data into an exported form 5-37
            Submit a form 5-42

CHAPTER 6: PUBLISHING TO THE IPAD

INTRODUCTION 6-2

LESSON 1
Install Software for Working with the iPad 6-4

Working with the Adobe Content Viewer iPad App 6-4
Downloading and Installing Digital Publishing Suite Desktop
   Tools 6-5
Tasks   Create an Adobe account on Adobe.com 6-6
           Install the Adobe Viewer app on an iPad 6-7
           Download DPS Desktop Tools CS6 6-9

LESSON 2
Set Up a Document for Upload to the iPad 6-12

Creating an InDesign Document for the iPad 6-12
Creating Articles 6-12
Tasks   View a document setup for upload to the iPad 6-14
           Save pages as articles for the iPad 6-16

LESSON 3
Use Folio Overlays 6-18

Placing Sound and Video Files for an iPad Presentation 6-18
Using the Overlays Panel to Play Audio and Video Files 6-18
Tasks   Set up a sound file in the Folio Overlays panel 6-22
           Set up video files in the Folio Overlays panel 6-24

LESSON 4
Upload to the iPad with the Folio Builder 6-26

About Folio Builder 6-26
Creating a New Folio 6-26
Adding Articles to a Folio 6-27
Naming the iPad Publication and Creating a Thumbnail 6-30
Tasks   Create a new folio in Folio Builder 6-31
           Name and create a cover for an iPad
              publication 6-32
           Add articles to a folio in the Folio Builder panel 6-32
           Preview contents in the Folio Builder panel 6-34
           View a folio on the iPad 6-37

CHAPTER 7: CREATING COMPLEX INTERACTIVITY IN AN IPAD PRESENTATION

INTRODUCTION 7-2

LESSON 1
Rotate Page Orientation on an iPad 7-4

Creating Alternate Layouts 7-4
Rotating a Layout on the iPad 7-6
Tasks   Create an alternate layout in a single document 7-7
           Create a folio that will change orientation on the
              iPad 7-10

LESSON 2
Pan and Zoom Images 7-14

Specifying Images to Pan and Zoom on the iPad 7-14
Tasks   Specify images to pan and zoom on the iPad 7-16

LESSON 3
Use Object States for iPad Interactivity 7-18

Creating Interactivity with Object States 7-18
Tasks   Work with interactive buttons 7-19
           Create a slideshow using object states 7-21

LESSON 4
Create a Scrollable Text Frame 7-24

Creating a Scrollable Frame 7-24
Tasks   Create a text file in Photoshop 7-26
           Create a scrollable text frame for the iPad 7-29

LESSON 5
Add an Image Sequence 7-32

Creating an Image Sequence 7-32
Tasks   Create an image sequence 7-34

LESSON 6
Incorporate Web Content 7-36

Using the Web Content Option on the Folio Overlays
   Panel 7-36
Tasks   Use the Web Content option on the Folio Overlays
              panel 7-37

INTRODUCTION 8-2

LESSON 1
Explore Apps And iPad Publishing 8-4

Defining Apps 8-4
About Apps and Publishing 8-5
iPad Publishing and the Individual 8-7

LESSON 2
Explore the Digital Publishing Suite 8-8

About the Digital Publishing Suite 8-8
Subscribing to Digital Publishing Suite 8-10
Purchasing a Subscription to the Digital Publishing
    Suite 8-12
Registering with Apple as an iOS Developer 8-14
Purchasing an Apple iOS Developer License 8-16
Obtaining Your iOS Development Certificate and
    Downloading Provisioning Documentation 8-20

LESSON 3
**Making the Leap from Indesign to the App
Store** 8-22

Exporting a Folio 8-22
Using the Viewer Builder Module 8-26
Testing the App 8-31

LESSON 4
Submitting Your App to the App Store 8-34

Downloading Your App from Viewer Builder 8-34
Uploading Your App to the App Store 8-36

DATA FILES 1

GLOSSARY 8

INDEX 11

How This Book Was Created

Chris Botello is the author of three other Revealed titles: *InDesign Revealed, Advanced Photoshop Revealed*, and *Illustrator Revealed*. Chris is also a professional graphic designer and has used InDesign, Photoshop, and Illustrator for years. Presently, Chris is the chair of the Media Arts department at Tabor Academy, a private high school on Cape Cod in Massachusetts, where he teaches classes in Photoshop and InDesign.

Dylan Dove is a junior at Tabor Academy with a strong interest in HTML coding and web programming. Chris and Dylan met when Dylan enrolled in Chris' InDesign class. The iPad was about a year old, and Adobe was repositioning InDesign as an interactive product able to publish to both the web and to the iPad. Many conversations happened spontaneously, and the idea of writing this book took shape.

About InDesign Websites

Think of everything you can do in InDesign, and then consider that the layout you create can be exported and uploaded as a website. If you compare InDesign as a web page layout tool with a standard HTML layout, InDesign changes the very idea of what a website can look like. All of InDesign's rich design and special effects capabilities can be leveraged to create a visually interesting and complex

web page. Figures 2 and 3 on this page and the next, for example, are both layouts for a website, both interactive, both easily uploadable and user friendly, and both unlike most any website you usually see.

InDesign websites are totally legit. You can use InDesign to create a complex and dependably functional website, complete with hyperlinks, buttons, rollover animation, button triggers, object animation, page transitions, and video.

Anyone seeking to create a personal or a family website or any small business seeking to put its presence online will find InDesign entirely satisfactory as a web page layout application. InDesign websites are easy to upload and easy to edit. You can't tell the difference between an InDesign website and one created in standard HTML, except that

the InDesign site usually is more visually interesting from a graphic design perspective.

If you want a more complex website, an InDesign site might not be the best choice. For example, if you want a site that is itself a business, one that shows and catalogues products, with a shopping cart and a credit card payment capability, that's a site you will want to have designed by a professional, and that professional will likely use the now standard combination of HTML, Flash, and Dreamweaver, not InDesign.

Using InDesign as the sole application to create a website is not yet standard, but it might be someday soon. Being able to use a layout program to create a multi-page website quickly and easily without having to code is revolutionary, a breaking-down of the barriers

Image courtesy of Chris Botello. Source Adobe® InDesign®, 2013.

to the Internet. With InDesign's interactive capabilities, more graphic designers can now also be web page designers, and InDesign may soon become the default software package to make it happen.

About InDesign Websites and the iPad

InDesign websites are Flash-based; they are exported from InDesign in the .swf format, which is Shockwave Flash. Any standard web browser like Internet Explorer, Firefox, or Safari will open SWF, but because the iPad doesn't support Flash, an InDesign website won't open on the iPad. For the same reason, InDesign animation from the Animation panel won't work on the iPad; nor will page transition animations. On the other hand, InDesign buttons, button triggers, hyperlinks, and object states all work in an iPad presentation.

About Interactive Forms

Interactive forms are an important and very practical component of InDesign's interactivity, and with the CS6 release, Adobe has upgraded InDesign's capability. In the previous paradigm, you would create only the layout for the form in InDesign, and you would then export the layout to Acrobat, where you would create the interactive functionality for the fields.

With InDesign CS6, both functions happen in InDesign. You can create text fields, check boxes, combo boxes, and radio buttons in InDesign, and you can apply actions to them—actions like printing or submitting a form.

Context needs to be considered when submitting the interactive form created in the lessons in this book. Using InDesign, you could post an interactive form to a website where users could enter information and click Submit. Similarly, you could email an interactive form to users, they could fill it out, then press Submit, and the data would be emailed to a URL where it could be collected in a database. However, both scenarios would require you to create code and set up a database to collect the data online.

Our goal in writing this book was to provide the graphic designer with interactive options that don't require coding, so our lessons in Chapter 5, Creating Interactive Forms, don't get into posting interactive forms on websites or submitting data to URLs. Instead, we offer lessons for the very practical option of emailing an interactive form as an attached PDF and having the filled-out form returned as an attached PDF. It's entirely digital—nothing gets printed out—but there's no coding and no database creation required.

About Publishing to the iPad

InDesign CS6 will publish to a number of tablet devices, most notably the Motorola Droid and the Apple iPad. The authors are

Photo illustration by Chris Botello. Source Adobe® InDesign®, 2013.

most excited about the iPad and, since Apple has always been the hardware of choice for professional graphic designers, we've focused more on the iPad than any other tablet.

Teachers will want to be clear about two levels, for lack of a better term, for publishing to the iPad. The free and built-in option involves using the Adobe Content Viewer app, which is downloadable from the Apple iPad App Store. In this paradigm, you upload layouts to your free Adobe account, then view the layouts through the Adobe Content Viewer app. The layout really isn't "published;" nobody can see it on the iPad except you. But it's a great way to preview what your work will look like on the iPad, a great way to show your friends and colleagues your work on the iPad, and a great way to practice and hone your design skills for the iPad.

The next level for publishing to the iPad involves purchasing an app on the iPad App Store then publishing your documents to that app. In this paradigm, your app is available for download by anyone who visits the App Store, and your documents are available to them in your app.

This is the debut of the methodology for publishing InDesign documents to the iPad, and the process will evolve and change. For example, the low-cost option for App publishing, which is $395 as we go to press,

has been rumored by Adobe to soon be free with a subscription to Adobe's Creative Cloud.

About Objective-C

The idea of using InDesign to publish to the iPad is relatively new (first released in InDesign CS 5.5). Most Apple iPad developers create apps in an object-oriented language called Objective-C, which is more than 20 years old and is an offshoot of the C programming language.

You're using InDesign to create a publication. And by putting your publication on the iPad, you're using the iPad differently than an Objective-C programmer tends to use it. With Objective-C apps, you're using the functionality of the iPad as a game, or as a clock, or as a grocery list, or as a music player. With InDesign, you're using the iPad as a reading device. InDesign is a well-established program for creating reading materials, and so the fact that it interfaces with the iPad, which itself was created to function as a presenter of reading materials, is logical, expected, and even classic.

About Paid Services in This Book

From the very first day, we established one single rule that we wouldn't budge on: we were going all the way. We feel that most

books on websites lead you only so far, then they drop the ball. They show you how to get started, and even how to get to the point of uploading a site, but then they say, "See ya. Good luck."

That's not what we wanted. We decided that if we were going to show you how to export a layout from InDesign that could be uploaded to the web, then we would have to actually show you how to upload it to the web. We'd have to show you how to purchase a domain name, show you how to purchase web hosting, show you how to upload your files. For us, there was no choice but to end our web section with our readers having a website live and online.

With that in mind, if you follow all the steps in Chapter 4, Creating a Website from an InDesign Layout, you'll actually purchase those services. The cost is not too expensive, under $100 to create a site and keep it live for a year. This may or may not be what you want to do today, but that's not a problem. The idea of Chapter 4 is that it's there if you want it and there if you need it.

If you don't want to actually purchase the services necessary to complete the chapter, you can step through as far as you can, then not purchase when it comes time to. If you're a teacher, you can be the demonstrator and perhaps be the only person in the class who steps through everything and purchases everything while your students watch and learn.

The same holds true for Chapter 8, Creating an App and Publishing it to the iPad, which concludes the book. For us, ending the book without showing the way to actually purchase app creation and publish to the App store would have been falling short of the goal.

You may or may not want to purchase the $395 single-edition publishing contract with Adobe or the $100 developer license with Apple. If you don't, no loss. It's free to read the whole chapter and learn how the process works for when you're ready to take the big leap.

About Chapter 8

In many ways, Chapter 8 is written as much for the instructor as it is for the student. InDesign CS6 is a revolutionary upgrade in terms of how it interfaces with the new Digital Publishing Suite to produce apps for the App Store. The process of doing so is essentially brand new; it's fairly complex and has many steps.

We decided to present this information in its own chapter as narrative with associated figures for illustration. We intentionally chose not to use a step-by-step approach: the cost of producing an app (approximately $500), the complexity of the process, and the near-certainty that the process will evolve and change sooner rather than later made the idea of presenting steps to achieve a certain outcome impractical. In addition, there are no testbanks or quizzes for Chapter 8.

Instead, we wrote the chapter to give instructors and students a full overview of how to go from a folio in the Folio Builder panel in InDesign to the App Store. The chapter is meant to be read more than it is meant to be followed or stepped-through. We feel that it is critical that any instructor using this text reads Chapter 8 thoroughly. Understanding the end-game of the DPS process is empowering and essential for understanding the context of folios, overlays and the Folio Builder panel in InDesign.

Chapter 8 offers readers a view of the authors' journey in publishing an app based on the exercises in this book. On many occasions we mention that, if you're doing this for real, utilize Adobe's Digital Publishing Suite tech support team. This is especially true for the Apple Developer certificates necessary to produce an app. These are the Apple components the DPS requires to finalize an app. Because you're doing this through Adobe's DPS, it's the DPS tech support team—not Apple—that you must rely upon to inform and support you through the process. They will, in fact, help you download and process the documentation you need from Apple.

Certification

For more information on ACE Certification for Adobe InDesign Interactive CS6 Revealed please visit www.cengagebrain.com.

CHAPTER 1

CREATING AN
INTERACTIVE DOCUMENT

1. Explore interactive documents
2. Set up an interactive document
3. Incorporate hyperlinks and buttons
4. Apply and view page transitions

1

CREATING AN
INTERACTIVE DOCUMENT

When computers were first invented, the only people who could use them were programmers. To work with a computer, you needed to know how to enter code and how to read code. Then, in the early 1980s, Steve Jobs and Steve Wozniak introduced the Apple computer.

With that one device, computing was made available to the masses. People who didn't know how to code could instead use menus and icons to interface with a computer. The coding was still happening in the background, but the concept of the "front-end user interface" made the computer a personal device.

By 2000, Adobe InDesign was emerging as the preeminent software package for print layout. But the Internet was the great new frontier in layout, and in order to create layouts for a website, you needed to know how to code in HTML. A whole generation of layout designers found itself shut out of this new medium: unless you could write HTML code, you really couldn't make layouts for the web. And many designers didn't want to be coders or programmers—they wanted to be designers.

Since those early days, programs like Dreamweaver and Flash became something of a bridge between traditional designers and the web, but the web ultimately remained the province of HTML and ActionScript coders, Java programmers, and other technicians skilled with computer languages.

InDesign CS6 represents a sea of change for traditional designers. The changes began in CS5, but with CS6 Adobe has redefined InDesign as a layout program for print, the web, and tablet devices like the iPad. With this release, Adobe makes it possible for designers to leverage all of the skills that were once reserved only for print and apply them to creating websites and publications for the iPad.

In addition to all the features that InDesign provides for print—imagery, illustration, and beautiful typography—CS6 offers buttons, hyperlinks, animation, object states, and video, all of which can be exported to the web or to the iPad.

This is truly a revolutionary release, because it puts the whole web and the whole new iPad universe into the hands of traditional designers—no coding, no scripting. A designer can quite literally use the same layout as a print document, as an interactive website, and as a publication on the iPad. That's the big picture:

Suddenly, InDesign looks like the future.

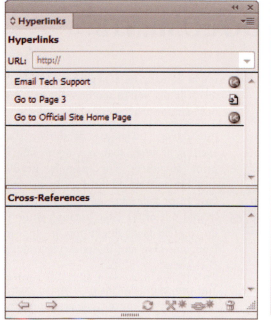

Source Adobe® InDesign®, 2013.

Explore INTERACTIVE DOCUMENTS

What You'll Do

Export SWF

General | Advanced

Export: ○ Selection
○ All Pages   ○ Range: 1
☑ Generate HTML File
☑ View SWF after Exporting

Size (pixels): ○ Scale: 100%
○ Fit To: 1024 x 768
○ Width: 612   ⫶ Height: 792

Background: ○ Paper Color   ○ Transparent
Interactivity and Media: ○ Include All   ○ Appearance Only
Page Transitions: From Document
Options: ☑ Include Interactive Page Curl

Embedded Fonts (Applicable for Flash Classic Text only)

Total Fonts: 0   Font Licensing Info

OK   Cancel

Source Adobe® InDesign®, 2013.

 In this lesson, you will read through an overview of interactive InDesign documents and learn how to create them, save them, and view them.

Defining an Interactive InDesign Document

Traditionally, an InDesign document was used to create a layout for print. Print documents contain four basic elements: text, color tints, illustrations, and imagery. Generally speaking, in a traditional InDesign document, text and color tints are created in InDesign, vector illustrations are imported from Adobe Illustrator, and bitmap images are imported from Photoshop.

An interactive InDesign document is everything that a traditional InDesign document is, with additional interactive features. For example, clicking an element on the page might activate an animation. Text on the page might actually be a hyperlink; clicking the text will take you to another page or spawn a new window that takes you to a website.

Interactive InDesign documents offer exciting features that you never saw in a print document. For example, headlines might fly in from off the page. Images might fade in or fade out—or they too might fly in and out of the page, rotating while they do so. Text fields might pop up, appearing from nowhere and disappearing when you click them.

You can make transitions between pages so that when you move from page to page, an animation occurs. Maybe one page dissolves to another, or maybe a page curls to reveal the next page beneath it. Figure 1 shows the interactive page curl feature that is available in Adobe InDesign.

In addition to animation and hyperlinks, you can incorporate movies and sounds in an interactive InDesign document. Imagine clicking a text box and hearing a voiceover reading the text on the page, or clicking a Play button and—wow!—you're watching a movie.

Identifying Destinations for an Interactive InDesign Document

When designing interactive layouts, the InDesign document is a means to an end. In other words, the interactive InDesign document is not the end product; it's the layout for the end product.

For all interactive layouts, the output medium will be a screen, such as a computer monitor, a cell phone, or a tablet device like an iPad. Whatever the destination might be, a screen is the means by which the layout is displayed.

The fact that a screen is the destination for interactive presentations has many implications for the choices you'll make when designing interactive layouts. For example, all of your image files should be in the RGB color mode, which is the **color space** for screen presentations; additionally, the minimum resolution for on-screen images is 72 pixels-per-inch. These are just two examples of how the rules, options, and features are very different when you are creating an interactive layout.

Understanding the Relationship Between InDesign and Flash

Adobe Flash is itself an interactive layout "authoring" software package. The interactive layouts you create in Adobe Flash can be as complex as any of the eye-popping websites you see on the Internet. Flash is the established software package for creating professional-level websites. In addition to its layout capabilities, Flash offers high-level ActionScript coding to create dramatic animation and complex interactivity with buttons, bells, and whistles.

Flash and InDesign are both Adobe products, and what you're seeing with interactive InDesign documents is an overlap between InDesign and Flash. Some designers design

Figure 1 *Interactive page curl feature*

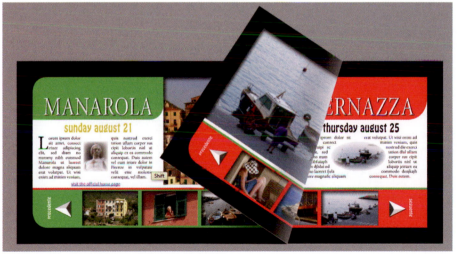

Image courtesy of Chris Botello. Source Microsoft® Internet Explorer®, 2013.

a layout from scratch in Flash. Traditional designers are often more comfortable in InDesign. For these latter designers, Adobe offers the capability to create a layout in InDesign and to export it to Flash for scripting and adding interactivity.

In this case, the best practice would be to create all of the interactivity in Flash. In other words, if the destination is Flash, use Flash to do what Flash does best. Use InDesign to create the layout, but use Flash to add the interactivity. This is, in most cases, the *only* choice because Flash offers limited support for interactive elements created in InDesign.

Note that choosing to export an InDesign layout to Flash is exactly that: a choice. With each new version, Adobe is strengthening InDesign's interactive capabilities. With CS6, you'll be able to create dynamic web-ready layouts without having to go through Flash. And remember, you can export your InDesign layouts to Apple's iPad, but the iPad does not support Flash animation.

Exporting InDesign Documents to Adobe Flash

You export your InDesign document to Flash using the FLA file format. When you do so, you can then open the document in Adobe Flash to edit its contents and use the Flash authoring environment to add such elements as animation, sound, complex interactivity, and video. Figure 2 shows the Export Flash (FLA) dialog box in InDesign.

Understand that the FLA format is proprietary to Adobe Flash. In other words, an FLA file is itself a Flash file. An FLA file cannot be opened or viewed directly in a web browser. It must first be exported from Flash to be viewed or otherwise presented.

Exporting a "Presentation-Ready" Interactive Document

If you're not a Flash designer or a Flash programmer, what you really want is to build your interactive presentation exclusively in InDesign and then export a file that's complete and ready for viewing.

When you're finished designing your interactive document in InDesign, or if you're just at a stage where you want to test it out, export the file as an SWF or an interactive PDF. These are "presentation-ready" formats: when you open the document to view it, the entire layout, all its pages, and all its interactivity is visible and ready to go.

Let's explore the two formats and the options available to you with each.

PDF, an acronym for **portable document format**, allows you to export a self-contained presentation complete with interactive components like buttons, movies, sound clips,

Figure 2 *Export Flash CS6 Professional (FLA) dialog box*

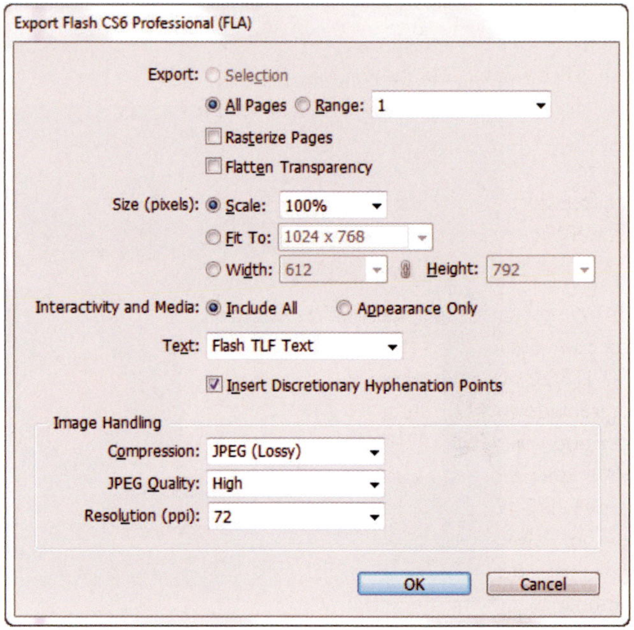

Source Adobe® InDesign®, 2013.

Creating an Interactive Document

hyperlinks, and page transitions all into a single, self-contained file. Adobe's Acrobat Reader is free software that you use to view PDFs.

Because a PDF is a single, self-contained file, and because Adobe's Acrobat Reader is widely used, PDF is a great format choice when you want to email your presentation to others for viewing.

InDesign's Animation panel offers a number of built-in animations that you use to create motion in your presentation. However, before choosing PDF as the format for output, be aware that InDesign animations are not supported by the PDF format.

SWF is an acronym for **Shockwave Flash**. For interactive InDesign documents that are destined for the web, SWF will be your export format of choice because it supports all InDesign interactivity, including animation. Opening an exported SWF file launches Adobe Flash Player, free software that you use to open and view the SWF.

A key component to SWF files is that they can be viewed through Internet browser software like Internet Explorer and Safari. Even though Adobe Flash Player is free and widely used, you'll want your presentation to be able to be viewed in these very popular browsers. When you export the SWF document, be sure to choose the Generate HTML file option in the Export SWF dialog box, shown in Figure 3. The browser software uses the HTML file to display the presentation in the browser window.

Keep in mind that, just because you're exporting your presentation as an SWF doesn't mean necessarily that you are uploading the presentation to the web. You can instead just view the presentation "locally," on your own computer. If you have an overhead display connected to your computer, an interactive InDesign document exported as an SWF file can make for a spectacular slideshow. You

could distribute your SWF presentation to multiple computers, such as in a classroom, for an interactive learning experience. You could also upload your SWF as content on your website or even as its own free-standing website to broadcast your presentation to a worldwide audience. And remember: this is all from InDesign. No programming in Flash is required!

Figure 3 *Export SWF dialog box*

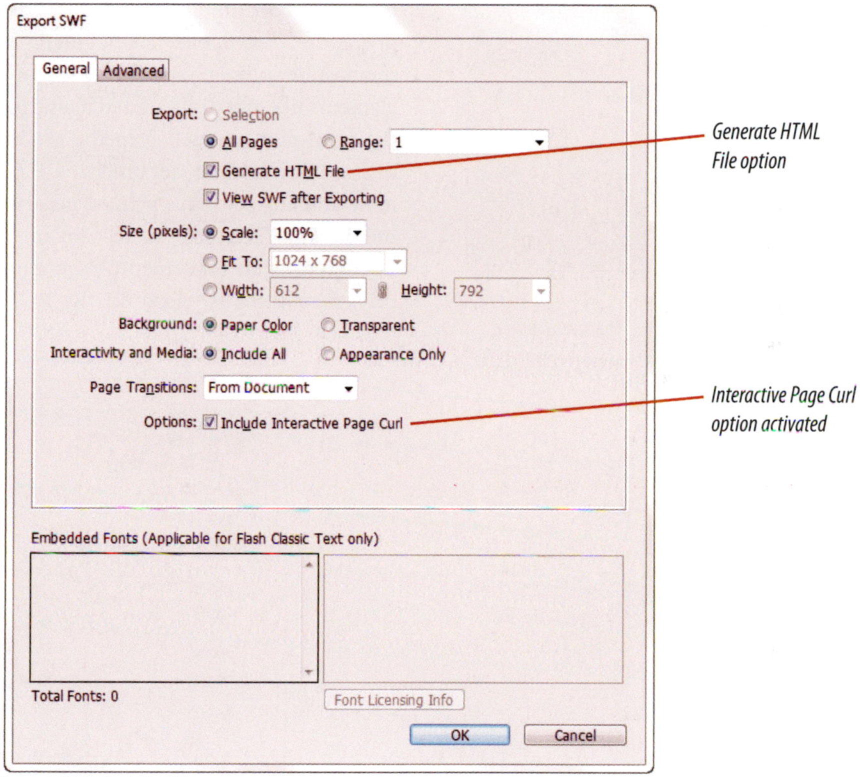

Source Adobe® InDesign®, 2013.

Set Up An
INTERACTIVE DOCUMENT

What You'll Do

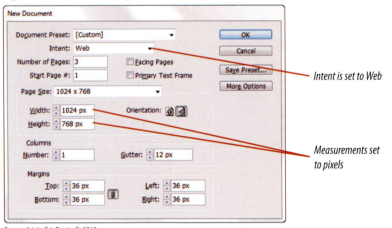

Source Adobe® InDesign®, 2013.

 In this lesson, you will set up an interactive document from scratch and you will modify an existing layout to be an interactive document.

Creating an Interactive Document

Designing in InDesign for either a print or interactive document is generally the same procedure: You create a document, specify the number of pages, and then create design elements like text, tints, and images. However, the print and interactive media are innately different. A printed document is a tangible item, and any color in a printed piece is based on the CMYK color model. An interactive document is an on-screen presentation, and on-screen color is based on the RGB color model. This is just one of many significant differences between a print and an interactive document.

When you set up a new interactive document, you must consider that the settings you enter are specific for on-screen presentations. For example, the page size of the presentation will be related to the size of a computer monitor.

Figure 4 shows the New Document dialog box in InDesign CS6. Note that the Intent option is set to Web. The Intent menu offers three

Figure 4 *New Document dialog box*

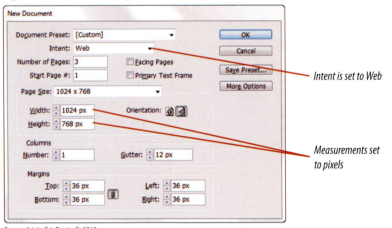

Intent is set to Web

Measurements set to pixels

Source Adobe® InDesign®, 2013.

options: Print, Web, and Digital Publishing. For interactive presentations, choose Web when you intend the presentation to be viewed on the World Wide Web or on a computer screen. Choose Digital Publishing when you intend the presentation to be viewed on a tablet device like an iPad.

Some websites are made up of one single page, but most websites are multiple pages. For example, when you click a link on a web page and that takes you to a different page, you have, at that point, seen two pages.

This scenario is represented in InDesign by multiple pages.

The Page Size menu offers standard document sizes for on-screen presentations. 1024 × 768 is an oft-chosen size because it's a universal size that will fit on almost every monitor.

Note that these page sizes are measured in pixels. **Pixels** are the smallest increment of an on-screen display, and they are the means by which monitors display color. The standard measurement for monitors—referred to as **monitor resolution**—is 72 pixels per inch.

You don't necessarily need to use the standard page sizes in the New Document dialog box when setting up an interactive document (though that's usually the best choice). You do, however, want to be sure that the document is sized so that it fits on a standard-sized screen. If your document is larger than the screen upon which it's being displayed, you'll need to scroll to see parts of the layout that are off screen, which will greatly diminish the impact of your presentation.

Working with Pixels

If I told you that a picture frame in your layout was 720 pixels by 360 pixels, would you know how big it is? At 72 pixels per inch, the frame would be 10″ × 5″. But even that relatively easy math requires that you run the numbers in your head. Imagine if I told you that a frame was 672.3 pixels by 123.7 pixels. Would you have any sense at all how big the frame is?

Some web designers feel comfortable working exclusively with pixels as their basis for measurements. If you don't, feel free to work with good old inches or picas and points. When you create a new document and specify it as a Web document, by default the ruler units are specified as pixels. That means every frame you create and all the positioning information for objects on the page will be specified in pixels. If you don't like that, don't feel that you have to live with it. Simply change your Units & Increments preferences to Inches. It will still be a Web document.

That being said, working with pixel measurements is standard for almost all web designers. If you plan on using InDesign to do a lot of web work, it's a good idea to get comfortable using pixels as your unit of measure.

Repurposing a Traditional Document as an Interactive Document

There's no defining line between a print InDesign document and an interactive InDesign document; they're both InDesign documents. It's the output method that determines a document's function.

In fact, you can have a single InDesign document doing double duty as a document that you both print and present on screen with interactivity. This is worth exploring. Let's say you had an 8.5" × 11" document with multiple images placed from Photoshop. In Photoshop, those images were saved in the CMYK color space designated for print. In InDesign, you've added a number of interactive elements to the layout, such as buttons, hyperlinks, and animation.

You could print this document on your personal color printer or even have it printed professionally in mass quantities. The interactive settings you applied would be inconsequential and wouldn't disrupt the printing process.

On the other hand, you could export the same document as an SWF and produce an on-screen presentation, complete with all the interactive elements you specified. All color on a screen is presented in RGB, because monitors display color in RGB. So even though the files were saved in CMYK in Photoshop, there's no problem presenting the layout on screen.

When repurposing print documents as inter-active documents, the two main considerations you should keep in mind are document size and transparency blend space.

As previously stated, you want your presentation document to fit on the screen upon which it's being presented. The width measurement is usually more critical than the height, because it's normal to scroll vertically on a web page, but seldom do you scroll horizontally. Verify that the width is small enough to fit on a standard screen. A standard 17" monitor has a screen width of 1024 pixels at 72 pixels per inch. Thus, ideally, you want your InDesign document to be no larger than 14.2 inches wide (1024 divided by 72 = 14.2).

It's often a smart choice to convert your Units & Increments preferences from inches to pixels when repurposing a print document.

In doing so, you'll get the exact number of pixels that make up the document's width and height. Figure 5 shows the Units & Increments Preferences dialog box set to Pixels.

The **transparency blend space** setting is a color setting that applies to transparency in your InDesign layout. When the layout is output—either as a print or an on-screen document—InDesign must define the colors of all overlapping transparent areas in the document. In other words, it must say, "Where this pink circle overlaps the yellow square, the overlapping color is X." To define that color, InDesign must refer to a color model or a color space. To avoid unexpected shifts in color, for on-screen documents, switch the transparency blend space from the default CMYK space to RGB. To do so, click the Edit menu and then chose Document RGB from Transparency Blend Space.

Figure 5 *Units & Increments Preferences dialog box*

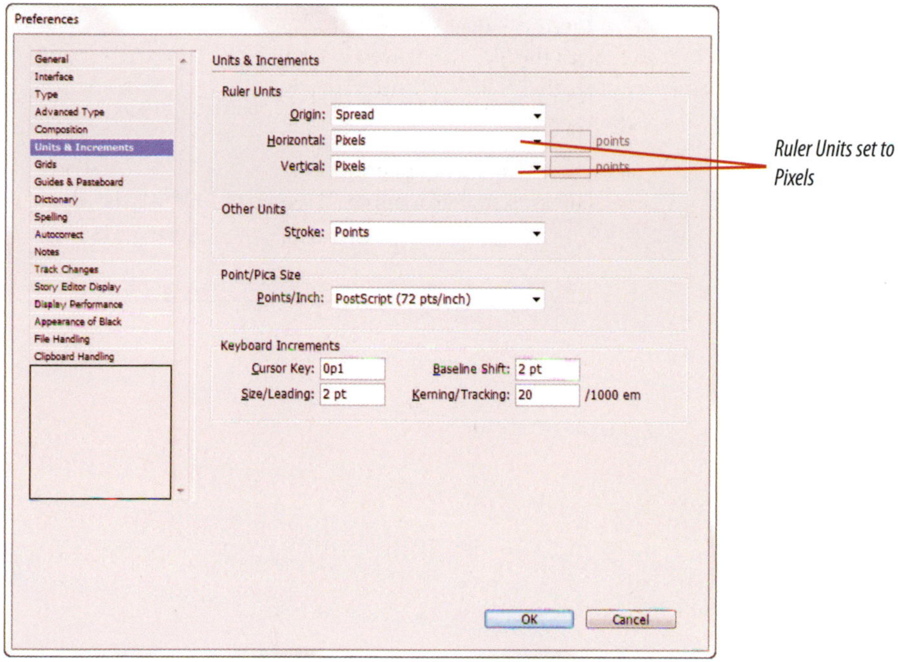

Source Adobe® InDesign®, 2013.

Create a new interactive document for the Web

1. Start InDesign and verify that no documents are open.

2. Click the **File menu**, point to **New**, then click **Document**.

   The New Document dialog box opens.

3. Click the **Intent list arrow**, then click **Web**.

4. Type **4** in the Number of Pages text box.

5. Verify that the **Facing Pages** and **Primary Text Frame check boxes** are not checked.

6. Click the **Page Size list arrow**, then click **1024 x 768**.

   Your New Document dialog box should resemble Figure 6.

7. Click **OK**.

8. Click the **Edit menu**, then point to **Transparency Blend Space**.

   Because the document was set up as a "Web" document, the Transparency Blend Space is automatically set to Document RGB.

9. Click the **Edit menu**, point to **Preferences**, then click **Units & Increments**.

   The document is automatically set up with Ruler Units set to Pixels.

10. Click **Cancel**.

11. Save the file as **Presentation Document**.

12. Close the file.

You created a new interactive presentation document from scratch. In the New Document dialog box, you specified the intent, the number of pages, and the page size for the document. Once the document was created, you noted the default transparency blend space and ruler units.

Figure 6 *New Document dialog box set up for a Web document*

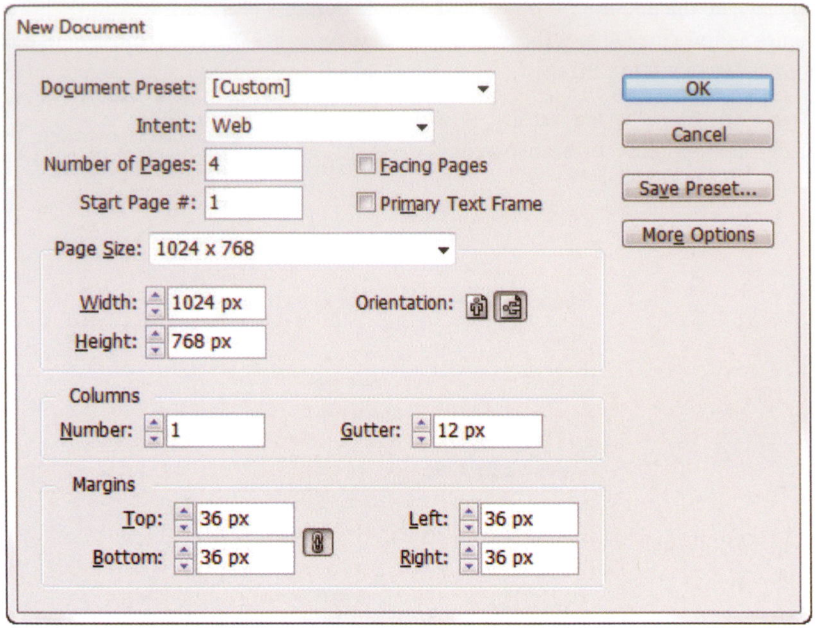

Source Adobe® InDesign®, 2013.

Figure 7 *Document Setup dialog box*

Document Setup

Intent: Print	OK
Number of Pages: 4 ☐ Facing Pages	Cancel
Start Page #: 1 ☐ Primary Text Frame	Fewer Options

Page Size: [Custom]

Width: 972 px   Orientation:
Height: 414 px

Measurements set to pixels

Bleed and Slug

	Top	Bottom	Left	Right	
Bleed:	0 px	0 px	0 px	0 px	
Slug:	0 px	0 px	0 px	0 px	

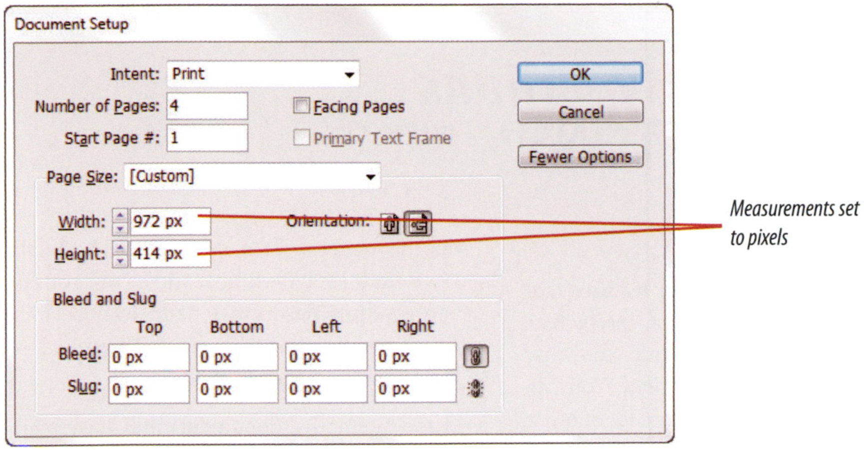

Source Adobe® InDesign®, 2013.

Repurpose a print document as an interactive document

1. Open **ID 1-1.indd**, then save it as **Italian Presentation**.

   This file was originally designed as a print document, with no thought given to any on-screen settings or interactive components.

2. Change the Horizontal and Vertical Ruler units to **Inches** in the Preferences dialog box.

   TIP Click the Edit (Win) or InDesign (Mac) menu, point to Preferences, then click Units & Increments.

3. Open the Document Setup dialog box, then compare your screen to Figure 7.

   At 972 pixels wide × 414 pixels in height, the document will fit on most monitors.

4. Click **Cancel**.

5. Click the **Edit menu**, point to **Transparency Blend Space**, then click **Document RGB**.

6. Click the **Window menu**, point to **Workspace**, click **[Interactive for PDF]**, then save your work.

   The Interactive for PDF workspace provides most of the necessary panels you need to work with interactive documents.

You opened an existing layout. You changed the ruler units to pixels to check the dimensions of the document in pixels, verifying that the width was less than 1024 pixels. You then changed the Transparency Blend Space to Document RGB and set the workspace to the Interactive for PDF workspace.

Incorporate Hyperlinks
AND BUTTONS

What You'll Do

Source Adobe® InDesign®, 2013.

In this lesson, you will incorporate hyperlinks and buttons to navigate within the document and to link to an online web page.

Working with Hyperlinks

Hyperlinks are one of the great features that make an interactive document interactive. With hyperlinks, you can jump to other pages in your InDesign document. You can also click a hyperlink to jump to another document, an email address, or to a website.

Hyperlinks have two components, the first of which is the **source**. The source is the linking element itself and, in InDesign, the source for a hyperlink can be text, a text frame, or a graphics frame. The second element is the **destination**, which is the place to which the hyperlink takes you. The destination can be another file, an email address, a website, or a page in the same document. Note that a hyperlink source can link to only one destination, but a destination can have any number of sources linking to it.

Hyperlinks in InDesign are created using the Hyperlinks panel, as shown in Figure 8. When you create a hyperlink, it appears on the panel with a default name, usually Hyperlink 1, Hyperlink 2, and so on. You can apply a more descriptive name to hyperlinks using the Rename Hyperlink command on the Hyperlinks panel menu.

Some interactive documents may have many hyperlinks. Imagine, for example, that you've produced an online cookbook. You might want to hyperlink an ingredient to a number of recipes that all require that ingredient. The Sort command on the Hyperlinks panel menu, offers options for viewing the links listed on the panel. Table 1 explains each option.

TABLE 1: OPTIONS FOR VIEWING HYPERLINKS IN THE HYPERLINKS PANEL	
Manually	Displays the hyperlinks in the order in which you created them.
By Name	Displays the hyperlinks in alphabetical order.
By Type	Displays the hyperlinks in groups of similar type, like page links and URL links.

© Cengage Learning 2013

Creating Buttons

Buttons perform actions when an InDesign document is exported to SWF or PDF formats. Clicking a button can take you to a different page in the document, open a website, play a movie, play a sound, or play an animation. Buttons you create are listed and formatted on the Buttons and Forms panel, shown in Figure 9.

You might be thinking that buttons sound a lot like hyperlinks. To a degree that's true, though buttons and hyperlinks are mutually exclusive in some things that they do. To make a clearer distinction in your head, think of buttons as *artwork* to which you apply an action.

Use any of the drawing tools such as the Ellipse tool or the Rectangle tool or the Pen tool to draw a shape for the button. You can design to your heart's content. Add fills, strokes, text, gradients, and effects. Or don't. Button artwork can be as simple as a rectangle or an ellipse with a fill.

Once you've created button artwork, select the artwork with the Selection tool. If the button artwork is created from multiple objects, group the objects first. With the artwork selected, convert it to a button in either of the following two ways:

- Click the Convert to Button icon on the Buttons and Forms panel.
- Click the Object menu, point to Interactive, then click Convert to Button.

The artwork will be converted to a button. A dotted line will appear around the artwork, and a small button icon will be positioned

Figure 8 *Hyperlinks panel*

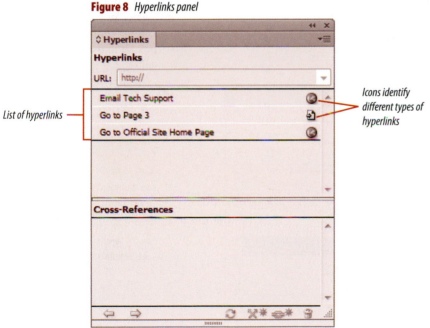

List of hyperlinks

Icons identify different types of hyperlinks

Source Adobe® InDesign®, 2013.

Figure 9 *Buttons and Forms panel*

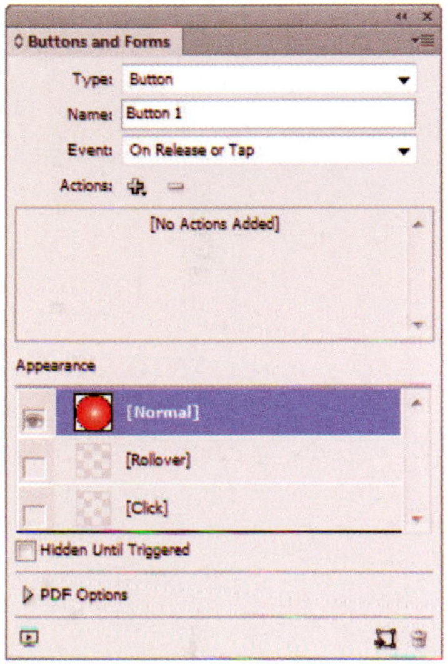

Source Adobe® InDesign®, 2013.

within the dotted line. The artwork will appear as Normal in the Appearance section on the Buttons and Forms panel, as shown in Figure 10.

Once you've converted artwork to a button, you can format it on the Buttons and Forms panel by doing any one or more of the following:

- Give the button a descriptive name to help you distinguish it from other buttons you create.
- Apply one or more actions to the button.
- Alter the appearance of the button to determine what it looks like when you "roll over" the button or click it in the SWF or PDF file.

At any time, you can convert button artwork back to regular artwork. Select the button artwork, click the Object menu, point to Interactive, then click Convert to Object.

Changing Button Appearances for Rollover and Clicking

Once you convert artwork to a button, you can format it with as many as three appearances, which are referred to as **states**: Normal, Rollover, and Click.

By default, the button you create starts out with a Normal appearance. In the exported file, the Normal appearance is used until the mouse pointer moves over the button, which triggers the Rollover appearance. Clicking the button triggers the Click appearance.

You don't necessarily have to assign different appearances to the three different states, but you'll find that having some sort of visual cue in place enhances the interactive experience with the buttons.

To define the appearance for a given state, select the button on the page, then click the state on the Buttons and Forms panel. Then, modify the button directly—typically you'll change its fill color—for each state.

Figure 10 *Converting artwork to a button*

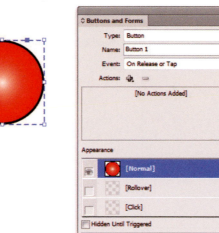

Source Adobe® InDesign®, 2013.

Figure 11 shows a red button in its Normal state. In Figure 12, the Rollover state is targeted on the Buttons and Forms panel, and a green gradient has been applied to the button. When the InDesign document with this button is exported as an SWF or PDF, the button will appear as red and then change to the green gradient appearance whenever a mouse pointer hovers over it.

In Figure 13, the Click state is targeted on the Buttons and Forms panel, and a blue gradient has been applied to the button. The button will appear blue when clicked in the exported document.

Note that the Click state color changes have very little visual impact because the jump to the destination happens so quickly that the visual change on the click is negligible. On the other hand, for buttons that don't change the page view, applying a color change to the Click state can be visually effective. For example, if you create a button that pauses a video on the page, having that button change color when the button is clicked can make for an important visual cue that the video is paused.

Figure 11 *Normal state on the Buttons and Forms panel*

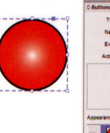

Source Adobe® InDesign®, 2013.

Figure 12 *Rollover state in the Buttons and Forms panel*

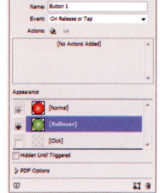

Source Adobe® InDesign®, 2013.

Figure 13 *Click state on the Buttons and Forms panel*

Source Adobe® InDesign®, 2013.

Adding Actions to Buttons

You use the Buttons and Forms panel to create, edit, and manage actions that you want to apply to buttons. **Actions** indicate what happens upon an event. An **event** is the specific interactive occurance that triggers the action of a button. Clicking a button and releasing a button are common events. Going to the next or previous page are common actions. The Buttons and Forms panel lists six events, as shown in Figure 14. Of the six events, four are standard, and are grouped separately in the Event menu. They are described in Table 2.

It's important to note that you can apply multiple actions to a single button. For example, you could specify that On Release or Tap, a sound is generated and the document moves to the next page.

To apply an action to a button, click the Add new action for selected event button on the Buttons and Forms panel to expose the list of

Figure 14 *Events list on the Buttons and Forms panel*

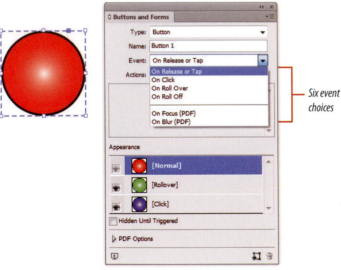

Six event choices

Source Adobe® InDesign®, 2013.

TABLE 2: COMMON EVENTS	
On Release or Tap	This is the default event. When the mouse button is released after being pressed, the action or actions applied to a button are triggered. This is the most commonly used event because it gives the user a last chance to not execute the action by not releasing the mouse button after clicking it.
On Click	When the mouse button is pressed down the action is triggered. Unless you have a specific reason for using this event, use On Release or Tap for the reason stated above.
On Roll Over	When the mouse pointer enters the area defined by the button's bounding box the action is triggered.
On Roll Off	When the mouse pointer leaves the area defined by the button's bounding box the action is triggered.

© Cengage Learning 2013

Creating an Interactive Document

preset actions, as shown in Figure 15. Note that some actions can be applied for SWF output only and others for PDF output only. The following is a list of the more commonly used actions:

■ **Go To First/Last/Next/Previous Page** Jumps to the specified page. Select an option from the Zoom menu on the Buttons and Forms panel to specify the magnification at which the page will be displayed.

■ **Go to URL** Opens the web page of the specified URL.

■ **Video** Lets you assign actions to buttons that allow you to play, pause, stop, or resume a selected movie. Only movie files that have been placed in the document appear in the Video menu on the Buttons and Forms panel.

■ **Sound** Lets you assign actions to buttons that allow you to play, pause, stop, or resume a selected sound clip. Also lets you apply a sound to an event, like clicking a button. Only sound files that have been placed in the document appear in the Video menu on the Buttons and Forms panel.

Figure 15 *Actions list on the Buttons and Forms panel*

Add new action for selected event button

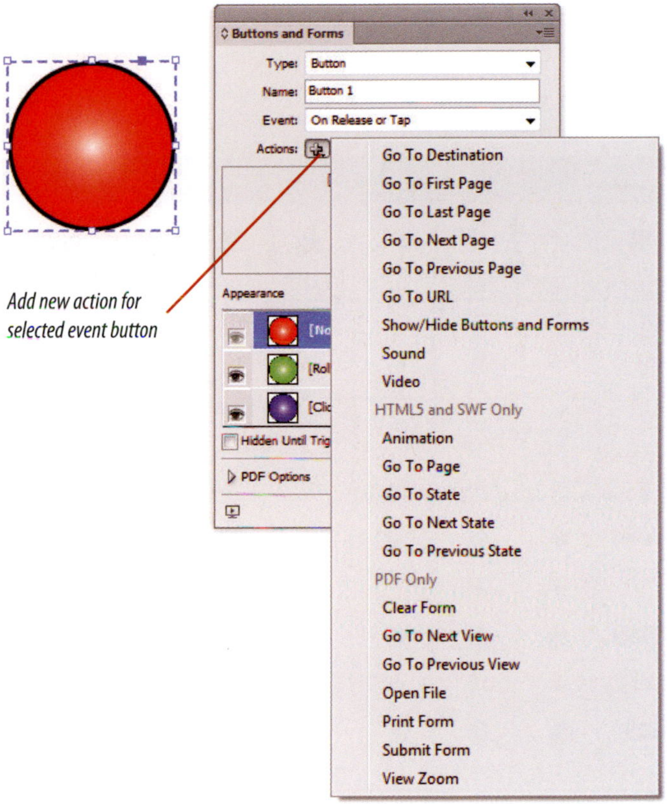

Source Adobe® InDesign®, 2013.

Using the Sample Buttons and Forms panel

As shown in Figure 16, the Sample Buttons and Forms panel is a great resource for quickly adding buttons to your presentation without having to design them yourself. The Sample Buttons and Forms panel contains dozens of buttons and arrows that are already formatted as buttons. Visually, they include effects such as gradient feathers and drop shadows, and each has a slightly different appearance preloaded for the Rollover appearance. The sample buttons also have actions assigned to them. For example, the arrow buttons have the Go To Next Page and Go To Previous Page actions built in. You can edit or delete these pre-assigned actions as necessary.

The Sample Buttons and Forms panel is a library. You can add the buttons you create to the panel and delete any you don't want. To access the panel, choose Sample Buttons and Forms from the Buttons and Forms panel menu. Simply drag buttons from the panel to the document. If you want to use the same button on every page of a multipage document, drag it to a master page.

Figure 16 *Sample Buttons and Forms panel*

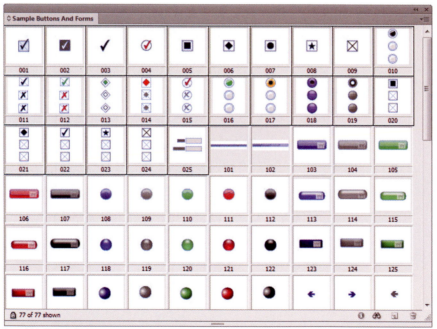

Source Adobe® InDesign®, 2013.

Assigning a Sound to a Button

Sounds and buttons are a match made in interactive heaven: Click a button, hear a sound. Sounds add a whole new layer of interactivity to a presentation.

Sounds are applied to buttons as actions on the Buttons and Forms panel. Click a button with the Selection tool, then choose Sound from the list of actions. In order for a sound to be listed and available on the Buttons and Forms panel, the sound file itself must be placed in the current InDesign document. You place sound files using the Place command on the File menu.

When you place a sound file, it is a nonprinting, invisible component of your presentation. A sound file is placed in an InDesign frame, so you can select and move the frame. But the frame will appear as an empty square unless you've chosen Show Edges on the View menu. In that case, a sound file will be represented as an icon, as shown in Figure 17.

Most designers position sound files on a master page so that they are available to be used on every page of the document.

Figure 17 *Sound file icon appears when edges are showing*

Source Adobe® InDesign®, 2013.

Create hyperlinks between pages in a document

1. Verify that guides are hidden.
2. Scroll through the four pages of the document to see the content on all four pages, then return to page 1.
3. Position the Hyperlinks panel somewhere on the page so that it remains open.
4. Click the **Type tool** T , then select only the word **Manarola** in the left column, as shown in Figure 18.
5. Click the **Create new hyperlink button** on the Hyperlinks panel.

   The New Hyperlink dialog box opens.
6. Click the **Link To list arrow**, then click **Page**.
7. Set the destination page to **3.**
8. Click the **Zoom Setting list arrow**, then click **Fit in Window**.

   With this zoom setting, when the hyperlink takes the viewer to page 3, page 3 will fit in the window.
9. In the Character Style section, click the **Style list arrow**, then click **Blue Text Links**.

   Blue Text Links is a Character Style that was created in this InDesign document. All character styles appear in the New Hyperlink dialog box so that they are available for formatting hyperlink text. Your New Hyperlink dialog box should resemble Figure 19.

   (continued)

Figure 18 *Creating a new hyperlink*

Selected text

Create new hyperlink button

Source Adobe® InDesign®, 2013.

Figure 19 *New Hyperlink dialog box*

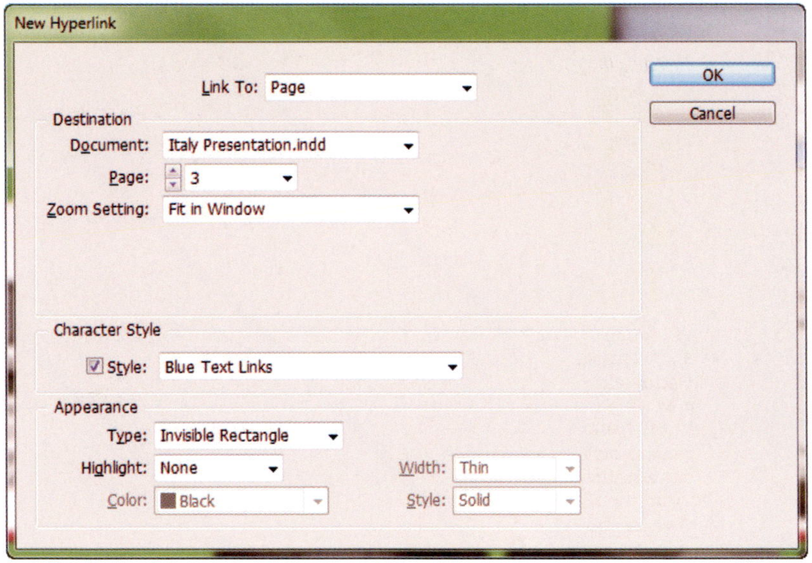

Source Adobe® InDesign®, 2013.

Figure 20 *Manarola hyperlink on Hyperlinks panel*

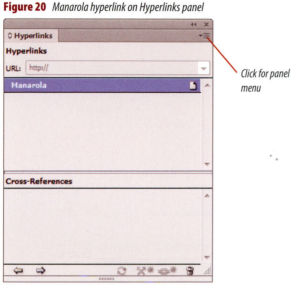

Click for panel menu

Figure 21 *Selecting the text frame to hyperlink*

Selected text frame

10. Click **OK**, then deselect the text in the document.

    Notice that the Blue Text Links character style is applied to the Manarola text and that a hyperlink named Manarola is listed on the Hyperlinks panel, as shown in Figure 20. When you create a hyperlink with text, the hyperlink is automatically named using the first word or words in the selected text.

11. Repeat the previous steps to hyperlink the word **Firenze** on page 1 to page 2 in the document.

12. Save your work.

You created a hyperlink from the word "Manarola" on page 1 to the Manarola feature on page 3. You then hyperlinked the word "Firenze" on page 1 to the Firenze feature on page 2.

Create a hyperlink to a web page

1. On page 1 in the document, select the **text frame** shown in Figure 21.

2. Click the **Create new hyperlink button** on the Hyperlinks panel.

3. In the New Hyperlink dialog box, click the **Link To list arrow**, then click **URL**.

(continued)

4. In the URL text box, click after **http://**, type **www.lecinqueterre.org/eng/** so that your dialog box resembles Figure 22, then click **OK**.

The word Hyperlink appears and is selected on the Hyperlinks panel.

5. Click the **Hyperlinks panel menu button** to open the Hyperlinks panel menu, then click **Rename Hyperlink**.

6. Rename the link as **Official Home Page**, then click **OK**.

At this point in the project, you would likely export the file as an SWF to test the hyperlinks. You will export the document at the end of Lesson 4, when you learn about viewing page transitions.

7. Save your work.

You created a hyperlink from a text frame to a web page. You renamed the hyperlink with a more descriptive name on the Hyperlinks panel.

Convert artwork to buttons

1. Position the Buttons and Forms panel somewhere on the page.

2. Select the **left triangle artwork** on page 1.

3. Click the **Object menu**, point to **Interactive**, then click **Convert to Button**.

The artwork appears in the Normal state in the Appearance section on the Buttons and Forms panel.

4. Enter **P1L** in the Name text box on the Buttons and Forms panel.

P1L stands for Page 1 Left. Your Buttons and Forms panel should resemble Figure 23.

(continued)

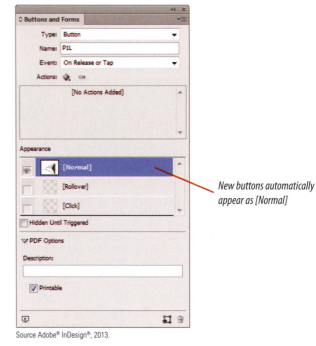

Figure 22 *Specifying the URL for the website*

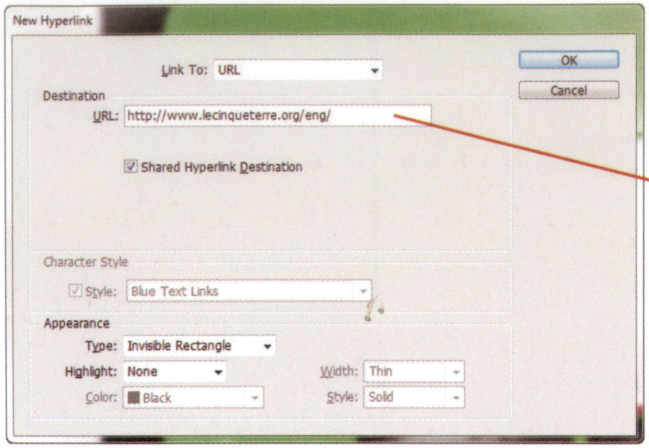

Website URL for hyperlink

Source Adobe® InDesign®, 2013.

Figure 23 *New button added to Buttons and Forms panel*

New buttons automatically appear as [Normal]

Source Adobe® InDesign®, 2013.

Creating an Interactive Document

Figure 24 *Changing the Rollover status fill color*

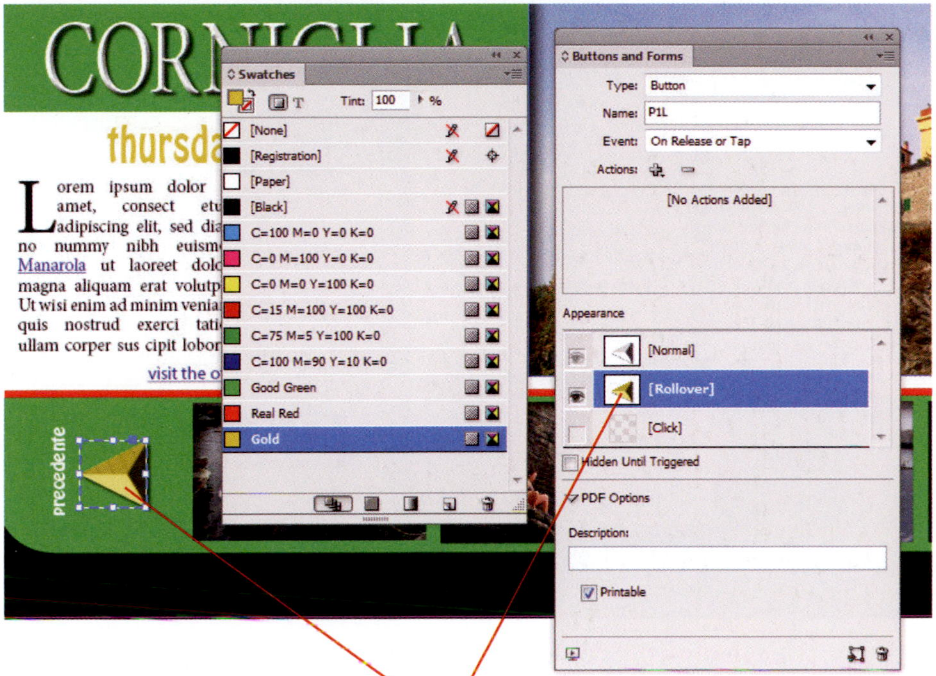

Source Adobe® InDesign®, 2013.

*Gold button appearance on
the panel and on the page*

5. Select the **right triangle artwork** on page 1.

6. Click the **Convert to Button icon** on the Buttons and Forms panel.

7. Enter **P1R** in the Name text box on the Buttons and Forms panel.

8. Go to page 2 in the document.

9. Select **both triangles** on the page, then click the **Convert to Button icon**.

   There's no relationship created just because both triangles are converted to buttons simultaneously; they will still be separate buttons.

10. Deselect, select the **left button**, then name it **P2L**.

11. Select the **right button** and then name it **P2R**.

12. Convert both triangles on page 3 to buttons, then name them **P3L** and **P3R** respectively.

13. Convert both triangles on page 4 to buttons, then name them **P4L** and **P4R** respectively.

14. Save your work.

You converted eight objects to buttons and gave them descriptive names.

Modify button appearances

1. Verify that the Swatches panel is expanded.

2. Scroll to page 1, then select the **left button**.

3. Click **[Rollover]** in the Appearance section on the Buttons and Forms panel.

   The Rollover status is activated and the triangle artwork appears as an icon on the panel.

4. Click **Gold** on the Swatches panel so that your screen resembles Figure 24.

(continued)

In the exported file, when the mouse pointer is positioned over the button, the button will change from silver to gold.

5. Select **[Click]** in the Appearance section on the Buttons and Forms panel to activate it.

6. Change the fill color of the button to **Good Green** so that your screen resembles Figure 25.

   In the exported file, when you click the button, it will change from gold to green. Note, however, you will find with the Click state that color changes have very little visual impact when you click a button that takes you to another page in the document.

7. Select the **right button** on page 1, change the Rollover status fill color to **Gold**, then change the Click status fill color to **Good Green**.

8. For all the buttons on pages 2 and 3 and 4, change the Rollover status fill color to **Gold**.

9. For both buttons on page 3, change the Click status fill color to **Good Green**.

10. For all the buttons on pages 2 and 4, change the Click status fill color to **Real Red**.

11. Save your work.

You changed the Rollover and Click appearances for different buttons in the document.

Apply actions to buttons

1. Scroll to page 1, then select the **left button** on the page.

2. Click the **plus button** on the Buttons and Forms panel, then click **Go To Last Page**.

(continued)

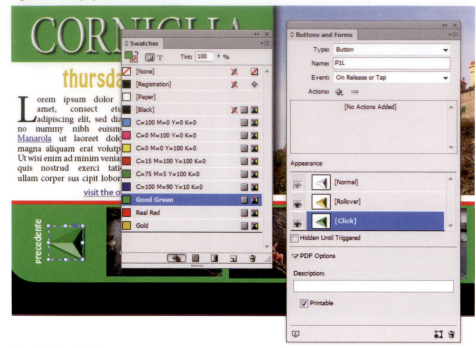

Source Adobe® InDesign®, 2013.

Figure 25 *Changing the Click status fill color*

Creating an Interactive Document

Figure 26 *The Go To Last Page action listed on the Buttons and Forms panel*

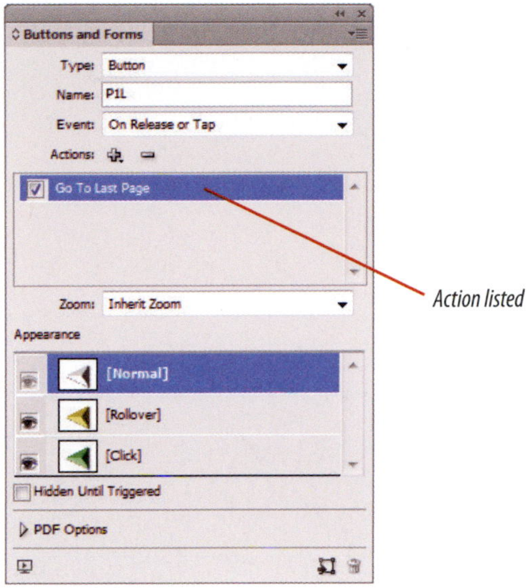

Action listed

Your Buttons and Forms panel should resemble Figure 26. The Go To Last Page action is listed on the panel and is checked. Note that, by default, the Event is listed as On Release or Tap. In the exported document, upon releasing the mouse pointer, the button will take you to the last page of the document. You may have a different appearance highlighted on your Buttons and Forms panel. The active appearance has no impact when you're applying an action to a button.

TIP The plus sign button name is Add new action for selected event, however we will refer to it as the plus sign button.

3. Click the **Zoom list arrow** to see the other options, then verify that **Inherit Zoom** is chosen.

   Inherit Zoom, which is the default setting, specifies that when the button takes you to the specified page, the new page will be displayed with the same magnification as the current page. In other words, it will "inherit" the zoom from the current page. You could choose a different view, like fitting the page in the window when you jump to the next page, but it can be annoying for the view to change every time you click a button.

4. Click the **P1R button** (right button) on the page, click the **plus sign button** on the Buttons and Forms panel, and then click **Go To Next Page**.

5. Apply the **Go To Next Page** action to buttons **P2R** and **P3R**.

6. Apply the **Go To Previous Page** action to buttons **P2L** and **P3L** and **P4L**.

(continued)

7. Apply the **Go To First Page** action to button **P4R**.

8. Save your work.

You applied actions individually to each of eight buttons, actions that will control how clicking each button moves the reader through the pages in the document.

Apply sounds to buttons

1. Scroll to page 1, click the **View menu**, point to **Extras**, and then click **Show Edges**.

2. On the Pages panel, double-click **A-Master**.

   As shown in Figure 27, two sound files have been placed on the master page. The source files (Click.mp3 and Squeak.mp3) are located in your Chapter 1 Data Files folder, and their format is MP3, a standard format for sound files.

3. Hide frame edges.

4. Double-click **page 1** on the Pages panel, click the **View menu**, then click **Fit Page in Window**.

5. Click the **Selection tool**, then click the **right button** on the page to select it.

6. On the Buttons and Forms panel, click the **plus sign button** , then click **Sound.**

7. Click the **Sound list arrow**, then click **Click.mp3**.

(continued)

Figure 27 *Sound files on the master page*

Source Adobe® InDesign®, 2013.

Creating an Interactive Document

Figure 28 *Click.mp3 sound clip on the Buttons and Forms panel*

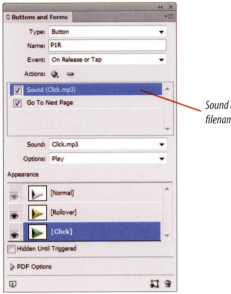

Sound action and sound filename listed

Source Adobe® InDesign®, 2013.

Figure 29 *Squeak.mp3 sound clip on the Buttons and Forms panel*

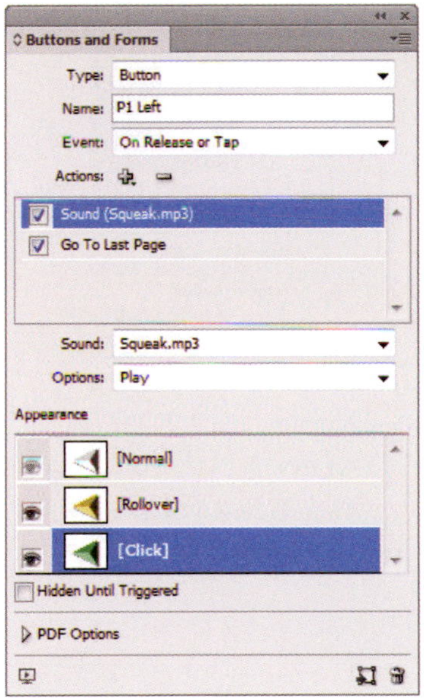

Source Adobe® InDesign®, 2013.

Your Buttons and Forms panel should resemble Figure 28. The two sounds are available on the Buttons and Forms panel because the sound files have been placed in the document (in this case, on the A master page). Remember that the sound, like any action, is tied to the event. In this case, the Click.mp3 sound will play On Release or Tap.

8. Using the same method, apply the **Click.mp3** sound to the **right buttons** on pages 2 and 3 and 4.

9. Go to page 1 then click the **left button** on the page to select it.

10. On the Buttons and Forms panel, click the **plus sign button** , then click **Sound.**

11. Click the **Sound list arrow**, then click **Squeak. mp3**.

    Your Buttons and Forms panel should resemble Figure 29. It doesn't matter what appearance is targeted when you apply a sound or any action, because actions are tied to events, not appearances.

12. Using the same method, apply the **Squeak.mp3** sound to the **left button** on pages 2 and 3 and 4.

13. Save your work.

You viewed two sound files placed on the master page. You applied the two sound files to buttons in the document.

Apply and View
PAGE TRANSITIONS

What You'll Do

Source Adobe® InDesign®, 2013.

In this lesson, you will apply page transitions and export an SWF file to view them.

Applying Page Transitions

Page transitions are just like classic video transition effects, such as dissolve, push, and wipe, that can be applied to your InDesign pages and that appear when you're moving from page to page in an exported SWF or PDF document. You can apply different page transitions to different pages in a single document, or you can apply a single transition to all the pages in the document. You cannot apply page transitions to master pages.

You apply page transitions with the Pages panel working in tandem with the Page Transitions panel. As shown in Figure 30,

Figure 30 *Applying page transitions*

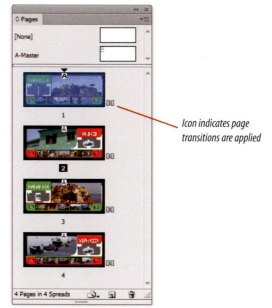

Icon indicates page transitions are applied

Images courtesy of Chris Botello. Source Adobe® InDesign®, 2013.

you target a page or multiple pages on the Pages panel, then choose the transition you want to apply on the Page Transitions panel. A page transition icon appears beside the page thumbnail on the Pages panel.

QUICK TIP

If you want to hide the page transition icon, deselect the Page Transitions check box in the Panel Options dialog box of the Pages panel.

The Page Transitions panel offers previews of how the transition looks when a page is turned. You can customize the transition to your liking by choosing options from the Direction and Speed menus.

If you select multiple page thumbnails on the Pages panel, the transition you choose will be applied to the selected pages. In many cases, you'll want to apply the same transition to all pages in a document. For example, if you're producing a slideshow, for visual consistency you'll likely want the same transition between each "slide." To apply the same transition quickly to all pages, select the transition, then click the Apply to All Spreads button on the Page Transitions panel, or choose Apply to All Spreads from the Page Transitions panel menu.

Exporting an SWF File

While you're working on your interactive document, you'll find yourself regularly exporting the document as an SWF and opening the exported file in your web browser software to test the interactivity.

Exporting to SWF is a smart, simple option because it supports all InDesign interactivity, including animation, and is opened quickly and easily by Internet Explorer and other browser software.

In InDesign, you don't save a file as an SWF, you export it. To do so, click the Export command on the File menu. Choose Flash Player (SWF) from the Save as type menu (Win) or Format menu (Mac) then click Save.

When you export the document, the Export SWF dialog box opens, as shown in Figure 31.

The dialog box has two tabs, General and Advanced. The General options are shown in Figure 31.

The following options are available to you on the General tab:

- **Export** allows you to determine whether to export the current selection, all pages in the document, or a page range. Choosing a specific page or page range can be a good idea in long documents when you are exporting only to test out interactivity on a specific page or area of the document.

Figure 31 *General options in the Export SWF dialog box*

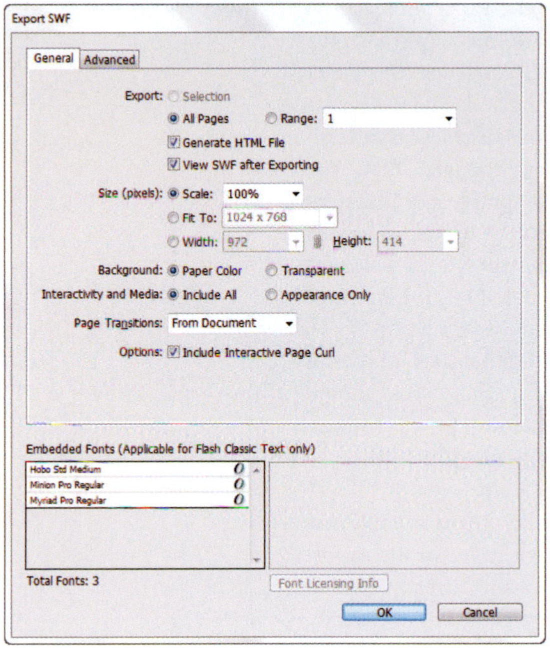

Source Adobe® InDesign®, 2013.

- **Generate HTML File** generates an HTML page that plays back the SWF file and is one that you should keep activated.
- **View SWF after Exporting** automatically opens the SWF for viewing in your browser.
- **Size (pixels)** specifies whether or not the SWF is scaled from the document size. If you build your document to a standard width for a standard monitor (see Lesson 1 in this chapter), you can feel comfortable that your layout will display properly on most computer screens without having to scale.
- **Background** specifies whether the background of the exported file is transparent or if it is the current Paper Color from the Swatches panel (almost always white). Generally speaking, you'll use the Paper Color option for most layouts, because a Transparent setting disables page transitions. Remember, though, that you have the option to specify a transparent background; it could be useful, especially for some object-level animations that aren't necessarily meant to be part of a layout or appear on a page.
- **Interactivity and Media** has a default Include All setting that you should keep activated to allow movies, sounds, buttons, and animations to be interactive in the exported SWF file.
- **Page Transitions** allows you to apply one page transition to all pages in the export document if you haven't already applied them to individual pages in the document. If you have already, leave the option as the default From Document to use the page transitions specified in the document.
- **Include Interactive Page Curl** applies to SWF output only (not PDF). When this option is selected, users viewing the SWF can manually drag a corner of the page layout, giving the effect that the page is turning like a page in a book. Think of this effect as being independent from the page transitions you set up in the document. For example, if you set a Wipe page transition for every page in the document, you could still implement the Include Interactive Page Curl feature. In the exported document, the Wipe transition would execute when you navigate from page to page, but you'd have the additional option of manually dragging pages with the Interactive Page Curl feature.

The following options are available to you on the Advanced tab, shown in Figure 32.

- **Frame Rate** directly affects the smoothness of animations. A higher number of frames per second creates smoother animations, but can also increase the file size. The default

Figure 32 *Advanced options in the Export SWF dialog box*

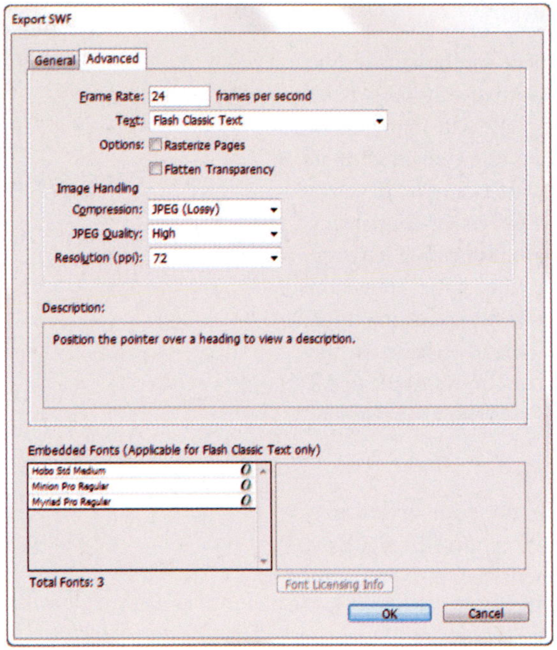

Source Adobe® InDesign®, 2013.

Creating an Interactive Document

frame rate, 24 frames per second, is usually satisfactory, especially for the animation presets on the Animation panel.

- **Text** specifies how InDesign text is output. Use the default Flash Classic Text to output searchable text that results in the smallest file size.
- **Rasterize Pages** converts all InDesign page elements into bitmaps. Unless you have a specific reason, keep this option in its default inactive state.
- **Flatten Transparency** removes transparent effects from the SWF document and preserves their appearance. However, it also removes all interactivity from the exported file, so keep this option in its default inactive state unless you have a specific reason for activating it.
- **Compression** determines how grayscale and color images will be compressed for quicker downloads. Compression is always a tug-of-war between download speed and image quality. JPEG (lossy) is the default compression algorithm and is generally suitable for grayscale or color images. **Lossy** refers to the fact that JPEG compression always removes image data to reduce file size. Sometimes that removal results in a degradation of image quality. Usually, JPEG compression works well, but if you notice an unacceptable reduction in image quality, use PNG ("ping"), which is a "lossless" compression algorithm.
- **JPEG Quality** specifies the amount of detail in exported images. The higher the quality, the larger the file size. Given today's robust Internet connections, you can feel free to choose Maximum.
- **Resolution** is the number of pixels per inch in a bitmap image. The more pixels per inch, the more detail in the image, and the higher the image quality. 72 pixels per inch (ppi) is the standard resolution for images presented on a monitor or screen. This setting in the Export SWF dialog box overrules the native resolution of placed images. In other words, if you place an image that has a 150ppi resolution and export it at this setting, the image in the exported document will have a 72ppi resolution. 72ppi is usually high enough resolution for all images. However, some animation presets allow you to zoom in on an image on the page, enlarging them substantially. Choosing a higher resolution is important to allow viewers to zoom-in on images, but can increase the file size significantly.

Too big to mail?

File size and image compression are always a consideration when exporting a document. When exporting an interactive document that will be emailed or presented online, you'll need to consider compressing bitmap images so that the overall file size won't be too large for email or for download.

In the early days of the Internet, slow download speeds made file size and image compression big issues to tackle. But times have changed. Today's robust Internet connections allow relatively large file sizes to download in a jiffy. Even mass market email services like Yahoo! mail allow for email attachments up to 25MB.

Keep this in mind when exporting your interactive presentations. Don't feel that you need to compress everything past the point of quality just to get your export file size under one megabyte. That's just overkill. Keeping your export file size under 5MB will allow you to maintain quality images and animations while still allowing for quick downloads and the ability to email the presentation.

Add page transitions

1. Verify that both the Pages panel and the Page Transitions panel are open.

2. Double-click the **page 1 thumbnail** on the Pages panel.

3. Click the **Transition list arrow** on the Page Transitions panel, then click **Blinds**.

4. Click the **Direction list arrow**, then click **Vertical**.

   Your panels should resemble those in Figure 33. Note the page transition icon beside the page thumbnail on the Pages panel.

5. Double-click the **page 2 thumbnail**, press and hold **[Ctrl]** (Win) or **[Command]** (Mac), then click the **page 3 thumbnail** so that both are selected.

6. Click the **Transition list arrow** on the Page Transitions panel, then click **Split**.

7. Verify that the Direction is set to **Horizontal In**.

8. Double-click the **page 4 thumbnail**.

9. Apply the **Wipe** transition in a **Down** direction with a **Medium** speed.

   Your panels should resemble those in Figure 34.

10. Save your work.

You applied three different transitions to pages in the document.

Figure 33 *Blinds transition in the Page Transitions panel*

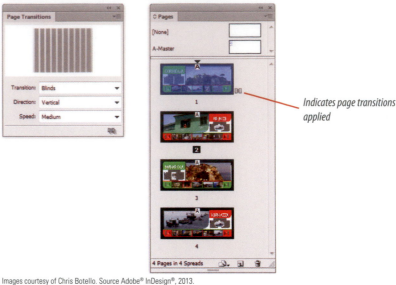

Indicates page transitions applied

Images courtesy of Chris Botello. Source Adobe® InDesign®, 2013.

Figure 34 *Wipe transition applied to page 4*

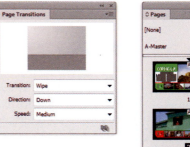

Images courtesy of Chris Botello. Source Adobe® InDesign®, 2013.

Creating an Interactive Document

Figure 35 *General options in SWF Output dialog box*

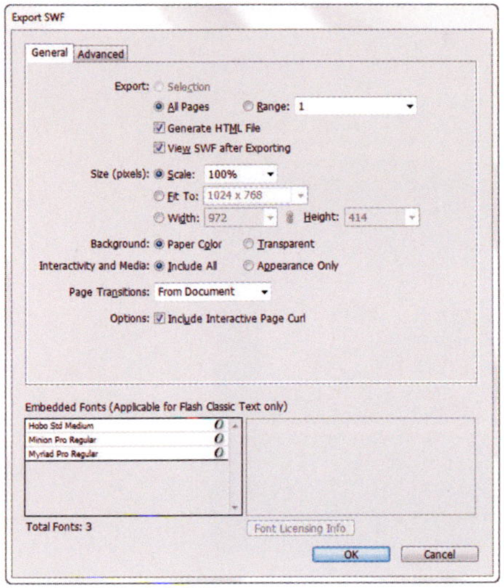

Source Adobe® InDesign®, 2013.

Figure 36 *Advanced options in SWF Output dialog box*

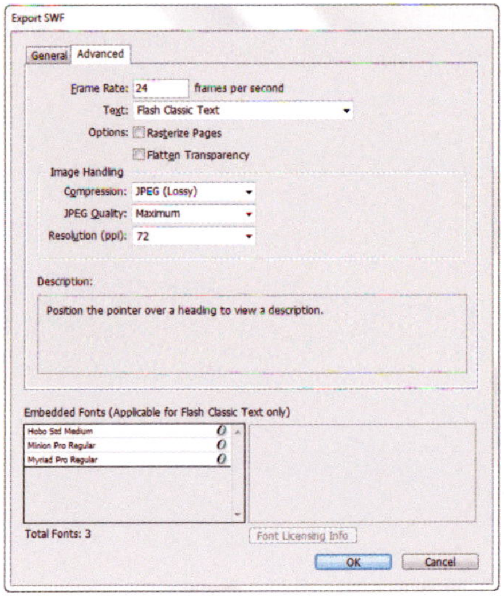

Source Adobe® InDesign®, 2013.

Export an SWF file

1. Click the **File menu**, then click **Export**.
2. Navigate to the folder on your computer in which you want to save the exported file.
3. Choose **Flash Player (SWF)** from the **Save as type menu** (Win) or **Format menu** (Mac) then click **Save**.

   The Export SWF dialog box opens.
4. Verify that your General export settings match those shown in Figure 35.

   Note that the Include Interactive Page Curl check box is checked. Note, too, that the View SWF after Exporting check box is checked. The file will open automatically in your browser software after exporting.
5. Click the **Advanced tab**, then enter settings that match those in Figure 36.

   Note that JPEG Quality has been set to Maximum.

(continued)

6. Click **OK**.

As shown in Figure 37, the document opens in your browser software. If your document doesn't open automatically, launch your browser software, then open the SWF file that you exported.

TIP If you get a warning dialog box saying pages in the document have overset text you should ignore it by clicking the Don't show again check box.

You applied three different transitions to pages in the document.

Figure 37 *SWF document displayed in Internet Explorer*

Image courtesy of Chris Botello. Source Microsoft® Internet Explorer®, 2013.

Creating an Interactive Document

Figure 38 *Viewing the Rollover appearance on the right button*

Image courtesy of Chris Botello. Source Microsoft® Internet Explorer®, 2013.

Button changes to Gold
on mouse rollover

Test interactive settings in an SWF file

1. Position your mouse pointer over the **right triangle button** on page 1.

   As shown in Figure 38, the button appearance changes to gold.

2. Click the **right triangle button**.

   The Click sound activates, and the page changes to page 2 using the Split page transition. The page transition is always that which has been applied to the *destination* page, and the Split page transition was applied to page 2.

3. Click the **left triangle button** on page 2.

   The Squeak sound activates, and the page changes to page 1 using the Vertical Blinds page transition.

4. Click the blue underlined word **Manarola** on page 1.

   The hyperlink takes you to page 3, the Manarola page, using the Split page transition, which was also applied to page 3.

5. Click the **right triangle button** on page 3.

   The Click sound activates, and the page changes to page 4 using the Wipe page transition.

6. Click the **right triangle button** on page 4.

   The button, formatted with the Go To First Page action, takes you to page 1 using the Vertical Blinds page transition.

   (continued)

7. Click the **visit the official home page link**.

   A new browser window opens displaying the web page. It is possible that the security settings in your browser or Adobe Flash Player will block the pop-up of the web page. If that occurs, go to the Read This Before You Begin section at the front of the book and follow the steps listed under the headline "Setting Flash Online Preferences."

8. In your browser, close all open tabs so that the only open window is that of the document we exported from InDesign.

9. Float the mouse pointer over the **bottom-right corner**, then click and drag to turn the page manually, as shown in Figure 39.

10. Turn pages to move back and forth through the document.

11. Close the browser window, then return to the Italian Presentation.indd document.

You tested the interactive settings in the SWF file by clicking buttons, verifying that sound files played, and using the Interactive Page Curl feature.

Figure 39 *"Turning the page" with the Interactive Page Curl feature*

Image courtesy of Chris Botello. Source Microsoft® Internet Explorer®, 2013.

Figure 40 *The Apply to All Spreads button*

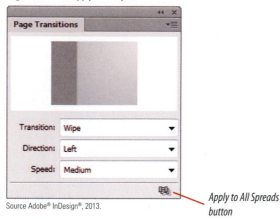

Source Adobe® InDesign®, 2013.

Apply to All Spreads button

Remove page transitions and apply a page transition to all pages in a document

1. Select all **four page thumbnails** on the Pages panel.
2. On the Page Transitions panel, click the **Transition list arrow**, then click **None** at the top of the list.

   The transitions are removed from all pages, and the page transition icons disappear from the thumbnails on the Pages panel.
3. Click the background area of the Pages panel to deselect all page thumbnails.
4. On the Page Transitions panel, click the **Transition list arrow**, then click **Wipe**.

   The transition is applied only to the page that is targeted on the Pages panel.
5. Click the **Direction list arrow**, then click **Left**.
6. Click the **Apply to All Spreads button** on the Page Transitions panel, shown in Figure 40.

   The transition is applied to all pages, and the page transition icons appear beside the thumbnails on the Pages panel. When using this method, page thumbnails do not need to be selected on the Pages panel for the transition to be applied.
7. Save your work.

You removed different page transitions then applied a single transition to all pages using the Apply to All Spreads button on the Page Transitions panel.

SKILLS REVIEW

Set up interactive documents.

1. Verify that no other documents are open.
2. Click the File menu, point to New, then click Document.
3. Click the Intent list arrow, then choose Web.
4. Enter 3 for the number of pages.
5. Verify that the Facing Pages check box is not checked.
6. Click the Page Size list arrow, then click 1024 x 768.
7. Click OK.
8. Click the Edit menu, then point to Transparency Blend Space, noting that because the document was set up as a "Web" document, the Transparency Blend Space is automatically set to Document RGB.
9. Click the Edit (Win) or InDesign (Mac) menu, point to Preferences, then click Units & Increments, noting that the Web document is automatically set up with Ruler Units set to Pixels.
10. Click Cancel.
11. Save the file as **Skills Presentation Document**.
12. Close the file.
13. Open ID 1-2.indd, then save it as **Maui Presentation**.
14. Click the Edit (Win) or InDesign (Mac) menu, point to Preferences, then click Units & Increments.
15. In the Ruler Units section, set the Horizontal and Vertical units to Pixels, then click OK.
16. Open the Document Setup dialog box again.

17. Click Cancel.
18. Click the Edit menu, point to Transparency Blend Space, then click Document RGB.
19. Click the Window menu, point to Workspace, then click [Interactive for PDF]. (*Hint:* If the workspace does not appear to change, click Window again, point to Workspace, then click [Reset Interactive for PDF].)
20. Save your work.

Incorporate hyperlinks and buttons.

1. If guides are showing, hide them.
2. Scroll through the five pages of the document to see the content on all five pages, then return to page 1.
3. Expand the Hyperlinks panel so that it remains open.
4. Click the Selection tool, then select the first image on page 1.
5. Click the Create new hyperlink button on the Hyperlinks panel.
6. In the New Hyperlink dialog box, click the Link To list arrow, then click Page.
7. Set the destination page to 2.
8. Click the Zoom Setting list arrow, click Fit in Window, then click OK.
9. Note that a hyperlink named Hyperlink is now listed on the Hyperlinks panel.

10. Using the same steps, hyperlink the image on page 2 to page 3
11. Hyperlink the image on page 3 to page 4, then hyperlink the image on page 4 to page 5.
12. Save your work.
13. Go to page 1, then select the Road to Hana text frame.
14. Click the Create new hyperlink button on the Hyperlinks panel.
15. In the New Hyperlink dialog box, click the Link To list arrow, then click URL.
16. In the URL text box, click after http://, then type **www.gohawaii.com/maui**.
17. Click OK.
18. Open the Hyperlinks panel menu, then click Rename Hyperlink.
19. Rename the link as **Visit Maui**, then click OK.
20. Save your work.
21. On the Pages panel, double-click the B-Master thumbnail to go to the B master page.
22. Expand the Buttons and Forms panel.
23. Click the Selection tool, then select the left arrow artwork.
24. Click the Object menu, point to Interactive, then click Convert to Button.

25. Type **LEFT** in the Name text box on the Buttons and Forms panel.
26. Select the right arrow artwork.
27. Click the Convert to Object button on the Buttons and Forms panel.
28. Type **RIGHT** in the Name text box on the Buttons and Forms panel.
29. Select the green circle artwork.
30. Click the Convert to Object button on the Buttons and Forms panel.
31. Type **HOME** in the Name text box on the Buttons and Forms panel.
32. Save your work.
33. Verify that the Swatches panel is expanded and available.
34. Select the left button.
35. Click [Rollover] in the Appearance section of the Buttons and Forms panel.
36. Use the Swatches panel to change the fill color of the left arrow to Green.
37. For the right arrow, change the [Rollover] status fill color to Green so that your screen resembles Figure 41.
38. Select the left arrow on the page.
39. Click the plus sign button on the Buttons and Forms panel, then click Go To Previous Page.
40. Click the right arrow, click the Add new action button on the Buttons and Forms panel, then click Go To Next Page.

41. Click the green circle, click the Add new action button on the Buttons and Forms panel, then click Go To First Page on the Actions menu.
42. Save your work.
43. Click the Selection tool, then select the left arrow on the page.

44. On the Buttons and Forms panel, click the Add new action button, then click Sound.
45. Click the Sound list arrow, then click Click.mp3.
46. Using the same method, apply the Click.mp3 sound to the right arrow.
47. Save your work.

Figure 41 *Changing the Rollover color*

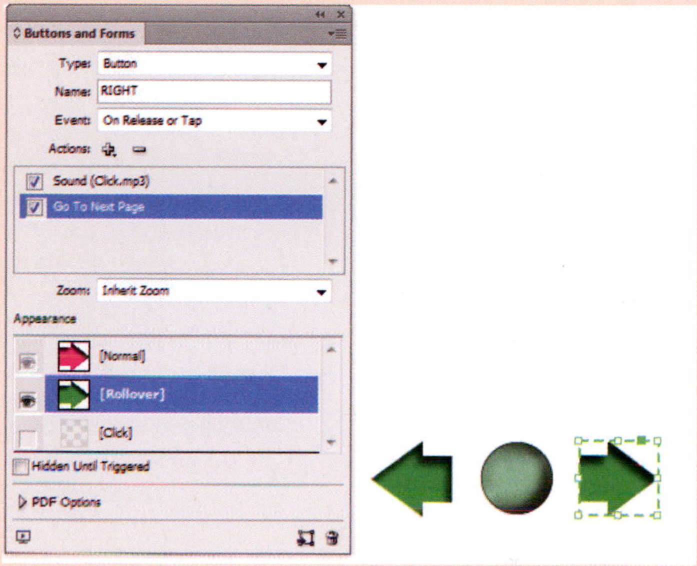

Source Adobe® InDesign®, 2013.

Apply page transitions.

1. Verify that the Page Transitions panel is expanded.
2. Double-click the page 1 thumbnail on the Pages panel.
3. Click the Transition menu on the Page Transitions panel, then click Blinds.
4. Click the Direction menu, click Vertical, then verify the Speed is set to Medium.
5. Click the Apply to All Spreads button on the Page Transitions panel.
6. Save your work.

Export an SWF file.

1. Click the File menu, then click Export.
2. Navigate to the folder on your computer to which you want to save the exported file.
3. Type **Maui** in the Name text box.
4. Choose Flash Player (SWF) from the Save as type menu (Win) or Format menu (Mac) then click Save.
5. Verify that your General export settings match Figure 42.

Figure 42 *General settings in the Export SWF dialog box*

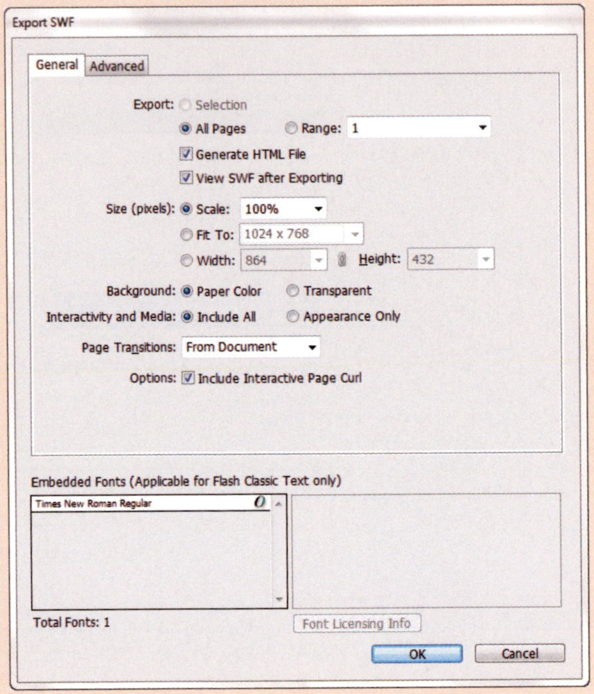

Source Adobe® InDesign®, 2013.

6. Click the Advanced tab, then verify that your Advanced export settings match Figure 43.
7. Click OK, then watch as the SWF opens automatically to page 1.
8. Click the leftmost image.

9. Click and drag to turn pages with the Interactive Page Curl feature.
10. Click the arrow buttons to move back and forth through the document.
11. Click the center button to go to the home page.

12. Return to the InDesign file and save your work.
13. Close Maui Presentation.indd.

Figure 43 *Advanced settings in the Export SWF dialog box*

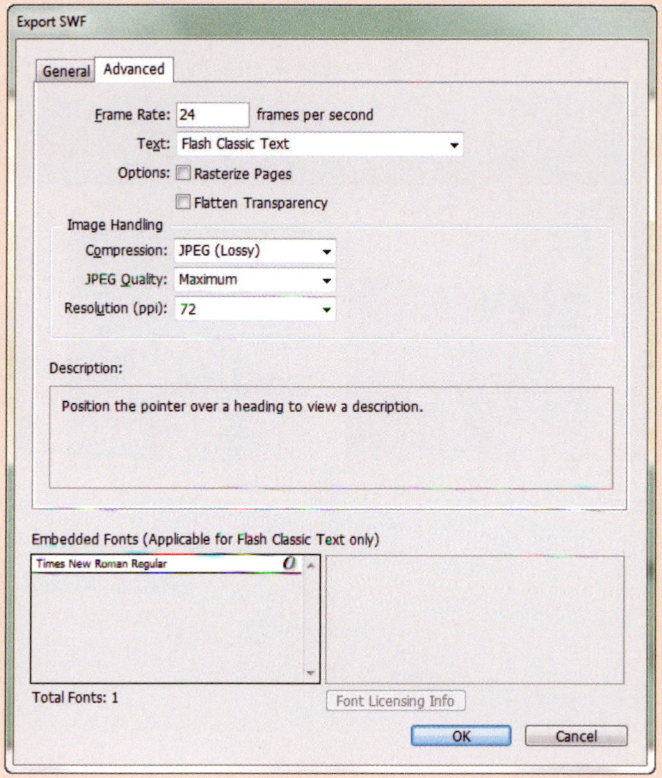

Source Adobe® InDesign®, 2013.

You're working on an interactive InDesign layout. Your creative director asks you to add some navigation buttons to the pages quickly. She tells you they should be in the same location on every page. Since you don't have time to design buttons, you decide to use the Sample Buttons and Forms panel.

1. Open ID 1-3.indd, then save it as **Sample Buttons**.
2. Open the Layers panel, then target the Buttons layer. (*Hint:* The buttons you create will be positioned on the Buttons layer.)
3. Open the Buttons and Forms panel, click the panel menu, then click Sample Buttons And Forms.
4. Drag button #114 onto page 1, then drag another copy of button #114 onto page 1.
5. Align the buttons and position them centered relative to the sub-headline as shown in Figure 44.
6. Select both buttons, then cut them.
7. Navigate to the A-Master page.
8. Click the Edit menu, then click Paste in Place.

Figure 44 *Positioning the buttons*

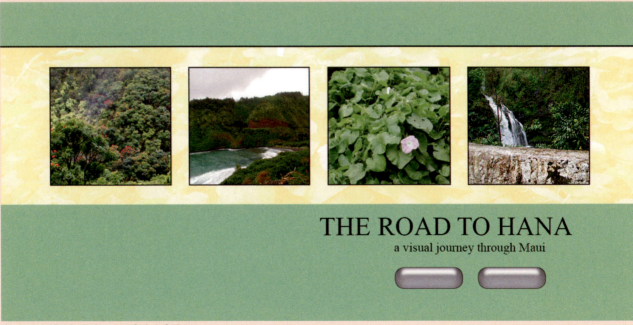

Image courtesy of Chris Botello. Source Adobe® InDesign®, 2013.

Creating an Interactive Document

9 Select the right button, then click Go To Next Page from the Actions menu on the Buttons and Forms panel.

10. Select the left button, then assign the Go To Previous Page action.

11. Scroll to the pasteboard on the right to locate the text frame with the word NEXT, click the Object menu, point to Arrange, then click Bring to Front.

12. Move the NEXT text frame from the pasteboard so that it is positioned over the right button.

13. Drag and drop a copy over the left button, then change the text to **PREV**.

14. Group the right button and the NEXT text frame.

15. Group the left button and the PREV text frame.

16. Double-click Page 1 on the Pages panel. The buttons appear on all pages, as shown in Figure 45.

17. Export an SWF file, and test out the buttons.

18. Save your InDesign work, then close the file.

Figure 45 *Viewing the buttons on a document page*

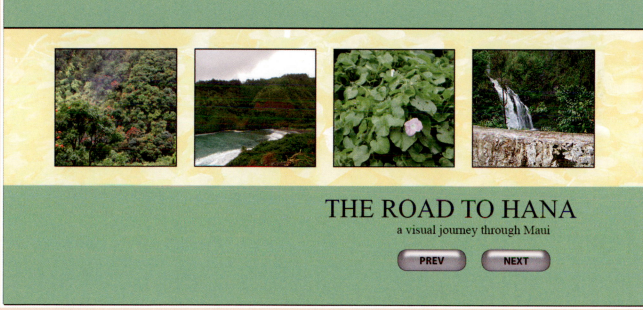

Image courtesy of Chris Botello. Source Adobe® InDesign®, 2013.

CHAPTER 2 ADDING ANIMATION
TO A PRESENTATION

1. Apply animation
2. Preview animation
3. Use the Timing panel to control animation
4. Use a button to trigger animation

CHAPTER 2 ADDING ANIMATION TO A PRESENTATION

It moves! That two word sentence might be the simplest way to describe how an interactive document is different from a traditional print document. The interactive document moves. Press a button, something happens. Load a page, something happens. Click a link, something happens. What happens? Something moves: the page changes, a new page opens, an element moves in from off the page, or an element on the page does something. In every case, movement is involved.

The Animation panel in InDesign offers built-in animation presets that allow you to quickly make things move in an interactive document. You can work with multiple presets to create complex animation, or you can work with a single preset to create simple, practical movement–like making a button disappear when you click it.

Keep the idea of 'movement' in mind when you're designing a layout for the web. Whether it's through animation, page transitions hyperlinks or some other strategy, movement puts the *active* in interactive.

Image courtesy of Chris Botello. Source Adobe® InDesign®, 2013.

Apply
ANIMATION

What You'll Do

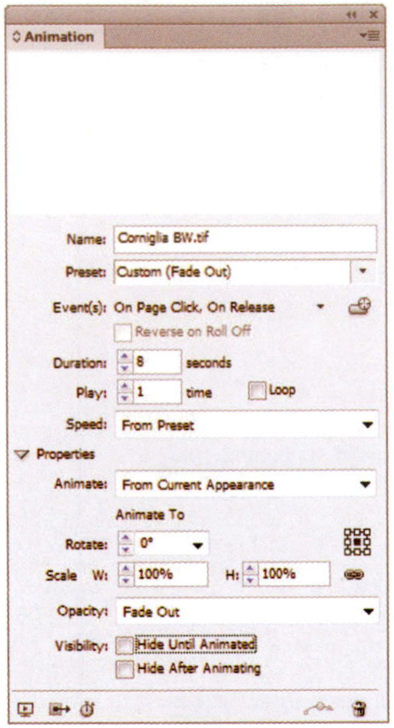

Source Adobe® InDesign®, 2013.

In this lesson, you will incorporate various animation presets to make objects in the layout move.

Using the Animation Panel

Animation is a great way to add life to your InDesign document. For example, you can make objects move and fade, appear and disappear, or fly in from one side of the screen in an exported document.

InDesign provides you with many predefined animations, called **presets**, which are available on the Animation panel and can be applied quickly and easily to objects in your layout.

Use the Animation panel, shown in Figure 1, to apply presets to objects, to change animation settings such as speed and duration, and to specify when an animation occurs. The Preset menu, shown in Figure 2, contains many fun and useful animations.

Figure 1 *Animation panel*

Source Adobe® InDesign®, 2013.

Figure 2 *Preset menu on the Animation panel*

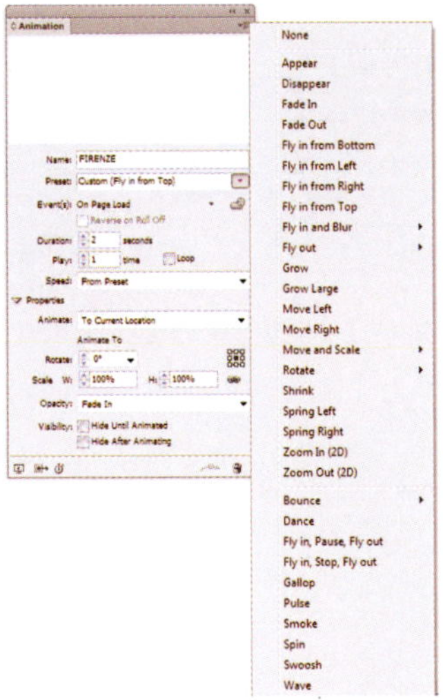

Source Adobe® InDesign®, 2013.

Adding Animation to a Presentation

Most are self-explanatory. For example, the Fade command expresses quite clearly what the preset does to an object. The Gallop and Smoke commands, on the other hand, hold a few surprises.

You'll find that working with presets on the Animation panel is intuitive, and a learn-as-you-go approach is effective for incorporating the various options you have with different animations. If you're the type of person who likes a tricky challenge, you'll find that creating animations can

be a test of strategy, and you'll often need to be inventive in duplicating objects and applying various presets in smart combinations to achieve the more complex animation effects.

Once you apply an animation to an object, use the Event(s) menu on the Animation panel, shown in Figure 3, to specify when the animation will occur. The default event is On Page Load, meaning the animation will begin when the page is loaded in your browser

or other software you're using to view the exported file.

You can apply multiple events to a single animation. For example, you can select an image on the page and apply a Fly In animation to it, and then specify that the animation will occur on page load and when you click the image. The ability to use more than one event to trigger an animation increases your options for making a more complex presentation.

Figure 3 *Event(s) menu on the Animation panel*

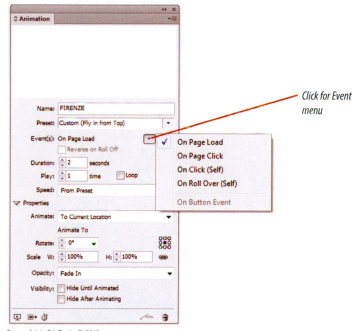

Source Adobe® InDesign®, 2013.

Apply Fly-in animations

1. Open the file **ID 2-1.indd**, then save it as **Italian Presentation Animated**.

   This file is identical to the file you created in Chapter 1 with the one exception that page transitions have been removed. Because page transitions are themselves a form of animation, you will often find that animations look best on their own, without page transitions.

2. Verify that you are on page 1 of the InDesign document, then expand the Animation panel.

3. Click the **Selection tool** , then select the **text frame** with the thursday august 11 text.

   The phrase "thursday august 11" automatically appears in the Name text box of the Animation panel.

4. Click the **Preset list arrow**, then click **Fly in from Left**.

   As shown in Figure 4, the options on the Animation panel are activated, and a motion path appears, attached to the text frame. The editable **motion path** indicates the default path the animated object will move along and the distance it will travel.

5. Click the **Event(s) list arrow** to expose the menu of options, then verify that the default **On Page Load** is chosen, as shown in Figure 5.

6. Set the duration to **2** seconds.

   TIP When you change the default options, the word Custom appears in the Preset text box preceding the animation name. This means that you have customized the default animation with your personal choices.

(continued)

Figure 4 *Animation panel and motion path*

Motion path

Image courtesy of Chris Botello. Source Adobe® InDesign®, 2013.

Figure 5 *Settings for Fly in from Left animation*

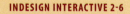

Source Adobe® InDesign®, 2013.

Adding Animation to a Presentation

Figure 6 *Animation panel settings*

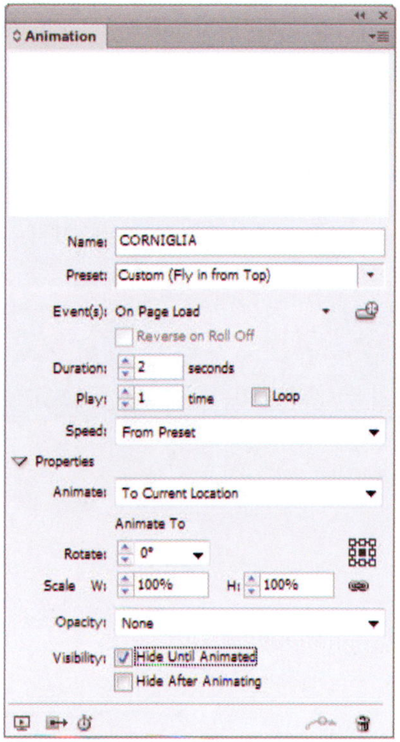

Source Adobe® InDesign®, 2013.

7. Expand the **Properties** section of the Animation panel, then make a note of the current Animate setting which is To Current Location.

   This setting specifies that when the animation is completed, the text frame's position will be at this current location.

8. Click the **Opacity list arrow**, then click **None**.

   No transparency changes will be applied to the text during the animation.

9. In the Visibility section, check the **Hide Until Animated check box**.

   The text frame will be hidden until the animation begins. The Hide Until Animated option is important because, without it, the text will appear for a split second when the page is loaded and spoil the effect that the text "flies in" from off the page. Your Animation panel should resemble Figure 6.

10. Select the **text frame** with the CORNIGLIA text.

11. Click the **Preset list arrow**, then click **Fly in from Top**.

(continued)

12. Use Figure 6 as a guide to choose the remaining settings for the Fly in from Top animation.

13. Save your work.

You applied two different fly-in animations to two different text frames.

Apply a Fade animation

1. Use the **Selection tool**  to select the **largest image** on the page.

2. Click the **Edit menu**, click **Copy**, click the **Edit menu**, then click **Paste in Place**.

    The copy of the image will serve as a placeholder for a black and white version of it.

3. Click the **File menu**, click **Place**, navigate to where your Chapter 2 Data Files are stored, navigate to the Links folder, then place the image **Corniglia BW.tif**.

    Your page should resemble Figure 7. Because the two images are exactly the same size and have the same number of pixels, the black and white version aligns perfectly with the color image beneath it.

4. With the frame still selected, click the **Preset list arrow** on the Animation panel, then click **Fade Out**.

5. Set the duration to **8** seconds.

6. Click the **Event(s) list arrow**, then click **On Page Click**.

    Notice that the On Page Click event is listed next to On Page Load on the Animation panel. This means the animation would happen on two events: when the page is loaded and when the page is clicked.

    (continued)

Figure 7 *Placing the grayscale copy of the Corniglia image*

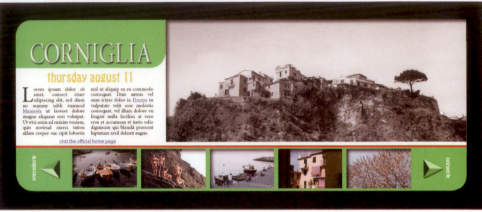

Image courtesy of Chris Botello. Source Adobe® InDesign®, 2013.

Figure 8 *Animation settings for Fade Out*

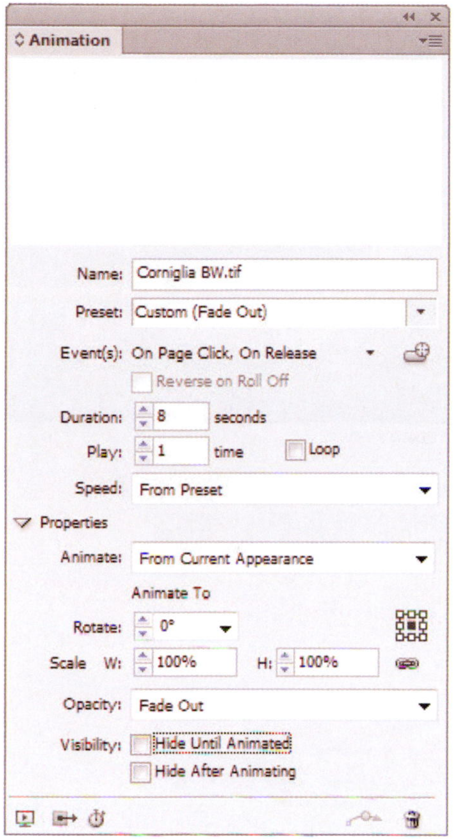

Source Adube® InDesign®, 2013.

7. Click the **Event(s) list arrow** again, then deselect **On Page Load** to remove the check mark.

8. Verify that both Visibility options at the bottom of the panel are unchecked.

   Your Animation panel should resemble Figure 8. When you click the black and white image, it will fade out over eight seconds to reveal the color image beneath it, creating the effect that the black and white image is "becoming" a color image.

9. Save your work.

You placed a grayscale copy of an image, then applied the Fade Out animation preset so that the grayscale image will fade when clicked.

Apply a Shrink animation

1. Use the **Selection tool** to select the **red horizontal line** on the page.

2. Copy the line, then paste it in place.

3. Use the Swatches panel to change the stroke color of the red line to **Gold**.

(continued)

Your page should resemble Figure 9.

4. With the line still selected, click the **Preset menu** on the Animation panel, then click **Shrink**.

5. Set the duration to **6** seconds.

6. Verify that the Event(s) menu is set to **On Page Load**.

7. In the Properties section, click the **Constrain the scale value icon** if necessary so that it appears unlinked or broken.

   We are going to shrink the line on the horizontal axis only. Removing the Constrain the scale value property allows you to affect just the horizontal axis and not the vertical axis.

8. Verify that the Opacity menu is set to **None**.

9. Click the **right-center button** on the origin chart, set the W (width) value to **0**, then set the H (height) value to **100%**.

   Your Animation panel should resemble Figure 10. On page load, the horizontal size of the line (the width) will shrink to 0%, using the right edge of the line as the point of origin for the transformation. The height of the line will not change.

10. Save your work.

You copied a line, changed its stroke color, then applied the Shrink animation to it.

Figure 9 *Gold line on page*

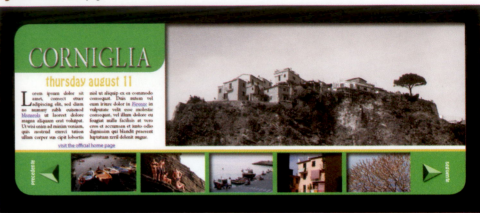

Image courtesy of Chris Botello. Source Adobe® InDesign®, 2013.

Figure 10 *Shrink animation settings for the gold line*

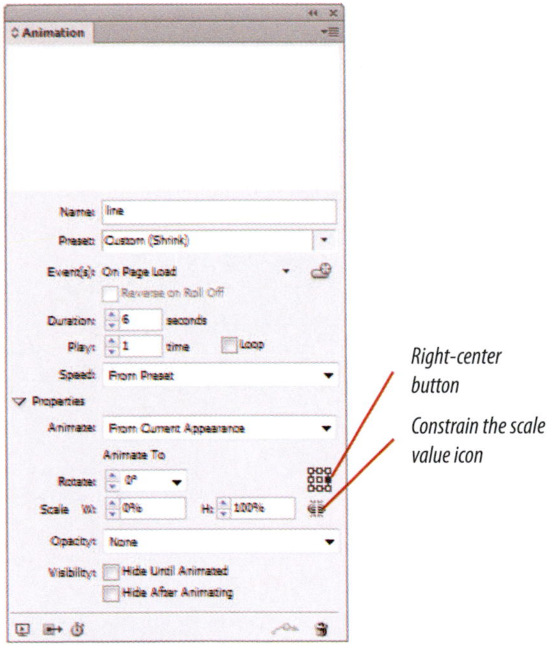

Right-center button

Constrain the scale value icon

Source Adobe® InDesign®, 2013.

Figure 11 *Settings for the Appear animation*

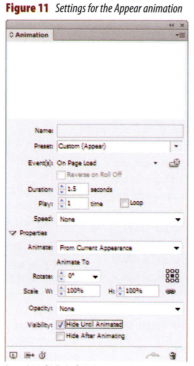

Source Adobe® InDesign®, 2013.

Apply an Appear animation

1. Use the **Selection tool** to select all five of the small images at the bottom of the page.

2. Click the **Preset menu** on the Animation panel, then click **Appear**.

3. Set the duration to **1.5** seconds.

4. Verify that the Event(s) menu is set to **On Page Load**.

5. Verify that the Opacity menu is set to **None**.

6. In the Visibility section, check the **Hide Until Animated check box**.

   Your Animation panel should resemble Figure 11.

7. Save your work.

You selected five images and set them to appear on page load.

Preview
ANIMATION

What You'll Do

Image courtesy of Chris Botello. Source Adobe® InDesign®, 2013.

In this lesson, you will use the SWF Preview panel to preview and test animations.

Previewing Animations

Applying animations can be simple or complex, depending on the goal toward which you are striving. As you work, you'll want to test out the animations you're applying to see whether you like the presets and whether they're working properly. Rather than export the file over and over again, you can use the SWF Preview panel, shown in Figure 12, for a quick preview of your work. You can resize the panel by dragging its lower corner, which makes all of the objects on the page large enough to test.

When you press the Play button on the SWF Preview panel, the page is reloaded on the panel, just as it would be in a browser window. The SWF Preview panel then "plays" the presentation, showing animations as they would occur in the exported file.

In addition to showing all animations, the SWF Preview panel displays button appearances and plays sounds that you've assigned to buttons. The mouse pointer will turn into the classic finger-pointer icon when it's positioned over a hyperlink on the SWF Preview panel.

The SWF Preview panel shows only the current page in the InDesign layout. Buttons and hyperlinks that take you to new InDesign pages will not open those pages on the panel. However, if you click a button or hyperlink that is linked to a website, a browser window will open and take you to the destination. This is a great way to quickly test that the URLs you've set as destinations are live and working without having to first export the file.

Figure 12 *SWF Preview panel*

Image courtesy of Chris Botello. Source Adobe® InDesign®, 2013.

Figure 13 *Page previewed in the SWF Preview panel*

Image courtesy of Chris Botello. Source Adobe® InDesign®, 2013.

Use the SWF Preview panel

1. Expand the SWF Preview panel, then drag the lower-right corner and the left edge to enlarge it.

   The preview might begin playing automatically when you open the panel.

2. Click the **Play button** 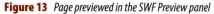.

   The eight animations occur sequentially: Fly in from Left, then Fly in from Top, then Shrink, then the five Appear animations. By default, animations are played in the order they were applied. The Fade animation on the black and white image doesn't play automatically because it is set to play when clicked, not on page load.

3. Click the **black and white image** in the Preview window.

   The black and white image fades away, revealing the color image beneath it, as shown in Figure 13. You can click anywhere on the page to launch this animation.

4. Float the mouse pointer over the right arrow at the bottom of the page.

   The arrow color changes to Gold, which is the color of the rollover appearance.

5. Click the **right arrow**.

   The Click.mp3 file sounds, but the link does not take you to the next page.

6. Click the **home page link**.

   Clicking the link launches your browser and takes you to www.lecinqueterre.org/eng, the official website of The Cinque Terre.

Use the Timing Panel
TO CONTROL ANIMATION

What You'll Do

Source Adobe® InDesign®, 2013.

In this lesson, you will use the Timing panel to change the order of animations and the timing of when they occur.

Using the Timing Panel

To work with animation, you need to think of the exported document as being a presentation displayed in a linear timeline. There is no actual timeline feature in InDesign, however, you can think of the moment when the exported page loads in the browser window as starting the timeline for the presentation. For example, if you set an animation to occur when the page is loaded, and you set the duration for the animation to be five seconds, you can think of the animation as playing for the first five seconds of the presentation.

This implies the question, "Then what happens?" The answer could be, "Nothing more happens." In some presentations, animations occur when the page is loaded, and that's it—after that, there are no more animations. You're left to read the page, view items on the page, or click links or buttons to take you to another page. But when you think of a presentation as occurring on a timeline, it opens the possibility of sequential animation. In other words, *first* this happens, *then* this happens, and *then* when I click this, this happens.

The Timing panel, shown in Figure 14, is used to control when animated objects play. Whenever you apply an animation to an object, that animation is listed on the Timing panel by its default name or the name you

Figure 14 *Timing panel*

Source Adobe® InDesign®, 2013.

apply to the animation. The Timing panel lists all the animations on a current spread, specifying the page event assigned to each animation. For example, the figure shows that the Boats.tif animation will occur on the On Page Load event.

One useful event is Page Click. Rather than clicking a specific button or link on the page, you can simply click any area of the page to execute animations set up as Page Click events. This can improve slide presentations by creating "invisible" launch events. In other words, rather than clicking a button, which is an obvious move to launch an animation, you can unobtrusively click anywhere on the page, making animations seemingly happen automatically.

By default, animated objects are listed on the Timing panel in the order they were created. Similarly, by default, animations listed for the Page Load event occur sequentially in the order they were created, one after the other with no pause in between. Animations specified as Page Click events occur sequentially every time the page is clicked.

Use the Timing panel to change the order of animations, to have animations play simultaneously, and to delay the start of animations.

Use the Timing panel

1. Expand the Timing panel, then click **thursday august 11** in the list.

   As shown in Figure 15, the event you specified for thursday, august 11—On Page Load—is displayed, and the Delay text box becomes available. Eight animations are listed on the Timing panel in the order that they were applied and the order in which they will play. The Fade animation is not listed, because it doesn't occur automatically.

2. Click the **up triangle** to set the delay to **3** seconds.

3. Click the **Play button**  on the SWF Preview panel.

   The animation is delayed for three seconds. The subsequent animations are therefore also delayed.

4. Set the delay on the thursday august 11 selection back to **0**.

5. Click and drag the **CORNIGLIA animation** above the thursday august 11 animation so that it is at the top of the Timing panel, as shown in Figure 16.

   The horizontal black bar that appears as you drag the animation on the panel indicates where the item being dragged will be positioned when you release the mouse pointer.

6. Click the **Play button** on the SWF Preview panel. The CORNIGLIA animation plays first.

7. Shift-click to select the **first three animations** on the Timing panel.

8. Click the **Play together button** on the Timing panel.

   As shown in Figure 17, a bracket indicates that the animations are grouped to play together.

9. Select the **five .tif files** listed on the Timing panel, then click the **Play together button**.

   (continued)

Figure 15 *Eight animations listed on the Timing panel*

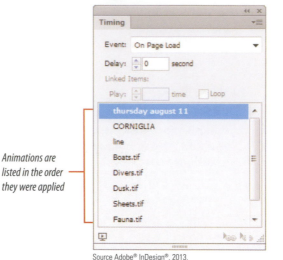

Source Adobe® InDesign®, 2013.

Animations are listed in the order they were applied

Figure 16 *CORNIGLIA animation moved to be the first in the list*

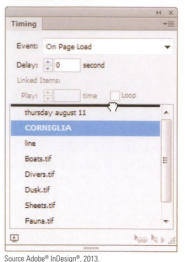

Source Adobe® InDesign®, 2013.

Figure 17 *Setting animations to play simultaneously*

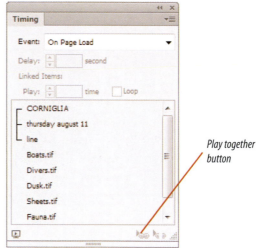

Source Adobe® InDesign®, 2013.

Play together button

Figure 18 *General settings in the Export SWF dialog box*

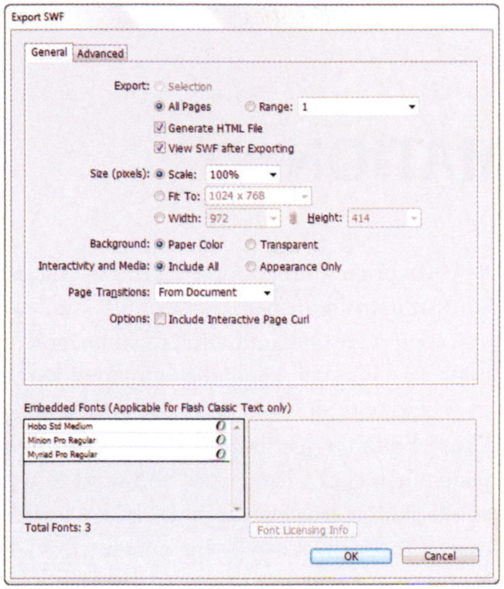

Figure 19 *Advanced settings in the Export SWF dialog box*

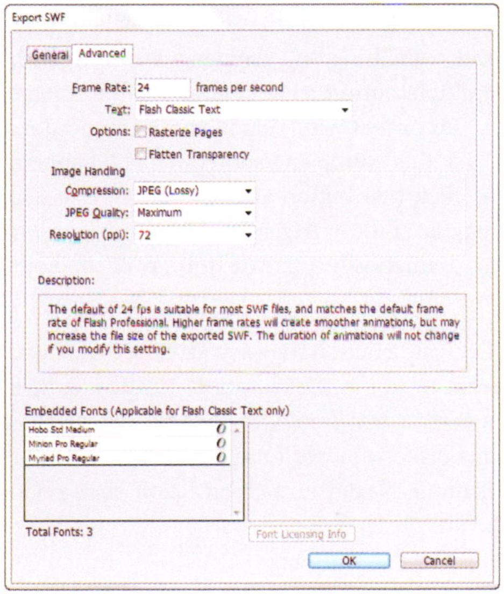

10. Click the **Play button** ▶ on the SWF Preview panel.

    The first three animations play simultaneously, then the five images appear simultaneously.

11. Save your work.

You used the SWF Preview panel to preview animations as you altered the document. You used the Timing panel to add a delay to an animation, to reorder animations, and to make three animations play simultaneously.

Export an animated document as an SWF

1. Click the **File menu**, then click **Export**.

2. Navigate to the folder on your computer in which you want to save the exported file.

    Choose **Flash Player (SWF)** from the Save as type menu (Win) or Format menu (Mac), then click **Save**.

    The Export SWF dialog box opens.

3. Verify that your General settings match those shown in Figure 18.

    Note that the Include Interactive Page Curl check box is not checked for this export.

4. Click the **Advanced tab**, then verify that your Advanced settings match those shown in Figure 19.

5. Click **OK**.

    The SWF file opens automatically. Three animations occur simultaneously upon page load, then the five small images appear simultaneously.

6. Click the **black and white image**.

    The black and white image fades slowly to reveal the color image behind it.

7. Return to the InDesign file and save your work.

You exported an animated document. You then clicked in the SWF to test the animations.

Lesson 3   Use the Timing Panel to Control Animation

Use a Button
TO TRIGGER ANIMATION

What You'll Do

Source Adobe® InDesign®, 2013.

In this lesson, you will use a button to make an animation play.

Using Buttons to Play Animations

The very essence of a button is to make something happen when you click it. In addition to navigating from page to page or launching a URL, buttons can be used to play animations. This is a very powerful option when you're designing a presentation, because the action triggered by the button will only occur if the viewer *chooses* to click the button.

The button plays the role of the signal or sign post, telling the viewer, "Click here and something will happen." Working with multiple button triggers allows you to create a "this or that" situation in your presentation: Click this button and something will happen, or click that button and something else will happen. Button triggers offer you the power to dramatically increase the scope of your presentation.

To create a button trigger, you choose what you want to use as the button. It can be a simple square, a text frame, or a placed image. For this discussion, we'll use a blue square as our example. Next, you apply an action, such as Go to URL, or an animation, such as Fly Out, to another item on the page. For example, let's say you apply a Fly Out animation to an image of a butterfly. Once you apply the animation to the item, and with the item still selected, click the Create button trigger button on the Animation panel, then click the artwork you want to use as the button trigger (the blue square in this case). The artwork will be converted to a button and it will be programmed to animate the butterfly image using the Fly Out preset, when clicked in the exported file.

Once you've created a button and formatted it to trigger an animation, you can apply an animation to the button itself. For example, in some cases, you'll want the button to disappear after it's been clicked. That's easy to do: Simply apply the Disappear animation to the button; then, when specifying the event that will trigger the Disappear animation, choose On Click (Self) from the Event menu. The result will be that, when the button is clicked, it will trigger an animation and the button itself will disappear.

Figure 20 *Positioning the finger-pointer artwork*

Image courtesy of Chris Botello. Source Adobe® InDesign®, 2013.

Figure 21 *Create button trigger button*

Create button
trigger button

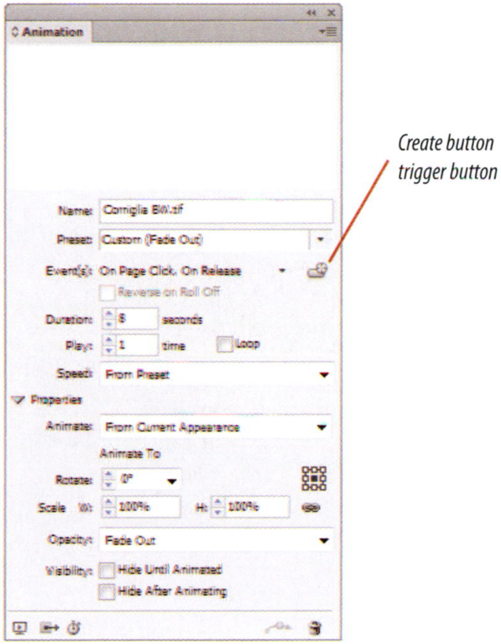

Source Adobe® InDesign®, 2013.

Use a button to trigger an animation

1. Verify that you're on page 1 of the InDesign document, then regard the black and white image.

   The black and white fade animation is very effective in the SWF. The only problem is that most people won't know to click the image to activate the animation. To remedy this we'll use a button to trigger the animation.

2. Find the **finger-pointer artwork** on the pasteboard.

3. Drag the **finger-pointer artwork** over the black and white image, click the **Object menu**, point to **Arrange**, then click **Bring to Front**.

4. Deselect then compare your screen to Figure 20.

5. Use the **Selection tool** to select the **black and white image**.

6. Click the **Create button trigger button** on the Animation panel, shown in Figure 21, then click the **finger-pointer artwork**.

   The finger-pointer artwork is converted to a button that will trigger the Fade animation on the black and white image.

(continued)

7. Note that the finger-pointer artwork is now a new button listed on the Buttons and Forms panel, as shown in Figure 22.

   In the figure, the new button is automatically named Button 11; yours might have a different number. Note that in the Actions section, the checked action is Animation and Corniglia BW.tif is identified as that which will be animated.

8. Note that the selected finger-pointer button is also listed on the Animation panel.

   Next, you will apply the Disappear animation to the finger-pointer button so that it will disappear after it is clicked and the color image will appear unobstructed.

9. Click the **Preset list arrow** on the Animation panel, then click **Disappear**.

10. Set the duration to **0.5** seconds.

11. Click the **Event(s) list arrow**, then click **On Click (Self)**.

    As opposed to the On Page Click event, which triggers an animation when the page is clicked anywhere, On Click (Self) will trigger the animation when the button itself is clicked.

12. Click the **Event(s) menu list arrow** again, then click **On Page Load** to deselect this option.

    We want the button to disappear only when it is clicked, not when the page is loaded.

    (continued)

Figure 22 *New button listed on the Buttons and Forms panel*

Source Adobe® InDesign®, 2013.

Figure 23 *Animation settings to make the button trigger disappear*

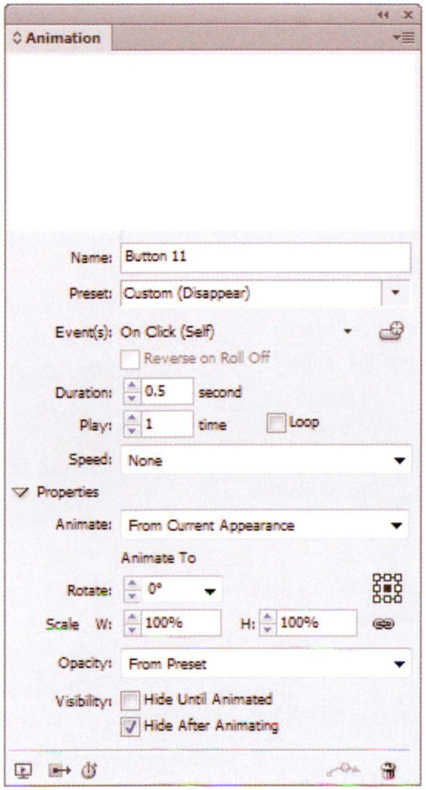

Source Adobe® InDesign®, 2013.

13. In the Visibility section of the Animation panel, check the **Hide After Animating check box** so that your Animation panel resembles Figure 23.

14. Save your work.

15. Export an SWF file with the same settings you last used.

16. Allow the automatic animations to execute.

17. Click the **finger-pointer button**.

    The button disappears when clicked and the black and white image fades, exposing the color image.

18. Return to InDesign, then close **Italian Presentation Animated.indd**.

You used artwork as a button to trigger an animation. You then applied a Disappear animation to the button so that it disappears when clicked.

Apply animations.

1. Open the file ID 2-2.indd, then save it as **Italian Presentation Animated SR**.
2. Go to page 2, then expand the Animation panel.
3. Click the Selection tool, then select the text frame for the tuesday august 16 text.
4. Click the Preset list arrow, then click Fly in from Right.
5. Verify that the Event(s) option is set to On Page Load.
6. Set the duration to 2 seconds.
7. Note the Location text box in the Properties section of the Animation panel.
8. Click the Opacity list arrow, then verify that Fade In is chosen.
9. In the Visibility section, click the Hide Until Animated check box.
10. Select the text frame for the FIRENZE text.
11. Click the Preset list arrow, then click Fly in from Top.
12. Set the duration to 2 seconds, then verify that your Animation panel settings match Figure 24.
13. Save your work.
14. Use the Selection tool to select the large image on page 2.
15. Click the Edit menu, click Copy, click the Edit menu again, then click Paste in Place.
16. Click the File menu, click Place, navigate to where your Chapter 2 Data Files are stored, navigate to the Links folder, then place Woman in Window BW.tif.
17. With the frame still selected, click the Preset list arrow on the Animation panel, then click Fade Out.
18. Set the duration to 8 seconds.
19. Click the Event(s) list arrow, then click On Page Click.
20. Click the Event(s) list arrow again, then click On Page Load to deselect this option.

21. Verify that both check boxes in the Visibility section of the Animation panel are not checked.
22. Save your work.
23. Use the Selection tool to select the green horizontal line on the page.
24. Copy the line then paste it in place.
25. Use the Swatches panel to change the stroke color to Gold.
26. With the gold line still selected, click the Preset list arrow on the Animation panel, then click Shrink.
27. Set the duration to 6 seconds.
28. Verify that the Event(s) option is set to On Page Load.
29. In the Properties section, click the Constrain the scale value icon if necessary, so that it appears unlinked or broken.
30. Verify that the Opacity option is set to None.
31. Click the left-center button on the origin icon, set the W (width) value to 0, then set the H (height) value to 100%.
32. Save your work.
33. Use the Selection tool to select all five of the small images at the bottom of page 2.
34. Click the Preset list arrow on the Animation panel, then click Appear.
35. Set the duration to 2 seconds.
36. Verify that the Event(s) option is set to On Page Load.
37. Verify that the Opacity option is set to None.
38. In the Visibility section, check the Hide Until Animated check box.
39. Save your work.

Preview animations.

1. Expand the SWF Preview panel, then drag the lower-right corner and the left edge to enlarge it.
2. Click the Play button to preview the eight animation sequences.
3. Click the black and white image in the Preview window.
4. Float over the right arrow at the bottom of the page to see the arrow color change to gold.
5. Click the right arrow to hear the Click.mp3 sound.

Figure 24 *Animation panel settings*

Source Adobe® InDesign®, 2013.

Adding Animation to a Presentation

Use the Timing panel.

1. Expand the Timing panel so that it stays open, then click tuesday august 16 in the list.
2. Click the up triangle to set the delay to 3 seconds.
3. Click the Play button on the SWF Preview panel.
4. Set the delay on the tuesday august 16 selection back to 0.
5. Click and drag the FIRENZE animation to the top of the Timing panel.
6. Click the Play button on the SWF Preview panel.
7. Shift-click to select the first three animations on the Timing panel.
8. Click the Play together button on the Timing panel.
9. Select the five .tif files in the list on the Timing panel, then click the Play together button.
10. Click the Play button on the SWF Preview panel.
11. Save your work.

Export an animated document as an SWF.

1. Click the File menu, then click Export.
2. Navigate to the folder on your computer in which you want to save the exported file.
3. Choose Flash Player (SWF) from the Save as type menu (Win) or Format menu (Mac) then click Save.
4. Verify that your General export settings match Figure 25. (*Hint*: Be sure to change the Range option to 2 to view page 2 only.)

Figure 25 *General settings*

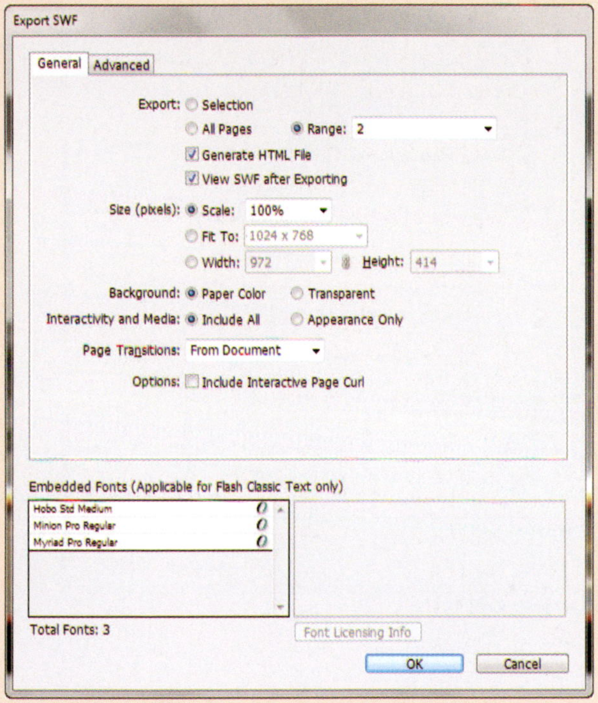

Source Adobe® InDesign®, 2013.

5. Click the Advanced tab, then verify that your Advanced export settings match Figure 26.
6. Click OK to preview the animations upon page load.

7. Click the main image to watch it fade slowly revealing the color image behind it.
8. Return to the InDesign file and save your work.

Use a button to trigger an animation.

1. Verify that you're on page 2 of the InDesign document, then regard the black and white image.
2. Find the finger-pointer artwork on the pasteboard, position it over the black and white image, then bring it to the front.

Figure 26 *Advanced settings*

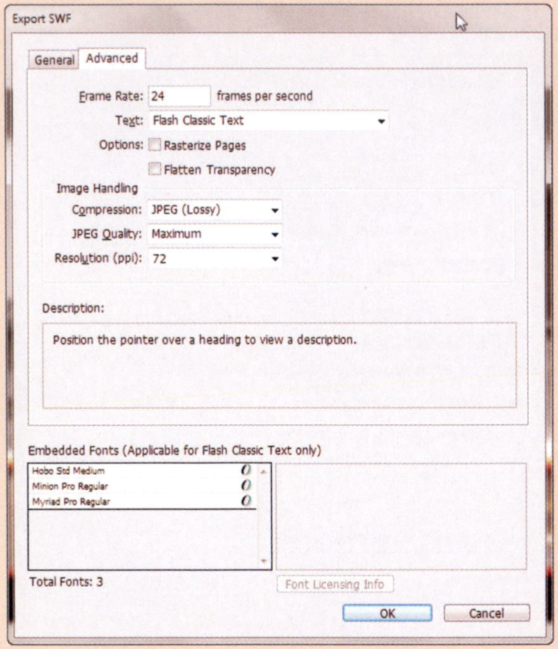

Source Adobe® InDesign®, 2013.

3. Use the Selection tool to select the black and white image.
4. With the image still selected, click the Create button trigger button on the Animation panel, then click the finger-pointer artwork.
5. Click the Preset list arrow on the Animation panel, then click Disappear.
6. Set the duration to 0.5 seconds.

7. Click the Event(s) list arrow, then click On Click (Self).
8. Click the Event(s) list arrow again, then click On Page Load to deselect this option.
9. In the Visibility section of the Animation panel, check the Hide After Animating check box so that your Animation panel resembles Figure 27.

10. Save your work.
11. Export an SWF file with the same settings you last used.
12. Allow the automatic animations to execute.
13. Click the finger-pointer button.
14. Return to InDesign, then close Italian Presentation Animated SR.indd.

Figure 27 *Settings for the Appear animation*

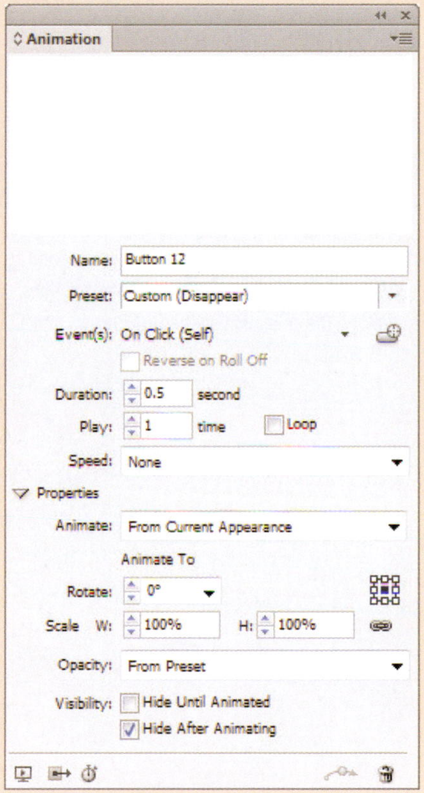

Source Adobe® InDesign®, 2013.

In most projects, you'll likely use only the basic fade, appear, and disappear animations because they're subtle and don't call too much attention to themselves. But the Animation panel has a number of unusual and exotic presets that are fun to investigate. In this project, you'll reinforce the skills you worked with in the chapter, but this time you'll have the opportunity to try out some of the more kooky and quirky animations that InDesign has to offer. When you're done, feel free to redo the project with other animations you want to investigate, and try to come up with strategies to make them interact with the layout in interesting ways.

1. Open the file ID 2-3.indd, then save it as **Maui Presentation Animated**.
2. On page 2, apply a 1.5-second Fly in from Top animation to the two middle images on the page.
3. Verify that the event is On Page Load and that the Opacity is set to Fade In.
4. Hide the images until they are animated.
5. Select the leftmost image, then apply the Fly in from Left animation.
6. Set the duration to 1.5 seconds, then verify that the Opacity option is set to Fade In.
7. Hide the image until it is animated.
8. Select the rightmost image, then apply the Fly in from Right animation.
9. Set the duration to 1.5 seconds, then verify that the Opacity option is set to Fade In.
10. Hide the image until it is animated.
11. Preview the animation on the SWF Preview panel.
12. On the Timing panel, select Flower.tif and Lagoon.tif, then specify that they play together.
13. On the Timing panel, select Tree coverage.tif and Waterfall.tif, then specify that they play together.
14. Preview the animation on the SWF Preview panel.
15. Save your work.
16. Go to page 2, then select the black and white image.
17. Apply the Smoke animation, then set the duration to 2 seconds.
18. Hide the images until they animate and after they animate.
19. On the Timing panel, click Tree coverage BW.tif, then set the delay to 2 (seconds).
20. Go to page 3, select the black and white image, then apply the Fly out Left animation.
21. Set the duration to 2 seconds, then hide it after animating.
22. On the Timing panel, click Lagoon BW.tif, then set the delay to 2 (seconds).
23. Go to page 4, select the black and white image, then apply the Shrink animation.
24. Set the duration to 2 seconds, then hide it after animating.

25. On the Animation panel, set the W value to 0%, set the H value to 0%.

26. On the Timing panel, click Flower BW.tif, then set the delay to 2 (seconds).

27. Go to page 5, then select the black and white image.

28. Apply the Gallop animation, set the duration to 2 seconds, then click Hide After Animating.

29. On the Timing panel, click Waterfall BW.tif, then set the delay to 2 (seconds).

30. Export an SWF file, then use the arrow buttons shown in Figure 28 to move from page to page and view the animations.

31. Return to InDesign, save your work, then close Maui Presentation.indd.

Figure 28 *Completed Project Builder 1*

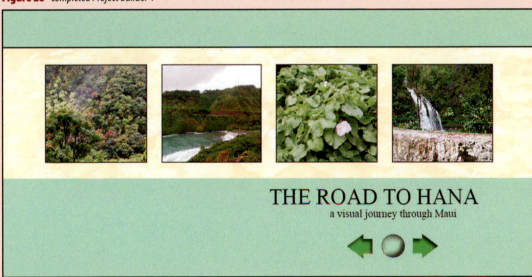

Image courtesy of Chris Botello. Source Adobe® InDesign®, 2013.

ADOBE INDESIGN CS6 INTERACTIVE

CHAPTER 3 WORKING WITH OBJECT STATES
AND VIDEO

1. Work with object states
2. Place video in a layout
3. Use buttons as video controls
4. Control video with navigation points

CHAPTER 3 WORKING WITH OBJECT STATES AND VIDEO

Object states are one of InDesign's most compelling features. They allow you to create different versions of the same object in one document. They play an especially powerful role with interactive presentations. You can think of object states as capturing a moment in time when you are designing a layout.

Video has been around for quite some time, but ever since YouTube debuted in the mid-2000s, video has been omnipresent on the web. Now, with InDesign CS6, video can become a central component of your interactive presentations.

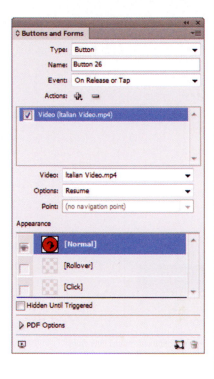

Image courtesy of Chris Botello. Source Adobe® InDesign®, 2013.

Work with
OBJECT STATES

What You'll Do

Source Adobe® InDesign®, 2013.

In this lesson, you will create object states then assign buttons to each state.

Understanding Object States

To best understand object states, let's use a real world example. Let's say you are designing a layout with a lot of images against a colored background. Your client tells you to try three different colors for the background: red, blue, and green. Without object states, you'd need to give the client three different documents with three different backgrounds: one red, one blue, and one green.

Using object states, you can instead save all three backgrounds on the Object States panel.

First, you would create a frame and fill it with one of the three colors to represent the colored background in the layout. The next step is to convert the object into a multi-state object using the Convert selection to multi-state object button on the Object States panel.

When you do so, two states will appear on the panel, as shown in Figure 1. To change the fill color of the second state, simply click it in the panel, then change the fill color. To create the third state, click the Create new state button on the Object States panel.

QUICK TIP

The Convert selection to multi-state object button becomes the Create new state button once an object has been converted to a multi-state object.

As shown in Figure 2, there are now three states of the rectangular frame. What's great about the Object States panel is that it's interactive. If you click on State 2, the frame on the page will change to blue. If you click on State 3, the frame on the page will change to Green. This means that you could send one InDesign file to your client, and your client could view the three options by clicking each state on the Object States panel. Or instead, you could create a free-standing button that the client could click to see all three backgrounds.

Assigning Buttons to Object States

The ability to assign buttons to object states creates a world of possibilities for interactive documents. You might not call them object states, but if you use the web, you use them all the time without realizing it. For example, let's say you go to a website and you see a shirt that you like. In the picture, the shirt is blue, but underneath the picture you see six colored squares which indicate the other colors that the shirt is available in. When you click a colored square, the picture of the shirt changes to that color.

In InDesign, that's done with object states. First create a graphics frame and convert it to a multi-state object—with six states for six different colors: let's say red, white, yellow, green, blue, and black. In State 1, place an image of the red shirt. In State 2, place an image of the white shirt. Move through the list and import a different color shirt image for

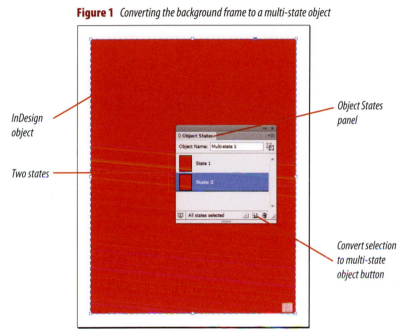

InDesign object

Two states

Object States panel

Convert selection to multi-state object button

Source Adobe® InDesign®, 2013.

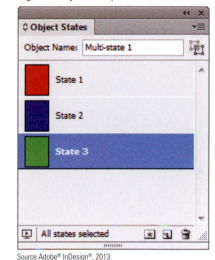

Source Adobe® InDesign®, 2013.

each state. Then, make six color squares—red through black—and convert them to buttons. On the Buttons and Forms panel, link each button with its corresponding state using the Go To State action as shown in Figure 3. When you choose the Go To State action, all of the states created in the document are listed in the States menu of the Buttons and Forms panel. In the exported file, when you click a colored square, the shirt with the corresponding color appears in the frame.

Imagination plays a big role here. Object states, like most of the interactive utilities in InDesign, aren't designed for a specific purpose or to be used in a specific way. They are a function of InDesign, but how you use them is limited only by your imagination.

Figure 3 *Linking a button to an object state*

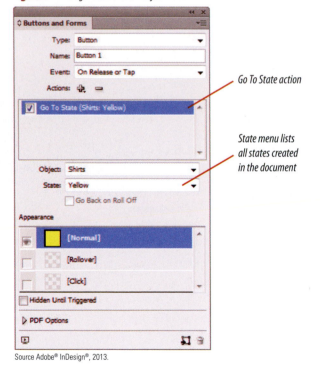

Go To State action

State menu lists all states created in the document

Source Adobe® InDesign®, 2013.

Figure 4 *Object States panel*

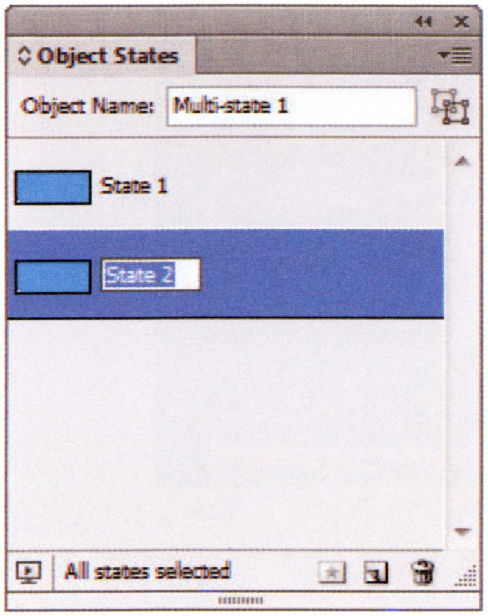

Object States

Object Name: Multi-state 1

State 1

State 2

All states selected

Source Adobe® InDesign®, 2013.

Figure 5 *Naming five object states*

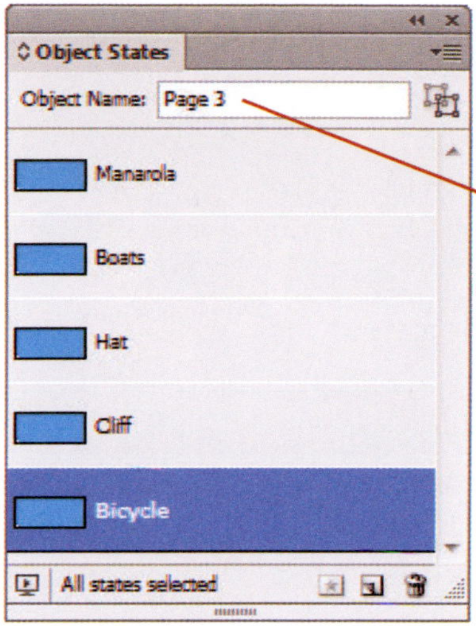

Object States

Object Name: Page 3

Manarola

Boats

Hat

Cliff

Bicycle

All states selected

Object Name identifies the multi-state object

Source Adobe® InDesign®, 2013.

Figure 6 *Positioning the Manarola image*

Image courtesy of Chris Botello. Source Adobe® InDesign®, 2013.

Create object states

1. Open the file ID 3-1.indd, then save it as **Italian Object States**.

   Pages 1 and 2 include all of the buttons, hyperlinks, and animations you created in Chapters 1 and 2.

2. Go to page 3, then display the Object States panel.

   TIP The Object States panel is in the Interactive section of the Window menu.

3. Click the **Selection tool** , then select the **large blue picture frame**.

4. Click the **Convert selection to multi-state object button** on the Object States panel.

   As shown in Figure 4, two states are created and listed on the panel.

5. Click the **Create new state button** three times to add three more states to the panel.

6. On the Object States panel, change the Object Name to **Page 3**.

   The object you are naming is the large blue frame that you just converted to a multi-state object.

7. Rename each of the states using the names provided in Figure 5.

8. Click to target the state named **Manarola**.

9. Click the **File menu**, click **Place**, navigate to the Links folder, then open the file named **Manarola**.

   The image will not appear in the frame. Instead, the loaded image icon appears as the cursor.

10. Click the **blue frame** to place the image.

11. Size and position the image so that it resembles Figure 6.

(continued)

12. Click the object state named **Boats** on the Object States panel.

    The Boats object state is targeted.

13. Place the **Boats image** as shown in Figure 7.

14. Click the object state named **Hat**.

15. Place the **Hat image** as shown in Figure 8.

16. Click the object state named **Cliff**.

(continued)

Figure 7 *Positioning the Boats image*

Images courtesy of Chris Botello. Source Adobe® InDesign®, 2013.

Figure 8 *Positioning the Hat image*

Images courtesy of Chris Botello. Source Adobe® InDesign®, 2013.

Figure 9 *Positioning the Cliff image*

Images courtesy of Chris Botello. Source Adobe® InDesign®, 2013.

Figure 10 *Positioning the Bicycle image*

Images courtesy of Chris Botello. Source Adobe® InDesign®, 2013.

17. Place the **Cliff image** as shown in Figure 9.
18. Click the object state named **Bicycle**.
19. Place the **Bicycle image** as shown in Figure 10.
20. Click randomly on each of the five states.

    Each state is different; when you click a state, the image you imported for that state appears in the large frame.
21. Save your work.

You created five states on the Object States panel, named them, then placed a different image for each state.

Assign buttons to object states

1. Select the five small images on page 3.

2. On the Buttons and Forms panel, click the **Convert to button icon** 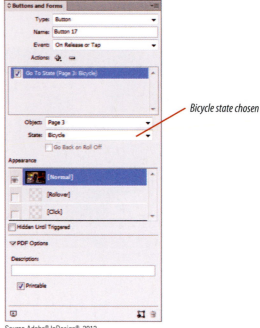.

   The five frames are converted to buttons.

3. Deselect all, then select only the small bicycle button.

4. On the Buttons and Forms panel, click the **plus sign button**, then click **Go To State**.

5. On the Buttons and Forms panel, click the **State list arrow** to view the five states, shown in Figure 11, then click **Bicycle**.

   Your Object States panel should resemble Figure 12.

   (continued)

Figure 11 *State menu showing the five object states created in this document*

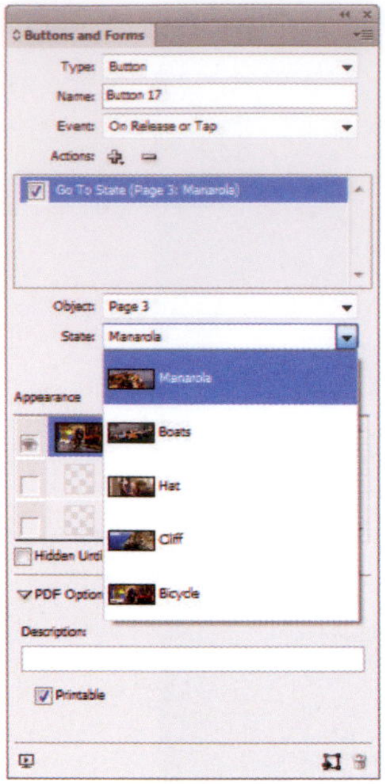

Source Adobe® InDesign®, 2013.

Figure 12 *Bicycle button linked to Bicycle state*

Bicycle state chosen

Source Adobe® InDesign®, 2013.

Working with Object States and Video

Figure 13 *Settings for exporting page 3 as an SWF*

Export SWF

General | Advanced

Export: ○ Selection
○ All Pages   ● Range: 3
☑ Generate HTML File
☑ View SWF after Exporting

Size (pixels): ● Scale: 100%
○ Fit To: 1024 x 768
○ Width: 972   Height: 414

Background: ● Paper Color   ○ Transparent
Interactivity and Media: ● Include All   ○ Appearance Only

Page Transitions: From Document

Options: ☐ Include Interactive Page Curl

Bicycle button linked to Bicycle state

Embedded Fonts (Applicable for Flash Classic Text only)

Hobo Std Medium
Minion Pro Regular
Myriad Pro Regular

Total Fonts: 3   Font Licensing Info

OK   Cancel

Source Adobe® InDesign®, 2013.

Figure 14 *Boats state displayed in the exported SWF*

Image courtesy of Chris Botello. Source Adobe® InDesign®, 2013.

6. Select the small cliff button, click the **plus sign button** 🔲 on the Buttons and Forms panel, then click **Go To State**.

7. Click the **State list arrow**, then choose **Cliff**.

8. Using the same steps, link the three remaining buttons to their respective states.

9. Save your work.

10. Export an SWF file of page 3 only, using the standard settings shown in Figure 13.

11. When the page opens in your browser, click one of the thumbnails on the page.

    As shown in Figure 14, when you click a thumbnail, the large image changes to the associated state.

12. Save your work.

You converted five images to buttons, then assigned the Go To State action to each button. You linked each button to its corresponding state so that, in the output file, clicking a thumbnail image button displayed the large version of the thumbnail in the large blue frame.

Place Video
IN A LAYOUT

Image courtesy of Chris Botello. Source Adobe® InDesign®, 2013.

 In this lesson, you will place a video file in an InDesign layout.

Placing Video Files

As InDesign evolves into an interactive as well as a print application, one remarkable feature is that you can import video files the same way that you import image files: using the Place command. When you click the loaded video cursor on the page or the pasteboard, a frame is created showing the first frame of the video as the preview, as shown in Figure 15. The frame is created using the same dimensions of the video file. You can resize the frame and the video within the frame as you would with a still image.

Figure 15 *A video placed using the Place command*

Frame is created at the same size as the video

Image courtesy of Chris Botello. Source Adobe® InDesign®, 2013.

You also have the option of placing a video file into a pre-existing frame. To do so, use the Place a video or audio file button on the Media panel, identified in Figure 16. You can then use the Fitting commands on the Object menu to fit the video in the frame.

Using the Fitting commands is a bit different for a video than it is for a placed image. With a placed video, the video is placed within a video frame inside the frame on the page. So, when fitting, you must fit *both* the video *and* the video frame inside the provided frame on the page. You can double-click the image preview repeatedly to select each component (the frame on the page, the video frame, and the video itself) then you can fit the two latter elements using the Fitting commands.

QUICK TIP

Videos placed in InDesign always play in a rectangular frame. If you place a video into a circular frame or a frame with rounded corners, the video will nevertheless play full-frame in a rectangle in the exported file.

Choosing the Poster Image

The Media panel is where you manage all the video files placed in an InDesign document. Here you can choose the option to play, pause, or restart a video when the page loads in your browser. You can also choose whether or not to have the video loop. **Loop** is a long-standing video term which means that a video plays continuously, restarting from the beginning over and over again.

The preview window on the Media panel shows one still image from the video, but if you press the Play button or drag the slider, you can see the entire video. Below the video are two time codes: the left time code is that of the current frame in the preview window; the right time code is the length of the entire video.

QUICK TIP

Time code is notated in InDesign in a standard format: hours, minutes, seconds and frames, separated by colons. For example, the time code notation 01:18:21:12 would identify a frame that is one hour, eighteen minutes, twenty-one seconds, and twelve frames into a video.

The term **poster** refers to the frame in the video that shows as a still image before the video plays. By default, the first frame of the video is specified as the poster. Often that is what you want, but sometimes the first frame may not be satisfactory as a poster image. For example, it might be all black or it might have a copyright line or other miscellaneous information that would be unappealing in your layout. Even if the poster frame is perfectly acceptable, there might be a much more interesting frame in your video that would make a more exciting poster.

Figure 16 *Media panel*

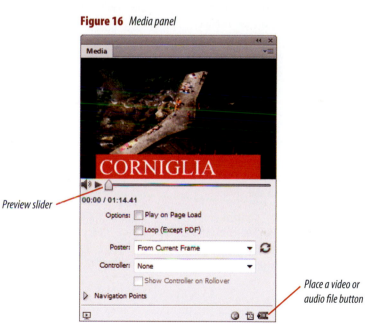

Image courtesy of Chris Botello. Source Adobe® InDesign®, 2013.

You can use the Media panel to change the poster quickly and easily. Verify that the Poster setting on the Media panel is set to From Current Frame, drag the preview slider to the frame of your choice, then click the refresh button, as shown in Figure 17.

Table 1 below describes the four options for choosing a poster using the Poster menu on the Media panel.

Adding Preset Controls to a Placed Video

When you export a video to a browser as an SWF or a PDF, clicking the poster image will cause the video to play. The video will play through to the end and stop, unless it is set to loop. Clicking the poster image is the only automatic interface you have with the video unless you apply a video controller to the video before exporting.

The Media panel includes many types of controller bars—too many to go into detail here—but the top option, SkinOverAll, gives you all the basic controls you need: Play, Pause, Stop, Rewind, and Forward buttons, a volume controller, and a slider to scrub the video.

To apply an automatic video controller to the video in your exported layout, click the Controller menu on the Media panel, as shown in Figure 18, then choose a controller.

Figure 17 *Choosing the poster*

Current frame

Click the refresh button to make the current frame the poster

Images courtesy of Chris Botello. Source Adobe® InDesign®, 2013.

Figure 18 *The Controller menu and its many options*

Controller menu lists a number of pre-designed controllers

Images courtesy of Chris Botello. Source Adobe® InDesign®, 2013.

TABLE 1: OPTIONS FOR CHOOSING A POSTER	
None	There is no preview. The frame containing the video will be transparent until you play the video.
Standard	A video icon appears in the top-left corner of the frame, which is otherwise transparent.
From Current Frame	The frame showing in the preview window will be the poster. This is the default setting.
Choose Image	You choose a still image to be the poster.

© Cengage Learning 2013

When you choose a controller, like SkinOverAll, you won't see it anywhere in your InDesign document; it only appears in the exported file when the video plays. Figure 19 shows an example of the SkinOverAll controller in an exported document.

One of the few problems you might have with controllers is that they appear over the video and therefore obscure part of the image. One very effective solution for this is to activate the Show Controller on Rollover option on the Media panel. With this option, the controller will be visible in the exported file only when the mouse pointer is positioned over the video frame.

Saving Video for Use in InDesign

When you download video files from a video camera, you usually view the files in software supplied from the camera manufacturer or in commercial video editing software like Adobe Premiere. All video software packages offer you many file format options for saving videos. When working with video to be placed in InDesign, your best option is to choose the H.264 file format. Files saved in the H.264 format will have .mp4 as their file suffix. Mp4 files are a standard format and widely used. They're the best choice for InDesign presentations because mp4s will play in an exported SWF presentation and they are also compatible if you want to upload your file to the iPad.

Figure 19 *The controller in the exported document*

Image courtesy of Chris Botello. Source Adobe® InDesign®, 2013.

Place a video file

1. Go to page 4.
2. Click the **File menu**, click **Place**, navigate to the folder where you store your Data Files, click **Italian Video**, then click **Open**.

   The cursor appears as a loaded media pointer.
3. Click anywhere on the pasteboard.

   As shown in Figure 20, the video is placed at full-size in a frame.
4. Press and hold [**Shift**][**Ctrl**] (Win) or [**Shift**] ⌘ (Mac), then drag any one of the resizing handles on the frame.

   The frame and the video within the frame are resized proportionally.
5. Size and position the frame and video as shown in Figure 21.
6. Save your work.

You placed a video using the Place command then resized and positioned it in the layout.

Figure 20 *Placed video file at full size*

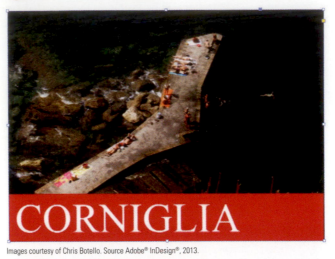

Images courtesy of Chris Botello. Source Adobe® InDesign®, 2013.

Figure 21 *Placed video resized and positioned in layout*

Images courtesy of Chris Botello. Source Adobe® InDesign®, 2013.

Working with Object States and Video

Figure 22 *Previewing the video on the Media panel*

Images courtesy of Chris Botello. Source Adobe® InDesign®, 2013.

Figure 23 *Choosing a frame to be the poster image*

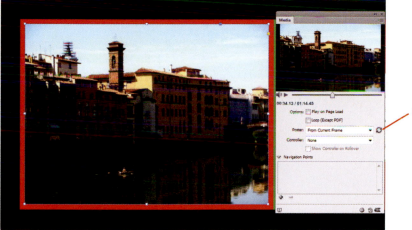

Refresh button

Images courtesy of Chris Botello. Source Adobe® InDesign®, 2013.

Specify the poster image

1. On the Media panel, drag the **slider** approximately half way until you see the frame shown in Figure 22.

2. Note that the default option for the Poster setting is From Current Frame.

   The poster is the frame that will be showing in the layout before the video begins playing.

3. Click the **refresh button** ⟳ to the right of the Poster menu.

   Clicking the refresh button defines the current frame in the preview window as the current poster frame. Your page and Media panel should resemble Figure 23.

4. Save your work.

You used the Media panel to choose a frame as the poster for the video.

Add a preset controller to a video

1. On the Media panel, click the **Controller list arrow**, then click **SkinOverAll**.

   Your Media panel should resemble Figure 24.

2. Save your work.

3. Export page 4 as an SWF.

4. When the page loads in your browser, note that the image in the frame is the one you chose as the poster.

   (continued)

Figure 24 *Choosing a controller type*

Controller menu

Image courtesy of Chris Botello. Source Adobe® InDesign®, 2013.

Figure 25 *The video and the controller in the exported file*

Image courtesy of Chris Botello. Source Adobe® InDesign®, 2013.

5. Click the image.

   The video plays and the video controller appears on the frame, as shown in Figure 25.

6. Use the controls on the video controller to pause, stop, and resume playing the video.

   While the controller is useful, for this video, it's not the best choice, because it obstructs the title cards with the city names.

7. Close the browser window when you are done, then return to the InDesign file.

8. On the Media panel, activate the **Show Controller on Rollover option**.

9. Export page 4 as an SWF.

10. When the page loads in the browser, click the image to play the video.

    The video controller will appear only when you position the cursor over the image.

11. Close the browser window when you are done, then return to the InDesign file.

12. Save your work.

You used the Controller menu on the Media panel to choose a controller for the exported video then applied the Show Controller on Rollover option.

Use Buttons as
VIDEO CONTROLS

What You'll Do

Source Adobe® InDesign®, 2013.

In this lesson, you will create buttons to play, pause, and restart a video.

Using Buttons to Control a Video

Sometimes, the preset video controls just aren't enough. When you're designing a layout with a placed video, you may want to design your own video control buttons. Why? Well, for one reason, it's fun to design cool-looking buttons. Buttons are fun. When compared with the perfunctory and somewhat cold look of preset video controls, well-designed and visually interesting buttons are more inviting to the person viewing your layout and will make it more likely that they want to interact with your video.

The power of the Buttons and Forms panel reveals itself once again, allowing you to format buttons to control video. Once you've converted artwork to a button, all you need to do is apply the Video action to your button. As shown in Figure 26, the Buttons and Forms panel displays options for playing the video.

Use the Video menu to choose which video in the document you want the selected button to control.

The Options menu, expanded in Figure 27, offers six basic controls that you can apply to buttons. Play, Pause, Stop, and Resume are all self-explanatory. Play from Navigation Point allows you to specify any frame in the video as the start frame. Stop All is useful when you have multiple videos in a single document: clicking a button formatted as Stop All will stop all the videos that are playing.

Working with Object States and Video

Figure 26 *Video action on the Buttons and Forms panel*

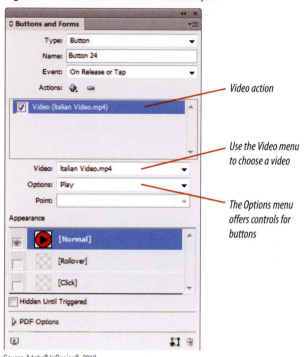

Source Adobe® InDesign®, 2013.

Video action

Use the Video menu to choose a video

The Options menu offers controls for buttons

Figure 27 *Choices on the Options menu*

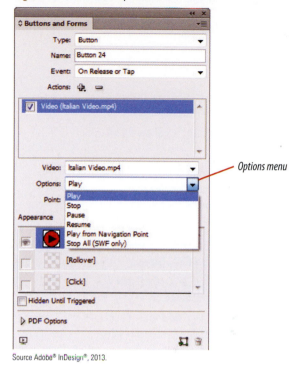

Source Adobe® InDesign®, 2013.

Options menu

Use buttons as video controls

1. Select the **frame** on the page that contains the video.

2. On the Media panel, click the **Controller menu**, then click **None**.

   If the layout were to be exported now, the video would not have a controller at the bottom.

3. Click the **Object menu**, then click **Show All on Spread**.

   Three red icons appear below the video frame.

4. Select the **three red icons**, then click the **Convert to Button icon** on the Buttons and Forms panel.

   All three red icons are converted to buttons.

5. Deselect all, then select the **left button**.

6. Click the **plus sign button** on the Buttons and Forms panel, then click **Video**.

   As shown in Figure 28, Italian Video is automatically loaded, because it is the only video placed in the document. Play, the default, is loaded as the option.

7. Select the **center button**, click the **plus sign button** on the Buttons and Forms panel, then click **Video**.

8. Click the **Options list arrow**, then click **Pause**.

9. Select the **right button**, click the **plus sign button** on the Buttons and Forms panel, then click **Video**.

(continued)

Figure 28 *Linking the button to the video*

Source Adobe® InDesign®, 2013.

Working with Object States and Video

Figure 29 *Applying the Resume option*

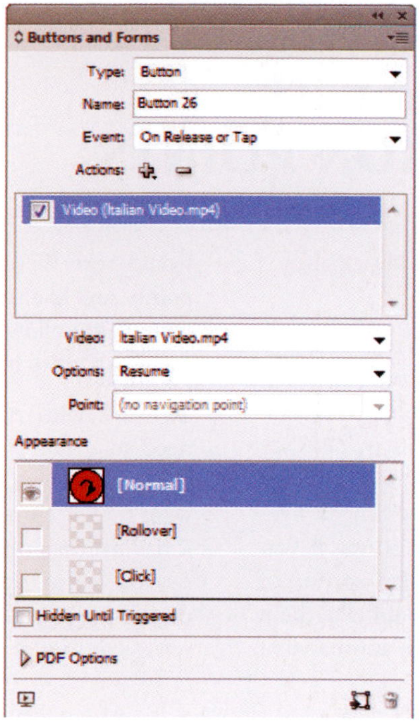

Source Adobe® InDesign®, 2013.

10. Click the **Options list arrow**, then choose **Resume**.

    Your Buttons and Forms panel should resemble Figure 29.

11. Export page 4 as an SWF.

12. When the page loads in your browser, click the **play button**.

13. Click the **pause button**.

14. Click the **resume button**.

15. Return to the InDesign file and save your work.

You created three buttons then used them to play, pause and resume the video.

Control Video with
NAVIGATION POINTS

What You'll Do

Image courtesy of Chris Botello. Source Adobe® InDesign®, 2013.

 In this lesson, you will create navigation points and format buttons to play video from those points.

Using Navigation Points to Play Video from a Specific Frame

Navigation points allow you to identify a specific frame in a video then format a button to play the video from that point. There are a number of uses for this strategy. Let's say you've created an online recipe book, and one page has a video for preparing a five-course meal. You could create a button that would take viewers to the "Soup" section of the video, and another that would take them to the "Salad" section, and still another that would take them to "Desserts." Navigation points are like scene selections in a DVD menu: They allow a viewer to get to a specific point in a video quickly and easily.

To work with navigation points, you first need to create them. On the Media panel, drag the preview slider to the frame that you want to play from. Then you are ready to set a navigation point. The Media panel has a section called Navigation Points. To add a navigation point, click the plus sign and a new navigation point will be created, as shown in Figure 30. Remember that the time code for a frame shows where the frame is in the video in minutes and seconds. Note that the time code that appears in the navigation point also appears in the preview at the top of the panel. The frame is 27 seconds and 9 frames into the video.

It's a good idea to apply a descriptive name to the navigation point. You'll often work with multiple navigation points simultaneously, so naming them clearly will improve your speed and organization.

Once you have created a navigation point, you are ready to link a button to it. With

Figure 30 *Creating a navigation point*

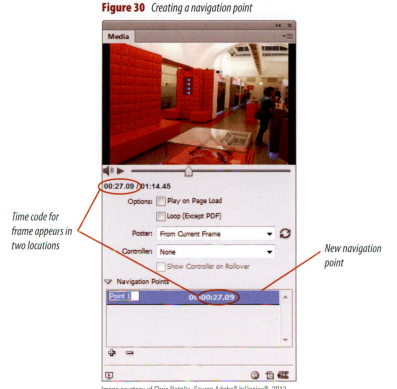

Time code for frame appears in two locations

New navigation point

Image courtesy of Chris Botello. Source Adobe® InDesign®, 2013.

the appropriate button selected, choose the Play from Navigation Point command from the Options menu on the Buttons and Forms panel. When you choose Play from Navigation Point, the Point menu offers you a choice of every navigation point you've created in the document. Pick a navigation point, as shown in Figure 31. In the output file, when the button is clicked, the video will play from that point.

Figure 31 *Specifying a navigation point for a button*

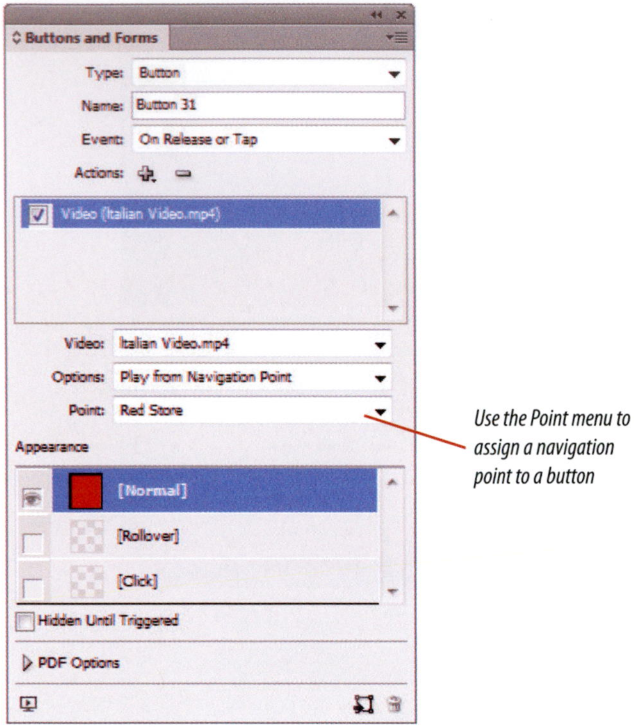

Use the Point menu to assign a navigation point to a button

Source Adobe® InDesign®, 2013.

Figure 32 *Navigation Points section of the Media panel*

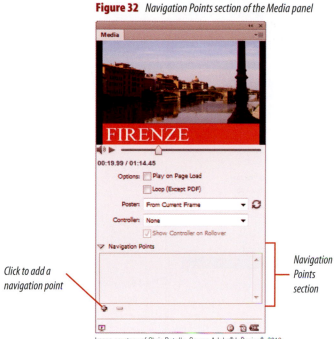

Click to add a navigation point

Navigation Points section

Image courtesy of Chris Botello. Source Adobe® InDesign®, 2013.

Create navigation points

1. Select the **frame** that contains the video.

2. On the Media panel, click the **Loop check box**.

   With the Loop option activated, the video will play continuously, as though it had no beginning or end.

3. Note the top image of the four thumbnail-sized images in the green column.

4. On the Media panel, click the **Play button** ▶ to play the Italian Video.

   When you click the Play button, it changes to a Pause button.

5. Click the **Pause button** ❚❚ when you see the same image as the top thumbnail.

6. Expand the Navigation Points section of the Media panel, if necessary, so that it resembles Figure 32.

(continued)

7. Click the **plus sign button** ⊞ in the Navigation Points section.

   As shown in Figure 33, a new navigation point is added identifying the current frame in the video. The name of the point is automatically highlighted.

8. Name the new point **Firenze**.

9. Drag the **video slider** all the way to the left.

   The first frame in the video is the same as the second thumbnail in the column.

10. Click the **plus sign button** ⊞ in the Navigation Points section, then name the new point **Corniglia**.

11. Click the **Play button** ▶ on the Media panel, then click the **Pause button** ❚❚ when you see the third thumbnail image.

12. Click the **plus sign button** ⊞ in the Navigation Points section, then name the new point **Manarola**.

13. Create the fourth navigation point and name it **Montorosso**.

14. Save your work.

You created four navigation points.

Link a button to a navigation point

1. Select the **four thumbnail images** in the green column and then convert them to buttons.

2. Deselect all, then select just the **top thumbnail image**.

3. Click the **plus sign button** ⊞ on the Buttons and Forms panel, then choose **Video**.

(continued)

Figure 33 *Creating a new navigation point*

Navigation point

Image courtesy of Chris Botello. Source Adobe® InDesign®, 2013.

Figure 34 *Linking a button to the Firenze navigation point*

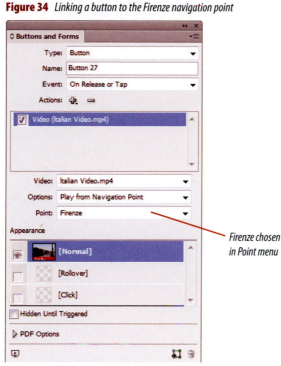

Firenze chosen
in Point menu

4. Click the **Options list arrow**, then click **Play from Navigation Point**.

5. Click the **Point list arrow**, then click **Firenze**.

   Your Buttons and Forms panel should resemble Figure 34.

6. Select the **second thumbnail image**.

7. Click the **plus sign button** ⊕ on the Buttons and Forms panel, then click **Video**.

8. Click the **Options list arrow**, then click **Play from Navigation Point**.

9. In the Point menu, choose **Corniglia**.

10. Using the same steps, link the remaining two buttons to their respective navigation points on the Buttons and Forms panel.

11. Save your work.

12. Export page 4 as an SWF.

13. When the page opens in the browser, click the **top thumbnail image**.

    The video will jump to that image and begin playing.

14. Click the **second thumbnail image**.

    The video will jump to that image and play from that point.

15. Return to the InDesign document.

16. Save your work, then close the document.

You linked four thumbnail images to four navigation points, giving you the option to play the video from those four points.

One of the best and most useful things about object states is that they allow you to showcase multiple images in a single interactive document. In the spirit of giving you a project that you would actually do in your real life, you will create an interactive, emailable holiday card using object states to showcase five photographs.

Apply object states to an image frame.

1. Open the file ID 3-2,indd, then save it as **Interactive Holiday Card**.
2. Expand the Object States panel, then select the black picture frame.
3. Convert the selection to a multi-state object on the Object States panel.
4. Add three more states to the panel.
5. Change the Object Name to **Image**.
6. Rename each of the states as follows: **Family Portrait**, **Julie**, **Jessica**, **Jillian**, **Three Girls**.
7. Target the state named Family Portrait.
8. Place the file named Family Portrait, into the black frame in the layout.
9. Click the Object menu, point to Fitting, then click Fill Frame Proportionally.

10. Use the same steps to import images for the Julie, Jessica, and Three Girls object states (skip the Jillian state).
11. Target the state named Jillian.
12. Place the file named Jillian.
13. Click the Object menu, point to Fitting, then click Fit Content Proportionally.
14. Change the fill color of the frame to Pantone 2975.
15. Click randomly through the states to see each.
16. Save your work.

Apply object states to a text frame.

1. Select the text frame under the large image.
2. Click the Convert selection to multi-state object button on the Object States panel.
3. Click the same button three times so that five states are listed on the panel.
4. In the Object Name text box at the top of the panel, type the name **Text**.
5. Rename each of the states as follows: **Family Portrait text**, **Julie text**, **Jessica text**, **Jillian text**, **Three Girls text**.
6. Click to target the state named Julie text.
7. Click the Type tool, then change the text to read as follows:
   Julie is very excited to be dancing in The Nutcracker this year.

8. Click the Selection tool, then click to target the state named Jessica text.
9. Click the Type tool, then change the text to read as follows:
   Jessica started first grade this year and loves her teacher.
10. Click the Selection tool, then click to target the state named Jillian text.
11. Click the Type tool, then change the text to read as follows:
    Jillian loves preschool and is learning sign language.
12. Click the Selection tool, then click to target the state named Three Girls text.
13. Click the Type tool, then change the text to read as follows:
    Our three sweet girls wish you the happiest of holidays.
14. Click the Selection tool, then click randomly through the states to see each.
15. Save your work.

Link buttons to multiple object states.

1. Select the five small images at the bottom, then convert them to buttons.
2. Deselect all, then select only the first button (far left).
3. Apply the Go To State action to the button.
4. Verify that Image is chosen in the Object menu, then choose Family Portrait in the State menu.
5. Apply the Go To State action to the button.
6. Click the Object menu, then click Text.
7. Click the State menu, then click Family Portrait text.
8. Repeat Steps 4-8 to link the remaining four buttons to their respective image and text states.
9. Save your work.
10. Export an SWF file.
11. When the page opens in the browser, click any of the thumbnails on the page. Figure 35 shows one screen of the completed project.
12. Save your work, then close the document.

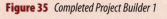

Figure 35 *Completed Project Builder 1*

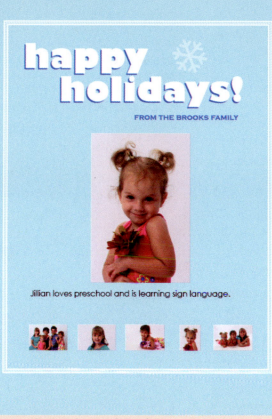

Images courtesy of Chris Botello. Source Adobe® InDesign®, 2013.

When creating an interactive project, don't forget all the options you have with InDesign: beautiful typography, blending modes, effects, transparency—all can be used in your interactive presentation. In the introduction to Lesson 2, you learned that a placed video always plays in a rectangular frame. In this project builder, you'll explore options for working around that issue, using compound paths and InDesign effects to play a video "inside" an old TV screen.

Place a video file.

1. Open ID 3-3.indd, then save it as **Retro TV**.
2. Open the Layers panel and verify that the Compound Path layer is targeted.
3. Place the file named Three Channels Video anywhere on the pasteboard.
4. Position the video frame over the blue rectangle.
5. Press and hold [Shift][Ctrl] (Win) or [Shift] ⌘ (Mac), then resize the frame so that it's just large enough to cover the blue rectangle.
6. On the Layers panel move the selected video file to the Video layer.
7. Select the blue rectangle.
8. Copy it, then paste it in place.
9. Fill the copy with [Paper] (white).
10. Click the Object menu, click Effects, then add an Inner Glow effect with the settings shown in Figure 36.

Figure 36 *Inner Glow settings*

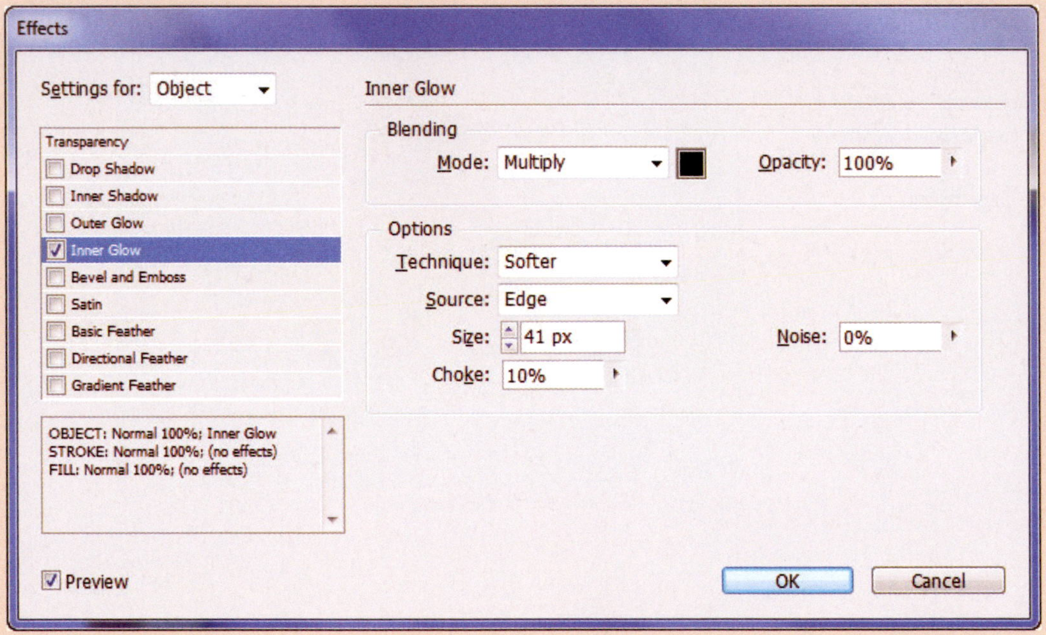

Source Adobe® InDesign®, 2013.

11. With the frame still selected, open the Effects panel, then change the blending mode to Multiply. Your artwork should resemble Figure 37.
12. Click the Object menu, then choose Hide.
13. Select the blue rectangle and the image frame that contains the image of the television.

14. Click the Object menu, point to Paths, then click Make Compound Path.
15. Click the Object menu, then click Show All on Spread. Your screen should resemble Figure 38.
16. Lock the Compound Path layer.
17. Save your work.

Use buttons as video controls.

1. Select the three circle icons at the lower left of the TV then convert them to buttons.
2. Deselect all, then select only the left play button.
3. Apply the Video action to the selected button.
4. Verify that the Options setting is set to Play.

Figure 37 *Inner Glow multiplied over the blue frame*

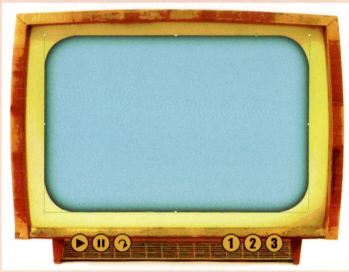

Image and illustration courtesy of Chris Botello. Source Adobe® InDesign®, 2013.

Figure 38 *Inner Glow multiplied over the first frame of the video*

Image and illustration courtesy of Chris Botello. Source Adobe® InDesign®, 2013.

5. Select the center pause button.
6. Apply the Video action to the selected button.
7. Click the Options list arrow, then click Pause.
8. Select the right resume button, then apply the Video action to it.
9. Click the Options list arrow, then click Resume.
10. Export the page as an SWF.
11. When the page loads in your browser, click the play button.

    Your page should resemble Figure 39.
12. Click the pause button.
13. Click the resume button.
14. Close the browser window.
15. Return to the InDesign file and save your work.

Figure 39 *The video playing "inside" the TV screen*

Image and illustration courtesy of Chris Botello. Source Adobe® InDesign®, 2013.

Create navigation points.

1. Select the frame on the page that contains the video. The video is a single video file, but it contains three different videos spliced together. The first is a scuba diving video, the second is a ceramics video, and the third is a sports montage video.
2. On the Media panel, click the Loop check box.
3. Create a new navigation point.
4. Name the new point **Scuba**.
5. On the Media panel, click the Play button to play the video.
6. Click the Pause button when you see the first frame of the ceramics video.
   (*Hint*: Don't worry if you don't pause exactly on the first frame.)
7. Create a new navigation point.
8. Name the new point **Ceramics**.

9. Play the video in the Media panel.
10. Click the Pause button when you see the first frame of the sports montage video.
11. Create a new navigation point, then name it **Sports**.
12. Save your work.

Link buttons to navigation points.

1. Select the **three numbered circle icons** at the lower right of the TV.
2. Convert them to buttons.
3. Select just the **number 1 button**, then apply the Video action to it.
4. On the Options menu, choose **Play from Navigation Point**.
5. On the Point menu, choose **Scuba**.
6. Select just the **number 2 button**, then apply the Video action to it.

7. On the Options menu, choose **Play from Navigation Point**.
8. On the Point menu, choose **Ceramics**.
9. Select just the **number 3 button**, then apply the Video action to it.
10. On the Options menu, choose **Play from Navigation Point**.
11. On the Point menu, choose **Sports**.
12. Save your work.
13. Export the file as an SWF.
14. When the page opens in your browser, click the number 2 button.
    The screen changes and the ceramics video plays.
15. Click the number 1 button.
16. Click the number 3 button.
17. Return to the InDesign document.
18. Save your work, then close the document.

CHAPTER 4 CREATING A WEBSITE FROM AN
INDESIGN LAYOUT

1. Register a domain name
2. Purchase website hosting
3. Upload an InDesign layout to the web

CHAPTER 4

CREATING A WEBSITE FROM AN INDESIGN LAYOUT

It's all about the SWF. The fact that you can export your InDesign layout as an SWF means that any web browser, like Safari, Internet Explorer or Google Chrome, can view that layout—complete with interactivity and animation.

Up to this point in this book, you've been viewing your exported InDesign layouts through your browser, but you've only been viewing them "locally." You've been exporting your layouts to your hard drive, then opening them with your browser, but your layouts have been accessible only on *your* computer.

In this chapter, you're going public. You're going to learn everything you need to know about uploading layouts to your own website, making them accessible to everyone on the Internet. You'll create a domain and purchase hosting, then you'll upload your work to create your own website.

This is, in many ways, a new frontier for InDesign as the application moves from being solely a print vehicle to one that you can use to create immersive, interactive websites.

Figure © GoDaddy.com 2013

Register
A DOMAIN NAME

Registering a Domain Name

Think of some of the great words and phrases that have become associated with the Internet. "Browser" dates back to the earliest days of the Internet's wide use, back when Netscape became one of the first browsers used to view web pages. "Surfing" went from being a water sport to something everyone does online. "Google" is both a noun and a verb: if you tell a friend to "Google me," she'll know exactly what you mean. Similarly, Facebook morphed the word "friend" from a noun to a verb, one that even has a past-tense: "I friended him." And Facebook also spawned a new word as the opposite of friend: to "unfriend."

"Domain" is another one of those words that has taken on a new life with the advent of the Internet. When you create a website, browser software identifies that site as a numerical Internet address. But people can't remember long strings of numbers, so a more friendly naming convention is necessary. A **domain name** is a humanly memorable name that people use to identify and access websites. A website and its domain name are the same thing: Ebay.com is a website, and Ebay.com is also a domain name.

Domain names are used in many different ways in an Internet network and address system. Generally speaking, a domain name is an easy-to-remember way of representing an **Internet Protocol (IP) address**, which is a hard-to-remember binary number. An IP address could be anything from a computer that's being used to access the Internet, to a server that's actually hosting a website, to the website itself. In any case, your domain name and your IP address are one in the same.

When you create a website, you must register a domain name for that site, and it must be a name nobody else has registered. Domain names are administered by **domain name registrars**, who sell this service online to the public. Domain name registration websites allow you to enter a domain name and find out if it's available. If no one is using it, it's available. You can purchase the domain for a monthly fee and use it as your personal space on the web to create a site. Though this is a financial transaction, no actual legal ownership has been conferred, but when you register a domain name, you legally have exclusive rights to use that domain name.

Domain name registration is a big business. Imagine that, in the early days of the Internet, you registered the domain name time.com. It would be perfectly legal for you to "own" that domain name, but clearly a company like Time/Warner would be very interested in taking control of that name from you. However, once you've registered a domain name, nobody can legally take it from you, and stories abound of private individuals selling domain names to corporations. Some have even sold for millions of dollars.

Domain name registration sites are accredited and overseen by the **Internet Corporation for Assigned Names and Numbers (ICANN)**. ICANN also oversees a registration database that lists all registrars for all registered domain names. This information is published as the *whois protocol*, which is accessible to anybody on the Internet. So you can think of registering a domain name as creating a public record, like purchasing a car or even a house. Someone somewhere knows you own it.

One important component of a domain name or IP address is the **top-level domain (TLD)**. The TLD is the highest level of the **domain name system (DNS)** on the Internet. TLDs are the same thing as **Internet address suffixes** like .com, .net, or .org. The .com (commercial) suffix was the first to be used by the public at large in the early days of the Internet.

The .com suffix is to the Internet what "Kleenex" is to facial tissues or "Band-Aid" is to bandages. It remains so synonymous with

the Internet that, if you say "she's in the dot-com business," almost everybody will know what you mean.

As the Internet took off and domain registrations increased dramatically, the need for more TLDs became evident. Suffixes like .org and .net became commonplace, while suffixes like .web and .tv became available but not as widely used. Today, the .com suffix remains the most coveted: If your friend John Smith had the choice to register either johnsmith.com or johnsmith.tv, he'd almost certainly choose johnsmith.com.

Receiving Email Through Your Website

When you register a domain name, you have the option to register email accounts associated with that domain name. For example, if I register the domain name chrisbotello.com, I can set up chris@chrisbotello.com as my email address. Thus, if I create a website—chrisbotello.com—where I upload my portfolio and my resume, I can create a link on the site for people to email me. As opposed to having a generic email address at Yahoo! or Hotmail or Gmail, having my own email address at my own domain name comes across as being professional. Having my domain name in my email address is also a good advertisement for the website itself.

Having an email account or multiple email accounts set up with your domain name is a function of registering a domain name. When you do, you'll be offered the opportunity to purchase email accounts a la carte with the

domain. Generally speaking though—and in the case of the lessons in this book—you will register a domain and purchase web hosting through the same service, and free email accounts are usually included when you purchase web hosting.

Creating a Website Using This Book

With the Adobe CS6 release, InDesign is a great choice for designing and managing a personal website because it allows you to create dynamic, visually interesting layouts without the need for coding or scripting. If you want a site to show family photos, to market your business, to advertise your resume, to display your portfolio, or to promote your professional services, InDesign is a smart choice.

At what point is InDesign not robust enough? When you want a complex, multi-feature site with a shopping cart and the ability to process credit card payments and perform e-commerce transactions, you'll need to hire a professional site developer because these features exceed InDesign's current capabilities.

But even that is changing. If you want to do relatively simple e-commerce transactions, you can create an InDesign website with a link to a payment service like Paypal. Using a third-party as the payment delivery for your site, you'll pay a fee to them for every transaction, but they'll be the ones managing and maintaining the complex programming and security issues involved with e-commerce, not you.

Domain name registration and website hosting is a commercial venture, no different than shopping for shoes or a shirt. You'll find many different domain name registration sites online that you can use to register a domain name, and each competes with the other in terms of pricing and services. For this book, we are using **GoDaddy.com**, shown in Figure 1, for both domain name registration and web hosting because it is a popular site that is dependable, easy to use, and because it features competitive pricing.

If you choose to step through this chapter and register a domain name and purchase web hosting, you should do so in one sitting. If you choose the same options that we do in the steps, the cost will be under $100 for a one-year domain registration and web hosting service.

Your other option is to work through the steps in order to learn the process without actually purchasing the service.

Figure 1 *GoDaddy.com home page*

Figure © GoDaddy.com 2013

Figure 2 *Domain services menu*

REGISTER OR TRANSFER

Domain Name Registration
Register a .COM, .NET or other domain name here.

Bulk Domain Registration
Save when you register 6 or more domains.

Transfer Domain
Transfer your domain & get 1 year FREE.

Bulk Domain Transfers
Transfer up to 1,000 domains at once.

Discount Domain Club
Register domains at a discount – join today!

ADVANCED DOMAINS

Domain Backordering
Be first in line when a domain becomes available.

Domain Buy Service
Want someone else's domain? We can help.

Internationalized Domains (IDN)
Register a domain in a language-specific alphabet.

REGISTRATION OPTIONS

Private Registration
Shield your personal information from public view.

Deluxe Registration
Promote your site & keep your privacy.

Business Registration
Publish an online business card on your domain.

Protected Registration
Keep your domain private, locked & protected!

MANAGEMENT

Domain Management
Organize, renew & upgrade your domains.

Figure © GoDaddy.com 2013

Register a domain name

1. Go to the website **www.godaddy.com**.

   You will need a username and password to log in and use the site. If you don't have an account, click the **Create Account link** at the top of the page and set up a username and password as you normally would for any site.

2. Log in to the site.

3. Position your cursor over the **Domains button** at the top-left of the web page.

   As shown in Figure 2, a window appears below the tab showing all the domain services available on the site.

4. In the REGISTER OR TRANSFER section, click **Domain Name Registration**.

   (continued)

5. Enter the name of the domain that you want to register.

In Figure 3, we have entered the name christopherbotello. Note that you don't enter any suffix, like .com or .org; by default, the site first searches for the .com suffix to go with the domain name that you entered.

6. Click **GO**.

If the domain you requested is available with the .com suffix, you will see the screen shown in Figure 4. If it is not available, you will see the

(continued)

Figure 3   *Entering a domain name*

Figure © GoDaddy.com 2013

.com suffix is automatically searched

Figure 4   *Available domain name screen*

Figure © GoDaddy.com 2013

Creating a Website from an InDesign Layout

Figure 5 *Unavailable domain name screen*

Search again link

.com is not available but other suffixes are

Figure 6 *Section 2 screen of the registration process*

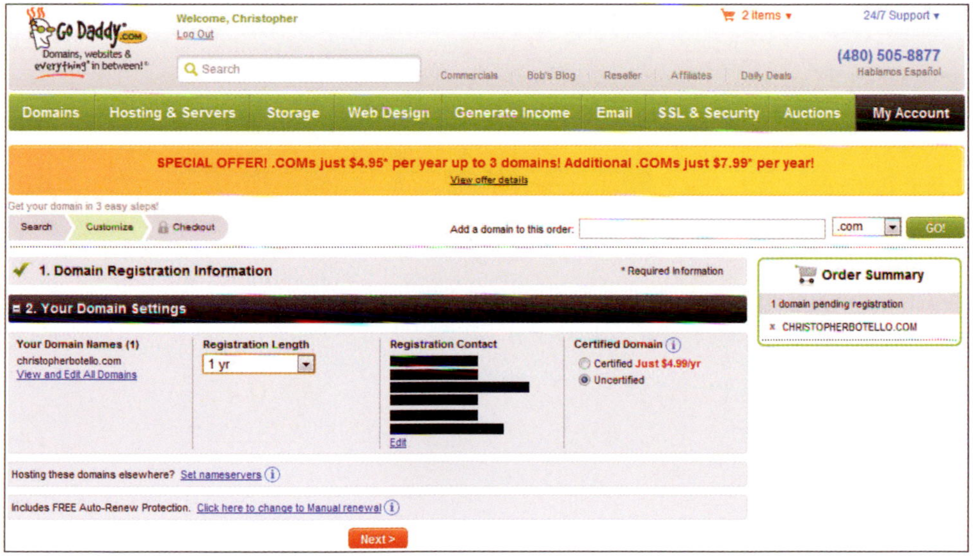

screen shown in Figure 5. In that case, you have two options: you can choose a different suffix that is available or click the search again link and enter a different domain name. Because dylandove.com is available, we will move forward with registering that domain.

7. Click the orange **Add button** under the .com suffix.

8. Click the **Continue to Registration button** in the Order Summary section.

    If a screen appears offering additional services, click No Thanks.

9. In Section 1, enter your information in the required (red star) fields.

10. Click the **Next button**.

    Section 1 will minimize and Section 2 will expand.

11. In Section 2, enter the settings shown in Figure 6.

    As shown in the figure, this domain is registered for just one year. If you register your domain for a longer period, the cost per year decreases. Note that the registration includes free auto-renew protection, meaning you will not lose the URL after the registration period expires. It will automatically renew and you will be billed.

    (continued)

12. Click **Next**.

13. In Section 3, shown in Figure 7, Standard Registration is listed as being already in your cart.

    You could opt for other types of registration, which are explained in the list of links at the left of the window, though for the purposes of this chapter, Standard Registration will suffice.

14. Click **Next**.

    Section 4 has two sections, one for adding email, and one for adding hosting. For the purposes of this chapter, we will skip this section and set up email and hosting in the next lesson.

15. Verify that no options are selected in Section 4, then click **Next**.

    Your shopping cart page opens, as shown in Figure 8. Stay on this page, and proceed to the next lesson to set up hosting.

You registered a domain at GoDaddy.com and chose preferences for the domain.

Figure 7 *Section 3 screen of the registration process*

Figure © GoDaddy.com 2013

Figure 8 *Shopping cart page listing one domain name registered for one year at $10.17*

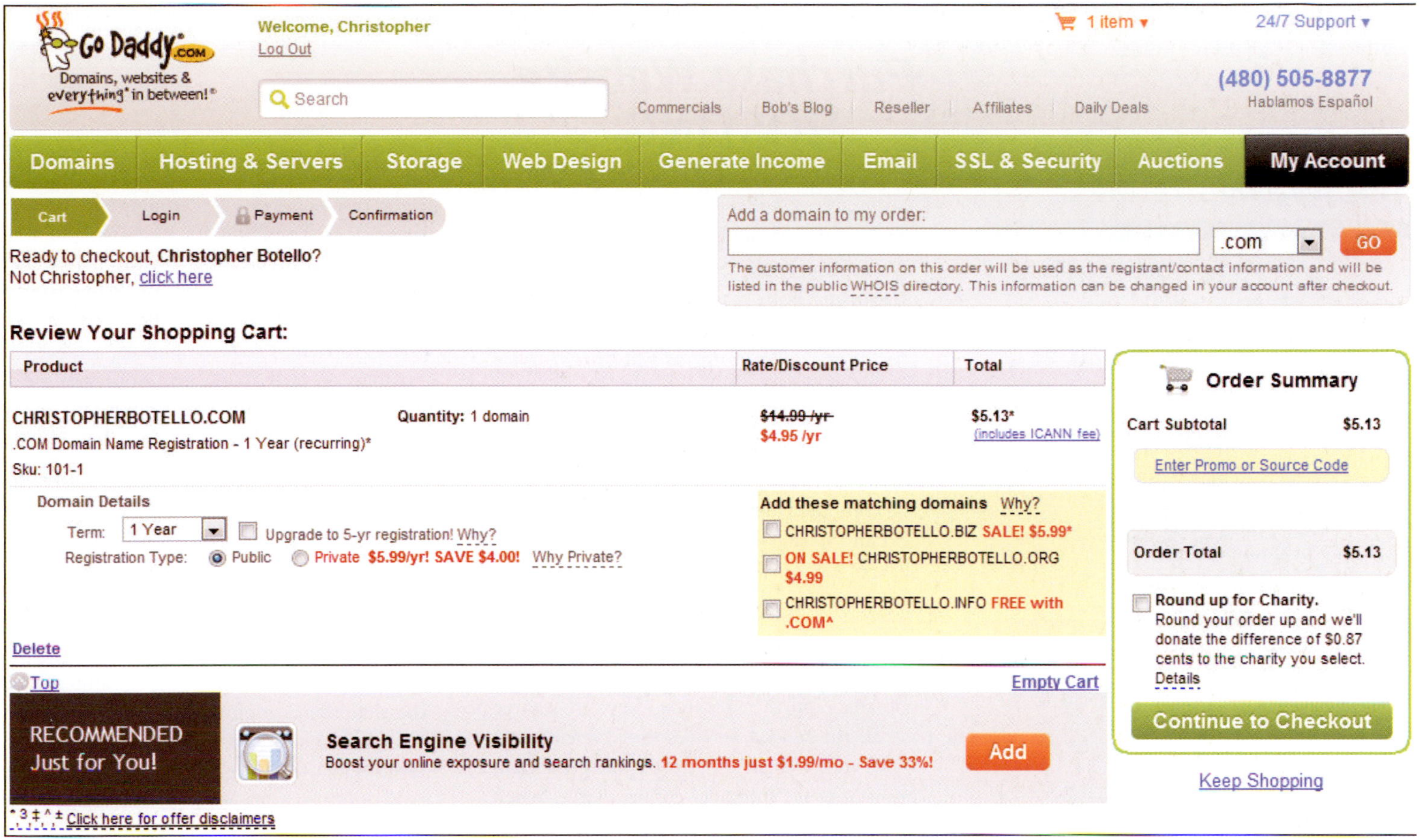

Purchase Website
HOSTING

What You'll Do

Figure © GoDaddy.com 2013

In this lesson, you will purchase hosting services for your website.

Purchasing Web Hosting

You can think of purchasing web hosting as purchasing both space and function on the World Wide Web. Web hosting companies are often referred to as **Internet Service Providers (ISPs)**, and they function somewhat like an agent: they provide a location—a space—on the web where your website exists. Remember that your website—any website— is a computer file (usually many related files), and an ISP sells you space on their computer servers where your computer files are stored and function as your website.

Just like a landlord charges rent for an apartment, ISPs make their money by leasing you space on their servers. They also charge for all the related services they provide that make your website function. One of the main functions is Internet connectivity: when someone types in the URL for your website and your main page appears in their browser, that service is set up and functions through the ISP. They maintain your website; they keep it up and running. If you were to go online and your site wasn't functioning, the first call you would make would be to your ISP.

The size and complexity of a website is a central factor in the ISP's role in hosting that site. Imagine for a moment the differences in complexity between your personal website— where you show family photos, perhaps a portfolio of your work, and your resume— and that of your state's Department of Motor Vehicles' site. The DMV site offers users, among many other things, the ability to track ticket numbers, to renew licenses, to file for permits, and to use a credit card to pay for fines and renewals. All of that functionality is based on complex programming, database systems, and security firewalls. Hosting and maintaining such a site requires substantial server space and full-time maintenance. The state must employ a full-time IT staff to maintain the site, and if it doesn't host the site itself on its own server network, the contract with an ISP must be complex and costly.

These are challenges you won't face with your personal website. Personal sites are usually small and require simple functionality like hyperlinks, email, image links, etc. Internet service providers charge a relatively low fee to manage personal websites, usually less than

$10/month. As with most utilities, the longer the contract term you agree to, the lower your monthly service fee will be.

When you purchase web hosting, email is a service that the ISP will provide as part of the hosting package. You can expect to receive 300-500 email accounts with the service, accounts that you can set up for yourself and for employees if you have them.

Data transfer is another built-in service that your ISP provides. When a user accesses your website, the ISP downloads your site from its server to the user's browser. You should expect unlimited data transfer as part of the monthly fee you pay to your ISP. If your ISP gives you a cap on data transfer, thus charging you after you reach that cap, choose a different ISP to work with.

Purchasing web hosting is much like purchasing anything else online. You need to have an account with the hosting service's website, complete with a username and a password. You'll have the option to choose from various hosting offers. These offers differ mainly on the space allotment and the complexity necessary to run your site. For a basic personal website, the lowest cost service will almost always suffice.

Once you choose your level of service, your choice goes into a shopping cart, and you enter credit card information to purchase the service.

Setting Up Your Web Hosting Account

Once you purchase web hosting, you need to set up your web hosting account. Essentially, this means creating a username and password for you to use as the administrator of the website. These credentials will be different from the username and password that you use for your user account with the website itself. The administration credentials give you access to your website on the hosting server. Whenever you want to modify your site, you'll need to enter your administration credentials, so it's a very good idea for you to write them down someplace secure.

Once you set up your administration account, you'll have an account management page that you can use to manage all areas and functions of your website. Figure 9 shows the My Account page on GoDaddy.com. The account management page is where you go to manage all areas of your site. For example, if you want to set up an email account for a new employee, this is where you'll start.

Figure 9 *My Account page*

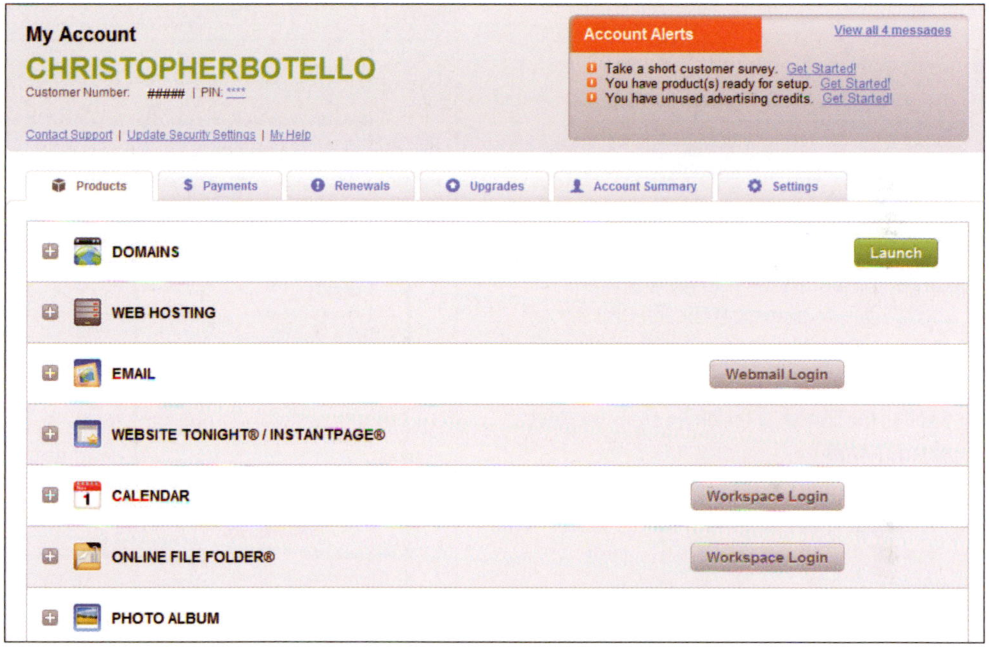

Figure © GoDaddy.com 2013

Purchase website hosting

1. Position your cursor over the **Hosting & Servers button** at the top of the web page.

   As shown in Figure 10, a window appears below the tab showing all the hosting services available on the site.

2. Click the top link: **Web Hosting**.

3. Click the leftmost of the three sections, **Economy 4GH**.

   When you click that section, a green frame appears around it.

4. In the Economy 4GH section, click the **menu list arrow**, then choose the **12 mo** (12 month) **option**.

5. Verify that **Linux** is selected as the operating system just above the Economy 4GH section.

   Linux is the operating system for the website itself, not your personal computer. Your screen should resemble Figure 11.

6. Click **Add to Cart**.

   Clicking this button will take you to a page of special offers to customize your order. For the purposes of this lesson, you won't choose any of these options.

7. Scroll to the bottom of the offers, then click **Next or No Thanks**.

   Clicking Next or No Thanks will take you to your shopping cart page, shown in Figure 12. Depending on current specials Go Daddy is offering, your price might differ slightly.

   (continued)

Figure 10 *Hosting services menu*

Figure © GoDaddy.com 2013

Figure 11 *Choosing the Economy 4GH option*

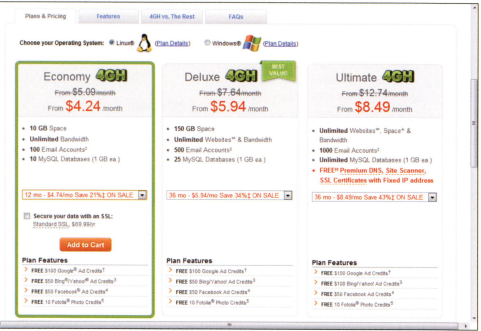

Figure © GoDaddy.com 2013

Creating a Website from an InDesign Layout

Figure 12 *Shopping cart page with one year domain name registration and one year web hosting at $70.45*

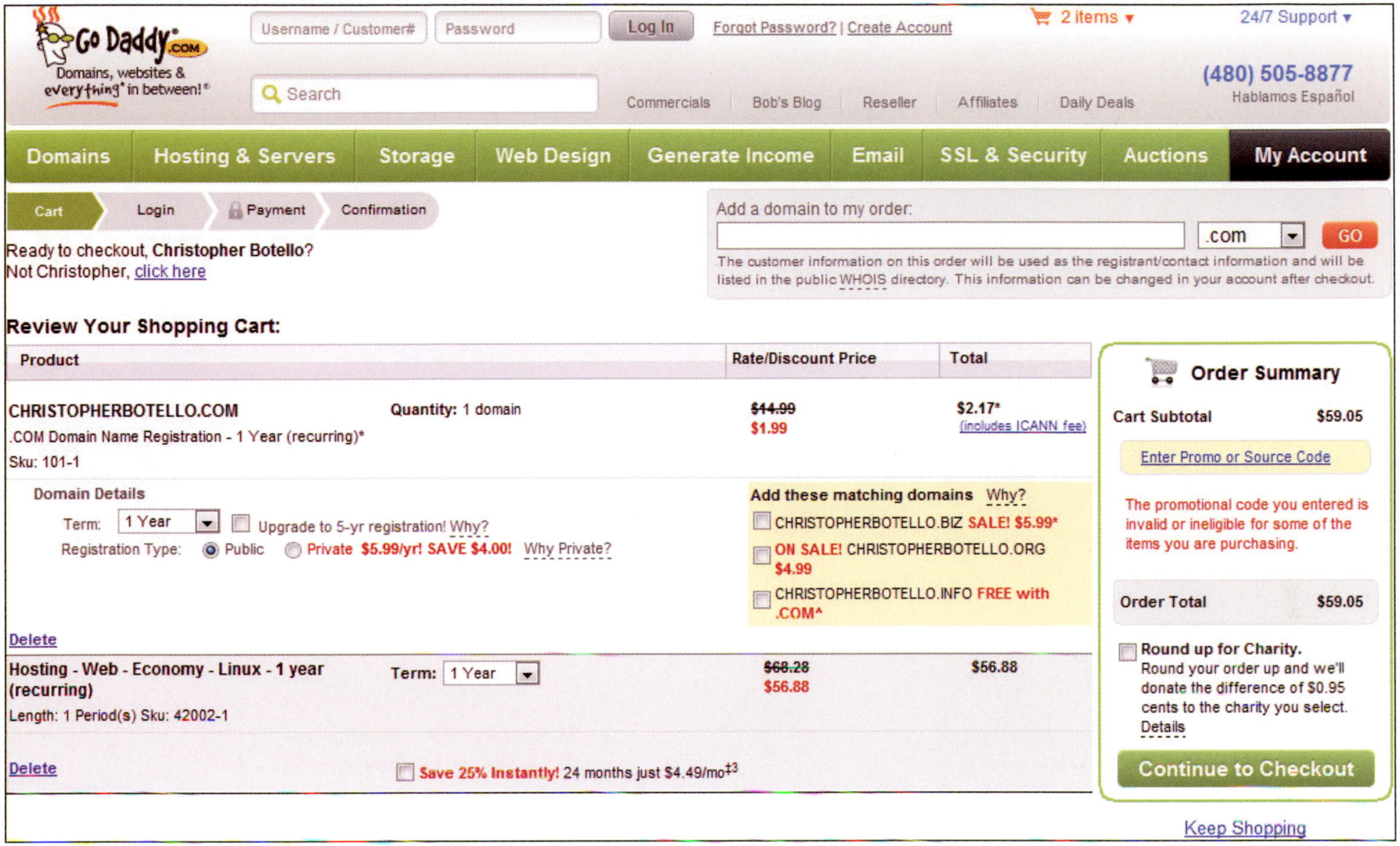

Figure © GoDaddy.com 2013

8. Click **Continue to Checkout**.

   If you're not already logged in with your username and password, clicking this button will take you to a login screen, where you should log in. If you are already logged in, you will go to a payment page.

9. Enter your payment information, as shown in Figure 13.

   Note that you must check the box to verify that you have read the terms of the agreement.

   (continued)

Figure 13 *Payment information screen*

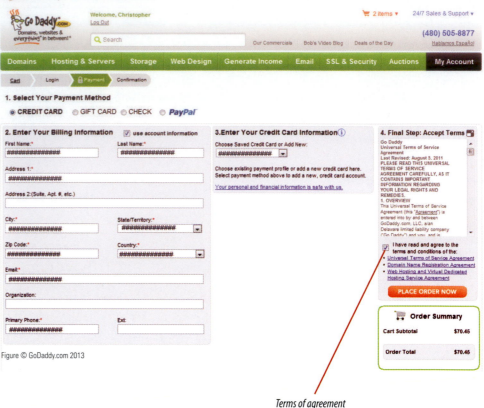

Figure © GoDaddy.com 2013

Terms of agreement check box

Figure 14 *Confirmation page*

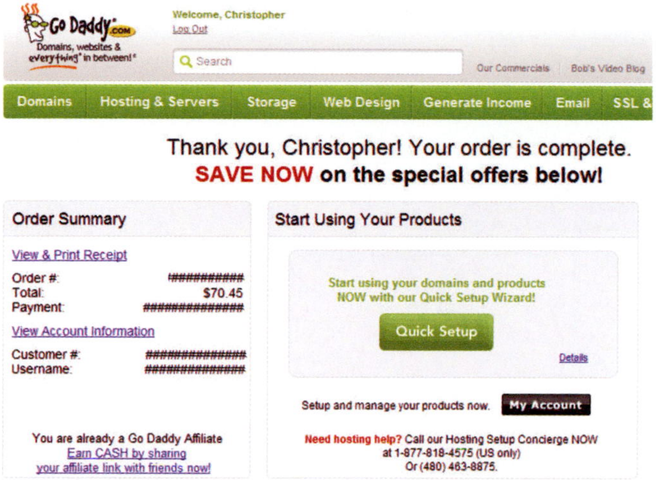

Figure © GoDaddy.com 2013

Figure 15 *Quick Setup Wizard window*

Figure © GoDaddy.com 2013

10. Click **PLACE ORDER NOW**.

    This will take you to the screen shown in Figure 14. You have completed your purchase.

11. Remain on this screen and then proceed to the next set of steps.

You purchased a 12-month hosting plan at GoDaddy.com.

Set up website email

1. Verify you are seeing the screen shown in Figure 14.

2. Click the **Quick Setup button**.

   This will open the Quick Setup Wizard window, shown in Figure 15.

3. Click **Email Setup**.

4. Enter the email address you want to use for yourself on the website.

(continued)

5. Choose and enter a password for your email account.

6. If there's an option for a free 1GB of online storage, check to activate that option.

7. Check the box to confirm that you have read and agree to the terms and conditions.

   Your window should resemble Figure 16.

8. Click **Finish** (Win) or **Save** (Mac).

   Once processed, you will receive a confirmation screen, shown in Figure 17.

   (continued)

Figure 16 *Entering your email address*

Figure © GoDaddy.com 2013

Figure 17 *Confirmation screen*

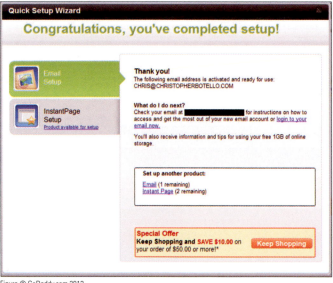

Figure © GoDaddy.com 2013

Creating a Website from an InDesign Layout

Figure 18 *Email login screen*

Figure © GoDaddy.com 2013

Figure 19 *Email inbox*

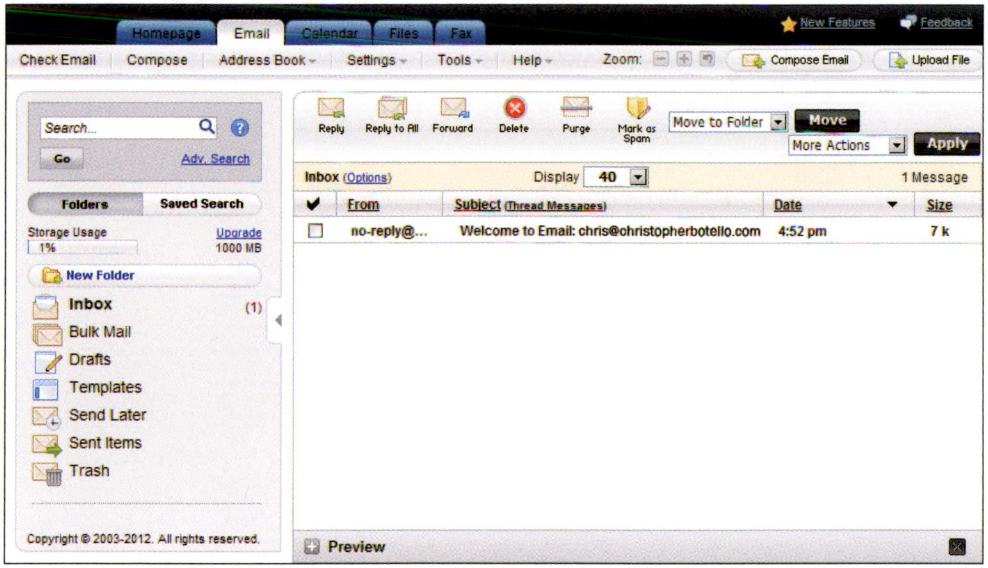

![Email inbox screenshot]

Figure © GoDaddy.com 2013

9. Click the **login to your email now** text link.

   This will open the email login screen, shown in Figure 18.

10. Enter your email address for this domain; enter the password you chose in Step 5, then click **LOG IN**.

    Your online email account opens and lists a welcome email, shown in Figure 19.

11. Open and read the welcome email for information about your account.

12. Proceed to the next lesson.

You created and setup an email account at GoDaddy.com.

Set up website hosting

1. Go to **godaddy.com** then log in with your username and password if necessary.

2. Position your cursor over the Hosting & Servers button, then click **Hosting Management**.

   This takes you to your hosting management page, shown in Figure 20. You will use this page often to manage your site. As shown in the figure, the page lists many sections of your site (such as domains, hosting, and email) that you can manage from this page.

3. Click the **plus sign** to expand the Web Hosting section.

   As shown in Figure 21, the web hosting you purchased is listed as NEW ACCOUNT.

4. Click the green **Launch button** to the right of NEW ACCOUNT.

   This will take you to the Hosting Control Center page, where you will set up login credentials for Go Daddy's FTP utility. These credentials are different from the username and password you set up when you created an account with GoDaddy.com. Be sure that you write down this information.

5. Enter the domain name that you created in the Enter domain text box.

6. Note the FTP username.

   GoDaddy.com provides you with a default FTP username. You should change that to a username you can remember.

7. Click **Change**.

8. Enter the username you would like to use.

   A pop-up balloon appears beside the text field stating the requirements for creating a username.

   (continued)

Figure 20 *Hosting Management screen*

Figure © GoDaddy.com 2013

Figure 21 *NEW ACCOUNT listed in Web Hosting section*

Figure © GoDaddy.com 2013

Figure 22 *Setting up a hosting account password*

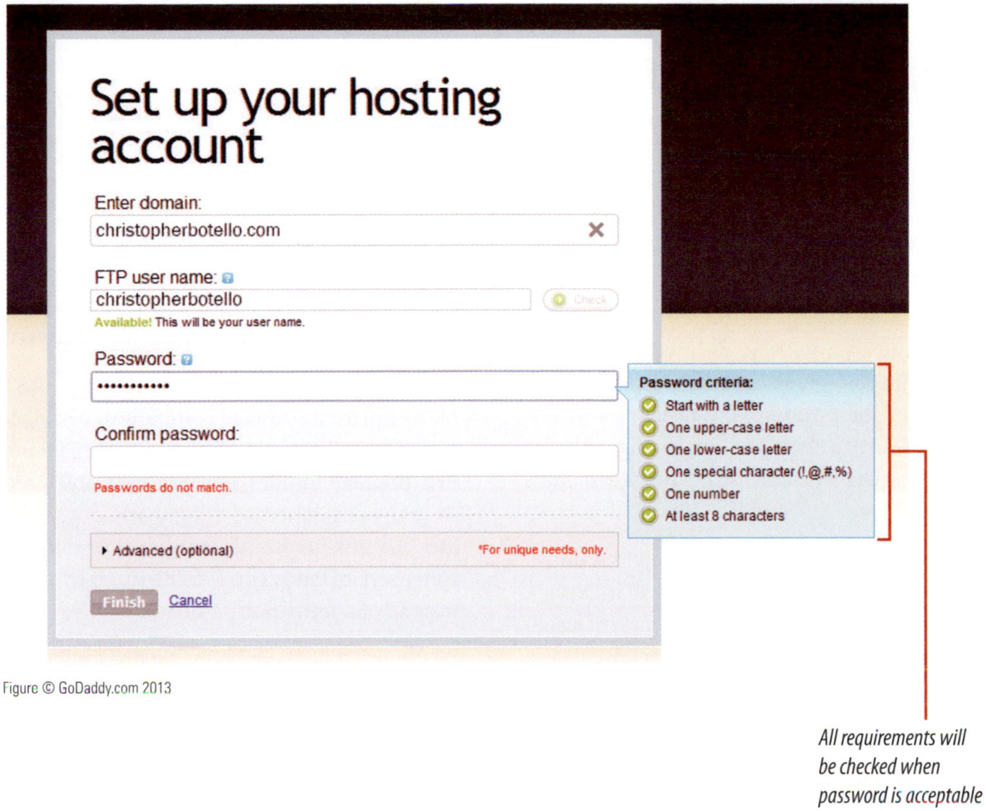

Figure © GoDaddy.com 2013

All requirements will
be checked when
password is acceptable

Figure 23 *Account List page*

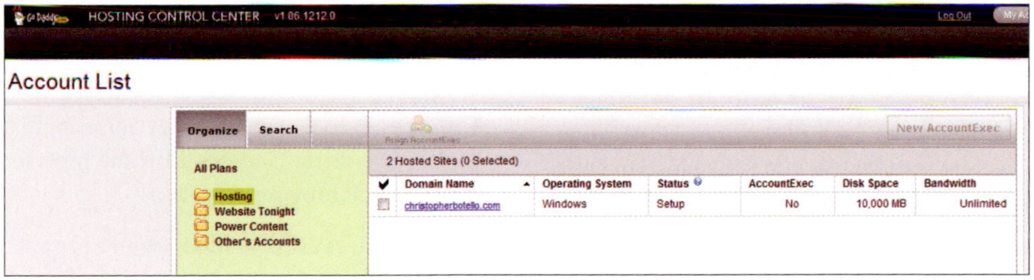

Figure © GoDaddy.com 2013

9. Enter the password you want to use.

The pop-up balloon lists all the requirements for creating a secure password. As shown in Figure 22, when you have entered an acceptable password, all the listed requirements will show a green check mark.

10. Enter a matching password in the Confirm password field.

11. Click **Finish**.

Your information will be uploaded. This might take some time. Once your information is uploaded, you will see the Hosting Control Center login window.

12. Enter your GoDaddy.com username and password (not the FTP credentials you just created).

This takes you to the Account List page in your Hosting Control Center, shown in Figure 23.

13. If you are not going immediately to the next lesson, you can log out of GoDaddy.com.

You went to the Hosting Management page on GoDaddy.com, where you set up an administration username and password to access GoDaddy.com's FTP utility.

Upload an InDesign Layout
TO THE WEB

What You'll Do

Figure © GoDaddy.com 2013

In this lesson, you will upload an InDesign layout to the web.

Packaging an InDesign Document for Upload to the Web

Before you export an InDesign document to upload to a website, do a quality-control check, just as you would before releasing it to a printer for printing. The primary concern you'll want to look out for is that all your placed images, sound files, and video links are updated.

One of the best ways to do a quality-control check is to use the Package feature in InDesign. When you package the document, InDesign creates a new folder for the document and a Links folder that contains all of the placed images. The Package function will warn you if any linked files are missing or need to be updated.

Uploading an exported InDesign document to your website

When you export an InDesign document in the SWF file format, two export documents are created: an SWF file and an HTML file. These are the two files you will upload to your website; essentially, they are your website.

Uploading is a process by which files are copied from your computer to the network

of computers the ISP is using to host your website. This is accomplished through a **file transfer protocol (FTP)** software utility. FTP software literally moves files between computers.

Many different software companies manufacture FTP utilities. FileZilla and CuteFTP are two popular utilities that are free and used by many developers to upload and download files. In this book and for these lessons, we will use GoDaddy.com's built-in FTP utility instead of a third-party FTP.

In the process of exporting an InDesign file, you will be given the option to name the exported files. As a standard procedure for exporting InDesign layouts for the web, name the export file index and be sure to use all lowercase letters. Thus, exporting to the SWF file format will create an **index.swf** file and an **index.html** file. Figure 24 shows an SWF and an HTML file generated from the export. (Note that the HTML file is identified as a "Chrome" HTML file; that's because in this lesson we're using Google's Chrome browser as our default browser software.)

Once these files are uploaded, when a browser accesses your website it will by default look for a file named index.html (all lowercase), which is a standard reference for the top page of a website. The browser uses the information in the index.html file to display the web page.

An HTML file is only a text file; it's code. If a web page has images, the HTML file contains code that references each image on the page by its filename. This code tells the browser where to go to look for those images. Thus, in a traditional setup using HTML only, you would need to upload every image on your site to the host server so that the browser could use the image references in the HTML file to display the images as part of the web page. The image files need to be there to be displayed.

When you use files exported from InDesign to create a website, the browser once again accesses the HTML file, but the HTML file then references the SWF file for all page layout information. Because all placed images are embedded in the SWF file, there's no need to upload loose image files. This explains why the SWF file size is larger: note in Figure 24 that the HTML file is only 11 KB while the SWF is 6,476 KB. The number of placed image files and their sizes are the greatest determining factors for the file size of an exported SWF.

In addition to placed images, the exported SWF contains all other functionality you have programmed for the site, including animation, hyperlinks, buttons, and object states. However, it's important to note that, unlike placed image files, placed video and sound files are not embedded in the exported SWF and therefore must be uploaded separately to the host site.

Uploading Video and Sound Files

When you export an SWF from an InDesign document containing video and/or sound files, an index_Resources folder is created as a function of the export. This folder is visible in Figure 24. The index_Resources folder is created automatically to hold all sound and video files that have been placed in the layout.

Figure 24 *Files generated from the export*

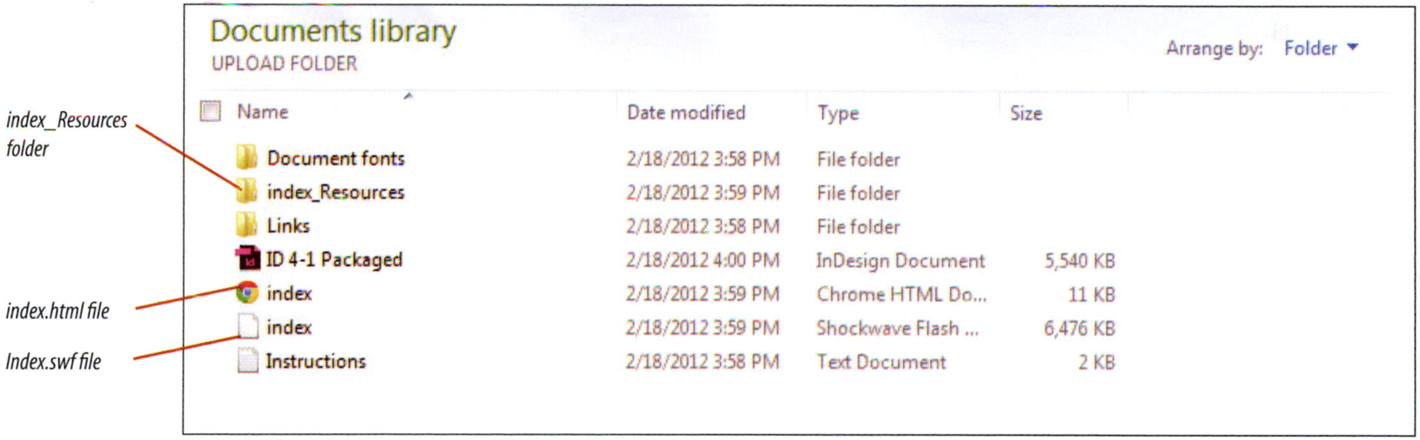

index_Resources folder

index.html file

Index.swf file

Documents library
UPLOAD FOLDER

Arrange by: Folder ▼

Name	Date modified	Type	Size
Document fonts	2/18/2012 3:58 PM	File folder	
index_Resources	2/18/2012 3:59 PM	File folder	
Links	2/18/2012 3:58 PM	File folder	
ID 4-1 Packaged	2/18/2012 4:00 PM	InDesign Document	5,540 KB
index	2/18/2012 3:59 PM	Chrome HTML Do...	11 KB
index	2/18/2012 3:59 PM	Shockwave Flash ...	6,476 KB
Instructions	2/18/2012 3:58 PM	Text Document	2 KB

Figure © GoDaddy.com 2013

The SWF file contains code that, essentially, tells the browser to look for and access the video and sound files in a folder named index_Resources. Because of the way HTML code functions, in order for the browser to find the index_Resources folder, the folder must exist in the same directory—the same window—as the index.html and the index.swf files.

When you use the built-in FTP utility on GoDaddy.com, as you will in these lessons, you can't simply upload an entire folder. You must create the index_Resources folder yourself then upload the sound and video files to that folder. Therefore, when the browser accesses the index.html file, and the index. html file accesses the SWF file, and the SWF file references the index_Resources folder as

the location of the sound and video files, the browser will go there to retrieve those files.

Figure 25 shows the FTP File Manager page on GoDaddy.com. Note that index.html, index. swf, and the index_Resources folder are all located in the same directory.

Figure 25 *FTP File Manager page*

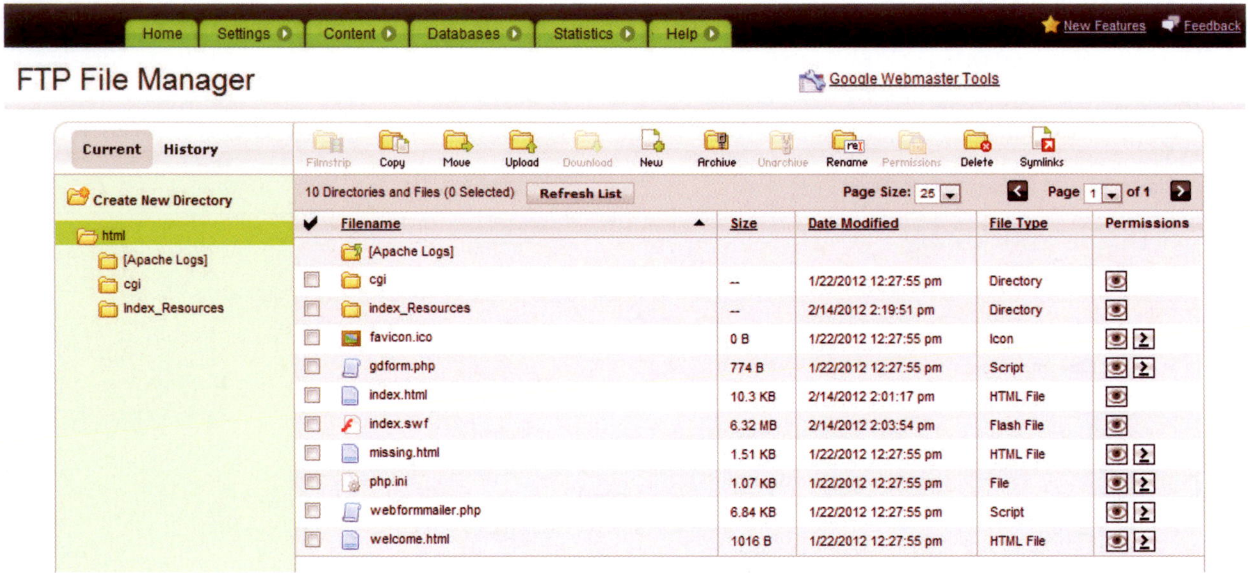

Figure © GoDaddy.com 2013

Creating a Website from an InDesign Layout

Figure 26 *Naming the folder for upload*

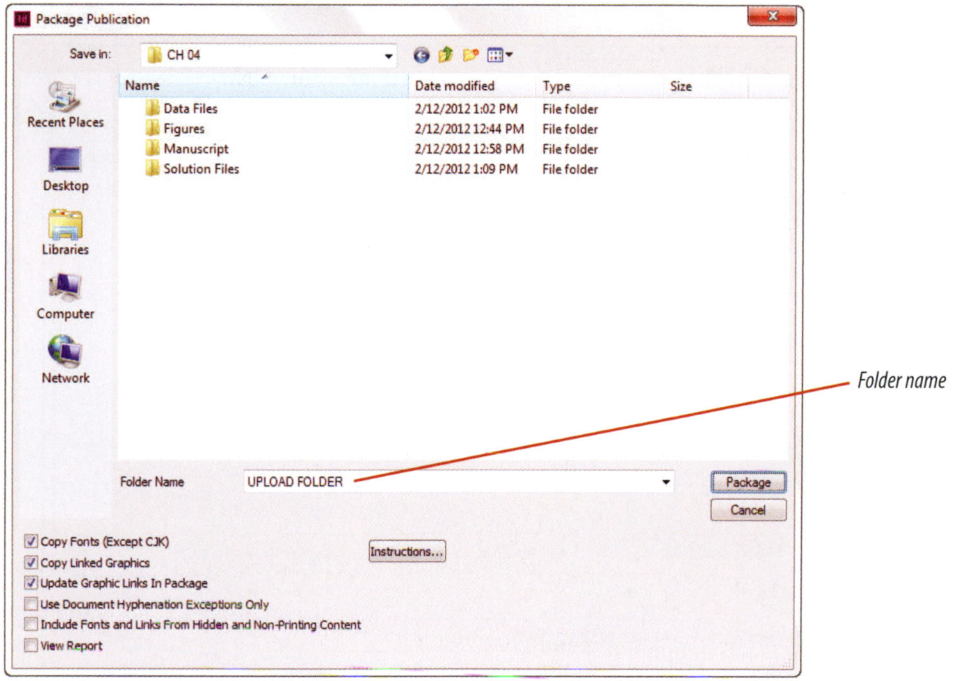

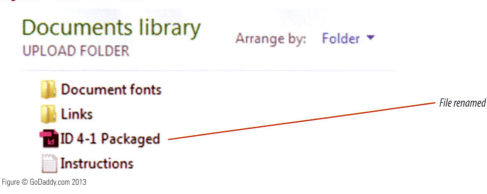

Folder name

Source Adobe® InDesign®, 2013.

Figure 27 *UPLOAD FOLDER window*

Documents library
UPLOAD FOLDER

Arrange by: Folder ▼

📁 **Document fonts**

📁 **Links**

📕 **ID 4-1 Packaged**   File renamed

📄 **Instructions**

Figure © GoDaddy.com 2013

Package and export an InDesign layout for upload

1. Open the file ID 4-1.indd.

2. Click the **File menu**, then click **Package**.

3. In the Package dialog box, click **Package**.

4. In the Printing Instructions dialog box, click **Continue**.

5. In the Package Publication dialog box (Win) or the Create Package Folder dialog box (Mac), type **UPLOAD FOLDER** in the Folder Name text box, as shown in Figure 26.

6. Save UPLOAD FOLDER to your desktop, then click the **Package button**.

   If you get a Warning dialog box, click **OK**.

7. Close ID 4-1.indd.

8. Go to your desktop, then open **UPLOAD FOLDER**.

9. Change the name of the InDesign file to **ID 4-1 Packaged** so that your window resembles Figure 27.

   Renaming the file is not necessary, but we're doing so in this case to distinguish the packaged InDesign file from the original data file.

   (continued)

10. Double-click **ID 4-1 Packaged.indd** to open it.

11. Click the **File menu**, then click **Export**.

12. In the File name text box, name the document **index**, then verify that you are saving it to UPLOAD FOLDER.

13. Click the **Save as type list arrow**, then click **Flash Player (SWF)**.

    The file must be named with all lowercase letters. Your Export window should resemble Figure 28.

14. Click **Save**.

(continued)

Figure 28 *Export dialog box*

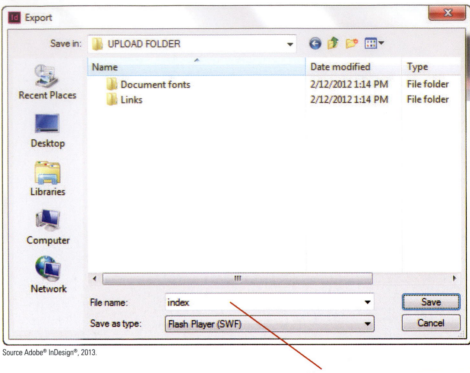

Source Adobe® InDesign®, 2013.

File name

Creating a Website from an InDesign Layout

Figure 29 *General settings of the Export SWF dialog box*

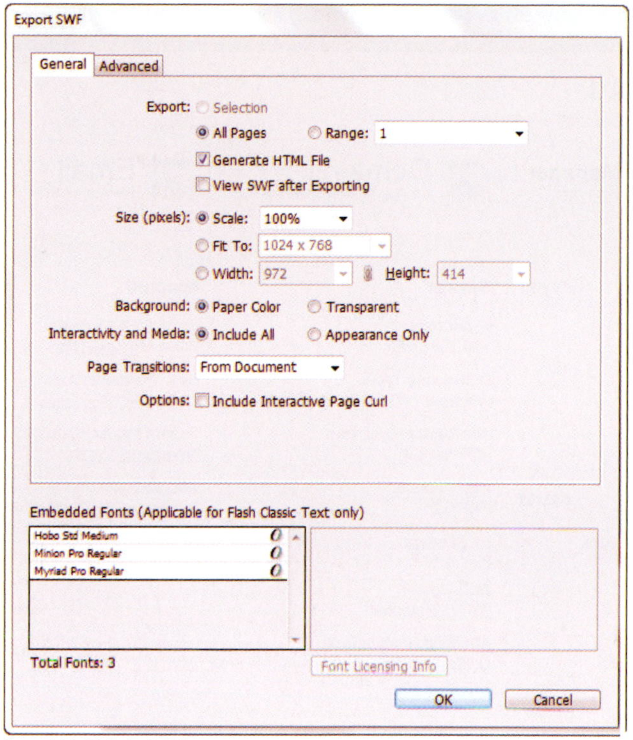

Source Adobe® InDesign®, 2013.

Figure 30 *UPLOAD FOLDER with exported files*

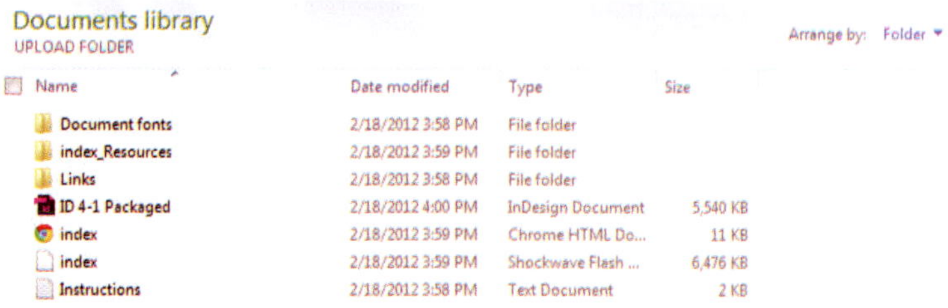

Figure © GoDaddy.com 2013

15. Enter the General settings shown in Figure 29.

    Note that the View SWF after Exporting and the Include Interactive Page Curl check boxes are not checked.

16. Click **OK**.

17. Close **ID 4-1 Packaged.indd** without saving changes.

18. Go to the desktop, open UPLOAD FOLDER, and compare it to Figure 30.

    As shown in the figure, InDesign exported two files named index into UPLOAD FOLDER. One is an SWF file, the other is an HTML file. It also created the index_Resources folder.

19. Open the index_Resources folder.

    The index_Resources folder contains files that are not embedded in the SWF document. In this case, it contains three files: the two sound clips and the placed video file.

You packaged an InDesign layout into a folder you named UPLOAD FOLDER. You then renamed the packaged InDesign file to distinguish it from the original file. You exported the packaged InDesign layout as an SWF named index to the same folder. You then looked in the folder, noting that the export created an SWF file, an HTML file, and a folder named index_Resources, which contains the two sound clips and the video file from the document.

Upload an exported InDesign layout

1. Go to **godaddy.com** and log in to your user account on the home page.

2. Float over the Hosting & Servers button, then click **Hosting Management**.

3. Expand the Web Hosting section if necessary.

   All accounts you've created with GoDaddy.com are listed in this window.

4. Click the green **Launch button** beside the domain name you registered.

   This opens the Hosting Dashboard page, shown in Figure 31.

5. Click the **FTP File Manager button** at the top-left of the window.

   FTP File Manager is GoDaddy.com's built-in FTP utility. Clicking FTP File Manager takes you to the FTP File Manager page where you can upload content to your website, as shown in Figure 32.

6. Click the **Upload folder icon**.

7. Click **Browse** (Win) or **Choose File** (Mac), then navigate to UPLOAD FOLDER on your desktop.

   (continued)

Figure 31 *Hosting Dashboard page*

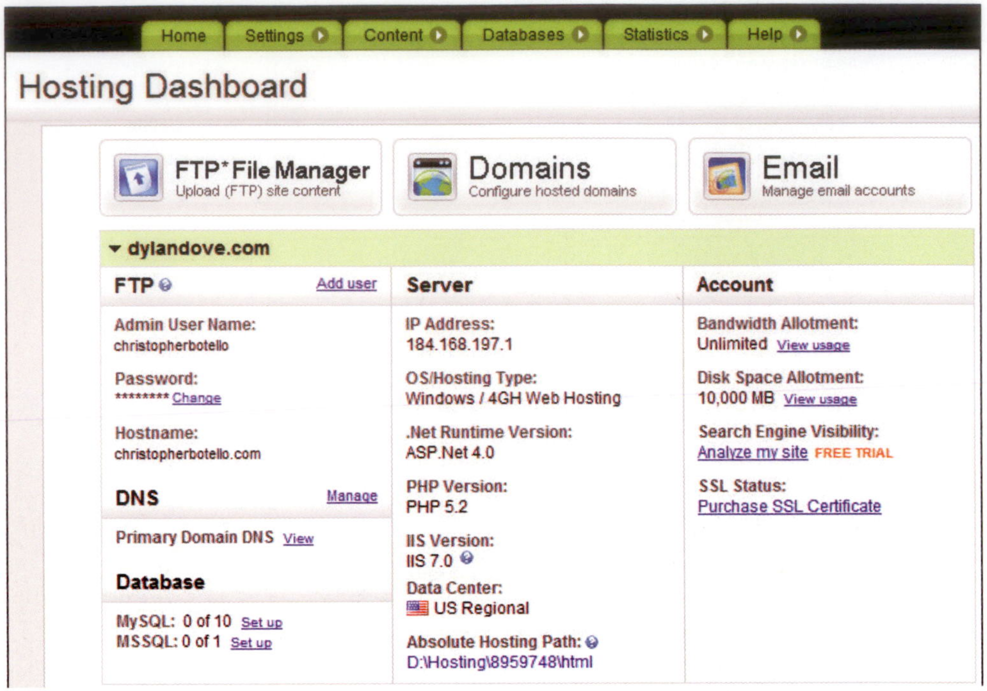

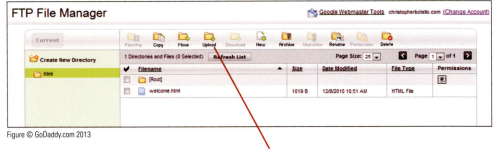

Figure © GoDaddy.com 2013

Figure 32 *FTP File Manager page on GoDaddy.com*

Figure © GoDaddy.com 2013

Upload folder icon

Figure 33 *index.swf file added to the Upload File(s) queue*

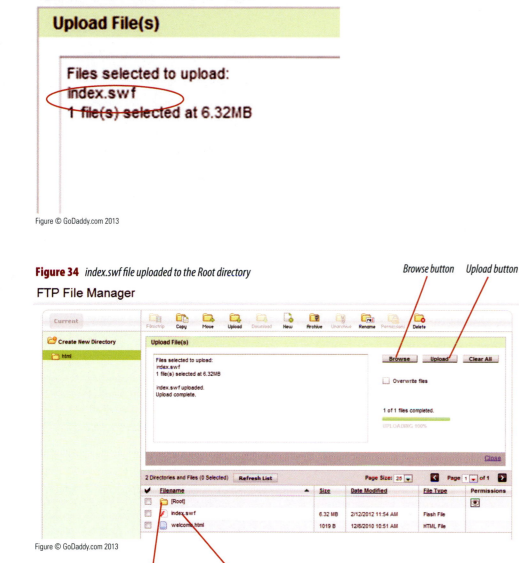

Figure © GoDaddy.com 2013

Figure 34 *index.swf file uploaded to the Root directory*

Figure © GoDaddy.com 2013

Root folder   Index.swf file

8. Select the **index.swf file**, then click **Open**.

   The file is added to an upload queue, shown in Figure 33. (The figure shows how the upload queue looks in Windows 7. If you're using a Mac, the GoDaddy.com queue screen will be slightly different.)

9. Click the **Upload button** (Win) or **OK** (Mac).

   The file is uploaded and listed in the **root directory** of your site, as shown in Figure 34. The root directory is the top-level folder that houses files for the entire site.

10. Click the **Browse button** (Win) or the **Choose File button** (Mac), then follow the same procedure to upload the **index.html** file.

    You might need to click the Refresh List button to see the HTML file in the list at the bottom of the window.

11. Proceed to the next set of steps.

You used the built-in FTP utility on GoDaddy.com to upload both index.swf and index.html.

Create a directory and upload video and sound files

1. Click **Create New Directory** at the upper-left of the window.

2. Type **index_Resources** in the name field so that your screen resembles Figure 35.

   The SWF file you exported is coded to access a folder within the directory named index_Resources to find the two sound files and the video file. You have now created a folder on GoDaddy.com with that name where you will upload the three files. It is critical when you create the directory that you name the folder exactly as it was named when it was created when exported.

3. Click **OK**.

   As shown in Figure 36, a directory folder named index_Resources is added to the root directory.

4. Click **index_Resources** to open the directory.

5. Click the **Upload folder icon**, click **Browse** (Win) or **Choose File** (Mac), then navigate to UPLOAD FOLDER on your desktop.

6. Select the sound file named **Click**, then click **Open**.

   The file is added to an upload queue.

7. Click the **Upload button** (Win) or **OK** (Mac).

   Because the index_Resources folder is open, the sound file will be uploaded to it.

8. Using the same steps, one file at a time, upload the file named **Squeak** and then upload the video file named **Italian Video**.

   The video file is relatively large in size and might take a couple of minutes to upload.

9. Proceed to the next set of steps.

Noting that the sound and video files weren't uploaded with the SWF file, you created a new directory folder in the root folder on

(continued)

Figure 35 *Entering the name for the new directory*

Figure © GoDaddy.com 2013

Figure 36 *index_Resources folder added to the Root directory*

Documents library
UPLOAD FOLDER

Arrange by: Folder ▾

Name	Date modified	Type	Size
Document fonts	2/18/2012 3:58 PM	File folder	
index_Resources	2/18/2012 3:59 PM	File folder	
Links	2/18/2012 3:58 PM	File folder	
ID 4-1 Packaged	2/18/2012 4:00 PM	InDesign Document	5,540 KB
index	2/18/2012 3:59 PM	Chrome HTML Do...	11 KB
index	2/18/2012 3:59 PM	Shockwave Flash ...	6,476 KB
Instructions	2/18/2012 3:58 PM	Text Document	2 KB

Figure © GoDaddy.com 2013

Creating a Website from an InDesign Layout

Figure 37 *The "Italy" layout live online in a web browser*

Image courtesy of Chris Botello. Source Microsoft® Internet Explorer®, 2013.

Figure 38 *The Cinque Terre website opens in a new window*

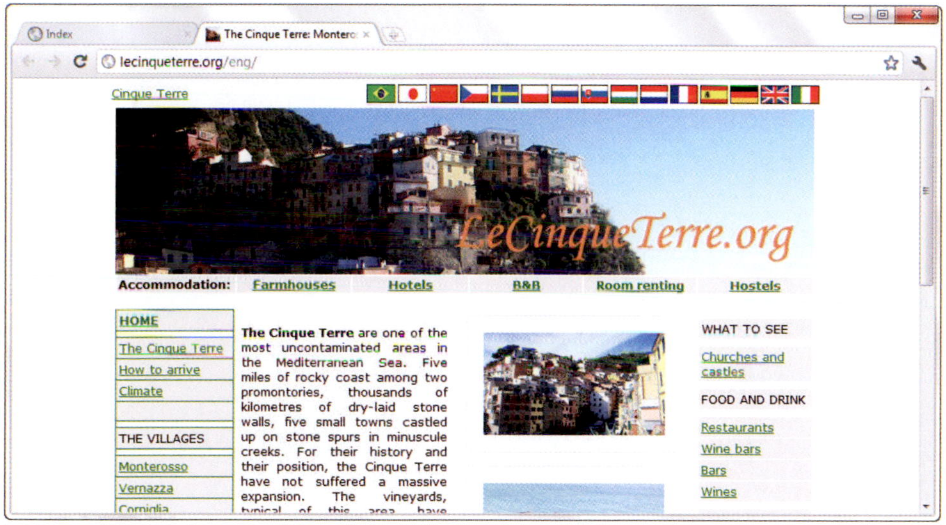

Image courtesy of Chris Botello. Source Microsoft® Internet Explorer®, 2013.

GoDaddy.com. You named the folder index_Resources, exactly the same name as the folder created on your computer when you exported your InDesign document as an SWF. You then uploaded the two sound files and the video file to the new directory folder online.

View the live website

1. Launch your browser.

   We are using Google's Chrome browser for the figures in this lesson.

2. Enter the URL of your registered domain name.

   As shown in Figure 37, page 1 of the InDesign file is the first page of your website.

3. Click the **finger pointer icon** to make the main image appear in color.

4. Click the **right arrow** to go to the next page.

   The Click sound plays.

5. Click the **right arrow** to go to page 3.

6. Click the **thumbnail images** at the bottom of the page.

   The object states you entered are live and active on the site and they change the large image.

7. Go to page 4, then click the **Play button** below the video.

   The video plays.

8. Click the **thumbnail images** in the green section to skip to different navigation points.

   You may experience a delay in this function until the video is downloaded entirely.

9. Click the **right arrow** to go to page 1.

10. Click the **visit the official home page link**.

    As shown in Figure 38, *The Cinque Terre website* opens in a new window.

You viewed your InDesign layout live online as an interactive website, and tested out links, animations, and object states.

ADOBE INDESIGN CS6 INTERACTIVE

CHAPTER 5 CREATING INTERACTIVE
FORMS

1. Explore strategies for designing an interactive form

2. Create text input fields

3. Create a pull-down list

4. Create check boxes and radio buttons

5. Create a submit form button

6. Enter information into an interactive form

CHAPTER 5 CREATING INTERACTIVE FORMS

As InDesign redefines itself as an interactive product that is able to produce websites and export layouts to the iPad, more and more designers are wanting to use InDesign to create interactive forms.

When you think of graphic design, you may not think of job applications or survey forms, but those layouts, like any other, must be designed. Utilizing InDesign's many options for line effects, arrows, drop shadows and beautiful typography, a savvy designer might see a lucrative opportunity in designing visually interesting forms for businesses.

Now consider making those forms interactive. The days of sending a form via snail mail are going, going, gone, and the days of going into a business to fill out a job application are almost a thing of the past. Forms are happening online. Job applications are found online: search for a job, fill out the form, press submit, and you're done.

As an alternative, a business can email a form to you, you can open it and fill it out on your computer, and then you can email it back. In either case, whether they exist online or are emailed to you, there's no paper involved; the forms are digital and interactive.

With InDesign CS6, Adobe has taken a giant step forward with its capabilities for producing interactive forms. In the past, a designer could use InDesign to design a form, but then the InDesign file needed to be opened in Adobe Acrobat, where interactive fields could be added and formatted. That's no longer the case.

With InDesign CS6, the design and the field formatting all happen in InDesign. The result is an interactive PDF file that is able to be posted to a website or emailed to a client list. This is a major upgrade, not only for InDesign itself, but also for the designer who can produce beautiful forms with the power of interactivity and the ability to collect data.

Buttons and Forms

Type: Combo Box
Name: student grade
Event: On Release or Tap
Actions: ➕ ➖

[No Actions Added]

☐ Hidden Until Triggered

▽ PDF Options

Description:

☑ Printable   ☐ Read Only
☐ Required   ☐ Sort Items

List Items   ➕ ➖

Freshman
Sophomore
Junior
Senior

Font Size: 14

Buttons and Forms

Type: Radio Button
Name: Radio Button 1
Event: On Release or Tap
Actions: ➕ ➖

☐ Hidden Until Triggered

▽ PDF Options

Description:

☑ Printable   ☐ Read Only
☐ Required   ☐ Selected by default

Button Value: Choice

✓ yes, I wan

choose ad

⊙ quarter-pag
⊙ half-page
⊙ full-page

Explore Strategies for Designing an
INTERACTIVE FORM

What You'll Do

Source Adobe® InDesign®, 2013.

In this lesson, you will examine an InDesign document set up for output as an interactive form.

Designing an Interactive Document

An interactive form created in InDesign is exported as an interactive Adobe PDF file. As explained in Chapter 1, you can think of a PDF as an "everything in one" document.

Consider an InDesign layout, with its different typefaces and placed graphic images. If you were to package the InDesign file, you'd get a folder containing the InDesign document itself and other folders containing the font files and the linked image and illustration files.

Not with a PDF: if you export the InDesign file as a PDF, you get one file, self-contained. All of the fonts, colors, and placed graphics exist in the PDF. Send the PDF to anybody, and they can open it using Adobe Reader or Adobe Acrobat.

When the InDesign file has been designed with interactive fields—like text fields or check boxes or pull-down lists—those frames and their functionality are included in the interactive PDF.

You'll find that designing an interactive layout is an acquired skill. You have to learn some of the basic rules—and restrictions—of working with interactive fields in InDesign to know how to best design a document so it looks good when it's exported.

You have six options for creating interactive buttons in a form: Check Box, Combo Box, List Box, Radio Button, Signature Field, and Text Field. Text Field is the most commonly used type and plays the most straightforward role: a text field is where you type text into a form. Text fields are the most basic data entry fields in interactive forms. Name, address, phone number, email—all of this type of information goes into text fields.

One of the key layout challenges in designing an interactive form is specifying text so that it will appear within a text field in a way that is visually pleasing. To create a text field in InDesign, you create a text frame and then convert it into a button using the Buttons and Forms panel. You then choose the type of button using the Type menu, as shown in Figure 1.

After you choose Text Field as the type of button, the Font Size menu becomes available, as shown in Figure 2. You can choose from the default font sizes, or enter a custom value, and that choice will carry through to the exported PDF.

Font size and vertical justification are the only two text formatting attributes that will carry over to the exported interactive form. No matter what typeface, type style, or horizontal alignment you choose in InDesign, the text formatting entered in the exported document is determined by end-user's default browser setting.

Figure 1 *The Buttons and Forms panel*

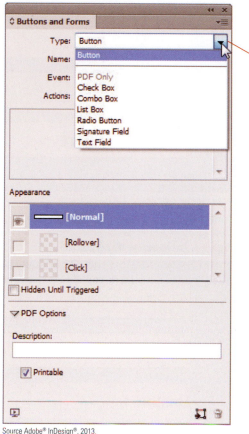

Type menu

Source Adobe® InDesign®, 2013.

Figure 2 *Options for Text Field button*

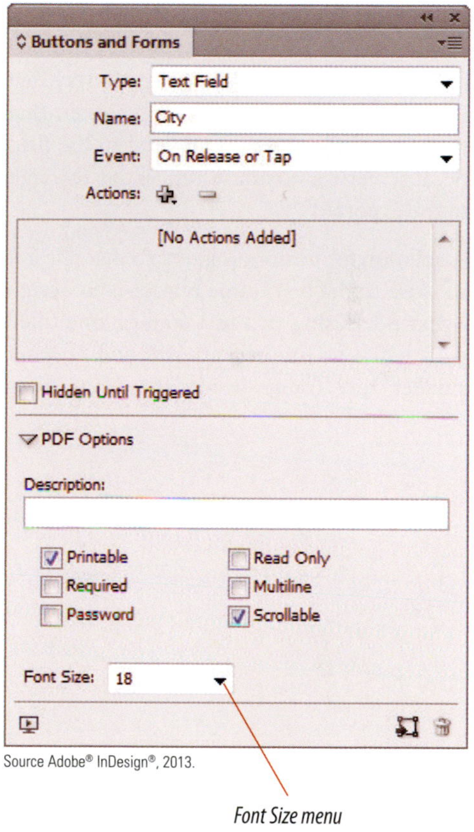

Font Size menu

Source Adobe® InDesign®, 2013.

Figure 3 shows the word *Test* in 16 pt Franklin Gothic Heavy, centered within a text field. It is vertically centered in the field. It would be ideal if, in the exported document, when a person types in this field, what they type would be in the same format as the word *Test*. Good idea, but it doesn't work.

Figure 4 shows an example of how the text would appear on another person's computer using their default browser settings. The size is different, and the typeface is different. The horizontal alignment is different—it's justified left in the field—and the first letter is jammed against the left edge of the field in a way that is visually unappealing. Note, however, that the text is still vertically centered in the field because vertical justification carries through to the exported PDF.

A solution for positioning text so that it is not so close to the text frame border is to design a text field using two text frames; one filled with white as the background and another smaller text frame inside the white-filled

Figure 3 *Formatted Test text in an InDesign document*

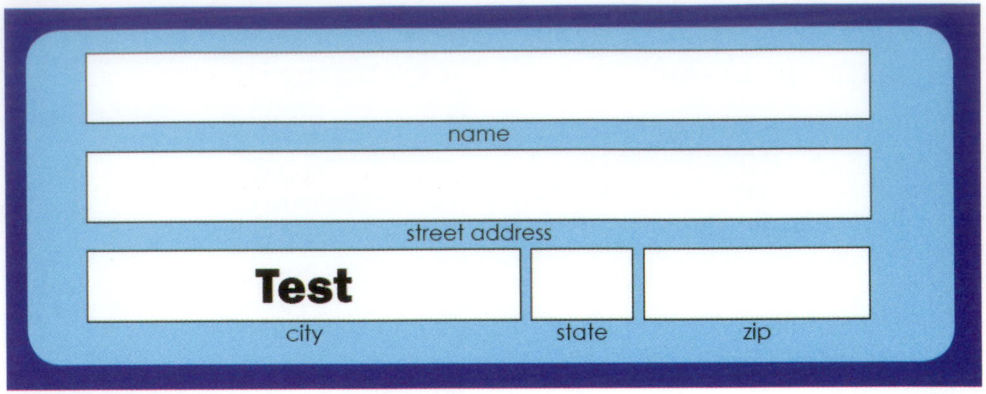

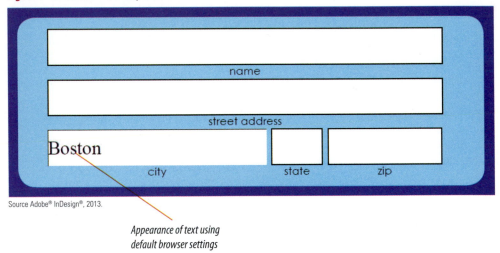

Source Adobe® InDesign®, 2013.

Figure 4 *Text entered into the exported PDF*

Source Adobe® InDesign®, 2013.

Appearance of text using default browser settings

frame. This will create some distance from the four edges of the white-filled frame, allowing you some control over how the text is positioned in the field.

Figure 5 shows an example of this frame-within-a-frame trick. Notice the smaller text field drawn within the larger white background frame. Figure 6 shows an example of text typed into the field in the export document. Note the indent on the left side is visually much more appealing.

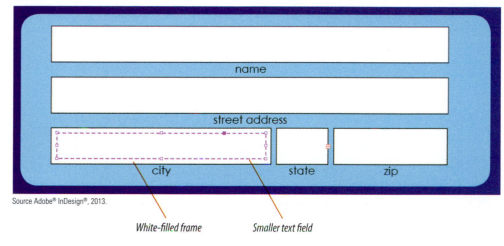

Source Adobe® InDesign®, 2013.

White-filled frame   *Smaller text field*

Figure 6 *Text with visually appealing position in text field*

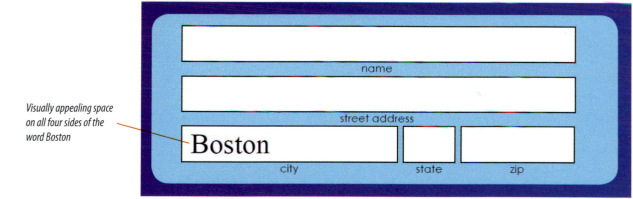

Visually appealing space on all four sides of the word Boston

Source Adobe® InDesign®, 2013.

Explore a layout for an interactive document

1. Open ID 5-1.indd, then save it as **Yearbook Order Form**.

2. Fit the page in the window, then compare your screen to Figure 7.

   The figure shows a visually interesting form created in InDesign. Placed images, gradients, illustrations, and dynamic typography—all of these can be exported as part of an interactive PDF form.

   (continued)

Figure 7 *Viewing the design of the Yearbook Order Form*

YEARBOOK & SHOUT–OUT
order form

① parent name

parent email address

② student name

student grade this year

③ yes, I want to purchase a yearbook

@ $50.00 per copy
# copies

④ yes, I want to purchase a shout-out ad

choose ad size
quarter-page
half-page
full-page

$
total

enter student's name as you wish it to appear

enter your shout–out message

FAQs

why buy more than one yearbook?
Some families purchase one copy for the student and an extra copy for mom and dad. Some even buy extra copies for grandparents.

what's a shout–out?
A shout-out is ad space that families purchase to send a personal message to a graduating senior. Most parents include a baby photo or a photo of their graduate as a young child. Shout-outs are a great way for families to say "we're so proud."

who are patrons and sponsors?
Patrons and sponsors are parents and alumni who make a donation to the yearbook. All contributions are a big help for the staff to produce a better book and defray the costs of color printing. All gifts are tax-deductible, and all patrons and sponsors are listed by name on the Patrons and Sponsors page in the yearbook.

I would like to make a contribution to the yearbook.

submit

Source Adobe® InDesign®, 2013.

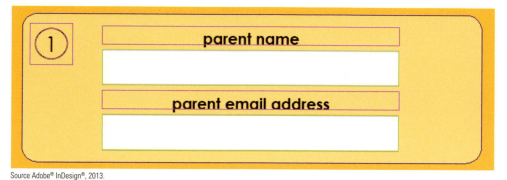

Source Adobe® InDesign®, 2013.

Figure 9 *Example of poor text alignment*

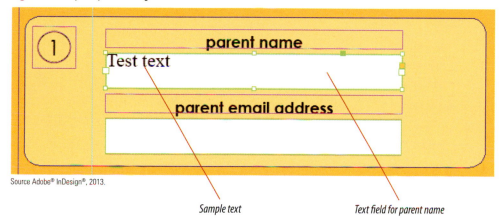

Source Adobe® InDesign®, 2013.

Sample text   Text field for parent name

3. Zoom in on section 1.

   As shown in Figure 8, section 1 has two text fields which are the white frames that are meant to be typed in by the person filling out the form. Above each text field is text that indicates what to type into the field. For example, **parent name** is positioned above the text field into which parents will enter their names. Note that the title is not *inside* the text field.

4. Open the Layers panel, then unlock the White Boxes layer.

5. Click the **Type tool** T, then type **Test text** into the white text field under the words **parent name**.

   Compare your result to Figure 9. The text is set at the upper-left corner of the text field. Because most formatting decisions you make in InDesign are not carried over to the exported PDF, you have very limited control over how text will appear and be positioned in a text field.

6. Delete the words **Test text**, then lock the White Boxes layer.

   (continued)

7. Show the Test Frames layer, then compare your screen to Figure 10.

The text looks much better. Rather than one frame for text entry, there is a text field (outlined in blue) within another white-filled frame (outlined in green). This "frame within a frame" approach creates space around all four sides of the text frame that is typed into, which is visually much more appealing.

8. Select the words **Sample text** in the text field under **parent name**.

The selected text is Times New Roman Regular, 14 pt. This sample text gives us an idea of the best and most visually appealing type size for the text that will be entered, even though the font may be different in the export document.

9. Click the **Object menu**, click **Text Frame Options**, then compare your dialog box to Figure 11.

Note that in the Vertical Justification section, the Align setting is set to Center. Vertical justification is one of the few formatting options that will carry through to the export document. In this example, when a user enters text into the **parent name** frame, that text will be vertically centered.

(continued)

Figure 10 *Visually appealing placement of text*

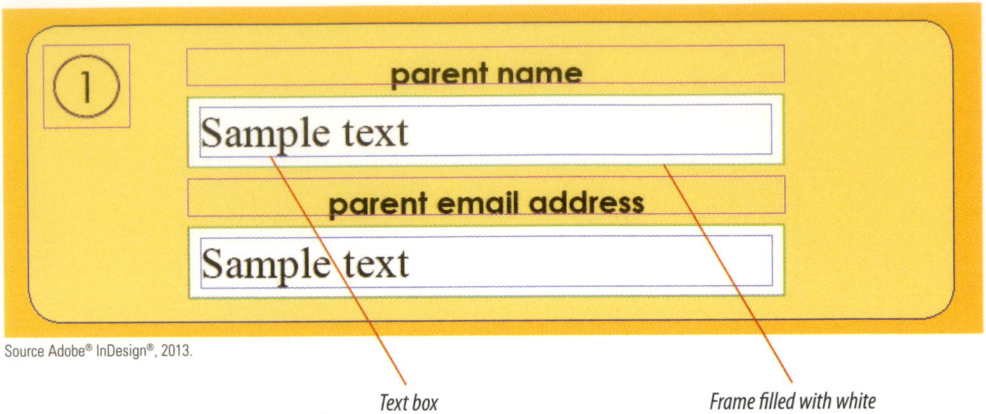

Source Adobe® InDesign®, 2013.

Text box

Frame filled with white

Figure 11 *Text Frame Options dialog box*

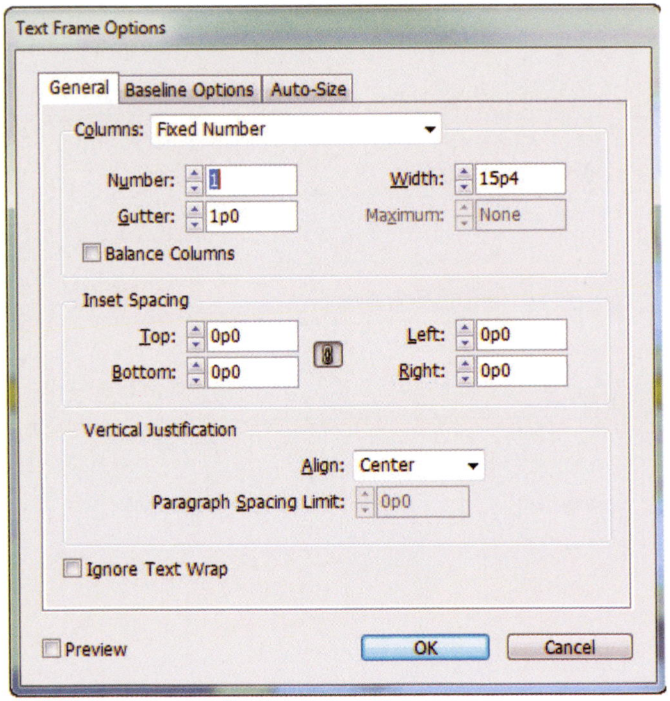

Source Adobe® InDesign®, 2013.

Creating Interactive Forms

Figure 12 *Determining how many words will fit at a given type size*

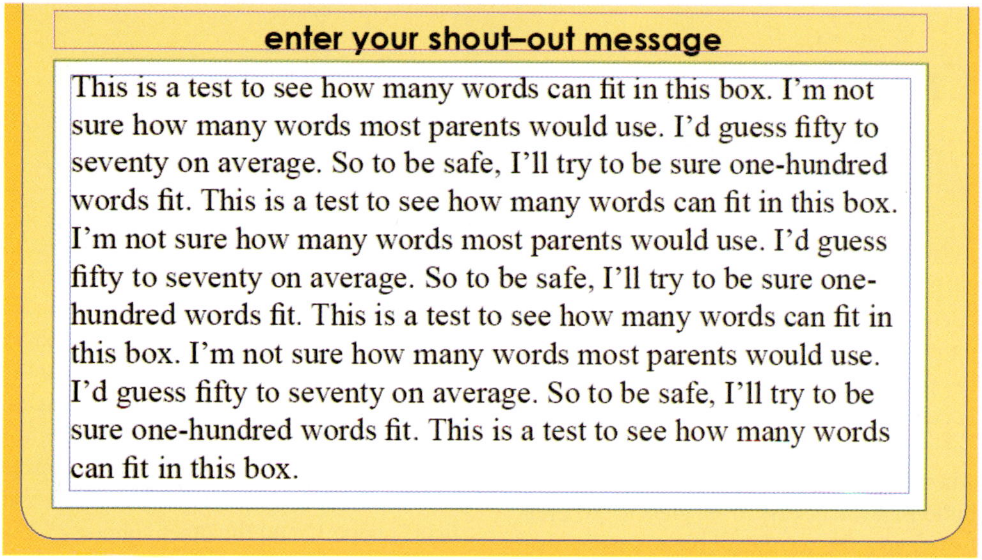

enter your shout–out message

This is a test to see how many words can fit in this box. I'm not sure how many words most parents would use. I'd guess fifty to seventy on average. So to be safe, I'll try to be sure one-hundred words fit. This is a test to see how many words can fit in this box. I'm not sure how many words most parents would use. I'd guess fifty to seventy on average. So to be safe, I'll try to be sure one-hundred words fit. This is a test to see how many words can fit in this box. I'm not sure how many words most parents would use. I'd guess fifty to seventy on average. So to be safe, I'll try to be sure one-hundred words fit. This is a test to see how many words can fit in this box.

Source Adobe® InDesign®, 2013.

10. Click **Cancel** to close the dialog box.

11. Zoom in on the text in the large, bottommost frame, as shown in Figure 12.

    This is an example of using sample text practically. The text is set at 10 pt. At this type size, approximately 140 words will fit in the box. Armed with this information, we could include instructions for filling out this form that "Shout-Out" copy should be approximately 120 words (leaving a little extra room if someone goes over).

12. Save your work.

You examined a document to find the best strategy for setting up text fields to look good when text is entered into them. You entered text into the text fields, noting that the text will not look good because it will be flush to the left edge. You then explored the frame-within-a-frame strategy for better text positioning. Finally, you explored the strategy of placing text and formatting it for size and vertical justification to get a good visual sense of how text will look and fit against the white background frame.

Create Text
INPUT FIELDS

What You'll Do

Buttons and Forms

Type: Text Field

Name: parent name

Event: On Release or Tap

Actions: ✥ ⚊

[No Actions Added]

☐ Hidden Until Triggered

▽ PDF Options

Description:

☑ Printable   ☐ Read Only
☑ Required   ☐ Multiline
☐ Password   ☐ Scrollable

Font Size: 14

Source Adobe® InDesign®, 2013.

 In this lesson, you will create text fields for an interactive form that will be exported as a PDF.

Creating Interactive Fields for Forms

All interactive fields in an interactive InDesign document are buttons. To make any frame into a field for a form, you must first convert the frame to a button using the Buttons and Forms panel. The new button is listed on the panel. (It's a good idea to name the button when you create it so that if you have multiple buttons, it will be easy to tell them apart. Even better, give the text field button a name that clearly describes the information that will be entered into the field.)

Interactive fields are used to collect data. All the data from a given form can be imported into a database, and databases use the names of fields to organize and sort data from those fields. For example, let's say you're designing a form that needs two phone text fields: one for a home phone number and one for a cell phone number. When you create the two fields in InDesign, don't name one text field "phone 1" and the other "phone 2." The terms are too non-specific, and you'll always need to keep in mind that phone 1 = home and phone 2 = cell. Instead, name the first text field "home phone" and the other "cell phone."

When you choose Text Field as the type of button, six options for the text field appear on the Buttons and Forms panel, as shown in Figure 13. Beneath the six options is the Font Size pull-down menu. Table 1 below describes the text field options.

Figure 13 *Six options for text fields*

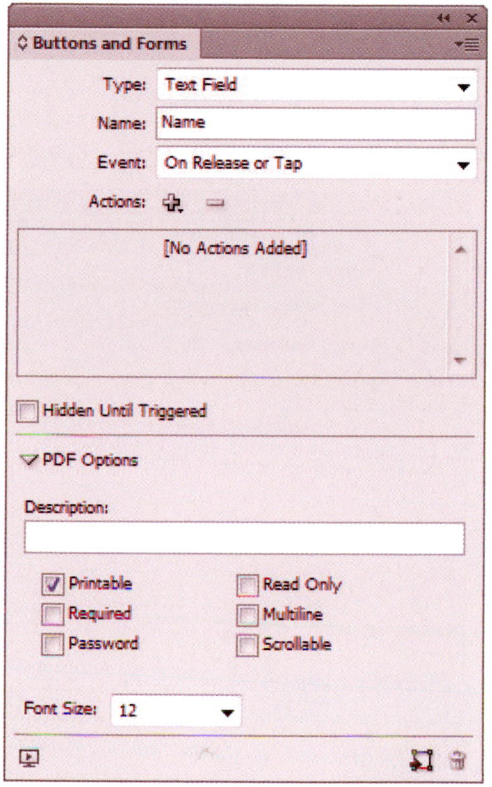

Source Adobe® InDesign®, 2013.

TABLE 1: TEXT FIELD OPTIONS	
Printable	When activated, data entered into a field will print. In almost all cases, you'll want this option checked.
Required	When activated, the form cannot be submitted if the Required field is left blank. This is a powerful feature for making sure the user gives you the information you need.
Password	When activated, text entered into the field will appear on screen and in a printed form as *******. The data from the form will read in normal text characters if imported into a database or when exported as data.
Read Only	When activated, text cannot be entered into the field.
Multiline	When you have fields that are meant to contain large amounts of data—like a paragraph—use this option so that the text will flow onto multiple lines.
Scrollable	When activated, scroll bars will appear on multiline fields when more text is entered than is visible in the frame.

© Cengage Learning 2013

Create text input fields

1. Hide the Test Frames layer, then show the Interactive Frames layer.

   The Interactive Frames layer contains empty frames that will be used for data entry in the export document.

2. Zoom in on the number 1 section, click the **Selection tool** then select the **frame** under **parent name**.

3. Open the Buttons and Forms panel, then convert the frame into a button.

4. Click the **Type list arrow**, then click **Text Field**.

5. Type **parent name** into the Name text box.

6. At the bottom of the panel, check the **Printable** and **Required check boxes**.

   With the Required option activated, the form cannot be submitted if this frame is empty.

7. Click the **Font Size list arrow**, then choose **14**.

   Your Buttons and Forms panel should resemble Figure 14.

8. Select the **frame** under **parent email address** then convert it to a button.

9. Enter the settings shown in Figure 15.

(continued)

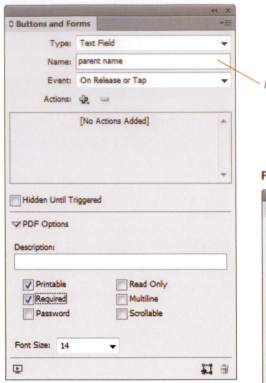

Figure 14 *Settings for the parent name text field*

Name of text field

Source Adobe® InDesign®, 2013.

Figure 15 *Settings for the parent email address text field*

Source Adobe® InDesign®, 2013.

Figure 16 *Settings for the student name text frame*

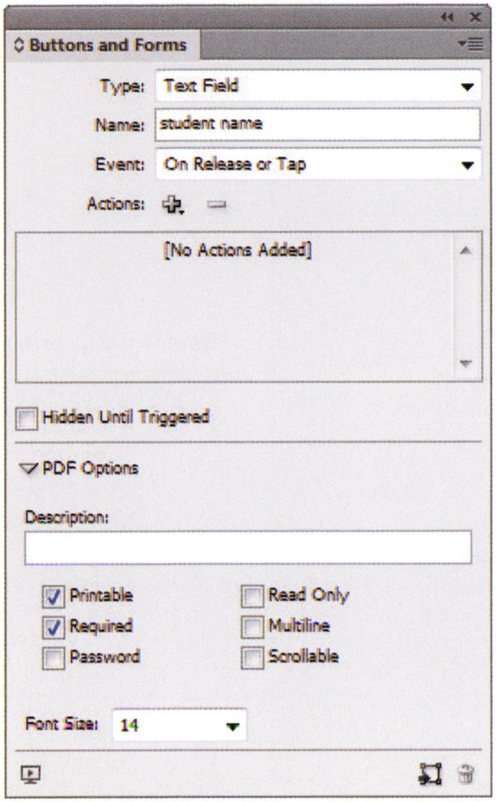

Buttons and Forms

Type: Text Field
Name: student name
Event: On Release or Tap
Actions: ➕ ➖

[No Actions Added]

☐ Hidden Until Triggered

▽ PDF Options

Description:

☑ Printable   ☐ Read Only
☑ Required   ☐ Multiline
☐ Password   ☐ Scrollable

Font Size: 14

Source Adobe® InDesign®, 2013.

Figure 17 *Selected frame for # of copies*

Source Adobe® InDesign®, 2013.

10. Select the **frame** under **student name** then convert it to a button.

11. Enter the settings shown in Figure 16.

12. Select the **frame in section 3**, as shown in Figure 17, then convert it to a button.

This frame is for the number of copies of yearbooks purchased. The frame is positioned so that the text entered will appear centered in relation to the white frame behind it.

(continued)

13. Enter the settings shown in Figure 18.

    Note that the Required check box is not checked because the user has the option to not purchase a yearbook.

14. In section 4, select the **frame** under **enter student's name as you wish it to appear** then convert it to a button.

15. Enter the settings shown in Figure 19.

(continued)

Figure 18 *Settings for the # of copies text field*

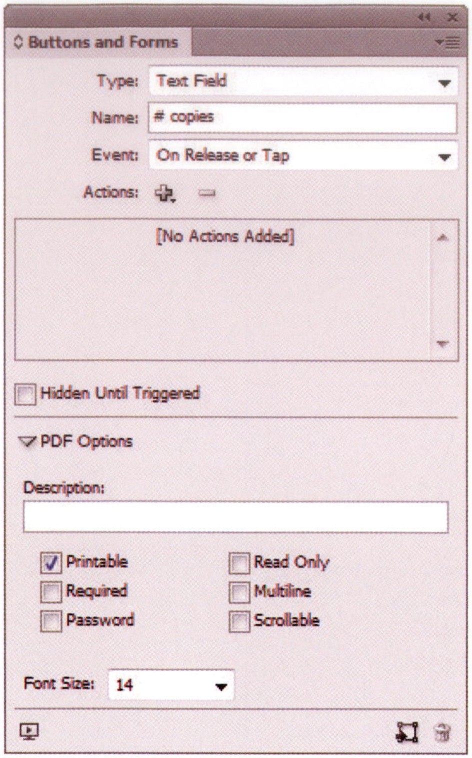

Source Adobe® InDesign®, 2013.

Figure 19 *Settings for the student shout-out name text field*

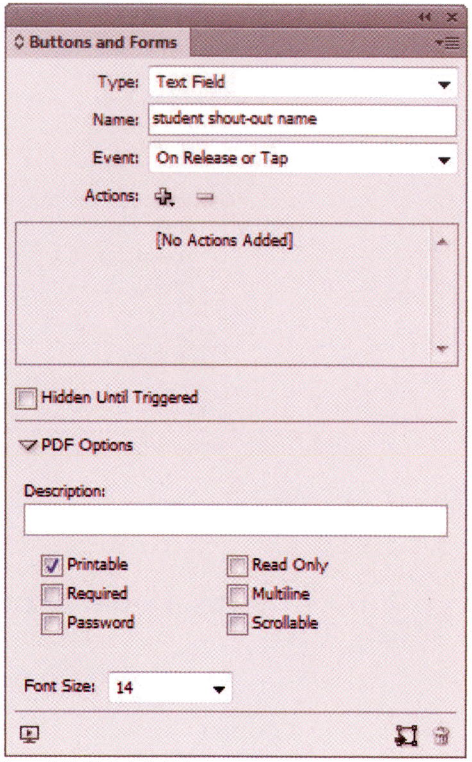

Source Adobe® InDesign®, 2013.

Creating Interactive Forms

Figure 20 *Settings for the shout-out message text field*

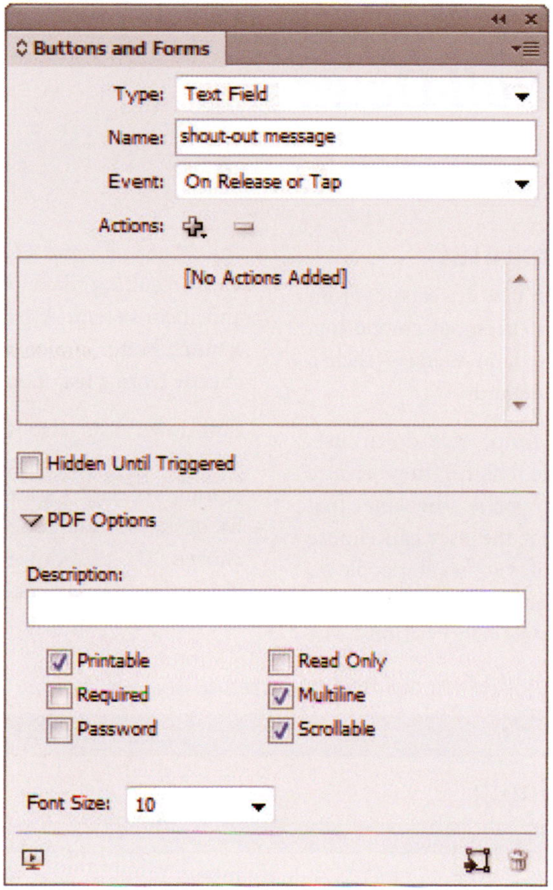

⬦ Buttons and Forms	▾≡
Type:	Text Field ▾
Name:	shout-out message
Event:	On Release or Tap ▾
Actions:	⊞ ⊟

[No Actions Added]

☐ Hidden Until Triggered

▽ PDF Options

Description:

☑ Printable   ☐ Read Only
☐ Required   ☑ Multiline
☐ Password   ☑ Scrollable

Font Size: 10 ▾

Source Adobe® InDesign®, 2013.

16. Select the **large frame** inside the large white frame at the bottom of section 4, then convert it to a button.

    This text frame is for the shout-out message text.

17. Enter the settings shown in Figure 20.

    Note that the Font Size is set to 10 pt, which is the size that was tested with the sample text. Save your work.

You converted six frames into buttons and specified their button types as Text Frame. You activated different options for the different fields and specified the font size for each field.

Create a Pull-Down LIST

What You'll Do

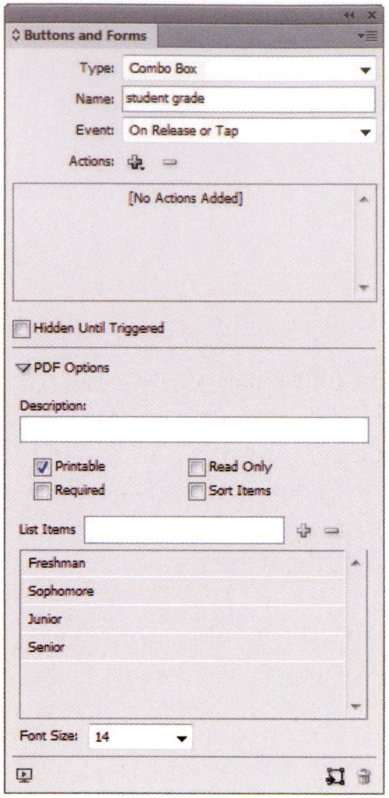

Source Adobe® InDesign®, 2013.

In this lesson, you will format a field as a pull-down list

Formatting a Pull-down List

Simply put, pull-down lists are classic. From the very beginning of personal computing, the interface was based on menus—click a menu, see a list of commands.

When designing a form, pull-down lists are a smart strategic choice; they ensure consistency because you're the one that creates a finite list that the user can choose from. For example, if you want people to enter what state they are from, you could end up with all kinds of state abbreviations: MA and MASS, FL and FLA, and CA and CAL. Your resulting data would be overlapping and inconsistent. A pull-down list would be a much better choice because users can only choose from a list of correct inputs.

Pull-down lists also offer a very practical solution for containing—and hiding—large amounts of data. Figure 21 shows a pull-down list of states, with the abbreviation for Arizona chosen. The pull-down list contains the long list of the other 49 states and keeps it hidden but easily accessible.

Figure 21 *AZ chosen in a pull-down list, with 49 other choices not showing*

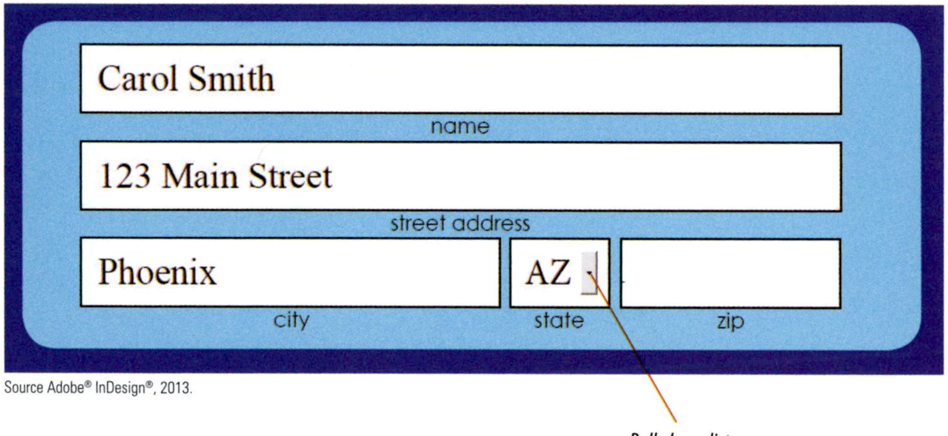

Carol Smith
name

123 Main Street
street address

Phoenix
city

AZ
state

zip

Source Adobe® InDesign®, 2013.

Pull-down list

Creating Interactive Forms

Figure 22 *Entering the first list item*

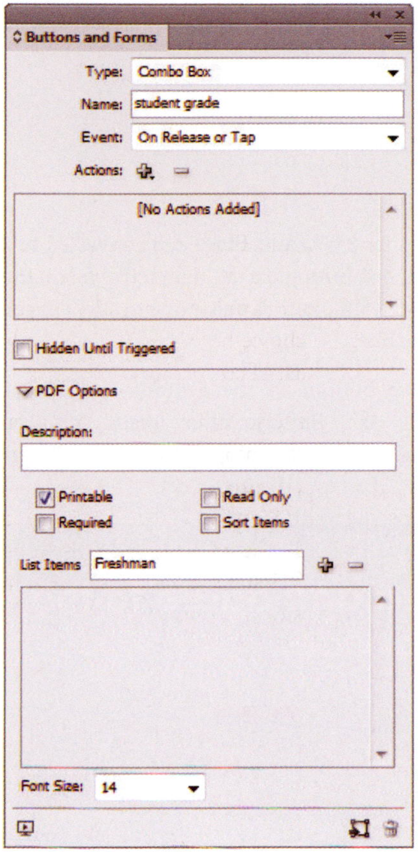

Source Adobe® InDesign®, 2013.

Figure 23 *Four list items for the student grade pull-down list*

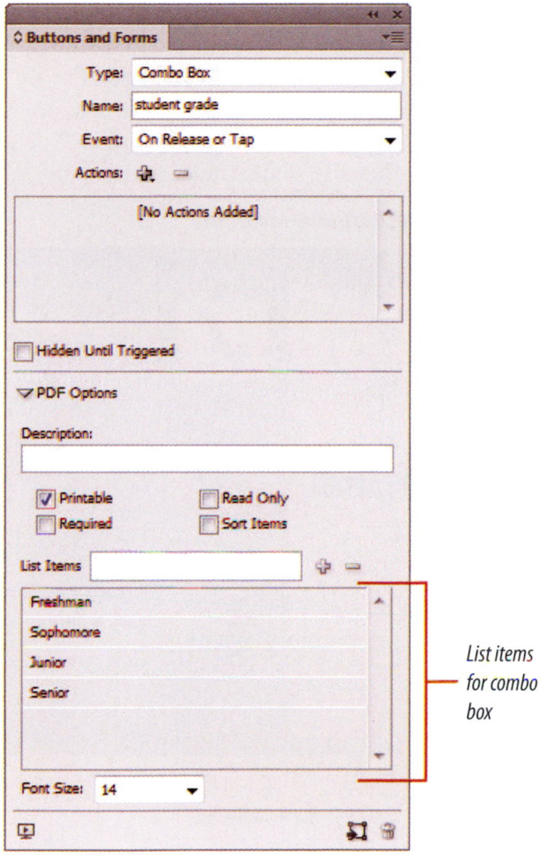

List items for combo box

Source Adobe® InDesign®, 2013.

Formatting a field as a pull-down list

1. In section 2, select the **frame** under **student grade this year**, then convert it to a button.

2. Click the **Type list arrow**, then click **Combo Box**.

   Combo Box is the type of button used for a pull-down list.

3. Type **student grade** into the Name text box.

4. Check the **Printable check box** under the Description field.

5. Click the **Font Size list arrow**, then click **14**.

6. Type **Freshman** in the List Items text box, as shown in Figure 22.

7. Click the **plus sign button** 🔣 to the right of the field.

   The word *Freshman* appears in the field below the List Items text box as the first available choice that will appear in the list of choices. Clicking the plus button allows you to add additional choices, such as Sophomore, Junior, and Senior.

8. Type **Sophomore** in the List Items text box, then click the **plus sign button** 🔣 .

9. Type **Junior** in the List Items text box, then click the **plus sign button** 🔣 .

10. Type **Senior** in the List Items text box, then click the **plus sign button** 🔣 .

    Your Buttons and Forms panel should resemble Figure 23. When you click the button in the export document, the four items will be selectable in a pull-down list.

11. Save your work.

To format a field with a pull-down list of options, you applied the Combo Box button type, then entered four items for the list.

Create Check Boxes and
RADIO BUTTONS

What You'll Do

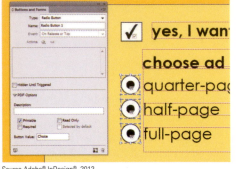

Source Adobe® InDesign®, 2013.

 In this lesson, you will format fields as check boxes and radio buttons.

Using Check Boxes and Radio Buttons

When utilized in a form—especially an interactive form—check boxes have a different connotation than radio buttons. Check boxes are affirmative; checking a box suggests that you are making a choice, choosing to opt in on an offer or identify with an item.

In Figure 24, a frame has been converted to a check box button. In the interactive form, the user can simply click the frame to add a check to the box.

At the bottom of the Buttons and Forms panel, the Button Value reads Yes (by default). Remember that when a user enters

Figure 24 *Frame converted to a check box*

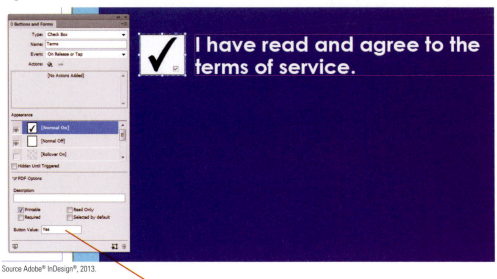

Source Adobe® InDesign®, 2013.

*Button Value reads
Yes (by default)*

information into a form, the form is essentially collecting data, and that data is stored as part of the saved document. In the case of check boxes, the button value of Yes means that if the box is checked, the data for the form will list Yes beside the button name.

Figure 25 shows five radio buttons, each identified with a different age group. With radio buttons, the function is usually that you can click only one button in the group, to the exculsion of all others. With check boxes, you'll often to be asked to "check all that apply."

When you format radio buttons, you must select all the buttons in the group and convert them into a button at the same time to make them function as a group. When they function as a group, only one radio button in the group can be selected or activated.

Using One Button to Trigger Another

When you convert a frame to a button, you can choose the Hide Until Triggered option, shown in Figure 26. With this option, a button will not be visible in the exported form until it is triggered by another button.

Check boxes and radio buttons are often used as triggers for hidden buttons. For example, you can put a check box button beside a text frame that says "check if you are finished." Beneath that line of text, you can create a second text frame that says "Thank you for filling out this survey." Convert the "Thank you..." frame to a button, then set it as hidden until triggered. You can then apply the Show/Hide Buttons and Forms action to the check box button and specify that it shows the "Thank you..." button when clicked.

Figure 25 *Five radio buttons; one selected*

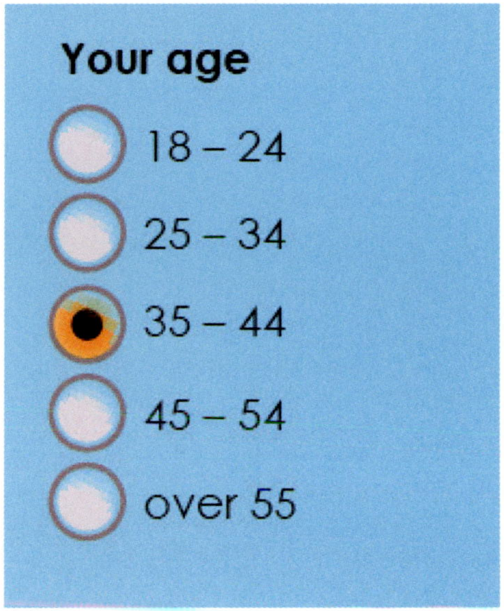

Your age

◯ 18 – 24

◯ 25 – 34

● 35 – 44

◯ 45 – 54

◯ over 55

Source Adobe® InDesign®, 2013.

Figure 26 *Hide Until Triggered option*

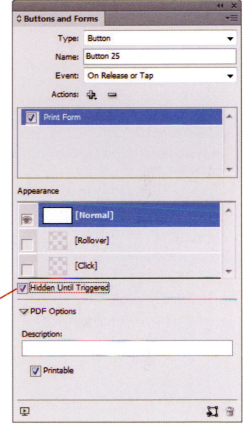

Hide Until Triggered check box

Source Adobe® InDesign®, 2013.

Formatting a field as a check box

1. Select the **white square frame** in section 3 beside the words **yes, I want to purchase a yearbook**.

2. Convert the frame to a button.

3. Click the **Type list arrow**, then click **Check Box**.

   A check mark appears inside the frame.

4. Type **yes yearbook** into the Name text box.

5. Check the **Printable check box** under the Description field.

   Your Buttons and Forms panel should resemble Figure 27.

6. Select the **white square frame** in section 4 beside the words **yes, I want to purchase a shout-out ad**.

7. Convert the frame to a check box button named **yes shout-out.**

8. Select the **white square frame** at the bottom of the right column of text beside the words **I would like to make a contribution to the yearbook.**

9. Convert the frame to a button, then apply the formatting as shown in Figure 28.

10. Save your work.

You converted three frames into buttons and specified their button types as check boxes.

Figure 27 *Formatting for the yes yearbook check box*

Figure 28 *Formatting for the yes contribution check box*

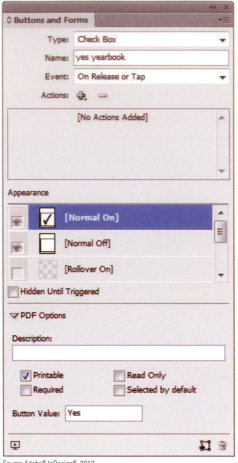

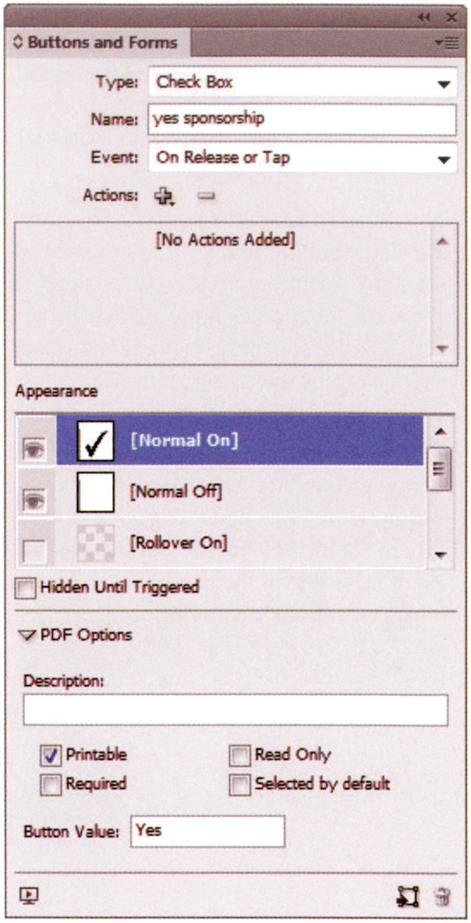

Source Adobe® InDesign®, 2013.

Source Adobe® InDesign®, 2013.

Creating Interactive Forms

Figure 29 *Settings for the radio buttons*

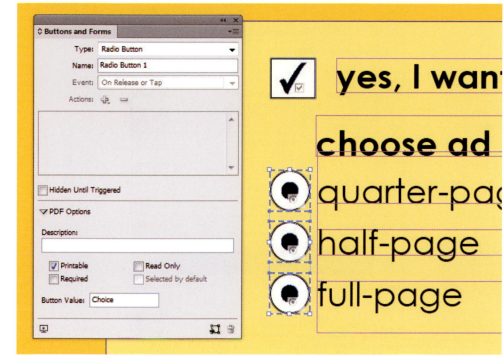

Source Adobe® InDesign®, 2013.

Create radio buttons

1. Select the **three white circles** in section 4.

   The circles are simple frames made with the Ellipse tool.

2. Convert the group of three white circles to buttons.

3. Click the **Type list arrow**, then click **Radio Button**.

   As shown in Figure 29, the three buttons are converted to radio buttons. Because all three were selected when converted to a button, the radio buttons are related—only one of the three can be selected. The radio buttons are for the three choices of shout-out ad sizes.

4. Type **choose ad size** into the Name text box.

5. Save your work.

You converted three ellipses into radio buttons.

Use radio buttons as triggers

1. In section 4, select the **frame with 300.00** in it, click the **Edit menu**, then click **Copy**.

2. Convert the frame to a button.

3. Name the button **300**.

4. Check the **Hidden Until Triggered check box** so that your Buttons and Forms panel resembles Figure 30.

   When the form opens, the 300 button will not be visible until it is triggered. If a person clicks the full-page ad radio button, the 300 button will appear in the $ text frame.

5. With the 300 button still selected, click the **Object menu**, then click **Hide**.

6. Click **Edit** on the Menu bar, then click **Paste in Place**.

7. Click the **Type tool** 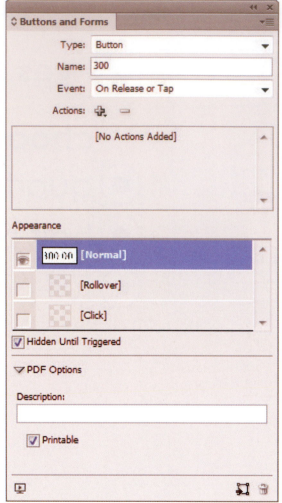, then change 300.00 to **150.00**.

8. Click the **Selection tool**, then convert the frame to a button.

9. Name the button **150**, then check the **Hidden Until Triggered check box**.

10. Click the **Object menu**, then click **Hide**.

    If a person clicks the half-page ad radio button, the 150 button will appear in the $ text frame.

(continued)

Figure 30 *Settings for the 300 button*

Source Adobe® InDesign®, 2013.

Creating Interactive Forms

Figure 31 *Settings for the 75 button*

Source Adobe® InDesign®, 2013.

11. Click **Edit** on the Menu bar, then click **Paste in Place**.
12. Click the **Type tool** T , then change 300.00 to **75.00**.
13. Click the **Selection tool** , then convert the frame to a button.
14. Name the button **75**, then check the **Hidden Until Triggered check box**.

    If a person clicks the quarter-page ad radio button, the 75 button will appear in the $ text frame. Your Buttons and Forms panel should resemble Figure 31.
15. Save your work.

(continued)

16. Click the **Object menu**, then click **Show All on Spread**.

    As shown in Figure 32, all three buttons are overlapped in the same location on the form. Note that the 75 button is still selected.

17. Press the **right arrow key** on your keypad until the decimal point on the 75.00 aligns with the other two, as shown in Figure 33.

18. Select the **top radio button**.

    (continued)

Figure 32 *Three buttons overlapped*

Source Adobe® InDesign®, 2013.

Figure 33 *Aligning the 75.00 decimal point*

Source Adobe® InDesign®, 2013.

Creating Interactive Forms

Figure 34 *The Visibility section becomes available with the Show/Hide Buttons and Forms action*

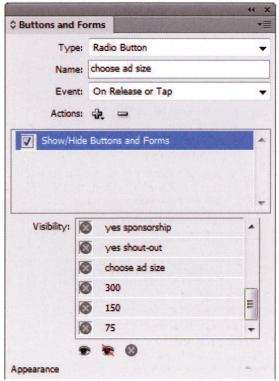

Source Adobe® InDesign®, 2013.

19. On the Buttons and Forms panel, click the **plus sign button** beside Actions, then click **Show/Hide Buttons and Forms**.

   The Visibility section appears, as shown in Figure 34.

20. In the Visibility section, click **300**, then click the **Hide button** .

(continued)

21. Click **150**, then click **Hide**.

22. Click **75**, then click **Show**.

    Your Visibility section should resemble Figure 35.

    (continued)

Figure 35 *Show/Hide strategy for the quarter-page radio button*

Source Adobe® InDesign®, 2013.

Figure 36 *Show/Hide strategy for the half-page radio button*

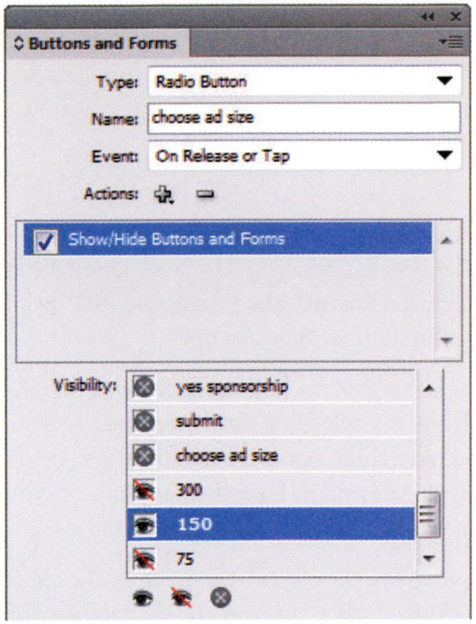

Source Adobe® InDesign®, 2013.

Figure 37 *Show/Hide strategy for the full-page radio button*

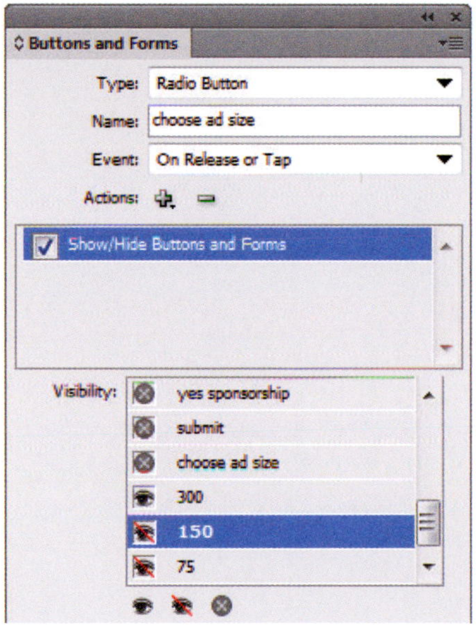

Source Adobe® InDesign®, 2013.

23. Select the **middle radio button**, activate **the Show/Hide Buttons and Forms** action, then set the Visibility section to match Figure 36.

24. Select the **bottom radio button**, activate the **Show/Hide Buttons and Forms** action, then set the Visibility section to match Figure 37.

25. Save your work.

You formatted three radio buttons to each show a different button when clicked.

Create a Submit
FORM BUTTON

What You'll Do

Source Adobe® InDesign®, 2013.

In this lesson, you will create a button to submit the form to an email address.

Creating a Submit Form Button

When you create an interactive form, two basic strategies you have to consider are how the form will be delivered to the user and how the user will return it to you.

You have two main options for delivering the form to your intended user: website or email. If you choose the website option, you can post the interactive PDF to a website where your users can go to fill out the form.

As an alternative, you can send an email to your user list with the interactive PDF as an attachment that they can open.

Once the form is delivered, the next step is getting the filled-out form returned to you. You have three options for data return: print, website, or email. For all three options, you can use a button to trigger the action.

Having the user print the form is the most low-tech option of the three, because the only delivery option with a printed form is for the user to fax the form to you or send it via snail mail. Either way, it's a bit of a chore.

To print the form, the user can click the Print command on their computer or you can include a "print" button in the form. To do so, convert a frame to a button, then apply the Print Form action to the button, shown in Figure 38.

Figure 38 *Print Form action ascribed to a button on the Buttons and Forms panel*

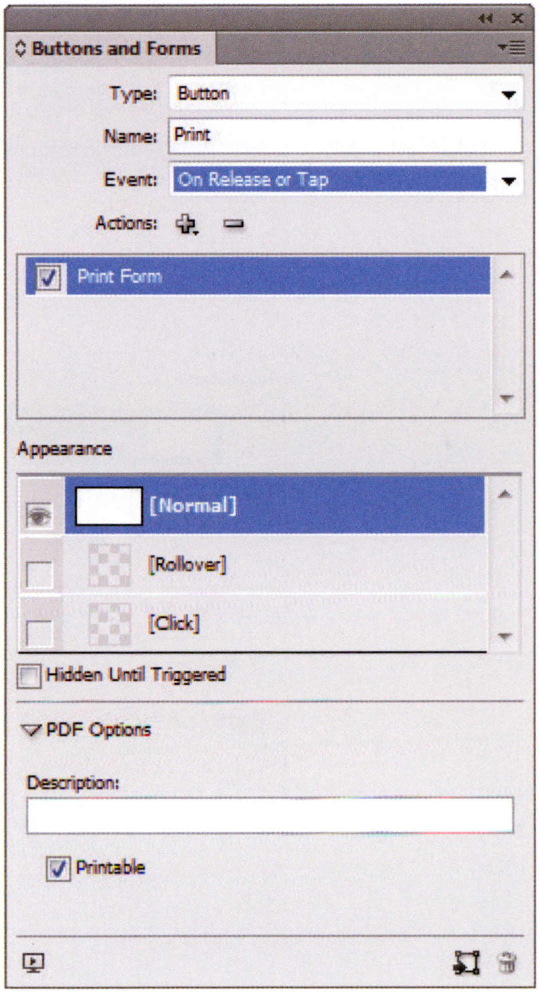

Source Adobe® InDesign®, 2013.

To have the form returned to a website or to an email address, apply the Submit Form action to a button, as shown in Figure 39. When you choose the Submit Form action, the URL text box becomes available on the Buttons and Forms panel. If you want the form delivered to a website, enter the URL for the page on the site that will accept and import the data from the form.

Using a website to collect data from a form is a great choice, because the data is imported into a database and is instantly sortable. However, professional-level coding skills are required to build a database on the site to accept the data from the form correctly into corresponding data fields.

Perhaps the most direct and easiest to set up option is to have the user return the form to you via email. When you choose the Submit Form action, type **mailto:** in the URL text box followed by the email address that you want the form to go to with no spaces. For example, you would enter **mailto:dylan@ dylandove.com** and Dylan would receive the form in his email inbox.

Figure 39 *Submit Form action ascribed to a button on the Buttons and Forms panel*

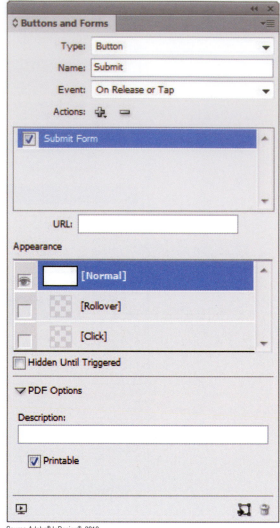

Source Adobe® InDesign®, 2013.

Creating Interactive Forms

Figure 40 *Formatting the button to submit the form to an email address*

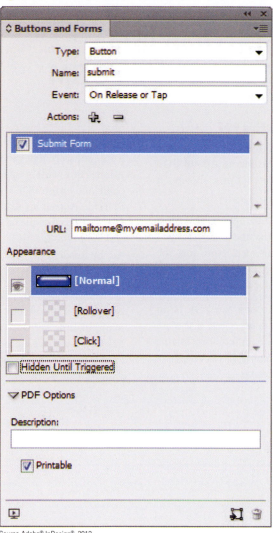

Create a button to submit a form to an email address

1. In the lower-right corner of the form, select the **blue rounded rectangle**.

2. Convert the artwork into a button.

3. On the Buttons and Forms panel, name the button **submit**.

4. Click the **plus sign** beside Actions, then click **Submit Form**.

5. In the URL text box, type your own email address. For example, you would type **mailto:john@ johnsmith.com.**

   Your Buttons and Forms panel should resemble Figure 40.

6. Save your work.

You formatted a button to submit a form to an email address.

Enter Information into
AN INTERACTIVE FORM

What You'll Do

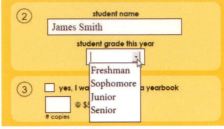

Source Adobe® InDesign®, 2013.

▶ *In this lesson, you will set the tab order, export the form as a PDF, enter information, then export the form as a deliverable file.*

Exporting an Interactive PDF

Once you're done designing and formatting a document, export the file as Adobe PDF (Interactive). Enter the options shown in Figure 41.

Note the Forms and Media option. This must be set to Include All so that the form fields you created will function as such. Note too, the View After Exporting option. This will open the PDF on your computer once it is generated.

The software that will open the PDF is an important consideration, especially if you are sending the PDF to many different recipients who will be using different types of computers with different configurations.

Most computer users have Adobe Reader installed on their computers. Adobe Reader is free software that can be downloaded from Adobe.com and is specifically designed to open and print PDF documents. Since the PDF file is itself an Adobe product, you can expect that the file you export will open and function exactly as you intend it to in Adobe Reader.

If the user has Adobe Acrobat installed, the file will automatically open in Acrobat. Adobe Acrobat is a proprietary PDF generation and manipulation software package. Since one has to pay to have Acrobat installed, you can expect fewer of your recipients to be viewing your PDF in Acrobat.

If the user does not have Reader or Acrobat installed, the PDF will open in a more generic application, like Preview on the Mac. In most cases, the form will function as you intend, but you can also expect some discrepancies.

Most are cosmetic: the type is positioned differently in the field, there's a color shift, or the fields don't align properly with one another. In worst-case scenarios, some buttons will not function properly or will

not function at all. For this reason, when you email the PDF to your recipients, you might want to consider including a message that the form is best viewed with Adobe Reader and include a link to **get.adobe.com/reader**.

Figure 41 *Export to Interactive PDF dialog box*

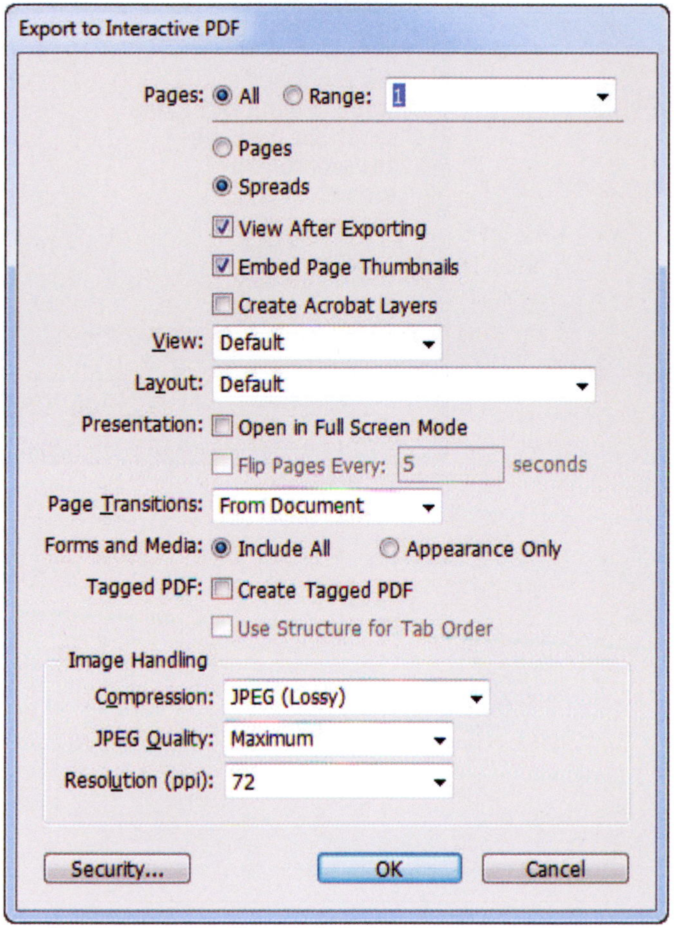

Export to Interactive PDF

Pages: ⦿ All ○ Range: [1 ▾]

　　　　○ Pages
　　　　⦿ Spreads
　　　　☑ View After Exporting
　　　　☑ Embed Page Thumbnails
　　　　☐ Create Acrobat Layers

View: [Default ▾]
Layout: [Default ▾]
Presentation: ☐ Open in Full Screen Mode
　　　　☐ Flip Pages Every: [5] seconds

Page Transitions: [From Document ▾]
Forms and Media: ⦿ Include All ○ Appearance Only
Tagged PDF: ☐ Create Tagged PDF
　　　　☐ Use Structure for Tab Order

Image Handling
Compression: [JPEG (Lossy) ▾]
JPEG Quality: [Maximum ▾]
Resolution (ppi): [72 ▾]

[Security...]　[OK]　[Cancel]

Source Adobe® InDesign®, 2013.

Set the tab order for an interactive form

1. Click the **Object menu**, point to **Interactive**, then click **Set Tab Order**.

   The Set Tab Order dialog box opens. The current tab order is listed from top to bottom in the window. By default, the tab order is created in the order you create buttons. In the case of this project, because you didn't create buttons from the top of the form to the bottom, the default tab order isn't satisfactory.

2. Click and drag **button names** up and down in the window so that your Tab Order dialog box resembles Figure 42.

   Note that the three radio buttons (all named **choose ad size**) and the buttons named 300, 150 and 75 are all at the bottom of the order. These are not fields you'll want to tab to, so they are at the bottom of the list.

3. Click **OK**, then save your work.

You set the tab order for fields in an interactive form.

Figure 42 *Tab Order dialog box*

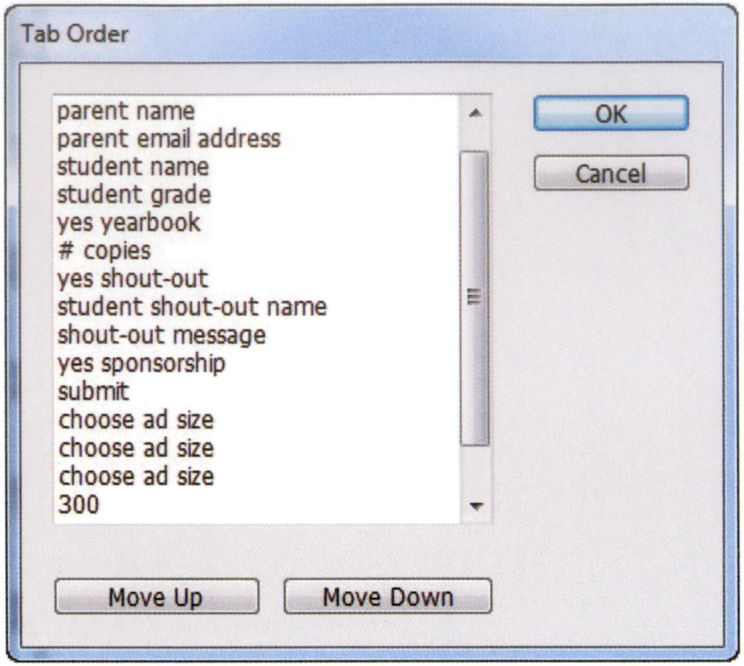

Source Adobe® InDesign®, 2013.

Creating Interactive Forms

Figure 43 *Export to Interactive PDF dialog box*

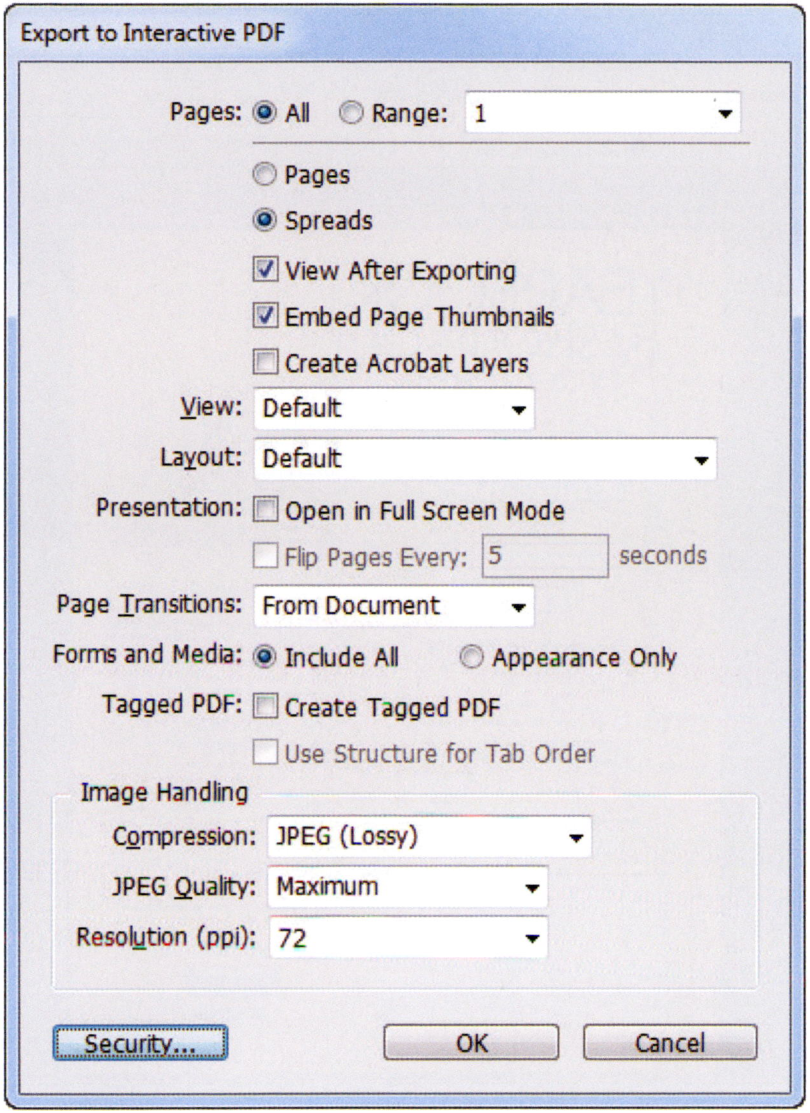

Export to Interactive PDF

Pages: ◉ All   ○ Range: 1 ▾

○ Pages
◉ Spreads
☑ View After Exporting
☑ Embed Page Thumbnails
☐ Create Acrobat Layers

View: Default ▾
Layout: Default ▾
Presentation: ☐ Open in Full Screen Mode
☐ Flip Pages Every: 5   seconds
Page Transitions: From Document ▾
Forms and Media: ◉ Include All   ○ Appearance Only
Tagged PDF: ☐ Create Tagged PDF
☐ Use Structure for Tab Order

Image Handling
Compression: JPEG (Lossy) ▾
JPEG Quality: Maximum ▾
Resolution (ppi): 72 ▾

Security...   OK   Cancel

Source Adobe® InDesign®, 2013.

Enter data into an exported form

1. Click the **File menu**, then click **Export**.

   The Export dialog box opens.

2. Click the **Save as type list arrow**, then choose **Adobe PDF (Interactive)**.

3. Click **Save**, then enter the settings shown in Figure 43.

   Note that the View After Exporting option is checked, and note that the Forms and Media option is specified as Include All. The Include All option must be chosen for the fields to be interactive in the exported PDF.

   (continued)

4. Click **OK**.

Because the View After Exporting check box was checked, the PDF will open automatically after it's been exported. Figure 44 shows the exported PDF opened in Adobe Acrobat X Pro, which is the most recent version of Adobe Acrobat. If you have Adobe Acrobat software installed, the file will open in Adobe Acrobat. If you don't, the file will open in Adobe Acrobat Reader. If you don't have Acrobat Reader installed, you should go to **get/adobe.com/reader/** to download the software, then finish this chapter.

(continued)

Figure 44 *The exported form in Adobe Acrobat X Pro*

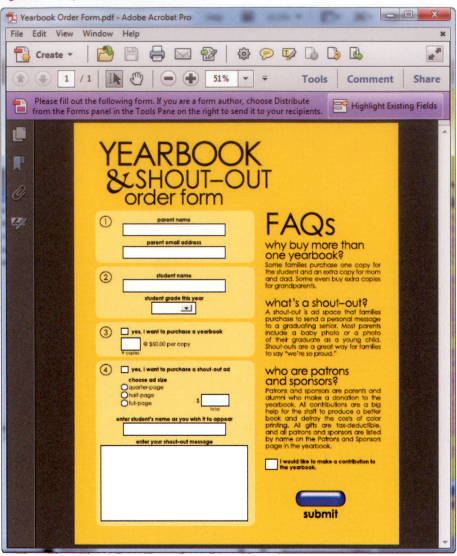

Source Adobe® Acrobat Pro®, 2013.

Creating Interactive Forms

YEARBOOK & SHOUT-OU order form

① parent name

John Smith

parent email address

5. Enter a name into the parent name field, but leave the parent email address field blank.

   As shown in Figure 45, the text appears to be indented in the white fields and is visually appealing.

   TIP Press [Tab] to move from field to field and [Shift][Tab] to move backwards.

6. Type **James Smith** in the student name field.

   (continued)

7. In the student grade this year field, click the **silver list arrow**, then compare your screen to Figure 46.

   A pull-down list appears showing the four list options.

8. Click **Senior** then press **Tab**.

9. In section 3, check the **yes ... option**.

(continued)

Figure 46 *List options revealed in the pull-down list*

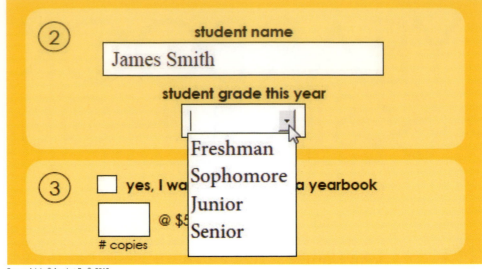

Source Adobe® Acrobat Pro®, 2013.

Creating Interactive Forms

Figure 47 *Check box checked and a number entered into the # copies field*

Figure 48 *Half-size radio button chosen and the half-price amount showing in the total field*

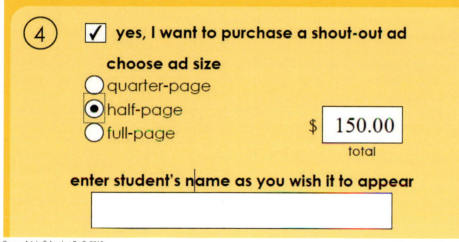

10. Type **2** in the # copies field, then compare your section 3 to Figure 47.

11. In section 4, check the **yes . . . option**, then click each of the radio buttons.

    As shown in Figure 48, when you click a radio button, the associated price appears in the total field.

12. Enter **Jimmy Smith** in the enter student name . . . field, then type a message into the large frame.

    The type in the frame is smaller than the other frames, and text enters on multiple lines.

You entered information into multiple fields, testing the formatting that you input.

Submit a form

1. Click the **submit button**.

   As shown in Figure 49, a warning dialog box appears informing that some required fields are empty. The three fields that were formatted with the required option appear with a red border.

2. Click **OK**.

3. Type **john@johnsmith.com** in the parent email address field.

   (continued)

Figure 49 *Warning that required fields are empty*

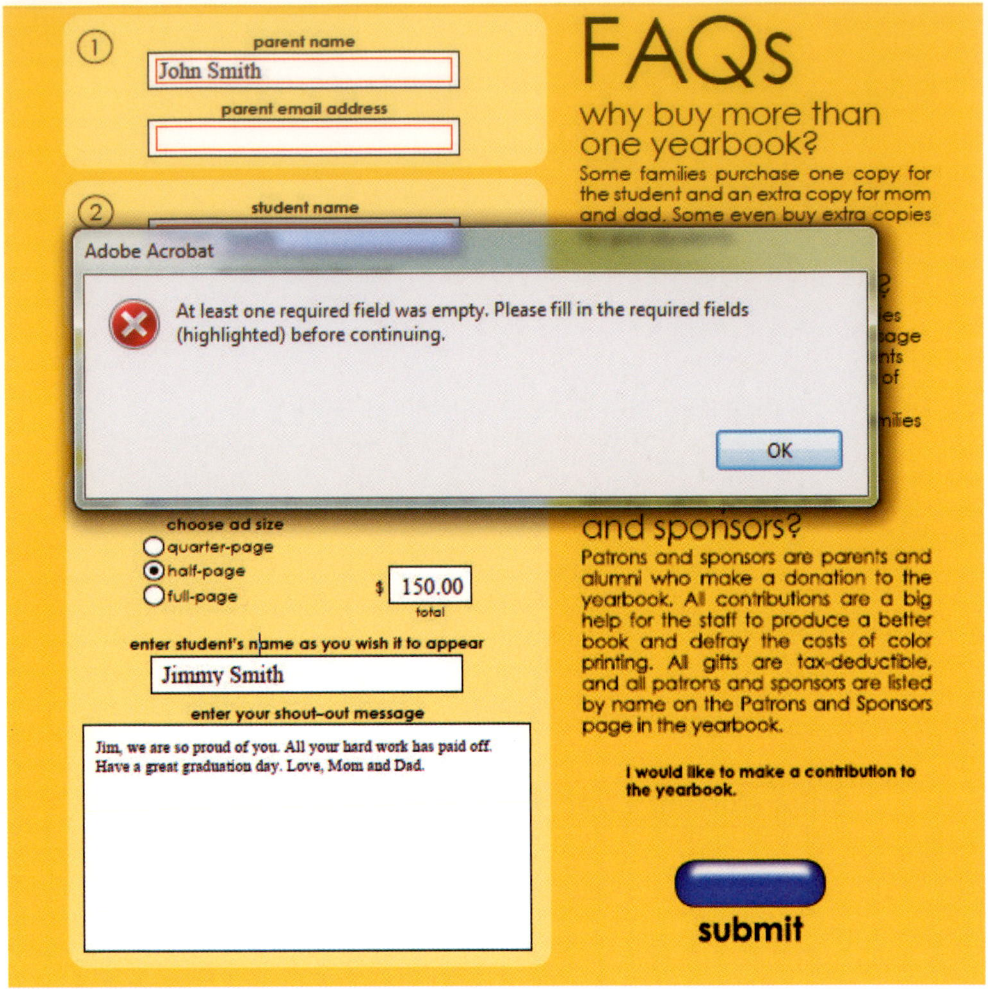

Source Adobe® Acrobat Pro®, 2013.

Figure 50 *Select Email Client dialog box after the submit button is clicked*

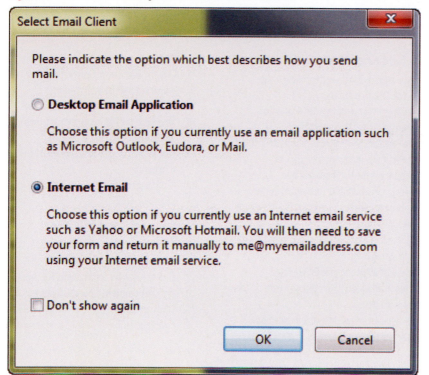

Source Adobe® Acrobat Pro®, 2013.

4. Click the **submit button**.

   As shown in Figure 50, the Select Email Client dialog box opens. Your options for sending the form are dependent on how you use email on your computer. If you have an email software application installed, like Eudora or Microsoft Outlook, click the Desktop Email Application option. If you email through a website such as Yahoo! or Google mail, click the Internet Email option. Because it is the most universally accepted option, you will finish the lesson with the Internet Email option.

5. Click **Internet Email**, then click **OK**.

   The Send PDF Data dialog box opens. You're being offered the ability to save the filled-out form as an emailable PDF. You can save over the file that you exported, or you can give this version a different name.

6. Type **Yearbook Order Form Complete** in the Save As textbox, then click **Save**.

   The file is saved to your computer. It can be attached to any email form and delivered as an attachment.

You clicked the submit button and needed to fill in a required field. Once done, you clicked the submit button again and saved the form as an emailable PDF.

Create text input fields

1. Open ID 5-2.indd then save it as **Skills Review**.
2. Zoom in on the white frames, then select the frame above name.
3. Open the Buttons and Forms panel, then convert the frame into a button.
4. Click the Type list arrow, then click Text Field.
5. Type **name** into the Name text box.
6. At the bottom of the panel, check the Printable and Required check boxes.
7. Click the Font Size list arrow, then choose 14.
8. Select the frame above email address then convert it to a button.
9. Click the Type list arrow, then click Text Field.
10. Type **email** into the Name text box.
11. Check the Printable checkbox only.
12. Click the Font Size list arrow, then choose 14.
13. Save your work.

Format a field as a pull-down list

1. Select the large rectangle under choose a date . . . then convert it to a button.
2. Click the Type list arrow, then click Combo Box.
3. Type **month** into the Name text box.
4. Click the Printable check box under the Description field.
5. Click the Font Size list arrow, then click 14.
6. Type **January** in the List Items text box.
7. Click the plus sign button to the right of the field.
8. Type **February** in the List Items text box, then click the plus sign button.
9. Type **March** in the List Items text box, then click the plus sign button.
10. Continue until all twelve months are listed.
11. Select the small square under choose a date . . . then convert it to a button.
12. Click the Type list arrow, then click Combo Box.
13. Type **day** into the Name text box.

14. Click the Printable check box under the Description field.
15. Click the Font Size list arrow, then click 14.
16. Type **01** in the List Items text box.
17. Click the plus sign button to the right of the field.
18. Type **02** in the List Items text box, then click the plus sign button.
19. Type **03** in the List Items text box, then click the plus sign button.
20. Continue until the list reads 01–31.
21. Save your work.

Format a field as a check box

1. Select the white square at the bottom below SEND.
2. Convert the frame to a button.
3. Click the Type list arrow, then click Check Box.
4. Type **yes email list** into the Name text box.
5. Click the Printable check box under the Description field.
6. Save your work.

Create radio buttons

1. Select the three white circles.
2. Click the Convert to Button icon on the Buttons and Forms panel.
3. Click the Type list arrow, then click Radio Button.
4. Type **choose group size** in the Name text box.
5. Zoom in on the three buttons, then open the Swatches panel.
6. Click the Direct Selection tool, then select and delete the three small black circles in each button.
7. Select just the top white circle.
8. Click [Normal Off] on the Buttons and Forms panel, then click Moon Gradient on the Swatches panel.
9. Click [Normal On] on the Buttons and Forms panel, then click Sunset Gradient on the Swatches panel.
10. Repeat the same procedure on the other two buttons.
11. Save your work.

Use a button as a trigger

1. Select the text frame at the bottom that says Please add me to your email list.
2. Click the Edit menu, then click Copy.
3. Convert the frame to a button.
4. Name the button **please add**.
5. Click the Object menu, then click Hide.
6. Click Edit on the menu bar, then click Paste in Place.
7. Click the Type tool, then change the message to read **Thank you, we'll be in touch**.
8. Click the Selection tool, then convert the frame to a button.
9. Name the button **thank you**, then check the Hidden Until Triggered check box.
10. Click the Object menu, then click Show All on Spread.
11. Select the check box.
12. On the Buttons and Forms panel, click the plus sign button beside Actions, then click Show/Hide Buttons and Forms.
13. In the Visibility section, click please add, then click Hide.
14. Click thank you, then click Show.
15. Save your work.

Create a button to submit a form to an email address

1. Select the frame that contains the word SEND.
2. Convert the frame into a button.
3. On the Buttons and Forms panel, name the button **SEND**.
4. Click the plus sign button beside Actions, then click Submit Form.
5. In the URL textbox, type **mailto:me@myemailaddress**.
6. Type your own email address. For example, you would type **mailto:john@johnsmith.com**.
7. Save your work.

Set the tab order for an interactive form

1. Click the Object menu, point to Interactive, then click Set Tab Order.
2. Click and drag button names up and down in the window so that your Tab Order dialog box resembles Figure 51.
3. Click OK, then save your work.

Figure 51 *Tab order*

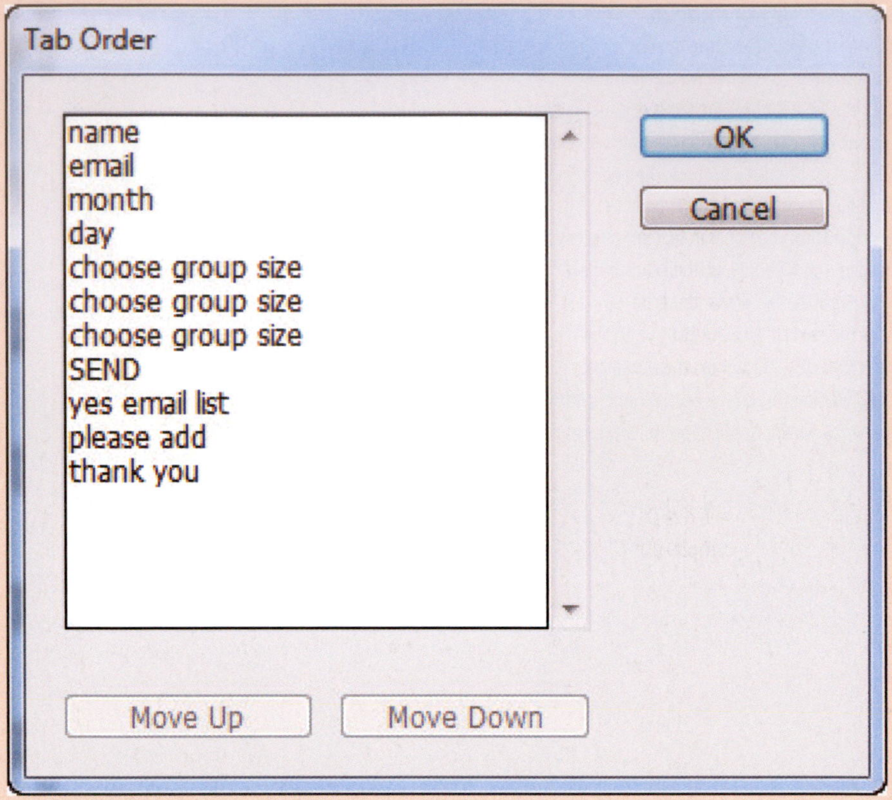

Tab Order

name
email
month
day
choose group size
choose group size
choose group size
SEND
yes email list
please add
thank you

OK

Cancel

Move Up   Move Down

Source Adobe® InDesign®, 2013.

Enter data into an exported form

1. Click File on the menu bar, then click Export.
2. Type **Skills Review** as the name, click the Save as type menu, then choose Adobe PDF (Interactive).
3. Click Save, then enter the same settings as the lesson from the chapter.
4. Click OK.
5. Type your name in the name field.
6. Type your email address in the email address field.
7. Click the silver list arrow, then choose a month.
8. Click the silver list arrow, then choose a day.
9. Click the more than 20 button.
10. Click inside the check box, then compare your form to Figure 52.

Submit a form

1. Click the submit button.
2. Click Internet Email, then click OK.
3. Type **Skills Review Complete** in the Save As text box, then click Save.

Figure 52 *Completed Skills Review*

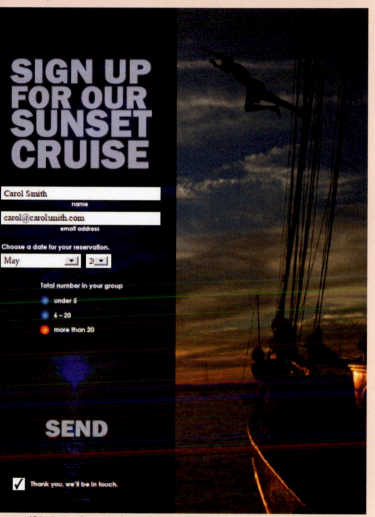

Image courtesy of Tabor Academy. Source Adobe® Acrobat®, 2013.

CHAPTER 6 PUBLISHING TO THE IPAD

1. Install software for working with the iPad
2. Set up a document for upload to the iPad
3. Use folio overlays
4. Upload to the iPad with the Folio Builder

CHAPTER 6 PUBLISHING TO THE IPAD

Downloading books isn't the only way the iPad is revolutionizing publishing. To fully appreciate the impact of the iPad, let's use *Entertainment Weekly* as an example.

The *Entertainment Weekly* website, EW.com, is a fun and much-trafficked site with lots of articles and information, blogs and message boards. But it's not *Entertainment Weekly* magazine. You can't sit with EW.com in your lap and page through *Entertainment Weekly* magazine. It's not a magazine; it's a website.

Furthermore, an advertisement in *Entertainment Weekly* magazine is not the same thing as an advertisement on EW.com. On the website, it's a banner ad or a pop-up ad. It doesn't take up the full web page; it's in the margins or across the top. And most importantly, if you click the ad, it *takes you away from* EW.com.

From this perspective, think of what the iPad delivers.

The *Entertainment Weekly* application (app) on the iPad is a magazine. It has a cover. You use your hand, not a mouse, to interface with it. It has "pages" you turn to read, just like a traditional magazine. It has illustrations, captions, charts, and sidebars—just like a magazine. The primary difference between the printed *Entertainment Weekly* and *Entertainment Weekly* on your iPad is the delivery system: one is printed on paper, purchased from a store or delivered to your mailbox, while the other is simply downloaded to your iPad.

The iPad is even more revolutionary when you consider it in terms of print advertising. Consider this statement: In the history of the Internet, the iPad is the first delivery system that restores advertising to its rightful place: in line with editorial.

If you read *Vanity Fair* magazine in 1950, the ads were on pages opposite the editorial. Read an article, turn a page, view an advertisement.

If you read *Vanity Fair* magazine on an iPad, the ads are on pages opposite the editorial. Read an article, turn a page, view an advertisement—it's the same experience. Except, on an iPad, you can interact with the editorial and interact with the ads; that's the difference.

Print is dead? Not so fast. If I have a subscription to *Entertainment Weekly*, I can read the printed magazine or read the magazine on my iPad. Same articles; different delivery system. The advertising reps for the magazine sell ad space for the printed version and for the iPad version. It's all revenue, and each pays for the other. They're not in competition with each other, and the advertising clients have their products advertised in both mediums. Because of the iPad, the supposed war between print and the Internet has actually resulted in a beautiful truce.

The tablet reader revolution also benefits the designer using InDesign. When we were just talking websites, the InDesign user often felt left out: to work on a website required Flash and Dreamweaver and HTML. But the iPad creates a whole new world of possibilities for the designer: create a layout in InDesign, print it, then publish it to the whole world on the iPad.

Folio Builder

Folios: All Local   Sort ▾ | ◯

Select New to create a local folio.

Sign In to Adobe Digital Publishing Suite with your Adobe ID, to create, distribute, monetize and optimize engaging publications for tablet devices.

Sign Up to create an account and access Digital Publishing Suite.

12.2.2.20120427_m_686742   8.0.6.20

Preview ▾ | New | 🗑 ⌁

Folio Overlays

◀ Audio & Video ⓘ

Audio:
Controller Files: 📁

☐ Show First Image Initially

☑ Auto Play

  Delay: [0] secs

Video:

☐ Auto Play

  Delay: [0] secs

☐ Play Full Screen

☐ Tap to View Controller

Preview | Reset   🗑 ⌁

New Folio

Folio Name:

[March 10 Issue]

Size:

[1024 x 768 ▾]

Width: | Height:

[1024] x [768]

Orientation: [▢] [▢] [▢]

☐ Create Local Folio

Default Format:

[Automatic ▾]

Default JPEG Quality:

[High ▾]

[Cancel] [OK]

Source Adobe® InDesign®, 2013.

Install Software for
WORKING WITH THE IPAD

What You'll Do

Source Apple®, 2013.

▶ *In this lesson, you will create an Adobe ID, download the Adobe Content Viewer app, and activate the Folio Builder panel in InDesign.*

Working with the Adobe Content Viewer iPad App

When you create a layout in InDesign, you use the Adobe Content Viewer app on the iPad to view the document. You install Adobe Content Viewer on an iPad just as you would any other app: click the App Store icon on the iPad, search the store for Adobe Content Viewer, then download and install the app. Figure 1 shows the Adobe Content Viewer icon.

You must have a user account with Adobe to open and run the Adobe Content Viewer app on your iPad. A user account is simple to create. Go to Adobe.com, then enter a username and password to create the account.

Once you have downloaded the app and created an Adobe ID, you're ready to use Adobe Content Viewer.

Figure 1 *Adobe Content Viewer app icon*

Source Apple®, 2013.

Downloading and Installing Digital Publishing Suite Desktop Tools

Uploading a layout to an iPad is done in InDesign using **Digital Publishing Suite Desktop Tools**. The **Digital Publishing Suite (DPS)** is a comprehensive software package that allows everyone from publishers and ad agencies to small businesses and individual designers to publish their content on tablet devices like the iPad.

DPS Desktop Tools CS6 functions in InDesign as the Folio Builder and Folio Overlays panels. You use the Folio Builder panel to upload layouts to the iPad, and you use the Folio Overlays panel to add functionality and interactivity to your iPad publication.

When you first install or use Adobe InDesign CS6, the DPS Desktop Tools software required to run the Folio Builder panel is not installed and the Folio Builder panel will appear as shown in Figure 2. Follow the directions in the panel to download and install the software.

When DPS Desktop Tools software is installed, the Folio Builder panel will prompt you to sign in with your Adobe ID. Once you do, the Folio Builder panel will be activated and appear as shown in Figure 3. Also installed is Adobe Content Viewer software, which allows you to preview on your computer the layouts you are uploading to your iPad.

Figure 2 *Folio Builder panel before downloading DPS Desktop Tools CS6*

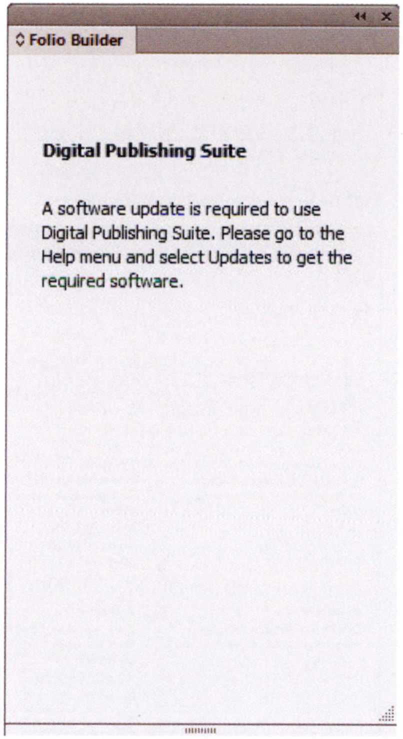

Digital Publishing Suite

A software update is required to use Digital Publishing Suite. Please go to the Help menu and select Updates to get the required software.

Source Adobe® InDesign®, 2013.

Figure 3 *Folio Builder panel activated*

Double circle indicates panel is signed-in

Source Adobe® InDesign®, 2013.

Create an Adobe account on Adobe.com

1. If you don't already have an Adobe account, go to Adobe.com.

2. Click the **Sign in link** in the top-right corner.

   This takes you to the Sign In page on the site, shown in Figure 4.

3. Click the **Create an Adobe Account button**.

4. On the Join Adobe page, enter all the necessary information to create an Adobe account.

5. Make a note of the username and password for your Adobe ID, as you will use it many times when working with the iPad.

6. Log in to Adobe.com so that you see the welcome page, shown in Figure 5.

TIP Sometimes, the Adobe Content Viewer doesn't recognize new accounts created at the Adobe.com site. To remedy this, after you create the account, go to Adobeacrobat.com and sign in using the same credentials. Doing so will verify your credentials across the Adobe platform and remedy any problems with Adobe Content Viewer rejecting your login.

You created a username and password for an Adobe ID.

Figure 4 *Sign In page on Adobe.com*

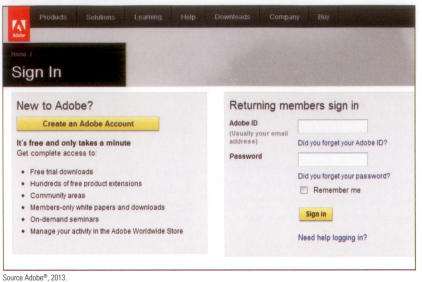

Source Adobe®, 2013.

Figure 5 *Welcome page on Adobe.com*

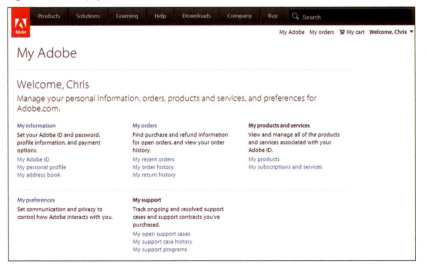

Source Adobe®, 2013.

Publishing to the iPad

Figure 6 *Suggestions list*

Source Apple®, 2013.

Install the Adobe Viewer app on an iPad

1. Click the **App Store button** on the main screen of the iPad.

2. In the Search field, type **adobe**.

   A Suggestions list appears, as shown in Figure 6.

   (continued)

3. On the Suggestions list, tap **adobe content viewer**.

   The Search results page opens as shown in Figure 7.

4. Tap **FREE**, then tap **INSTALL APP** for the Adobe Content Viewer for iPad app.

   An Apple ID Password dialog box opens showing your username.

5. Enter your password, then click **OK**.

   (continued)

Figure 7 *Search results page*

Source Apple®, 2013.

Figure 8 *Adobe Content Viewer installed*

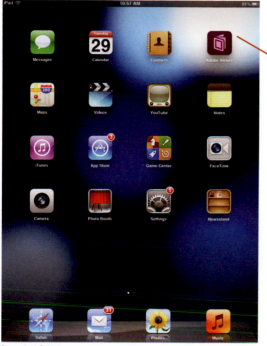

Adobe Viewer

Figure 9 *Folio Builder panel*

6. Find the Adobe Content Viewer app on your iPad.

7. Note in Figure 8 that the name of the app is simply Adobe Viewer.

You installed the Adobe Content Viewer app on your iPad.

Download DPS Desktop Tools CS6

1. Launch InDesign CS6.

2. Click the **Window menu**, then click **Folio Builder**.

   If this is the first time you are trying to use the Folio Builder panel, it will appear as shown in Figure 9. It appears this way because the DPS Desktop Tools software is not installed automatically when you purchase and first open InDesign CS6.

(continued)

3. Click the **Help menu**, then click **Updates**.

   The Adobe Application Manager dialog box opens, as shown in Figure 10. Note the DPS Desktop Tools CS6 item in the Updates list.

4. Verify that **DPS Desktop Tools CS6** is checked, then click **Update**.

   When the software is installing, you will be prompted to quit InDesign to enable the software installation.

   (continued)

Figure 10 *Adobe Application Manager dialog box*

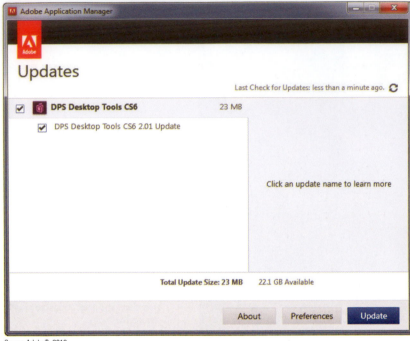

Source Adobe®, 2013.

Publishing to the iPad

Figure 11 *Folio Builder panel after DPS Desktop Tools CS6 installation*

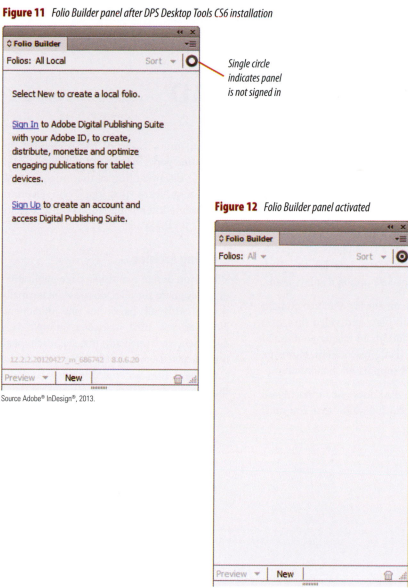

Single circle indicates panel is not signed in

Figure 12 *Folio Builder panel activated*

Double circle indicates panel is signed in

Source Adobe® InDesign®, 2013.

Source Adobe® InDesign®, 2013.

5. After the software is installed, launch **InDesign CS6**, then compare your Folio Builder panel to Figure 11.

6. Click the **Sign In link**.

   The Sign In dialog box opens prompting you to sign in using your Adobe ID.

7. Enter your username and password, click the **Stay signed in check box**, then click **Sign In**.

8. Once you are signed in, compare your Folio Builder panel to Figure 12.

9. Position the cursor over the target icon at the top-right of the panel.

   The target icon indicates that you are signed in and the panel is connected to Adobe.com.

You installed the DPS Desktop Tools CS6 software, which includes the Folio Builder and Folio Overlays panels.

Set Up a Document for
UPLOAD TO THE IPAD

What You'll Do

Image courtesy of Tabor Academy. Source Adobe® InDesign®, 2013.

 In this lesson, you will set up an InDesign document for upload to the iPad.

Creating an InDesign Document for the iPad

When you create an InDesign document for upload to the iPad, you choose the Digital Publishing option as the intent in the New Document dialog box, as shown in Figure 13. Doing so will create a 1024 pixels × 768 pixels document, which is standard for the iPad. Note that the Page Size option displays iPad.

An InDesign document for iPad can contain hyperlinks, sound files, and video files. You can also create buttons to trigger sound and video files in an iPad presentation. However, the iPad does not support Flash animation.

The fact that the iPad does not support Flash is an important consideration that you must keep in mind. None of the presets in the Animation panel in InDesign will work on the iPad. As disappointing as that might sound, you'll soon learn that the Folio Overlays panel offers interesting and fun interactivity options for the iPad.

Creating Articles

When you design a multiple page publication in InDesign for the iPad, do so as you normally would, with all pages in one document. However, you can't upload a multiple-page document to the iPad. Instead, each page must be saved as a standalone file. When those standalone files are uploaded in the Folio Builder panel, they are referred to as **articles**.

Figure 13 *Digital Publishing option in the New Document dialog box*

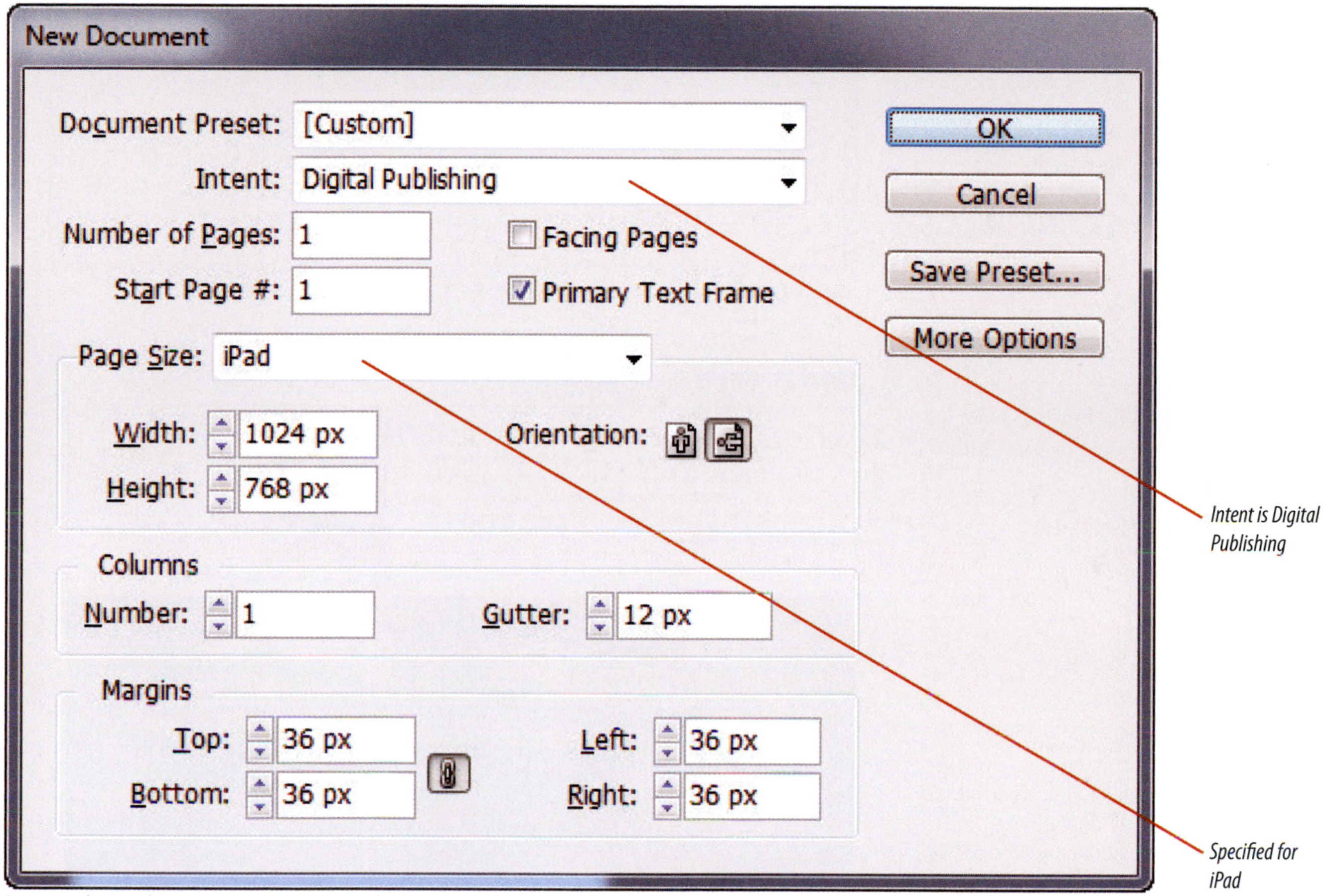

New Document

Document Preset: [Custom] ▼

Intent: Digital Publishing ▼

Number of Pages: 1   ☐ Facing Pages

Start Page #: 1   ☑ Primary Text Frame

OK

Cancel

Save Preset...

More Options

Page Size: iPad ▼

Width: ⬍ 1024 px   Orientation: 🔲 🔲

Height: ⬍ 768 px

Columns

Number: ⬍ 1   Gutter: ⬍ 12 px

Margins

Top: ⬍ 36 px   Left: ⬍ 36 px

Bottom: ⬍ 36 px   🔒   Right: ⬍ 36 px

Intent is Digital Publishing

Specified for iPad

Source Adobe® InDesign®, 2013.

View a document setup for upload to the iPad

1. Open ID 6-1.indd, then save it as **Tabor Lookbook**.

2. Scroll through the pages of the document.

3. Click the **File menu**, then click **Document Setup**.

   As shown in Figure 14, the document is 1024 pixels × 768 pixels, and the Digital Publishing option is selected. All of the placed images have a resolution of 72 ppi and are saved in the RGB format.

4. Click **Cancel** then go to **page 1**.

5. In the maroon column on the left, note the yellow Tabor Academy url.

   This text has been formatted as a hyperlink to the Tabor website.

6. Go to **page 5**.

7. Note the video on the page, identified in Figure 15.

   (continued)

Figure 14 *Document is set up for the iPad*

Document Setup

Intent: Digital Publishing ▼   OK

Number of Pages: 10   ☐ Facing Pages   Cancel

Start Page #: 1   ☐ Primary Text Frame   More Options

Page Size: iPad ▼

Width: 1024 px   Orientation:

Height: 768 px

Source Adobe® InDesign®, 2013.

Figure 15 *Video file placed in document*

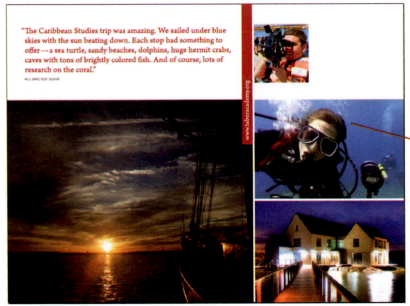

Video file

Image courtesy of Tabor Academy. Source Adobe® InDesign®, 2013.

Publishing to the iPad

Figure 16 *Sound file on pasteboard*

Sound file

Image courtesy of Tabor Academy. Source Adobe® InDesign®, 2013.

8. Go to **page 8**.

9. Note the placed sound file on the pasteboard, shown in Figure 16.

Tip If you don't see the sound file, click the View menu, point to Extras, then click Show Frame Edges.

10. Drag the **sound file** and position it over the top-right corner of the image so that the sound file is completely on the page.

   When uploading a document that contains sound for the iPad, the sound file must be positioned on a document page.

11. Save the file.

You viewed the document and its attributes. You moved a sound file from the pasteboard onto a document page.

Save pages as articles for the iPad

1. Open the Links panel, then verify that all the linked files are updated.

2. Click the **File menu**, then click **Package**.

3. In the Package Publication dialog box, click **Package**.

4. Click **Continue**.

5. In the Folder Name text box, type **To iPad**, then choose the location where you store your Data Files before clicking Package.

   Your dialog box should resemble Figure 17.

6. Click **Package**.

7. In the Warning dialog box, click **OK**.

8. Close Tabor Lookbook.indd.

9. Go to the location where you stored the To iPad folder, then open it.

(continued)

Figure 17 *Package Publication dialog box*

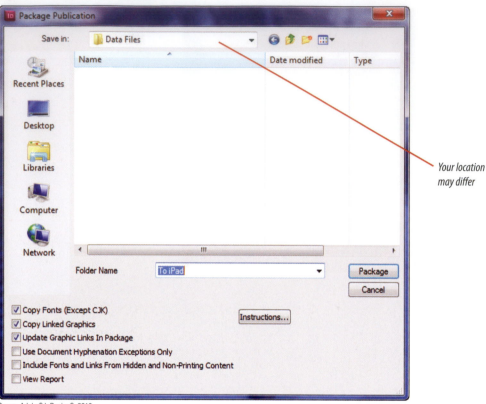

Your location may differ

Source Adobe® InDesign®, 2013.

Figure 18 *Ten copies of Tabor Lookbook.indd*

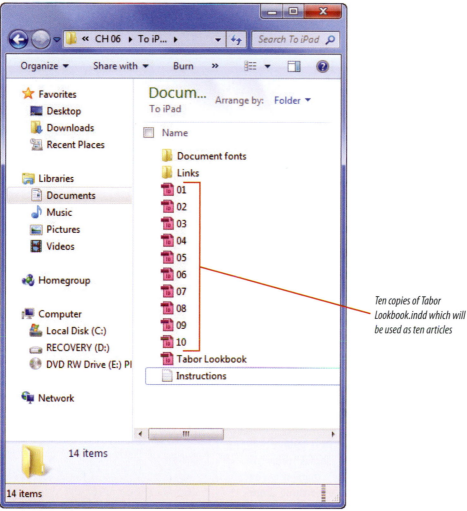

Ten copies of Tabor Lookbook.indd which will be used as ten articles

Source Adobe® InDesign®, 2013.

10. Make ten copies of the Tabor Lookbook.indd file.

11. Rename each of the ten copies from **01** to **10**, so that your To iPad folder resembles Figure 18.

    Each copy will become a one-page article.

12. Open each file and delete all pages other than the title number page.

    For example, file 01.indd should contain only page 1; file 02.indd should contain only page 2, and so on.

You packaged the document. You made ten copies of the packaged document, then deleted the unwanted pages from each copy in order to create ten articles.

Use Folio
OVERLAYS

What You'll Do

Source Adobe® InDesign®, 2013.

In this lesson, you will use the Folio Overlays panel to specify sound and video files to play.

Placing Sound and Video Files for an iPad Presentation

When you're designing an InDesign publication for the iPad, you place sound and video files as you normally would, with one important exception: in order for a sound or video file to play, it must be on the document page. In Chapter 3, you learned that you had the option to place a sound file off the page in the pasteboard, and it would play in the exported SWF file. That's not an option when designing for an iPad presentation.

Using the Overlays Panel to Play Audio and Video Files

When you download DPS Desktop Tools CS6, the Folio Overlays panel is downloaded and installed. You use the Folio Overlays panel, shown in Figure 19, to specify when sound and video files play in a publication on the iPad. The panel shows different categories of interactivity that can be utilized in a presentation, everything from simple hyperlinks to panoramas and image sequences.

Figure 19 *Folio Overlays panel*

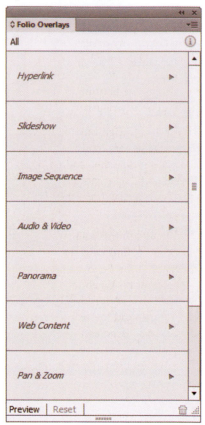

Source Adobe® InDesign®, 2013.

In Chapter 3 of this book, you learned how to create buttons to play sound and video files in an SWF file or on a website; you can create buttons the same way to play sound and video files on an iPad presentation. These can be a great design option for iPad presentations. However, you also need to remember that InDesign animation will not play on the iPad, because InDesign doesn't support Adobe Flash.

This has a big impact on buttons because you can't specify that a button disappears after it's been clicked. So any design work you do with buttons to play sound or video in an iPad presentation has to be done with the consideration that the button will remain on the page after it's been triggered.

Rather than use InDesign buttons to trigger events, many designers prefer to use the controls available on the Folio Overlays panel. These controls are more standard for iPad and tablet device presentations than button triggers.

When you open an InDesign article that contains a placed sound or video file, select the placed file and the Folio Overlays panel changes to Audio & Video mode, shown in Figure 20. If the Auto Play check box is checked, the sound or video will play whenever the page is accessed. In an iPad

presentation, pages are accessed when you finger swipe from one page to another.

While auto-playing sound and video files is fairly common in iPad presentations, you'll find many times that you don't want them to play automatically. For example, imagine how annoying it would be if you designed a document that you wanted people to browse through on their iPads, and every time a page

was accessed, the same video file played from the same starting point.

If you leave the Auto Play check box unchecked, sound and video files will play only when tapped. This solves any issues you might have with files playing automatically, but it also creates a new problem: How will a reader know sound and/or video files are available to be played?

Figure 20 *Audio & Video mode in the Folio Overlays panel*

Audio & Video mode

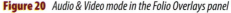

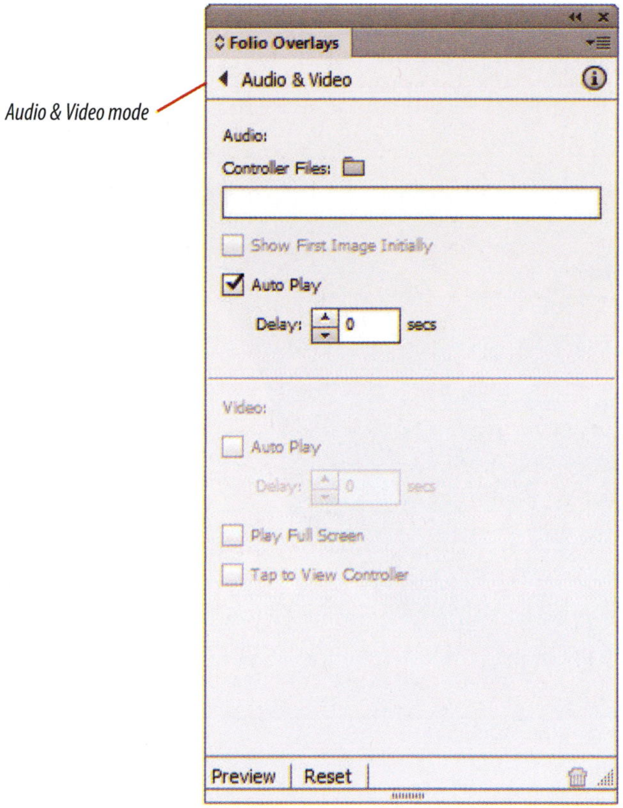

Source Adobe® InDesign®, 2013.

In Figure 21, it appears that the page shows four images. Actually, the image of the building is a video, not just a still image. If you had designed this layout for the iPad, how would you indicate that to your reader? One option would be to add artwork of a "play" button, like a triangle in a circle, to the first frame in the video. When a user taps the video and it plays, the triangle disappears—because it's only on the first frame of the video. An easier alternative would be to simply put a small line of text above the video that says something like, "Click the image to play the video."

Sound files pose a different problem: they're invisible on the presentation page. If you choose to not auto play a sound, you have no

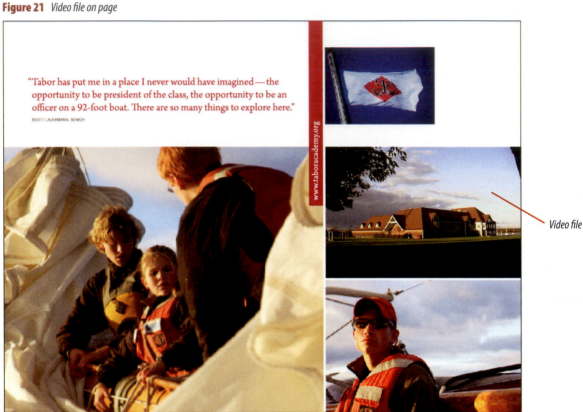

Video file

other choice than to have some artwork to call a reader's attention to it.

In Figure 22, the artwork indicates that clicking the icon will play a sound. The sound file has been positioned in front of the icon artwork so that when the reader taps the icon, he's really tapping the sound file.

Figure 23 shows a better solution: the icon has been formatted as a button that will trigger the sound file when tapped. It remains visible on the page, and when tapped again, it will stop the sound.

Figure 22 *Sound file positioned where user is told to tap*

Sound file positioned in front of icon artwork

Figure 23 *Button formatted to trigger sound file*

Button triggers sound file when tapped

Sound file

Set up a sound file in the Folio Overlays panel

1. Open the file 08.indd.

2. Click the **Window menu**, then click **Folio Overlays**.

3. Click the **sound file** to select it.

   When you select the sound file, the Folio Overlays panel shows Audio & Video controls.

4. Click the **Auto Play check box**.

   Your Folio Overlays panel should resemble Figure 24. When this page is accessed on the iPad, the sound file will play automatically.

   (continued)

Figure 24 *Audio controls in the Folio Overlays panel*

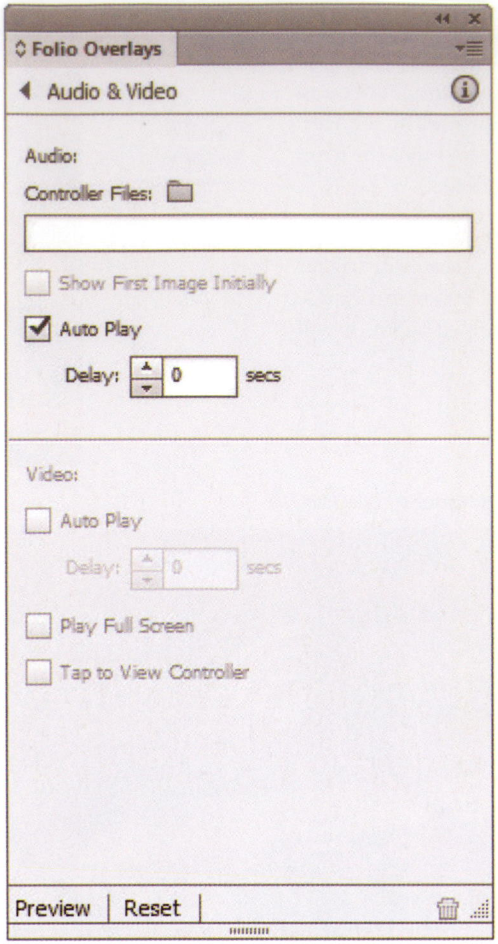

Source Adobe® InDesign®, 2013.

Figure 25 *Adobe Content Viewer window previewing Article 08*

Adobe® Content Viewer @ 75%

File   Edit   View   Help

CONSIDER TABOR YOUR SECOND HOME

Students and faculty members alike share life and laughter, everyday triumphs and significant achievements. Lifelong friendships are forged across class years and across cultures.

At Tabor you'll join a long line of students and graduates who have all gazed out across Sippican Harbor, felt the rush of excitement from a Seawolf victory, learned to ask insightful questions, found inspiration in a senior's Chapel speech, and become part of something larger than themselves.

Image courtesy of Tabor Academy. Source Adobe® InDesign®, 2013.

5. Click **Preview** at the bottom of the Folio Overlays panel.

The page opens in Adobe Content Viewer, as shown in Figure 25, and the sound file automatically plays. Adobe Content Viewer on your computer previews what Adobe Content Viewer will display on your iPad.

6. Close Adobe Content Viewer, save the changes to 08.indd, then close 08.indd.

You used the Folio Overlays panel to specify that a sound file auto plays when the page is accessed. You previewed the page and the sound in Adobe Content Viewer on your computer.

Set up video files in the Folio Overlays panel

1. Open the file 05.ind.

2. Click the **video file** (the underwater scuba diver image) to select it.

   When you select the video file, the Folio Overlays panel shows video controls.

3. Click the **Auto Play check box**.

   When this page is accessed on the iPad, the video file will play automatically.

4. Click the **Tap to View Controller check box**.

   When you tap the video on your iPad, a pause/play control button will be revealed, along with timecode and a mute button.

5. Click **Preview** at the bottom of the Folio Overlays panel.

   The page is previewed in Adobe Content Viewer, and the video begins playing as shown in Figure 26.

6. Click the **image** repeatedly to hide and show the controller.

7. Close the Adobe Content Viewer window, save the changes to 05.indd, then close 05.indd.

8. Open the file 09.indd.

9. Note the type above the video file (the image of the building) that instructs the reader to tap the image to play the video, as shown in Figure 27.

(continued)

Figure 26 *Video previewed in Adobe Content Viewer*

Video playing in preview

Image courtesy of Tabor Academy. Source Adobe® InDesign®, 2013.

Figure 27 *Text indicates to tap the video to play and stop it*

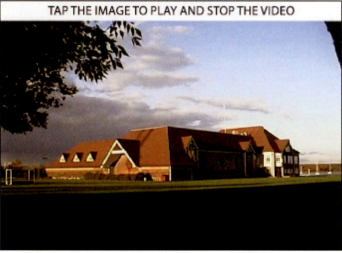

Image courtesy of Tabor Academy. Source Adobe® InDesign®, 2013.

Figure 28 *Video previewed in Adobe Content Viewer*

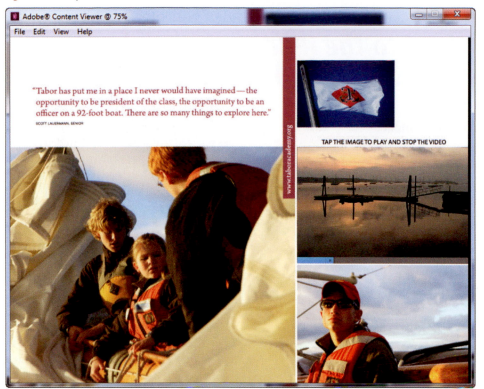

Image courtesy of Tabor Academy. Source Adobe® InDesign®, 2013.

10. Click the **video file** to select it.

11. Verify that the Auto Play check box is not checked.

12. Verify that the Tap to View Controller check box is not checked.

13. Click **Preview** at the bottom of the Folio Overlays panel.

    The page is previewed in Adobe Content Viewer. The video does not begin playing.

14. Click the **video**.

    The video begins playing as shown in Figure 28.

15. Close the Adobe Content Viewer window, save your work, then close 09.indd.

You used the Folio Overlays panel to specify different control settings for two different videos.

Upload to the iPad
WITH THE FOLIO BUILDER

What You'll Do

Source Adobe® InDesign®, 2013.

In this lesson, you will use the Folio Builder panel to upload a folio to your iPad

About Folio Builder

The key to understanding the relationship between InDesign and the iPad is to remember that the Folio Builder panel is live—it's connected to the Internet. When you click the Sign In option on the Folio Builder panel, the panel connects to your Adobe account using your Adobe ID and password.

You can think of your Adobe account as storage space that you have online with Adobe. When you create a folio on the Folio Builder panel, that content is automatically uploaded to your Adobe account. The Adobe Content Viewer app on your iPad displays the folio that you upload to that Adobe account.

Once you understand that the Folio Builder panel is live, you start to see the panel as an interface between the InDesign files on your desktop and your Adobe account. When you create a folio in or add articles to the Folio Builder panel, those actions are simultaneously updating to your Adobe account, and therefore to your iPad.

Your first step in the process is to create a new folio. The term **folio** has a long history

in printing and publishing. Traditionally, it has referred to a sheet of paper folded once to make two leaves—or four pages—of a book. In the Folio Builder panel, the folio is the complete publication—and it contains all the articles in the publication.

Let's use *Time* magazine as an example. Let's say you've designed the March 10 issue with 64 pages. You'd save each of the 64 pages as individual documents which would then become 64 articles. In the Folio Builder panel, you'd create a new folio—to which you'd want to give a descriptive name, like March 10 Issue. (Since *Time* publishes every week, at the end of the year you'd have 52 folios listed on the Folio Builder panel.) The Folio Builder panel is the one place that holds every folio you create.

Creating a New Folio

When you click the New button on the Folio Builder panel, the New Folio dialog box opens. Shown in Figure 29, the New Folio dialog box is where you specify basic settings for the folio, such as its name and size. Note that the panel also offers three options for Orientation.

Tablet presentations—like those on an iPad—have three basic orientations: Portrait Only Folio, Landscape Only Folio, and Portrait and Landscape Folio. You specify which orientation you'll be using when you set up an InDesign document.

It's important that the orientation you choose in the New Folio dialog box is the same as the orientation of the articles that will be added to the folio. Note that in this chapter, you will be working with only portrait orientation articles, so you will set up the new folio as Portrait Only Folio.

Adding Articles to a Folio

For the purposes of this book, we will refer to the Folio Builder panel as having two modes: **Folios Mode** and **Articles Mode**. All folios you create are listed on the Folio Builder panel. Figure 30 shows three folios listed on the panel, one for each issue of a publication. We will refer to this view of the Folio Builder panel as **Folios Mode**—a list of all folios. You can think of the folio as the publication itself. Articles are what are "inside" the folio. The folio is the shell, and the articles are the content.

Figure 29 *New Folio dialog box*

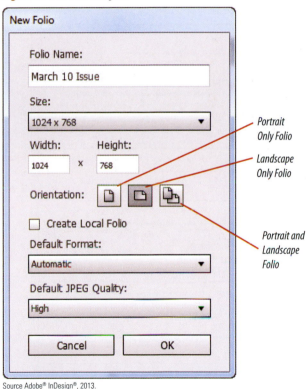

Source Adobe® InDesign®, 2013.

Portrait Only Folio

Landscape Only Folio

Portrait and Landscape Folio

Figure 30 *Three folios in Folios Mode of the Folio Builder panel*

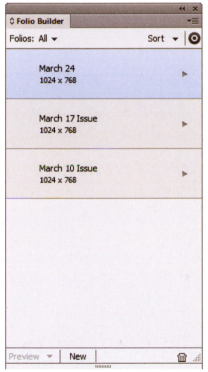

Source Adobe® InDesign®, 2013.

In Figure 31, the top of the Folio Builder panel shows the name March 10 Issue. March 10 Issue is the folio name. Beside the name is the word *Articles*. When you see the word *Articles*, you can think of yourself as being "inside" a given folio—this is the mode you are in when you add articles to a folio. We will refer to this view of the Folio Builder panel as **Articles Mode**—where all articles for a given folio are added and listed.

To add articles to a given folio, you first open the InDesign documents that you want to add as articles. Then, you click the Add button at the bottom of the Folio Builder panel. The active open document will be added to the folio and the New Article dialog box opens, as shown in Figure 32. This is where you give the article a name, and specify its default format. In this example, the article is named Page 1.

The Default Format menu is a clue to how InDesign interfaces with the Folio Builder panel to produce documents for tablet devices. The formats listed in the menu are JPEG, PNG, and PDF. These are all image formats. This is because InDesign documents are converted to images when they're added to a folio as articles. If you choose JPEG, for example, when the InDesign document is converted to an image, it will be added

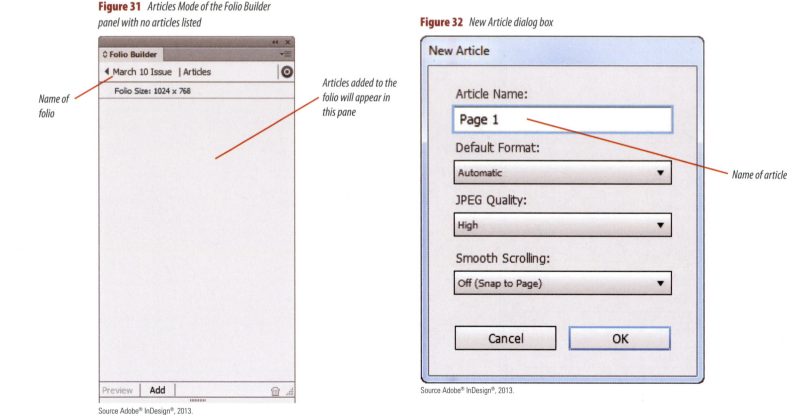

Figure 31 *Articles Mode of the Folio Builder panel with no articles listed*

Name of folio

Articles added to the folio will appear in this pane

Source Adobe® InDesign®, 2013.

Figure 32 *New Article dialog box*

Name of article

Source Adobe® InDesign®, 2013.

to the folio in the JPEG format. In the case of JPEGs, you can use the Quality menu to specify the quality of the JPEG image in the tablet presentation.

The Smooth Scrolling option controls how you swipe from page to page (article to article) on your tablet device. If Smooth Scrolling is activated, you could have half of one page and half of the subsequent page both visible on your tablet screen. Generally speaking, that's not an option you want to activate, and you'll usually use the default Off (Snap to Page) option, which forces a full page to "snap" into the tablet window. When you click OK, you will see status bars in the Folio Builder panel, as shown in Figure 33. This is another example of how the panel is "live": the article is being uploaded to the folio in your Adobe account.

Figure 34 shows the Articles Mode of the Folio Builder panel with two articles added. The articles are named Page 1 and Page 2, and they are articles within the folio named March 10 Issue. To switch to Folios Mode and see the March 10 Issue folio listed in the panel with any and all other folios, click the black triangle beside the folio name.

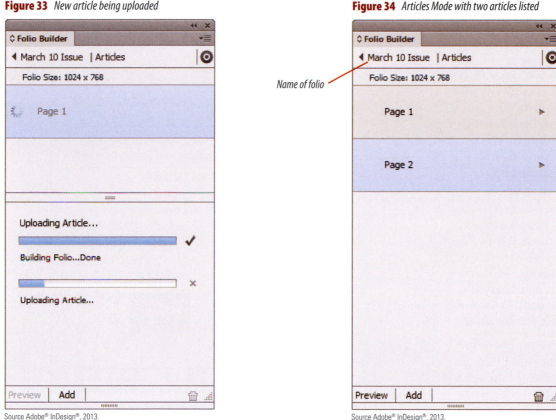

Figure 33 *New article being uploaded*

Source Adobe® InDesign®, 2013.

Figure 34 *Articles Mode with two articles listed*

Name of folio

Two articles

Source Adobe® InDesign®, 2013.

Once you have finished adding articles to a folio, you can view the folio on your iPad using the Adobe Content Viewer app. Simply sign in to your Adobe account.

Back in InDesign, it's interesting to note that you do not save the folios you create. They exist in your online Adobe account and will be accessible in Folios Mode in your Folio Builder panel whenever you open InDesign and are connected to the Internet.

Naming the iPad Publication and Creating a Thumbnail

Whenever you create a new folio in the Folio Builder panel, you give the new folio a name. That name refers only to the work you do in InDesign and only to the name of the folio in the Folio Builder panel. Naming a folio in the Folio Builder panel does not mean that you've named the publication that will be uploaded to the iPad. The publication file will remain untitled until you name it.

You might be asking, "Why would there be a different name for the folio in the Folio Builder panel and the actual publication on the iPad?" The reason might be best explained with the words *private vs. public*. For a number of reasons, you might want the name of the folio on your computer to be different from the publication name. Let's say you produce a monthly newsletter called *John's Newsletter*. When you create a folio for this month's issue, you might have an internal naming convention for the folio—something like issue010716. That's certainly not the name you want to appear on the iPad. On the iPad, the folio might better be named John's Newsletter Issue 01/07/16.

When you name a folio in the Folio Builder panel, you are not naming the publication. To name the publication, click the Folio Builder panel menu, then click Properties. This opens the Folio Properties dialog box. The name you enter here will be the name that appears on the article on your tablet.

You use the Folio Properties dialog box to specify the thumbnail artwork that will identify the folio—in both horizontal and vertical orientations. Figure 35 shows the Folio Properties panel with an image placed for the horizontal orientation of the thumbnail.

The artwork you use for the thumbnail should be proportional to 1024 pixels × 768 pixels—and be no larger than that size.

Figure 35 *Folio Properties panel*

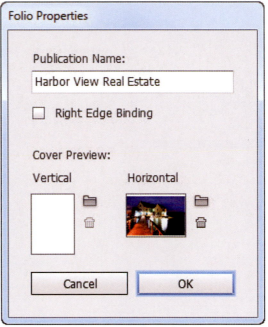

Image courtesy of Tabor Academy. Source Adobe® InDesign®, 2013.

Figure 36 *New Folio dialog box*

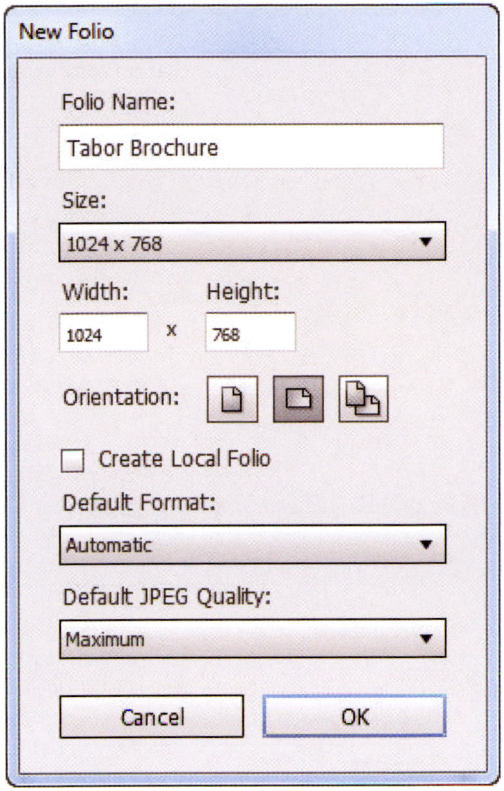

New Folio

Folio Name:

Tabor Brochure

Size:

1024 x 768 ▼

Width: Height:

1024   x   768

Orientation: ☐ ☐ ☐

☐ Create Local Folio

Default Format:

Automatic ▼

Default JPEG Quality:

Maximum ▼

Cancel   OK

Source Adobe® InDesign®, 2013.

Figure 37 *New folio listed in the Folio Builder panel*

◇ Folio Builder

◀ Tabor Brochure | Articles   ◉

Folio Size: 1024 x 768

Preview   Add   🗑 ▪

Source Adobe® InDesign®, 2013.

Create a new folio in Folio Builder

1. Verify that no files are open in InDesign.

2. Open the Folio Builder panel, then verify that you are signed in by hovering over the target icon.

   If you are not signed in, click the **Folio Builder panel menu button** ▾▤, click **Sign In**, then sign in using your Adobe ID username and password.

3. Click **New** at the bottom of the Folio Builder panel.

   The New Folio dialog box opens.

4. Type **Tabor Brochure** in the Folio Name text box.

5. In the Orientation section, click the middle icon named **Landscape Only Folio**.

   Because the original InDesign file and the ten article files have only landscape orientations, that same orientation must be specified here when setting up the folio.

6. Set the Default JPEG Quality setting to **Maximum** so that your New Folio dialog box resembles Figure 36.

7. Click **OK**.

   As shown in Figure 37, the folio name, Tabor Brochure, appears at the top of the Folio Builder panel.

In the Folio Builder panel, you created a new folio file, giving it a name and specifying the quality setting for JPG images in the file.

Name and create a cover for an iPad publication

1. Click the **Folio Builder panel menu button** ≡ , then click **Properties**.

   The Folio Properties dialog box opens. In this dialog box you will choose a cover image and a name for the publication as it will appear on the iPad.

2. Type **Tabor Brochure** in the Publication Name text box, then click the **folder icon** next to the Vertical thumbnail in the Cover Preview section.

3. Navigate to your Chapter 6 Data Files folder, open the Cover Images folder, then click **Vertical Cover.jpg**.

   Your Folio Properties panel should resemble Figure 38.

4. Using the same method, place the image for the horizontal cover using the file named **Horizontal Cover.jpg**, then click **OK**.

   When you click OK, the information is uploaded to your Adobe account. The folio on your iPad will be named Tabor Brochure and the thumbnail image will show in both horizontal and vertical orientations.

In the Folio Properties panel, you entered a name for the publication and specified two thumbnail images as its cover.

Add articles to a folio in the Folio Builder panel

1. Click the **File menu**, click **Open**, navigate to the **To iPad folder** that you packaged, then open all ten article files (01.indd – 10.indd).

2. Verify that 01.indd is the active document.

3. Click **Add** at the bottom of the Folio Builder panel.

   The New Article dialog box opens.

4. Type **01** in the Article Name text box so that your New Article dialog box resembles Figure 39.

(continued)

Figure 38 *Vertical cover specified in the Folio Properties dialog box*

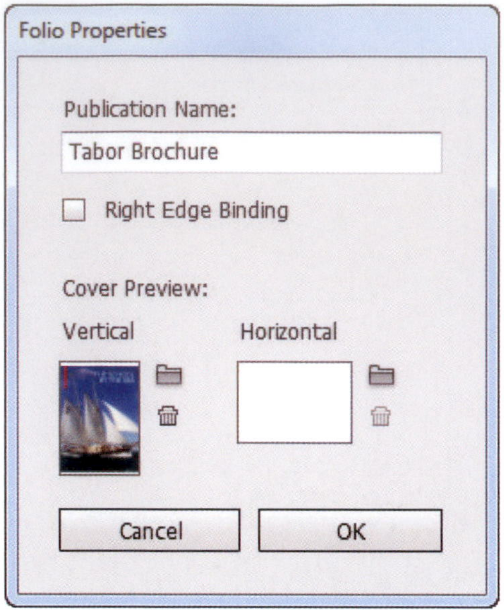

Image courtesy of Tabor Academy. Source Adobe® InDesign®, 2013.

Figure 39 *Naming an article in the New Article dialog box*

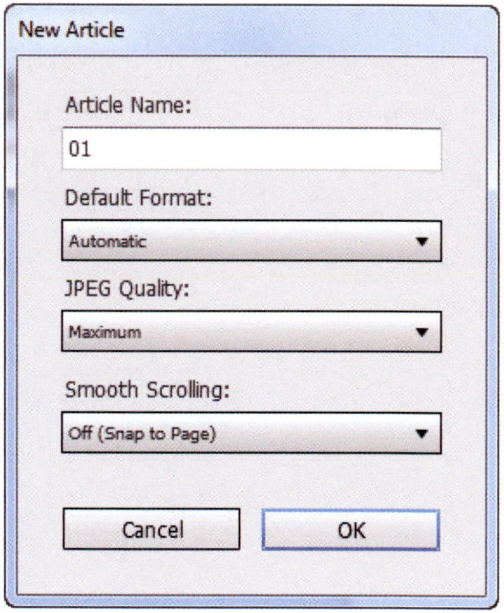

Source Adobe® InDesign®, 2013.

Figure 40 *Folio Builder panel with article 01 added and listed*

Source Adobe® InDesign®, 2013.

Figure 41 *Ten articles added to the folio*

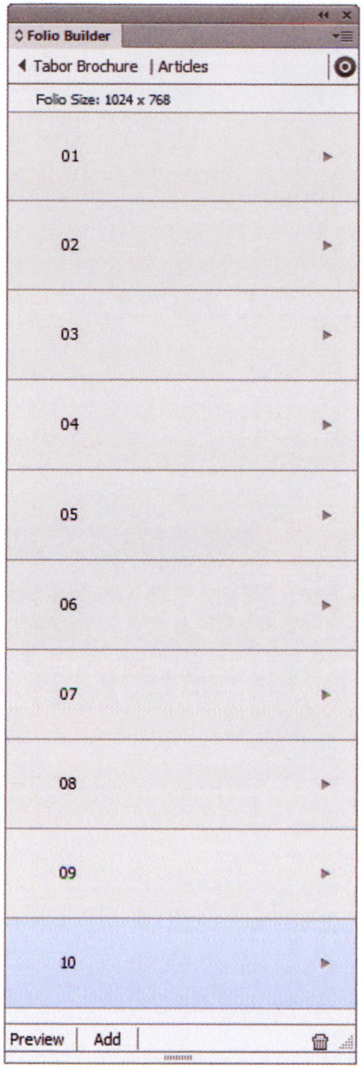

Source Adobe® InDesign®, 2013.

5. Click **OK**.

   When you click OK, the article is uploaded to your Adobe account. Your Folio Builder panel should resemble Figure 40.

6. Close the 01.indd document.

7. Click **Add** at the bottom of the Folio Builder panel.

8. Type **02** in the Article Name text box.

9. Click **OK**.

10. Close the 02.indd file.

11. Using the same procedure, add articles 03-10 to the Tabor Brochure folio so that your Folio Builder panel resembles Figure 41.

You added ten articles to the Folio Builder panel.

Preview contents in the Folio Builder panel

1. Click **article 07** to select it.
2. Click **Preview** at the bottom of the panel.

   The Adobe Content Viewer window opens showing page 07.

3. Click and drag the **image** left or right.

   As shown in Figure 42, no other pages show, because only article 07 was selected to preview.

   (continued)

(continued)

Figure 42 *Previewing a single article in the folio*

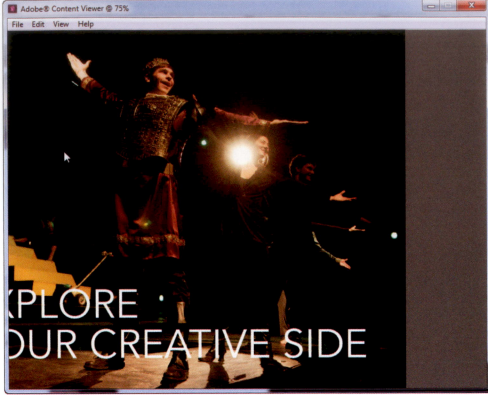

Image courtesy of Tabor Academy. Source Adobe® InDesign®, 2013.

Publishing to the iPad

Figure 43 *The Tabor Brochure folio selected in the panel*

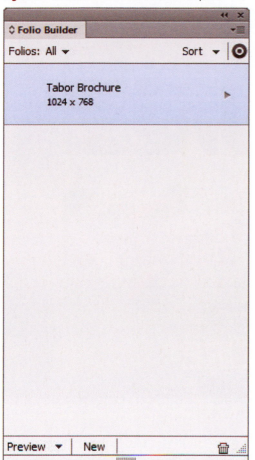

Source Adobe® InDesign®, 2013.

4. Return to InDesign.

5. At the top of the Folio Builder panel, click the **black triangle** beside the name Tabor Brochure to switch to Folios Mode.

   The panel changes to show all the folios that have been created. As shown in Figure 43, the panel lists only Tabor Brochure, because that's the only folio that you created.

   (continued)

6. On the Folio Builder panel, click the **Preview button arrow**, then click **Preview on Desktop**.

The Adobe Content Viewer window opens, showing the first page of the folio.

7. Click and drag the **page** to the left.

As shown in Figure 44, you can scroll through all the pages in the folio.

You previewed a single article and then previewed the entire folio on your computer.

Figure 44 *Previewing the entire folio*

Image courtesy of Tabor Academy. Source Adobe® InDesign®, 2013.

Figure 45 *The folio on the iPad*

Image courtesy of Tabor Academy. Source Adobe® InDesign®, 2013.

View a folio on the iPad

1. Launch the Adobe Content Viewer app on the iPad.

2. Click the **Sign In button** in the top-left corner.

3. Enter your **Adobe ID username** and **password**.

   When you sign in, an alert appears telling you that Tabor Brochure is now available. The Tabor Brochure thumbnail is visible.

4. Click the **Download button** beside the Tabor Brochure thumbnail, then click **View**.

   As shown in Figure 45, the entire folio appears as an interactive document on the iPad.

5. Finger swipe to article 05.

   The video file begins playing when you access the page.

6. Go to article 08.

   The sound file plays when you access the page.

7. Go to article 09, then tap the video.

   The video plays.

You signed in to the Adobe Content Viewer app on the iPad, then viewed the folio.

CHAPTER 7

CREATING COMPLEX
INTERACTIVITY IN AN
IPAD PRESENTATION

1. Rotate page orientation on an iPad

2. Pan and zoom images

3. Use object states for iPad interactivity

4. Create a scrollable text frame

5. Add an image sequence

6. Incorporate web content

CHAPTER 7

CREATING COMPLEX INTERACTIVITY IN AN IPAD PRESENTATION

It's interesting to think that the iPad is so new, yet so much about it is already so classic. In fact, you might say it was an instant classic.

InDesign, having been around for more than a decade and now the preeminent layout program, is itself something of a classic. But it's also new: Adobe has reinvented InDesign as a layout tool for the web and the iPad. As you get used to the idea of InDesign as an iPad publishing tool, you can also marvel at how nimble it is at creating classic iPad interactive features.

Alternate layouts are an instant solution for creating a layout that rotates orientation when you hold your iPad horizontally or vertically. Object states let you create a slideshow on the iPad.

The Folio Overlays panel is where much of the iPad magic is set up in InDesign. Applying the Pan & Zoom option allows you to finger-swipe images in your iPad presentation, to move them in their frames, and to resize them with a pinch of your finger and thumb. The Web Content option lets you use a graphic frame as a window for a live, interactive web page. And the Image Source option is great for placing frames from a video as a movie on your iPad, a movie that you can play forward and backward with a swipe of your finger.

From this perspective, InDesign CS6 is an instant classic: it's brand new, but it already does all the things you want it to do, and it does them so well.

Create Alternate Layout

Name: iPad H

From Source Pages: iPad V

Page Size: iPad

Width: 1024 px   Orientation:

Height: 768 px

Options

Liquid Page Rule: Off

☐ Link Stories

☐ Copy Text Styles to New Style Group

☑ Smart Text Reflow

Cancel   OK

Object States

Object Name: Slideshow H

01

02

03

04

Folio Overlays   **Folio Builder**

◀ Web Content

URL or File: 🗀

http://taboracademymycrew.blogspot.com/

☑ Auto Play

Delay: 0 secs

☐ Transparent Background

☑ Allow User Interaction

☑ Scale Content to Fit

Preview | Reset   🗑

Source Adobe® InDesign®, 2013.

Rotate Page Orientation
ON AN IPAD

What You'll Do

Images courtesy of Tabor Academy. Source Adobe® InDesign®, 2013.

In this lesson, you will use the alternate layout feature to create a vertical version of a horizontal layout for page rotation on an iPad.

Creating Alternate Layouts

As new as the iPad is to the marketplace, there are already some classic features. One of those is image rotation: turn the iPad to the opposite position, and the page rotates to the new orientation.

If you think this is a result of a single layout readapting itself from one orientation to the other, that's not the case. Image rotation on the iPad relies on the **alternate layouts** feature in InDesign. When designing for the iPad, creating alternate layouts is almost always part of the process, because you need one layout for the vertical orientation of the iPad and another for the horizontal layout.

InDesign offers the very useful option of creating alternate layouts in a single document. Let's use a layout for the iPad as an example. If you create a new single-page document using the iPad size and the Portrait page orientation, you will create a document that is 1024 pixels in height by 768 pixels wide. As shown in Figure 1, iPad V appears above the thumbnail of the page on the Pages panel, indicating that the page has a vertical orientation and has the iPad size

applied. The alternate of this size is iPad H (horizontal).

You can create an alternate layout using the Create Alternate Layout command on the Layout menu or by clicking the black triangle next to iPad V on the Pages panel and then choosing Create Alternate Layout. Doing either opens the Create Alternate Layout dialog box, shown in Figure 2. Notice that the default name, iPad H, is automatically entered because the alternate layout is based on iPad V. Both the name and the page size can be modified in the dialog box.

When you create an alternate layout based on a page that has artwork, all of the artwork on the base page is copied to the alternate layout. The idea here is that you can then resize the artwork to create the alternate layout.

The Create Alternate Layout dialog box offers useful options for how elements are copied and how objects on one layout relate to objects on the other.

If you click the Link Stories check box, text frames from the original layout are linked to text frames in the alternate layout. If you make changes to the text in the original layout, the text frame in the alternate layout will alert you that you can update the text in the frame on the alternate layout. If you do so, the changes you made to the text on the base layout will be reflected in the alternate layout. This feature can be very useful for maintaining consistency between layouts.

The Liquid Page Rule options control how objects are sized or resized when copied between layouts. If the option is turned off, the artwork from the base layout is copied at the same size and with the same physical relationships—to the alternate layout. The other options are designed to make it easier to adapt content from one layout to an alternate layout by adapting the artwork to the new size, orientation, and aspect ratio. For example, if you choose the Scale option, the artwork from the base layout is scaled in proportion to the width of the alternate layout.

QUICK TIP

If you're designing a document with an alternate layout for print, both layouts will print using the default print settings. You also have the option of choosing, in the InDesign Print dialog box, which of the two layouts you want to print at a given time.

Figure 1 *Viewing a single-page document on the Pages panel* **Figure 2** *Create Alternate Layout dialog box*

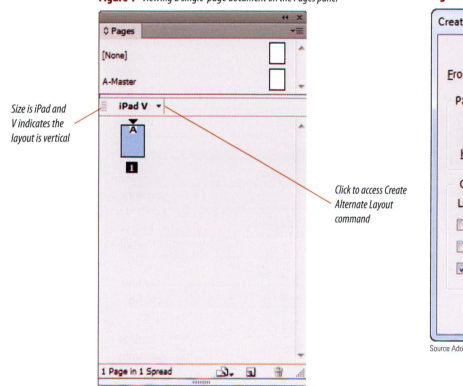

Size is iPad and V indicates the layout is vertical

Click to access Create Alternate Layout command

Source Adobe® InDesign®, 2013.

Source Adobe® InDesign®, 2013.

When you click OK to close the Create Alternate Layout dialog box, a thumbnail for the alternate layout is added to the Pages panel, as shown in Figure 3. In this example, the alternate layout is iPad H. You can simply double-click a thumbnail to toggle between each of the two layouts.

Rotating a Layout on the iPad

Once you've created an alternate layout, you're ready to create an article and add it to a folio for upload to the iPad.

When you add an article file to a folio, the New Article dialog box opens. As shown in Figure 4, when the article file contains iPad V and iPad H alternate layouts, the New Article dialog box, by default, identifies the alternate layouts as the portrait and landscape orientations. When the article is added to the folio, those alternate layouts are accessed when the iPad is held in a vertical or horizontal orientation.

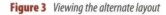

Figure 3 *Viewing the alternate layout*

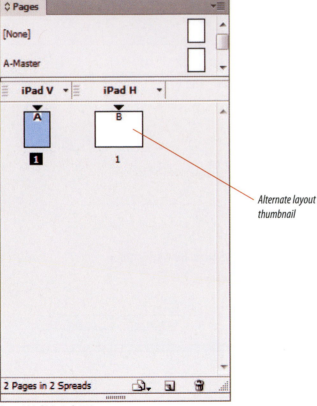

Alternate layout thumbnail

Source Adobe® InDesign®, 2013.

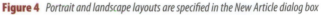

Figure 4 *Portrait and landscape layouts are specified in the New Article dialog box*

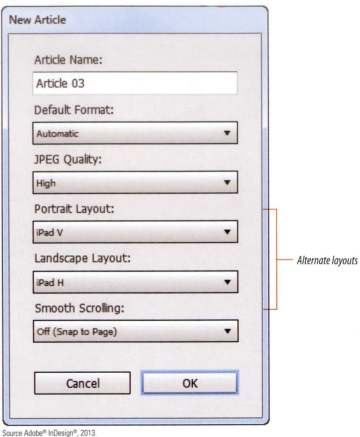

Alternate layouts

Source Adobe® InDesign®, 2013.

Creating Complex Interactivity in an iPad Presentation

Figure 5 *Document Setup dialog box*

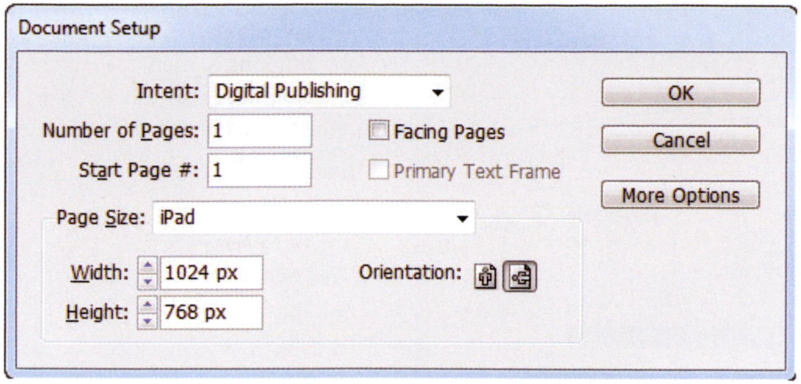

Document Setup
Intent: Digital Publishing
OK
Number of Pages: 1
Facing Pages
Cancel
Start Page #: 1
Primary Text Frame
More Options
Page Size: iPad
Width: 1024 px
Orientation:
Height: 768 px

Source Adobe® InDesign®, 2013.

Figure 6 *Pages panel with a single-page thumbnail*

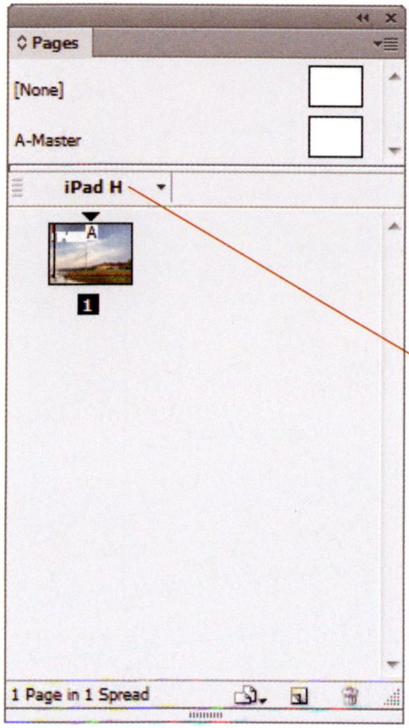

Pages
[None]
A-Master
iPad H
A
1
1 Page in 1 Spread

Document is set up with Landscape (horizontal) orientation

Image courtesy of Tabor Academy. Source Adobe® InDesign®, 2013.

Create an alternate layout in a single document

1. Open ID 7-01.indd, click **Update Links**, then save it as **Article 01**.
2. Click the **File menu**, then click **Document Setup**.

   As shown in Figure 5, the document is set up with Digital Publishing as the Intent. Its Orientation is specified as Landscape, and its Page Size is specified as iPad.
3. Click **Cancel**.
4. Open the Pages panel.

   As shown in Figure 6, the panel shows a horizontal thumbnail. On your Pages panel, the thumbnail might or might not be labeled as iPad H, as shown in the figure.
5. Click the **Layout menu**, then click **Create Alternate Layout**.

   The Create Alternate Layout dialog box opens.

(continued)

6. Click the **Liquid Page Rule list arrow**, then click **Off**.

Your dialog box should resemble Figure 7. Note that the alternate layout will automatically be named iPad V and that the Orientation has been set to Portrait.

7. Click **OK**.

As shown in Figure 8, a second thumbnail is added to the Pages panel.

(continued)

Figure 7 *Create Alternate Layout dialog box*

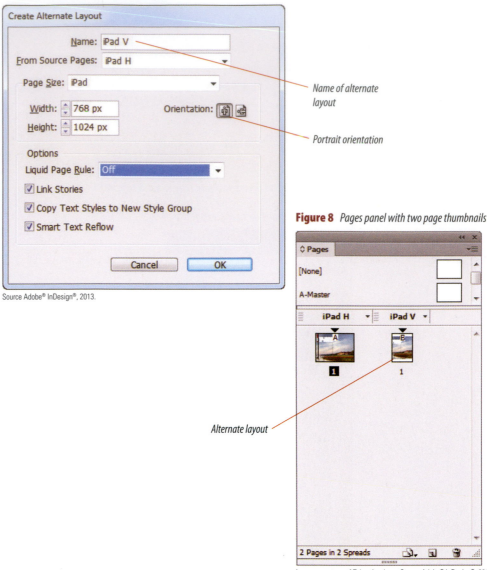

Source Adobe® InDesign®, 2013.

Name of alternate layout

Portrait orientation

Figure 8 *Pages panel with two page thumbnails*

Alternate layout

Images courtesy of Tabor Academy. Source Adobe® InDesign®, 2013.

Creating Complex Interactivity in an iPad Presentation

Figure 9 *Alternate vertical layout*

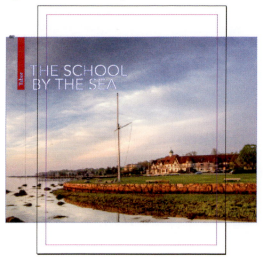

Image courtesy of Tabor Academy. Source Adobe® InDesign®, 2013.

Figure 10 *Alternate vertical layout with scaled artwork*

Image courtesy of Tabor Academy. Source Adobe® InDesign®, 2013.

Figure 11 *Redesigned vertical page*

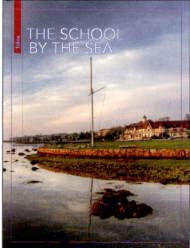

Image courtesy of Tabor Academy. Source Adobe® InDesign®, 2013.

8. Double-click the **new thumbnail**, apply the **Fit in Window** command, then compare the alternate layout to Figure 9.

   The horizontal artwork appears at the same size on a vertical page.

9. Click the **Edit menu**, then click **Undo Create Alternate Layout**.

10. Click the **small black triangle** next to iPad H on the Pages panel, then click **Create Alternate Layout**.

    The Create Alternate Layout dialog box opens.

11. Click the **Liquid Page Rule list arrow**, then click **Scale**.

12. Click **OK**, then switch to the alternate layout.

    As shown in Figure 10, the horizontal artwork is scaled to the width of the vertical page.

13. Redesign the layout so that the artwork fills the page.

    Figure 11 shows a sample layout.

14. Save your work.

    Because you made an alternate layout, the file is now defined as a portrait and landscape document. It's neither one nor the other; it's both.

You used the Create Alternate Layout command to create a vertical layout based on a horizontal layout. The first time you created it, you turned off the Liquid Page Rule option, and the artwork was identical on both pages. The second time, you used the Scale option and the artwork was scaled down to the width of the vertical page.

Create a folio that will change orientation on the iPad

1. Open the Folio Builder panel, then click **New**.

   For this and the remaining lessons in the chapter, you'll need to be signed-in to your Adobe account on the Folio Builder panel and in the Adobe Content Viewer app on your iPad.

2. In the New Folio dialog box, type **Tabor Waterfront** in the Folio Name text box.

   The size, 1024 × 768, is consistent with the size specified for the article file.

3. In the Orientation section, click the **Portrait and Landscape Folio option** so that your New Folio dialog box resembles Figure 12.

   Choosing the Portrait and Landscape Folio option specifies that this article can be rotated and viewed horizontally and vertically on the iPad.

4. Click **OK**.

5. On the Folio Builder panel, switch to Folios Mode, then verify that the **Tabor Waterfront folio** is selected.

6. Click the **Folio Builder panel menu button** , then click **Properties**.

   The Folio Properties dialog box opens. Here you can choose a name for the publication.

7. Type **Tabor Waterfront** in the Publication Name text box.

8. In the Cover Preview section, click the **folder icon** next to the Vertical thumbnail.

   You will be prompted to choose an image on your hard drive that will serve as the cover image for the iPad publication.

   (continued)

Figure 12 *New Folio dialog box*

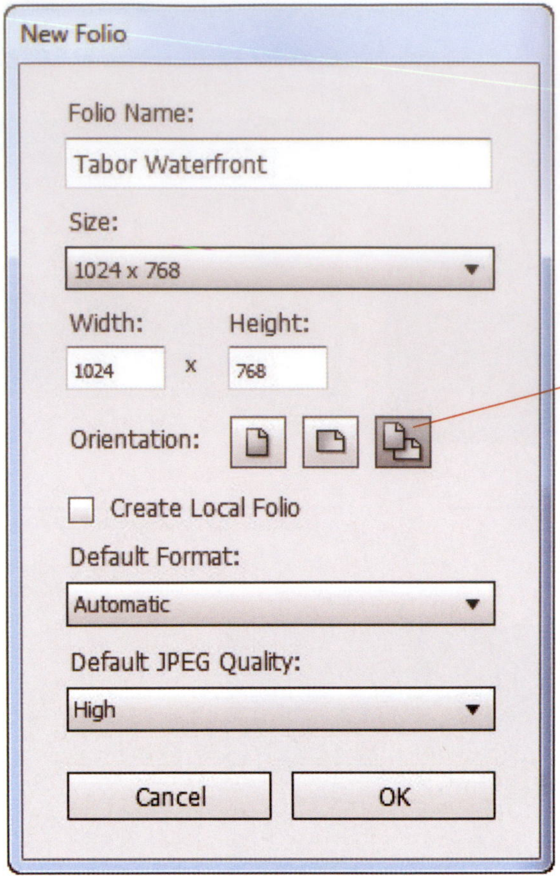

Portrait and Landscape
Folio option

Source Adobe® InDesign®, 2013.

Figure 13 *Folio Properties dialog box*

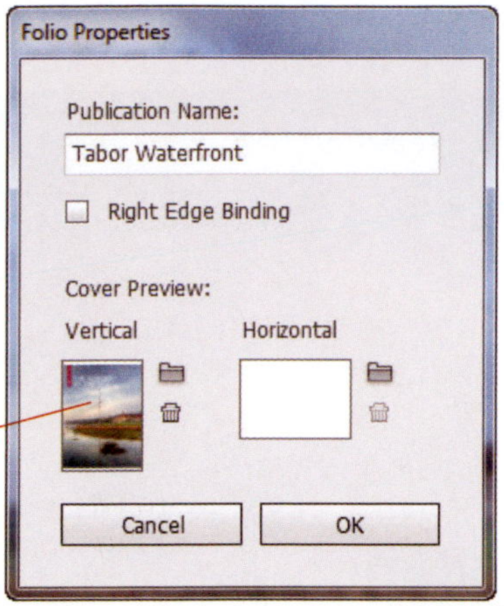

Cover artwork
for the vertical
layout

Image courtesy of Tabor Academy. Source Adobe® InDesign®, 2013.

Figure 14 *New Article dialog box*

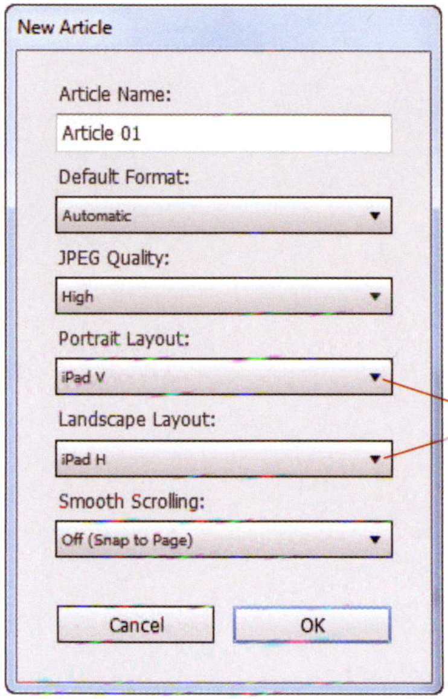

Pull down menus
allow you to
choose layouts

Source Adobe® InDesign®, 2013.

9. Navigate to the Chapter 7 Data Files folder, open the Cover Images folder, then click **Vertical Cover.jpg**.

   Vertical Cover.jpg will be the cover of the Tabor Waterfront publication. Your Folio Properties panel should resemble Figure 13.

10. Using the same method, use the **Horizontal Cover.jpg** for the horizontal cover, then click **OK**.

11. Switch to Articles Mode on the Folio Builder panel, then click **Add**.

   The New Article dialog box opens. You will use Article 01 as the single-page article for the Tabor Waterfront folio.

12. Type **Article 01** in the Article Name dialog box, then compare your New Article dialog box to Figure 14.

   Note that the New Article dialog box contains Portrait Layout and Landscape Layout menus. The iPad V layout is specified as the Portrait Layout, and the iPad H layout is specified as the Landscape Layout.

(continued)

13. Click **OK**.

Status bars appear on the Folio Builder panel as the article uploads to your Adobe account.

14. Open the **Adobe Content Viewer app** on your iPad.

15. When the library is done updating, press the **Download button** next to the Tabor Waterfront publication.

16. Hold the iPad horizontally, press **View**, then compare your horizontal view of the layout to Figure 15.

(continued)

Figure 15 *Horizontal orientation of Tabor Waterfront*

Image courtesy of Tabor Academy. Source Adobe® InDesign®, 2013.

Creating Complex Interactivity in an iPad Presentation

Figure 16 *Vertical orientation of Tabor Waterfront*

Image courtesy of Tabor Academy. Source Adobe® InDesign®, 2013.

17. Rotate the iPad to the vertical orientation, then compare the view to Figure 16.

18. Save your work, then close Article 01.indd.

You created a new folio specified as a Portrait and Landscape Folio. You then added a single-page article that contained both a landscape and vertical layout. Once uploaded, you held the iPad at different orientations and noted that the layout rotated accordingly.

Pan and
ZOOM IMAGES

What You'll Do

Source Adobe® InDesign®, 2013.

In this lesson, you will use the Pan & Zoom option on the Folio Overlays panel to specify that images can be panned, enlarged, and reduced on the iPad.

Specifying Images to Pan and Zoom on the iPad

Two other classic interactions with the iPad are done with your fingers: there's the "swipe" and the "pinch/split."

The **swipe** occurs when you drag your finger over an image, and the image moves with your finger. The **pinch/split** occurs when you put your thumb and index finger on an image and then pinch them together or spread them apart, either reducing or enlarging the image.

When preparing an article in InDesign for the iPad, you specify images to pan and zoom by clicking the Pan & Zoom option on the Folio Overlays panel, shown in Figure 17. This opens the Pan & Zoom options pane on the Folio Overlays panel, which offers simple controls for turning Pan & Zoom on or off for a selected graphics frame.

The Pan & Zoom option is only available when an image in a graphics frame is larger than the frame; in other words, when only part of

Figure 17 *Folio Overlays panel*

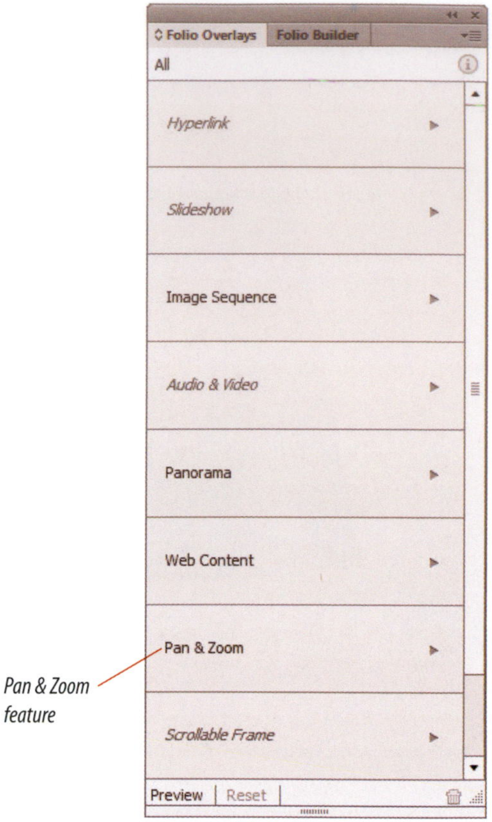

Pan & Zoom feature

Source Adobe® InDesign®, 2013.

the image is showing in the frame. Figure 18 shows an example. The graphics frame, indicated by the blue border, is cropping the larger image. The brown selection border is the actual size of the image. This image could be panned and zoomed when the page is uploaded to the iPad.

In Figure 19, the image is smaller than the graphics frame that contains it, and the Pan & Zoom option is not available on the Folio Overlays panel. You can't pan or enlarge (zoom) the image because the whole image is already showing.

Figure 19 *Example of graphic that is smaller than frame*

Image courtesy of Tabor Academy. Source Adobe® InDesign®, 2013.

Source Adobe® InDesign®, 2013.

Figure 18 *Example of graphic that is larger than frame*

Graphics frame crops image so that you don't see all of it

Brown frame indicates size of graphic

Image courtesy of Tabor Academy. Source Adobe® InDesign®, 2013.

Specify images to pan and zoom on the iPad

1. Open ID 7-02.indd, click **Update Links**, then save it as **Article 02**.

   The document contains an iPad H layout and an iPad V layout.

2. On the Folio Builder panel, verify that you are in Articles Mode so that you see Article 01 in the panel.

3. Click the **Add button**, enter the settings shown in Figure 20, then click **OK**.

   Article 02 is added to the Tabor Waterfront folio and uploaded to your Adobe account.

4. Update and view both articles in the Tabor Waterfront folio on your iPad.

   On the iPad, articles exist side by side. Regardless of what orientation you're viewing the folio, you finger swipe left to right—or horizontally—to move from article to article.

5. Return to the Article 02.indd document, double-click the **iPad H layout** on the Pages panel, click the **Selection tool** , then select the **top small image**.

6. Open the Folio Overlays panel, then click **Pan & Zoom**.

7. Click the **On option button** on the Folio Overlays panel, as shown in Figure 21.

   (continued)

Figure 20 *Settings for Article 02*

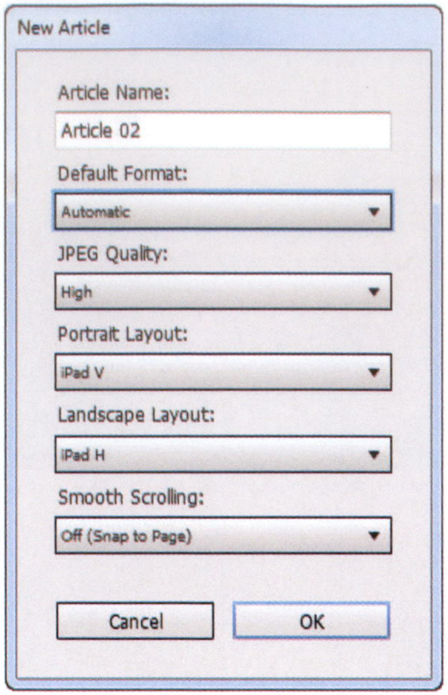

Source Adobe® InDesign®, 2013.

Figure 21 *Activating Pan & Zoom on the Folio Overlays panel*

Pan & Zoom is on

Image courtesy of Tabor Academy. Source Adobe® InDesign®, 2013.

Creating Complex Interactivity in an iPad Presentation

Figure 22 *Panning an image on the iPad*

Image courtesy of Tabor Academy. Source Adobe® InDesign®, 2013.

8. Select the other **small image**, click **Pan & Zoom**, then click the **On option button**.

9. Using the same method, apply the **Pan & Zoom folio overlay** to the two small images on the iPad V layout.

10. Save the Article 02.indd document.

11. On the Folio Builder panel, verify that **Article 02** is selected, click the **Folio Builder panel menu button** , then click **Update**.

12. Update and view the Tabor Waterfront publication on your iPad.

13. Go to the **Article 02 page**, then tap the **top image**.

14. Drag your **finger** across the image.

   As shown in Figure 22, the image moves within its frame.

15. Pinch and expand your thumb and index finger to reduce and enlarge the image.

16. Return to the Article 02.indd file, then close the file.

You added a second article to the Tabor Waterfront folio then noted that articles on the iPad move horizontally from article to article. You specified four images to Pan & Zoon, then updated the article in the Folio Builder panel.

Use Object States for
IPAD INTERACTIVITY

What You'll Do

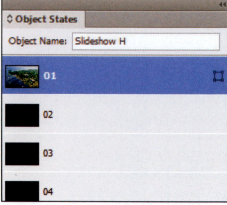

Image courtesy of Tabor Academy. Source Adobe® InDesign®, 2013.

 In this lesson, you will use object states in InDesign to create an interactive slideshow on the iPad.

Creating Interactivity with Object States

In Chapter 3, you learned the power of object states for creating complex interactivity on a website. You selected a large graphics frame and then specified five object states for the frame. You placed a different image into each state, then linked the small thumbnail image buttons at the bottom of the page to each state. In the exported swf, clicking the thumbnail image button triggered a given object state to become active in the larger graphics frame.

This functionality works exactly the same way on the iPad and makes for great interaction with a page.

Object states are also used when you want to make a slideshow for an iPad presentation.

Create a multi-state object with many states, then click Slideshow on the Folio Overlays panel. The Slideshow pane, shown in Figure 23, offers a number of controls for the slideshow, including delays, transitions, and the ability to loop the show. When you choose Auto Play, the slideshow plays from the beginning whenever the page is accessed on the iPad.

Figure 23 *Controls in the Slideshow pane on the Folio Overlays panel*

Source Adobe® InDesign®, 2013.

Figure 24 *Viewing the active object states in the landscape layout*

Five object states

Image courtesy of Tabor Academy. Source Adobe® InDesign®, 2013.

Work with interactive buttons

1. Open ID 7-03.indd, click **Update Links**, then save it as **Article 03**.

   The document contains a landscape and a portrait layout.

2. Verify that you're viewing the portrait layout.

   This page has been set up with object states and buttons, similar to those you created in Chapter 3. The large image frame beside the text frame has been converted to a multi-state object containing five object states. The text frame is also a multi-state object; it contains five different versions of text. The five thumbnail images at the bottom are buttons that link to their respective image and text descriptions.

3. Open the Pages panel, then double-click the **iPad H thumbnail** to view the landscape layout.

4. Open the Object States panel, then click the **graphics frame** with the photo of the crew member to the left of the text description.

   As shown in Figure 24, the five object states associated with the frame are listed on the Object States panel. When the horizontal alternate layout was created, all of the object states and button links were copied over automatically; there was no need to recreate them.

   (continued)

5. Double-click the **iPad V thumbnail** to view the portrait layout.

6. Open the Folio Builder panel, then click **Add** to add a new article.

   The New Article dialog box opens.

7. Enter the settings for Article 03 shown in Figure 25, then click **OK**.

8. When the new article is done uploading, update the Tabor Waterfront folio on your iPad.

9. View the folio in portrait orientation.

(continued)

Figure 25 *Settings for Article 03*

New Article

Article Name:

Article 03

Default Format:

Automatic

JPEG Quality:

High

Portrait Layout:

iPad V

Landscape Layout:

iPad H

Smooth Scrolling:

Off (Snap to Page)

Cancel   OK

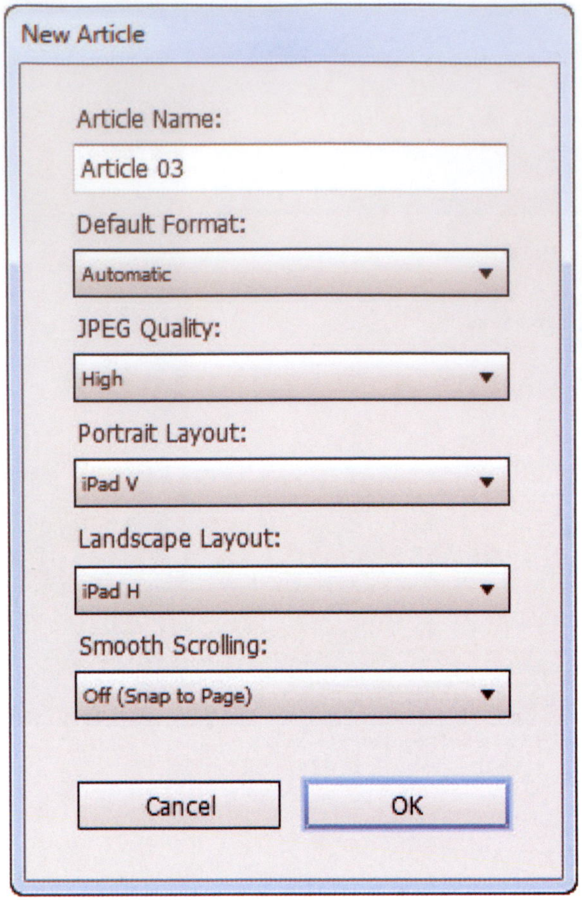

Source Adobe® InDesign®, 2013.

Creating Complex Interactivity in an iPad Presentation

Figure 26 *Interacting with the Article 03 layout*

Image courtesy of Tabor Academy. Source Adobe® InDesign®, 2013.

10. Touch each **thumbnail image** at the bottom of the screen.

    As shown in Figure 26, when you touch a thumbnail, both the large image and the text frame change.

11. Rotate the iPad to horizontal orientation, then touch a **thumbnail image**.

    The layout changes to the horizontal layout, and the interactivity functions the same way.

12. Return to InDesign and keep the Article 03.indd file open.

You opened an InDesign file that was set up with object states and buttons linking to those states. You uploaded the document as a new article, then tested the button interactivity with the object states.

Create a slideshow using object states

1. Open ID 7-04.indd, click **Update Links**, then save it as **Article 04**.

   The document contains a landscape and a portrait layout.

2. Verify that you're viewing the portrait layout.

3. Open the Object States panel, if necessary, then select the **black frame** on the page.

4. Click the **Convert selection to multi-state object button** at the bottom of the Object States panel ten times so that you have a total of 12 states in the panel.

5. Renumber each state **01–12**.

6. Type **Slideshow H** in the Object Name text box at the top of the panel.

7. Select **state 01** on the Object States panel.

(continued)

Lesson 3   Use Object States for iPad Interactivity

8. Click the **File menu**, click **Place**, navigate to the location of the Chapter 7 Data Files folder, open the folder named **Slideshow Images**, then open the file named **Helicopter Shot**.

9. Place the file into the black frame so that your page and Object States panel resemble Figure 27.

10. Click the **Fill frame proportionally button** on the Control panel, if necessary.

11. Using the same method, place the remaining eleven images in any order that you like into the remaining eleven object states.

12. Deselect all, then save your work.

13. Click the **Selection tool** , then select the **frame** on the page.

14. On the Object States panel, click the **frame icon** next to the object state name at the top of the panel.

    The Folio Overlays panel displays controls for a slideshow.

15. On the Folio Overlays panel, click **Slideshow**.

16. Click the **Auto Play check box**.

17. Click the **Tap to Play/Pause check box**.

18. Verify that Delay is set to **0**, set the Interval to **2**, then click the **Loop check box**.

19. Click the **Cross Fade check box**, then set the Speed to **0.5**.

    Your Folio Overlays panel should resemble Figure 28.

(continued)

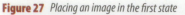
Figure 27 *Placing an image in the first state*

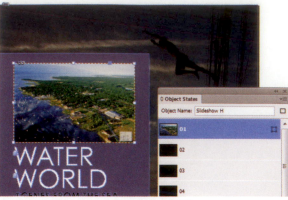

Image courtesy of Tabor Academy. Source Adobe® InDesign®, 2013.

Figure 28 *Slideshow controls on the Folio Overlays panel*

Image courtesy of Tabor Academy. Source Adobe® InDesign®, 2013.

Creating Complex Interactivity in an iPad Presentation

Figure 29 *Viewing the slideshow*

Image courtesy of Tabor Academy. Source Adobe® InDesign®, 2013.

20. Save your work.

21. Add Article 04 to the list of articles on the Folio Builder panel.

22. After the article uploads, update the Tabor Waterfront folio on your iPad.

23. Hold the iPad vertically, then go to the fourth article.

    The slideshow begins playing when you access the article and continues to play because the loop option is activated.

24. Compare your iPad to Figure 29.

25. Return to InDesign, and keep Article 04.indd open.

You created twelve object states for a frame and placed twelve images. You then applied slideshow controls using the Folio Overlays panel and viewed the slideshow on your iPad.

Create a Scrollable
TEXT FRAME

Source Adobe® InDesign®, 2013.

▶ *In this lesson, you will learn a trick for making text that scrolls within its frame on an iPad.*

Creating a Scrollable Frame

Let's say you're holding your iPad in Portrait (vertical) position, and you're paging through a folio that contains ten articles. To move from article to article, you finger swipe left or right. In other words, articles are positioned side by side, or horizontally.

When you're reading a single article, you read top to bottom, or vertically. Since the screen on an iPad isn't nearly long enough to show, say, a magazine article or a newspaper editorial, it's only natural that what's on the screen needs to scroll.

With a scrollable frame, you can finger swipe as you read and the text scrolls so that you can continue reading. Other elements of the page—like the headline or a photo—remain stationary.

Scrollable text in a scrollable frame is really just a trick, but in order to understand that trick, you first need to understand what you're looking at when you're seeing an InDesign layout on an iPad screen: you're looking at a picture.

An InDesign layout is created with frames into which you place images, illustrations, and text—text that can be selected and edited. The images and illustrations too can be edited: they can be enlarged, rotated, flipped, etc.

When that InDesign layout is uploaded as an article to a folio, the layout is essentially exported as a jpeg, which is what you see when you see the layout on the iPad. You're seeing a picture of a page.

But it's more than just a flat, static picture. As you saw with panning and zooming, for example, you can tap a picture and finger swipe to see more of the picture that lies outside of the frame.

That's the trick—panning—that's used for scrollable "text" in a scrollable frame. Create the text in Photoshop or Illustrator at the width of the frame into which it will be placed in the InDesign layout, but allow the height to be as long as you need it to be to contain all of the text.

When you export the file to InDesign, the "text" is actually an image file of text, an image that's taller than the frame that contains it. Apply the Scrollable Frame option on the Folio Overlays panel, shown in Figure 30, and when you upload the layout as an article, the "text" can be finger swiped. It is image panning—just with a different name—and it's a cool, practical option.

The Scrollable Frame option can be applied to any frame, not just a frame containing an image of text. Additionally, the frame can be set to scroll in more directions than just vertically. Click the Scroll Direction menu for more options.

Figure 30 *Scrollable Frame controls on the Folio Overlays panel*

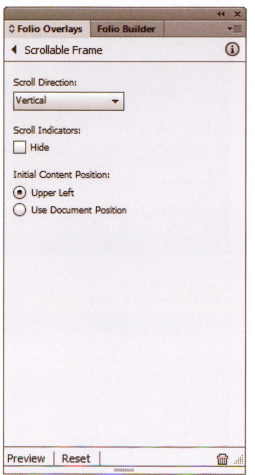

Source Adobe® InDesign®, 2013.

Create a text file in Photoshop

1. In Article 04.indd, select the **large blue frame** on the page, then open the Swatches panel.

2. Note that the frame's fill color is R95 G99 B128.

   Because the document's intent is Digital Publishing, all colors on the Swatches panel are specified as RGB by default.

3. Select the **text frame** that contains the white text, and note its width in the Control panel.

   The width of the text frame is 354 pixels and the height is just over 392 pixels. As shown in Figure 31, the text frame contains overset text; there's more text than can fit in the frame.

4. Open the Paragraph Styles panel, double-click the **White Copy style**, then note in the dialog box how it has been formatted.

   The White Copy paragraph style is Font=**Arial**; Font Size = **16pt**; Leading =**21pt**; Alignment = **Justified**; Space After = **7px**; Color = **White**.

   TIP Because the document is set up with Desktop Publishing as its intent, units in the Paragraph panel are specified as pixels (px).

5. Close the Paragraph Styles dialog box, click the **Type tool** T, then click anywhere in the white text.

6. Press [**Ctrl**][**A**] (Win) or ⌘ [**A**] (Mac) to select all, click the **Edit menu**, then click **Cut**.

   The text is cut to the clipboard.

7. Open Photoshop, click the **File menu**, then click **New**.

   The New dialog box opens.

8. Type **Vertical Text** in the Name text box, type **354** in the Width text box, then type **1000** in the Height text box, so that your New dialog box resembles Figure 32.

   (continued)

Figure 31 *Noting the specifications of the text frame*

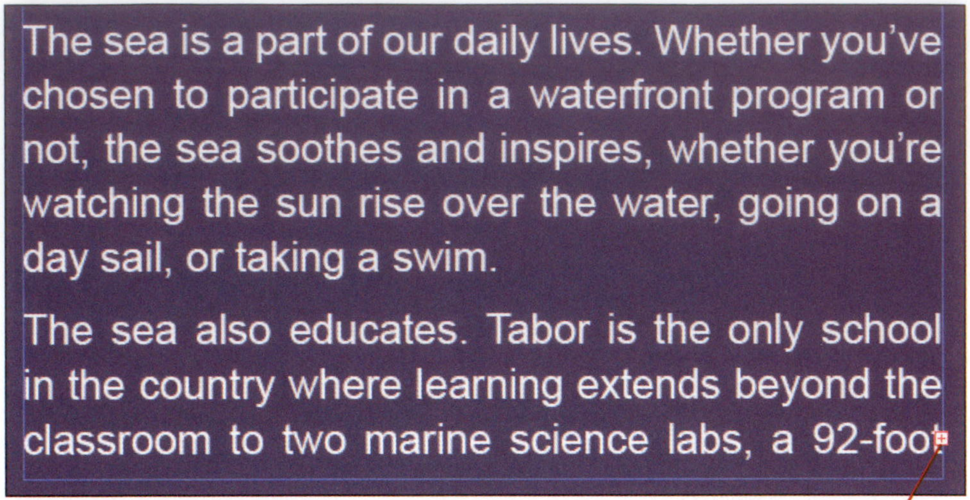

The sea is a part of our daily lives. Whether you've chosen to participate in a waterfront program or not, the sea soothes and inspires, whether you're watching the sun rise over the water, going on a day sail, or taking a swim.

The sea also educates. Tabor is the only school in the country where learning extends beyond the classroom to two marine science labs, a 92-foot

Source Adobe® InDesign®, 2013.

Overset text icon

Figure 32 *New dialog box in Photoshop*

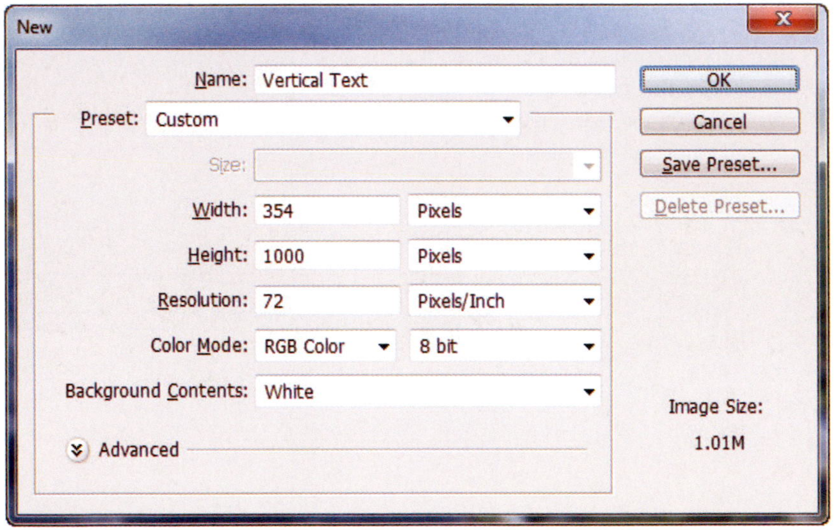

Source Adobe® InDesign®, 2013.

Figure 33 *Color Picker*

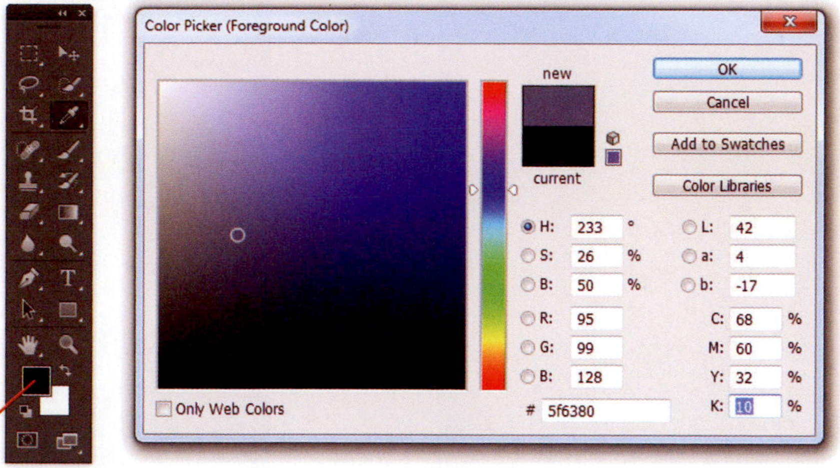

Set foreground
color button

Source Adobe® InDesign®, 2013.

Figure 34 *Fill dialog box*

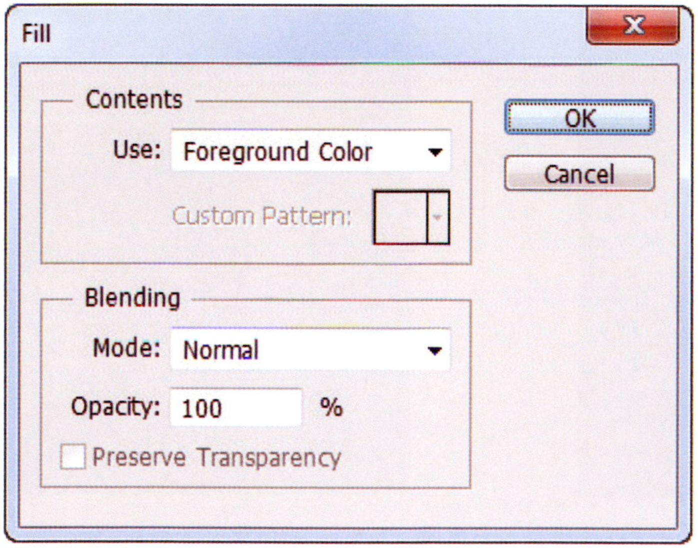

Source Adobe® InDesign®, 2013.

Lesson 4   Create a Scrollable Text Frame

It's important that the width of the Photoshop file is the same as the width of the text frame in InDesign that you want to use as a scrollable frame. The height value needs to be enough to contain all of the text.

9. Click **OK**, then verify that you can see the entire canvas in the window.

10. Click the **Set foreground color button** on the Tools panel to open the Color Picker, then type **95** in the Red text box, **99** in the Green text box, and **128** in the Blue text box.

Your Color Picker should resemble Figure 33.

11. Click **OK**, click the **Edit menu**, then click **Fill**.

12. Enter the settings shown in Figure 34, then click **OK**.

The canvas fills with the same color as the large blue frame in the InDesign layout.

(continued)

13. Click the **Type tool** , position it at the top-left corner of the canvas, then click and drag to create a text box that is exactly the same size as the canvas.

    Your canvas should resemble Figure 35.

14. Click the **Edit menu**, then click **Paste**.

    The text that you cut from the InDesign document is pasted into the text frame in Photoshop.

15. Select all of the text.

16. Open the Character and Paragraph panels, then format the text as it was formatted in InDesign (Font=**Arial**; Font Size = **16pt**; Leading =**21pt**; Alignment = **Justified**; Space After = **7pt**; Color = **White)**.

    TIP Enter the Space After value in Photoshop as points (pt).

17. When you're done formatting the text, deselect, then compare your canvas to Figure 36.

18. Click the **File menu**, click **Save As**, then save the file in the Photoshop (.psd) format as **Vertical Text**.

    It's a good idea to keep a layered version.

19. Click the **Layer menu**, then click **Flatten Image**.

20. Click the **File menu**, click **Save As**, then save the file in the JPEG (.jpg) format as **Vertical Text**.

    When asked to choose a quality setting for the JPEG, choose the highest setting.

You created a Photoshop file to contain an entire block of text too long to fit in a text frame in InDesign. You built the Photoshop file at the exact same width as the text frame in InDesign, but you specified the height to be long enough to fit all the text. You filled the background with the same color as the background in the InDesign document. You then saved the file as a high-quality JPEG.

Figure 35 *Creating a text frame in Photoshop*

Text box

Source Adobe® InDesign®, 2013.

Figure 36 *The formatted text in Photoshop*

The sea provides a dramatic backdrop for everything we do at Tabor. At our marine science laboratories, you can literally wade right into the ecosystem you're studying. After a hard-fought soccer game, dive off the docks for a swim. Take out a kayak and explore the nearby coves. The beauty of our seaside campus will take your breath away, but the splendor is only one piece of the Tabor experience, which offers unlimited opportunities to learn, grow and become the person you want to be.

The sea is a part of our daily lives. Whether you've chosen to participate in a waterfront program or not, the sea soothes and inspires, whether you're watching the sun rise over the water, going on a day sail, or taking a swim.

The sea also educates. Tabor is the only school in the country where learning extends beyond the classroom to two marine science labs, a 92-foot sailing vessel, a tidal salt marsh — and even the coral reefs of the Caribbean.

While we all work hard at our studies, there's always room in the schedule for fun. You can dive in the ocean after class or practice. You can head to the Beebe Grill to grab Tabor's popular cheese fries, listen to a student band, or watch the action through the window overlooking the Tabor hockey rink. Join in one of the big campus events — Springfest, Asian dinner, or the semi-formal winter dance. Then there are open mic nights, comedians, concerts, late night snacks in the dorms, advisee dinners and more.

Source Adobe® InDesign®, 2013.

Creating Complex Interactivity in an iPad Presentation

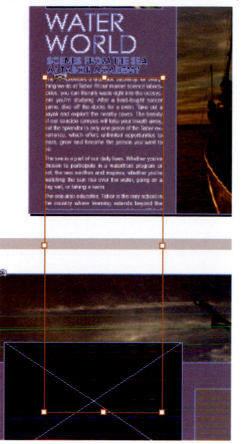

Figure 37 *Viewing the perimeter of the image outside of the graphic frame*

Source Adobe® InDesign®, 2013.

Create a scrollable text frame for the iPad

1. Return to InDesign, click the **Selection tool** , then select the **text frame**.

2. Click the **Object menu**, point to **Content**, then choose **Graphic**.

   The frame is changed from a text frame to a graphic frame.

3. Place **Vertical Text.jpg** into the graphic frame.

4. Click the **Object menu**, point to **Fitting**, then click **Fill Frame Proportionally**.

5. On the Control panel, verify that the **top left reference point** is selected, as shown in this icon .

6. Double-click the **image** so that the Control panel displays the X+ and Y+ values.

7. Verify that the X+ value on the Control panel is **0 px**, enter **0** in the Y+ text box, then press [**Enter**] (Win) or [**return**] (Mac).

   The top edge of the placed image is now aligned with the top edge of the frame that contains it.

8. Zoom out so that you can see how much longer the image is than the frame that contains it, as shown in Figure 37.

9. Deselect all.

10. Select the **text frame** again, open the Folio Overlays panel, then click **Scrollable Frame**.

(continued)

11. Click the **Scroll Direction list arrow**, then click **Vertical**.

12. Click the **Hide check box** under Scroll Indicators.

    Your Folio Overlays panel should resemble Figure 38.

13. Save Article 04.indd.

14. Select **Article 04** on the Folio Builder panel, then update it.

15. When Article 04 is uploaded, update the Tabor Waterfront folio on your iPad.

(continued)

Figure 38 *Scrollable frame controls on the Folio Overlays panel*

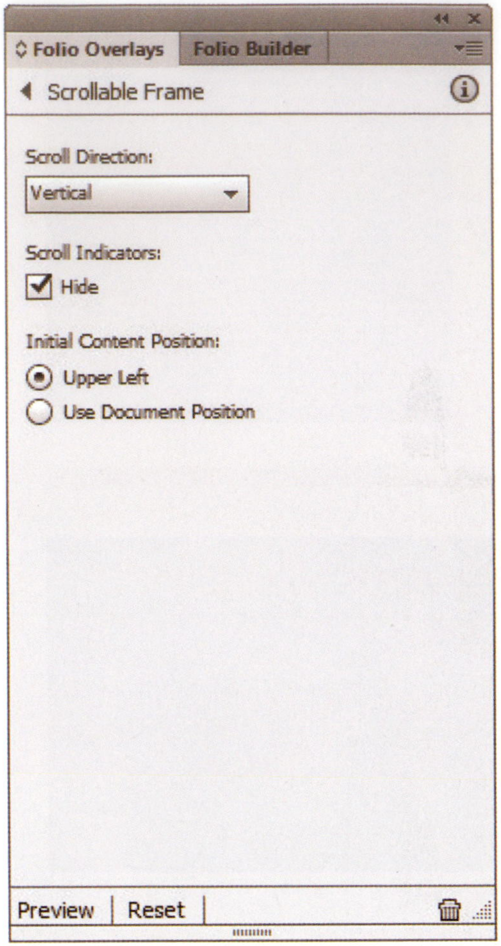

Source Adobe® InDesign®, 2013.

Creating Complex Interactivity in an iPad Presentation

Figure 39 *Finger swiping the text*

Image courtesy of Tabor Academy. Source Adobe® InDesign®, 2013.

16. Hold your iPad in portrait orientation, then go to Article 04.

17. Finger swipe vertically to scroll the text in the frame.

    As shown in Figure 39, you can scroll the text all the way to the end of the story.

18. Return to InDesign, then save Article 04.indd.

You placed an image of text into a graphic frame in InDesign. Noting that the image was longer than the frame itself, you aligned the top of the image with the top of the frame. You used the Folio Overlays panel to specify the frame as a scrollable frame, then uploaded the article to the iPad. On the iPad, you were able to read all the text in the frame by scrolling the image within the frame.

Add an Image
SEQUENCE

What You'll Do

Image courtesy of Tabor Academy. Source Adobe® InDesign®, 2013.

 In this lesson, you will import a series of frames from a video and use them as an interactive image sequence on the iPad.

Creating an Image Sequence

One of the coolest options in the Folio Overlays panel is Image Sequence.

When the layout is uploaded to the iPad, finger swiping across the frame rapidly moves from one image to the next, both forward and reverse.

An image sequence is one of the easiest options to apply. Select a frame in your layout, click Image Sequence, then navigate to a folder on your computer that contains the images that you want in the sequence. All of the images in the folder you select will be included in the sequence. Figure 40 shows the Image Sequence pane on the Folio Overlays panel.

An image sequence is really powerful when you use frames from a video as the image sequence. On the iPad, finger swiping the image sequence becomes like playing a movie forward and reverse, making the movie move at the speed of your fingertip.

One thing to keep in mind when creating an image sequence: size matters, both the size of the images in the sequence and the size of the frame that contains them. Your best bet, in most cases, is to make all the images in your sequence the same size. You'll also find it easier if the size of your images is the same as the frame in InDesign that the image sequence will go into, or at least directly proportional.

Figure 40 *Image sequence options on the Folio Overlays panel*

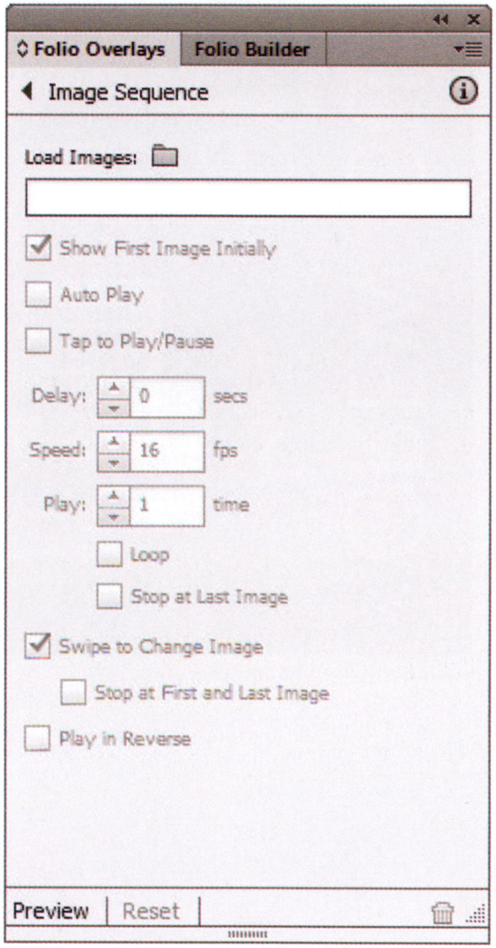

Source Adobe® InDesign®, 2013.

Create an image sequence

1. Go to the **iPad V layout** in Article 03.indd.

2. Select the **large black frame** at the top of the page, then note its width and height.

   The frame is 508 pixels in width and 286 pixels in height.

3. On the Folio Overlays panel, click **Image Sequence**.

4. Click the **folder icon** beside Load Images.

   The Browse For Folder dialog box opens. You will specify the folder that contains the images for the image sequence.

5. Navigate to the Chapter 7 Data Files folder, open it, select the folder named **Crew Regatta Images**, then click **Open**.

   The folder contains 90 images captured from a video. Each frame is sized to 508 pixels × 286 pixels (reduced from the standard 1280 pixels × 720 pixels). The black frame is also 508 pixels × 286 pixels to match the size of the images.

6. Click the **Show First Image Initially** and **Swipe to Change Image check boxes**, if necessary.

7. Compare your Folio Overlays panel and your page to Figure 41.

8. Save Article 03.indd.

9. On the Folio Builder panel, select **Article 03**, then update it.

   (continued)

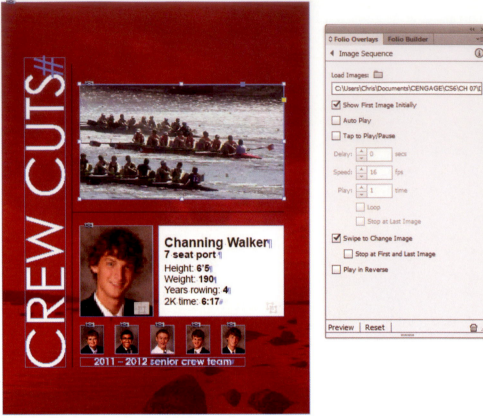

Image courtesy of Tabor Academy. Source Adobe® InDesign®, 2013.

Creating Complex Interactivity in an iPad Presentation

Figure 42 *Finger swiping the image sequence on the iPad*

Image courtesy of Tabor Academy. Source Adobe® InDesign®, 2013.

10. Update the Tabor Waterfront folio on your iPad.

11. Hold the iPad vertically, then go to Article 03.

12. Finger swipe the **image sequence** at the top of the page.

   As shown in Figure 42, the images move forward and in reverse as you move your finger over the frame.

13. Return to InDesign, then save Article 03.indd.

You selected a frame then used the Image Sequence option in the Folio Overlays panel to specify a folder that contains the images to be used in the image sequence.

Incorporate
WEB CONTENT

What You'll Do

![Folio Overlays panel showing Web Content pane with URL field http://taboracademycrew.blogspot.com/, Auto Play checked, Delay 0 secs, Transparent Background unchecked, Allow User Interaction checked, Scale Content to Fit checked]

Source Adobe® InDesign®, 2013.

 In this lesson, you will use a frame as a window to a website in an iPad presentation.

Using the Web Content Option on the Folio Overlays Panel

The Web Content option on the Folio Overlays panel allows you to use a frame in an InDesign layout as a window to a website. When the article is uploaded to the iPad, the website appears in that frame on the iPad screen.

Figure 43 shows the Web Content pane on the Folio Overlays panel. Simply enter the URL you want to link to into the URL or File text box, and the link is established. That's all you gotta do.

It doesn't take long to think of all the many ways this option can be useful. You can show a YouTube video in an iPad presentation. You could show your Twitter feed scrolling at the side of your layout or link to a web cam, or show your personal website or the Google home page.

What's even more exciting is that the web page in the frame on the iPad screen is live and interactive. So if you link to Google's home page, you can do a Google search right there in your own layout in your own iPad presentation!

Figure 43 *Web Content pane on the Folio Overlays panel*

![Folio Overlays panel showing Web Content pane with empty URL field, Auto Play unchecked, Delay 0 secs, Transparent Background unchecked, Allow User Interaction checked, Scale Content to Fit unchecked]

Source Adobe® InDesign®, 2013.

Creating Complex Interactivity in an iPad Presentation

Figure 44 *Web Content options on the Folio Overlays panel*

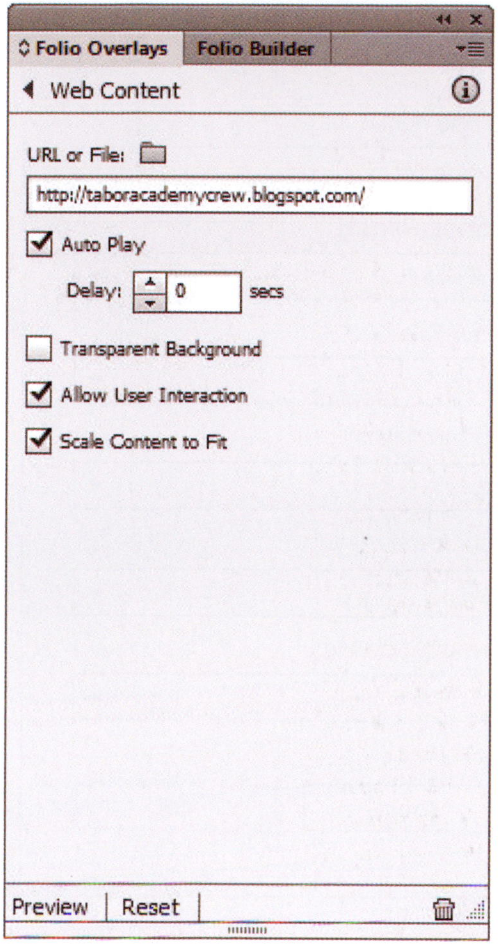

Source Adobe® InDesign®, 2013.

Use the Web Content option on the Folio Overlays panel

1. Open ID 7-05.indd, click **Update Links**, then save it as **Article 05**.
2. Verify that you're on the iPad V layout.
3. Select the **large white frame** on the page.
4. On the Folio Overlays panel, click **Web Content**.
5. Type **http://taboracademycrew.blogspot.com/** in the URL or File text box.
6. Click the **Auto Play check box**.
7. Verify that the **Allow User Interaction check box** is checked.
8. Click the **Scale Content to Fit check box**.

   Your Folio Overlays panel should resemble Figure 44.

(continued)

9. Switch to the iPad H layout, then select the **large white frame**.

10. Repeat Steps 4-8.

11. Save your work.

12. On the Folio Builder panel, click **Add**.

    The New Article dialog box opens.

13. Enter the settings shown in Figure 45, then click **OK**.

14. After the new article uploads, update the Tabor Waterfront folio on your iPad.

(continued)

Figure 45 *Settings for Article 05*

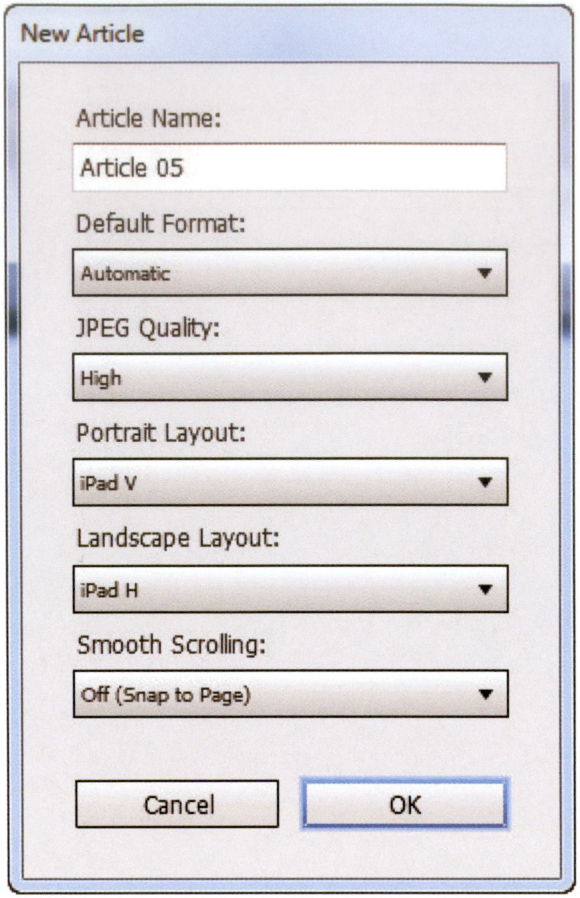

Source Adobe® InDesign®, 2013.

Creating Complex Interactivity in an iPad Presentation

Figure 46 *Viewing the website in the frame*

Image courtesy of Tabor Academy. Source Adobe® InDesign®, 2013.

15. View the folio and go to Article 05.

As shown in Figure 46, the website automatically appears in the frame and is interactive.

16. Return to InDesign, save your work, then close Article 05.indd.

You linked the frame on the horizontal and vertical layouts to the same URL. When you viewed the article on your iPad, the website opened in the frames.

You're asked to create a layout for the iPad that contains scrollable text in a scrollable frame. When you meet with your client, you realize that the project will provide you with an added challenge: he wants you to format the page so that the text scrolls over an image. This will require you to do an extra trick in Photoshop so that the "text" image is placed in the InDesign layout with a transparent background.

1. Open ID 7-06.indd, then save it as **Article 06**.
2. Verify that you are viewing the iPad V layout, then select the text frame that contains the white body copy.

   The text frame has a None fill and stroke, so it is transparent. Behind the frame is a second frame (locked) filled with a semi-transparent black. This second frame is there only to darken the image behind the white text.
3. Note the width and height of the selected text frame.

   The width of the text frame is 334 pixels and the height is just over 370 pixels. The text frame contains overset text; there's more text than can fit in the frame.

4. Open the Paragraph Styles panel, double-click the White Copy style, then note in the dialog box how it has been formatted.

   The White Copy paragraph style is Font=Arial; Font Size = 16pt; Leading = 21pt; Alignment = Justified; Space After = 7px; Color = White.
5. Close the Paragraph Styles dialog box, click the Type tool, then click the cursor anywhere in the white text.
6. Enter [Ctrl][A] (Win) or [⌘][A] (Mac) to select all, click the Edit menu, then click Cut.
7. Switch to Photoshop, click the File menu, then click New.
8. Type **Vertical Transparent BKG Text** in the Name text box, enter **334** in the Width text box, then enter **1000** in the Height text box.
9. Click OK, then verify that you can see the entire canvas in the window.
10. Fill the Background layer with black.
11. Click the Type tool, then create a text box that is exactly the same size as the canvas.
12. Click the Edit menu, then click Paste.

    Your canvas should resemble Figure 47
13. Select all the text.

Figure 47 *White text pasted into the Photoshop file*

Source Adobe® InDesign®, 2013.

Creating Complex Interactivity in an iPad Presentation

14. Open the Character and Paragraph panels, then format the text as it was formatted in InDesign.

    Refer back to Step 4 for the formatting. Note that in Photoshop, text color is applied in the Character panel.

15. When you're done formatting, deselect, then compare your canvas to Figure 48.

16. Click the eye button on the Background layer to hide the Background layer.

17. Click the File menu, click Save As, then save the file in the Photoshop (.psd) format as **Vertical Transparent BKG Text**.

18. Return to InDesign, click the Selection tool, then select the text frame.

19. Convert the text frame to a graphic frame.

20. Place Vertical Transparent BKG Text.psd into the graphic frame.

21. On the Control panel, verify that the top left reference point is selected, as shown in this icon .

22. Click the Fitting command, then click Fill Frame Proportionally.

23. Double-click the image so that the image is selected and the X/Y coordinates in the Control panel read X+ and Y+.

Figure 48 *Text formatted in the Photoshop file*

Source Adobe® InDesign®, 2013.

24. Verify that the X+ text box in the Control panel reads 0 px, enter **0** in the Y text box, then press [Enter] (Win) or [return] (Mac).
25. Deselect all.
26. Select the text frame again, open the Folio Overlays panel, then click Scrollable Frame.
27. Click the Scroll Direction list arrow, then choose Vertical.

28. Click to activate the Hide option under Scroll Indicators.
29. Save Article 06.
30. In the Folio Builder panel, add Article 06 to the Tabor Waterfront folio.
31. When Article 06 is uploaded, update the Tabor Waterfront folio on your iPad.
32. Hold your iPad in portrait orientation, then go to Article 06.

33. Finger swipe vertically to scroll the text in the frame.

    As shown in Figure 49, the background image is visible behind the scrollable frame.
34. For further experience, repeat the entire exercise on the horizontal layout.
35. Return to InDesign, save Article 06, then close the document.

Creating Complex Interactivity in an iPad Presentation

Figure 49 *Scrollable text in a scrollable frame with a transparent background*

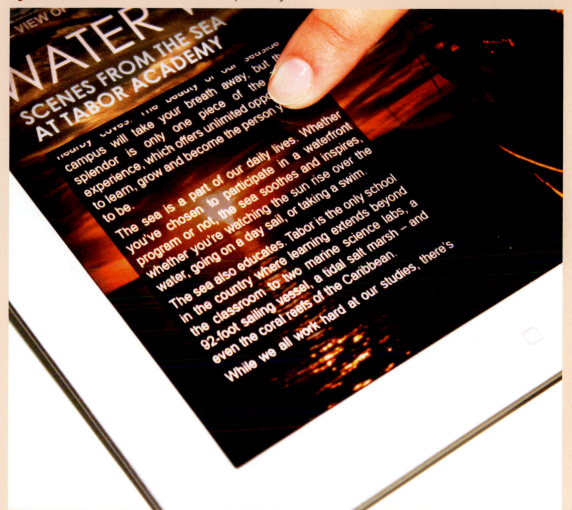

Image courtesy of Tabor Academy. Source Adobe® InDesign®, 2013.

CHAPTER 8 CREATING AN APP AND PUBLISHING TO THE IPAD

1. Explore apps and iPad publishing.

2. Explore the Digital Publishing Suite.

3. Making the leap from InDesign to the App Store.

4. Submitting your app to the App Store.

CHAPTER 8 CREATING AN APP AND PUBLISHING TO THE IPAD

Up to this point in this book, you've been uploading layouts to the iPad and viewing them through the Adobe Content Viewer application. You can think of this as a "local" view of the layout. It's not published, and it's not accessible to anyone other than you.

In this chapter, we're going to explore the world of Adobe's Digital Publishing Suite and creating an app on the iPad App Store. With an app, you can make your documents available on the iPad and publish, quite literally, to the world.

This is a new frontier. The iPad itself is new on the scene, and the system for users to publish to the iPad is in its infancy. It's stunning to think of how well it works already, and we're only in the beginning stages. That being said, this is an evolving process, one that will be upgraded and changed regularly over the next couple of years.

With that in mind, we are not going to give you a step-by-step walk-through of the tablet publishing procedure as it stands today, because we know those steps may change as soon as tomorrow. Instead, we're going to give you an overview of the process, identify the main stages, and give you a solid understanding of how this is all set up to work.

To streamline the discussion, we're going to use Apple's iPad as the tablet device we're publishing to, but you can extrapolate these examples to include other tablet devices.

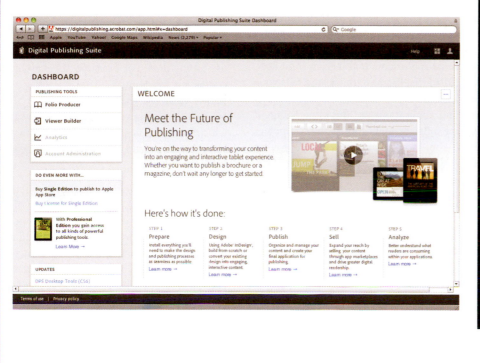

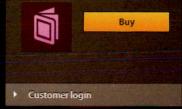

Source Adobe®, Digital Publishing Suite®, 2013.

Explore Apps And
IPAD PUBLISHING

What You'll Do

Source Apple®, 2013.

 In this lesson, you will examine what an app is and consider concepts in iPad publishing.

Defining Apps

Apps are programs that run on the iPad. App is short for application, but the term *app* has taken on an identity of its own. Photoshop is a traditional application, but Shazam is an app on the iPad that listens to music and tells you the song title and who sings it. Technically, apps and applications are the same thing—both are software applications for a computer device—but when you say "app," you're talking about software that runs on a tablet or a smart phone.

The app is central to the iPad. Everything that you do on an iPad, indeed everything the iPad itself does, is based on apps. Without apps, the iPad would be nothing more than a hand-held web browser.

The iPad comes equipped with default apps, like maps, the camera, and a clock. To add additional functionality, you can download and purchase other apps from the App Store

on the iPad. Figure 1 shows a search in the App Store.

All kinds of businesses—including web businesses—are creating apps for you to use on the iPad. For example, the App Store contains a free download for the eBay app. Rather than use the browser on your iPad to go to eBay.com, you can use the eBay app, which has been customized to give you the eBay experience on your iPad, as shown in Figure 2.

It's interesting to consider the distinction between using the browser on your iPad to go to a website vs. using an app to go to the same entity. For example, you could use the browser to go to BankofAmerica.com, or you could download the Bank of America app. Both routes will allow you to access your banking account, so what's the difference?

The difference is that the Bank of America website was designed for a traditional computer or laptop. That's a different delivery system than a tablet device like the iPad. So you can think of apps as giving you access to an online entity in a way that has been customized for the tablet experience.

About Apps and Publishing

You can't really say that eBay or Bank of America is "publishing" to the iPad, even though they do have apps. Essentially, both companies are giving you their website experience through an app; it's just a customized way of surfing their sites.

The role of an app is clarified and becomes more interesting when you consider publications that are distributed via apps on the iPad.

Figure 1 *Shopping for apps in the App Store*

Source Apple®, 2013.

Figure 2 *eBay app on the iPad*

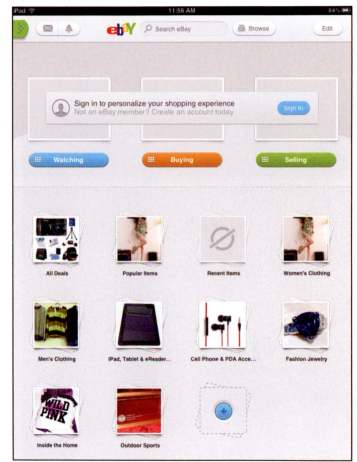

Source Apple®, 2013.

Figure 3 shows the thumbnail for *Time* magazine's app on the iPad, and Figure 4 shows the library of issues available to subscribers for download. When you open an issue on the iPad, the experience is like having a digital magazine in your hands. You can read articles, turn pages, see advertisements, and so on.

Take a moment to consider how revolutionary this is. Up until the advent of the iPad and tablet devices, *Time* magazine had a website and could therefore be accessed digitally via a computer, but consider how much that website was not the same experience as reading *Time* magazine. The articles on the website, in long scrolling HTML pages, sure didn't look like a magazine. And even though an article on the website might have been word-for-word the same as the article printed in the magazine, you didn't lay on your couch reading the website, looking at traditional magazine page layouts, turning pages, and seeing full-page advertisements.

Figure 3 *TIME magazine app icon*

Source Apple®, 2013.

Figure 4 *TIME magazine library*

Source Apple®, 2013.

That is what makes the iPad the publishing revolution that a website never was. The fact that the iPad can deliver a traditional magazine- or book-reading experience is both subtle and profound. It's a new publishing paradigm, and the immense power of this new delivery system is that it's the first to successfully mimic all of the comfort and familiarity of the traditional paradigm.

iPad Publishing and the Individual

The other big part of the iPad revolution is the transformation in who is doing the publishing. If the App Store is a vast marketplace where anyone in the world can purchase an app, and if anyone in the world can create an app and publish to it, then anyone in the world can self-publish—to the whole world!

For a representative case in this discussion, we are going to use Tabor Academy, the school where Chris teaches and where Dylan is a student.

Tabor Academy is a boarding high school in Marion, Massachusetts. Approximately 500 students attend the school. Some are local and some come to the school from as far away as China, Korea, and Thailand.

Like any school, Tabor generates a great number of publications. Every year, the school produces a brochure, a course of studies manual, a student handbook, and a photography-based "look book." Less from a marketing perspective and more from a practical one, Tabor generates a number of forms for parents of students to sign:

healthcare forms, school banking forms, sports waivers, dormitory Internet access forms, and so forth.

In addition to all of this, students produce their own publications. Every month a new issue of *The Log,* the school newspaper, is published. Then, at graduation, the full-color yearbook is distributed, and the Art department prints *The Bowspirit*—a portfolio of all the artwork the students have produced in the school year.

Think of all those publications, and then consider that Tabor Academy is not a publisher. If you define the traditional view of "publisher" as an entity in business to manufacture and distribute readable materials, Tabor Academy does not fall into that category. Instead, Tabor must outsource these functions. Tabor hires a design agency to produce marketing materials. Tabor contracts with a printer to produce those designs as printed pieces. Tabor then uses the U.S. Post Office to distribute those printed pieces.

And that's just for the marketing pieces. Internal publications like the student handbook, the school newspaper, and the *Bowspirit* are unlikely to reach a parent in Bangkok or Shanghai or even Chicago, unless a student physically brings them home.

All of this changes when you consider the idea that Tabor can create a Tabor Academy app on the iPad and publish to that venue. From this perspective, the view of the iPad as a powerful one-stop distribution channel becomes clear.

Distribution has always been the element of publishing that no individual or small business could duplicate. But with the iPad, packaging and trucking to magazine outlets and book stores all over the country (or all over the world!) disappears. Instead, the individual or small business can publish to the iPad. Print costs are greatly reduced, if not removed entirely, because this is a digital publication. Publications are uploaded to the indvidual's or small business's app in the App Store, and then the publication can be downloaded and read by anybody with a tablet.

Think of how this could change Tabor Academy's publications. Rather than pay for long print runs, Tabor could instead print a small number of copies in-house for people who visit the campus; all other versions would be digital. Rather than take on the physical labor of packaging mailings and the cost of actually mailing publications, Tabor could upload everything to the Tabor Academy app on the iPad. All of the brochures, handbooks, forms, newspapers, and other student publications could be distributed via the iPad and other tablet devices, available for all of the students and their parents (and even potential students and their parents) to access at any time, from any city or country in the world.

What's the glitch? There's only one: Tabor cannot expect realisitically that all of their students and parents have an iPad or a tablet device. That glitch means that the iPad and tablet devices are not yet widespread enough to become Tabor's sole source of publishing, but that's changing rapidly.

Explore the Digital
PUBLISHING SUITE

What You'll Do

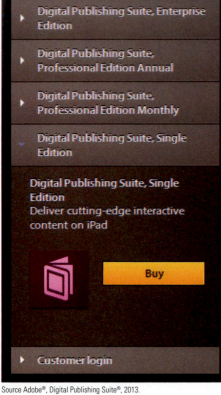

Source Adobe®, Digital Publishing Suite®, 2013.

In this lesson, you will explore the role the Digital Publishing Suite plays in publishing to the iPad.

About the Digital Publishing Suite

InDesign as a publishing platform for the iPad is itself a major part of the digital publishing revolution.

Think of all the apps on your iPad. Most of them are not produced via InDesign or through Adobe at all. Creating and producing apps for the iPad is done through Apple's **iOS Developer Program**. The iOS refers to the operating system for the iPhone and the iPad. Figure 5 shows the iOS Developer member page.

Apple iOS Developers create apps for the iPhone and the iPad. For this discussion, we'll be talking about developing apps for the iPad. Developers create apps for the iPad in a coding language called Objective-C. **Objective-C** is an object-oriented programming language that first appeared in 1983 and which you can think of as an offshoot of the C programming language.

This book is not about computer programming, but what you need to know as a graphic designer is that, unless you can code in Objective-C, you were shut out of creating apps and publishing to the iPad before Adobe introduced the Digitial Publishing Suite.

The Digital Publishing Suite (DPS) is a subscription-based publishing service provided by Adobe to users who want to publish InDesign publications to the iPad. If you're not a coder, or if you can't code in Objective-C, the DPS gets your foot in the door. Objective-C programmers don't use the Digital Publishing Suite. The Digital Publishing Suite is there to help you, the graphic designer, publish to the iPad without having to code.

And that's a big part of the revolution: the barrier to entry has been lifted. We are at a pivotal moment when graphic designers can publish to an Internet-based distribution device without having to code. This moment represents evolution and advancement, and it represents the way of the future. Whereas the graphic designer working in InDesign only a couple of years ago was shut out entirely from designing for the Internet, and whereas layouts that mimicked traditional magazine layouts were also shut out entirely from the Internet, the iPad—through Adobe's DPS—is now a venue to which graphic designers can publish traditional publication layouts and distribute them across the Internet, with no coding required.

If you really think about this, the iPad is re-creating the revolution of the very first Apple Macintosh back in 1984. Not too long ago, computer use was limited to those who could program, because you needed to know a programming language to use a computer. Then, Steve Jobs and Apple introduced the Apple Macintosh with its revolutionary interface of icons and pull-down menus and trash cans. That interface was the middleman between the user and the code, allowing non-programmers to use a computer.

Flash forward to the present day iPad and the Digital Publishing Suite. In many ways the same barrier is being broken again. Since the advent of the Internet as a household entity, only programmers could produce content that could be distributed on the Internet. Today, a graphic designer can use a single layout in InDesign as both a printed piece and an interactive publication on the iPad. A whole new future has opened up.

Figure 5 *Apple's iOS developer page*

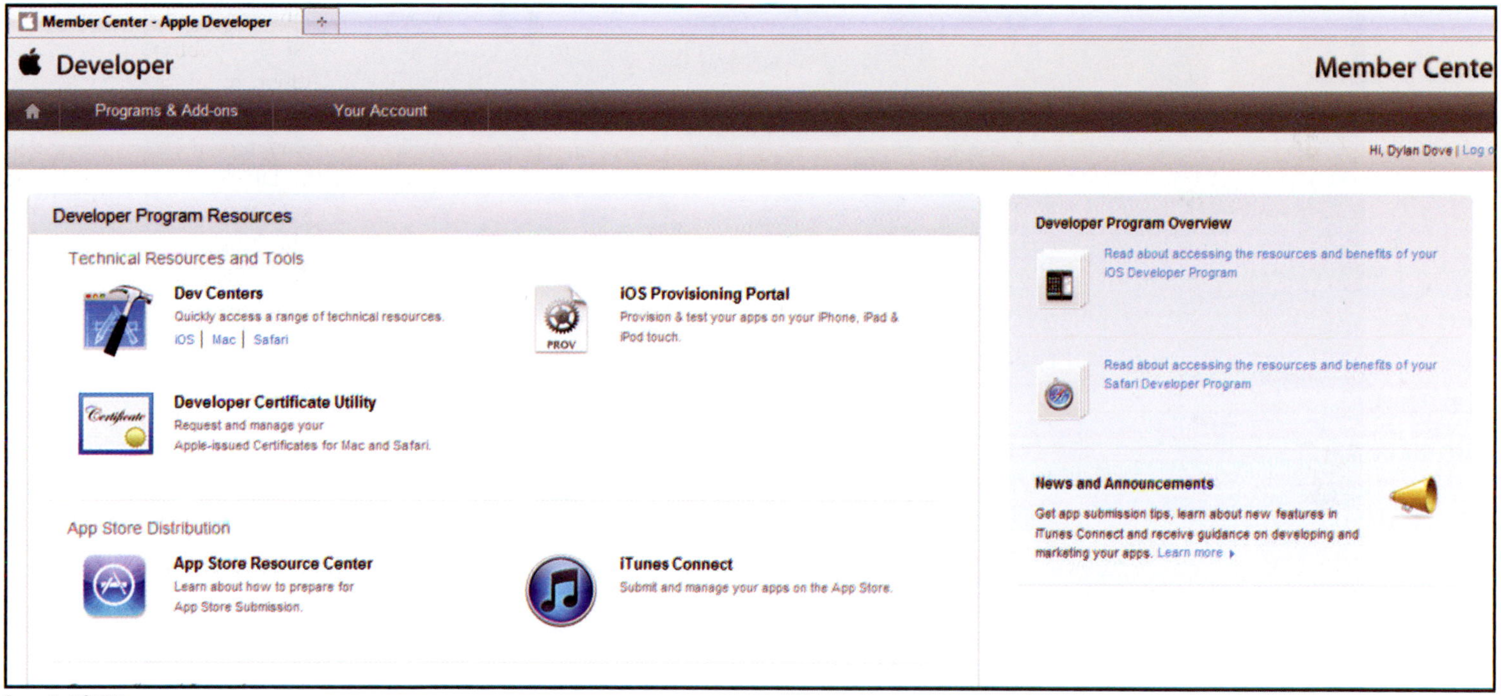

Source Apple®, 2013.

Subscribing to Digital Publishing Suite

Figure 6 shows the Digital Publishing Suite home page on Adobe.com. Digital Publishing Suite offers three different subscription models: Enterprise Edition, Professional Edition, and Single Edition. All editions ultimately lead to the same goal—publishing to the iPad—but each is defined by the scope of a user's publishing goals. How many publications you want to publish, how often you want to update the app and the publications in the app, and how many times the contents of the app will be downloaded are all factors in choosing which edition to subscribe to.

Unless you're the CEO or creative director of a worldwide ad agency or a media conglomerate, the Enterprise Edition is most likely way beyond the scope of your digital publishing goals. The **Enterprise Edition** is designed for major publishers, like Condé Nast and Martha Stewart Living Omnimedia,

Figure 6 *Digital Publishing Suite home page*

Source Adobe®, 2013.

Creating an App and Publishing to the iPad

to incorporate digital publishing as a new distribution channel for their titles. The annual fee for a suscription to the Enterprise Edition of the DPS run in the tens of thousands of dollars.

(All prices quoted in this narrative are quoted at press-time and are likely to change. The DPS—and digital publishing in general—is a brand-new game, and all prices and scenarios quoted in this narrative will almost certainly change and change again. For example, Adobe is already saying that, by the end of 2012, the Single Edition of DPS will be included with a subscription to Creative Cloud, but it's not included as we go to press.)

The **Professional Edition** is designed for mid-size businesses and organizations. With a subscription to the Professional Edition, a school like Tabor Academy can create a Tabor Academy app on the iPad and then upload multiple publications—newspapers, brochures, etc.—to the app. A subscritption to the Professional Edition is close to $6,000 annually, but there's also a monthly à la carte subscription available for $495 per month.

The monthly subscription to the Professional Edition is based on a pay-as-you-go scenario. If a small business or a school like Tabor Academy were able to upload all of their publications for the entire year in the same month, the charge would be $495 for that month. However, after that month passes, if the business wants to update any of the publications or if it wants to add or remove a publication, it will have to pay a second fee of $495.

The idea behind the monthly subscription to the Professional Edition is that a small business can save money by not making changes to the app every month of the year. For example, if a business only makes quarterly changes to the app, the annual subscription fee will be $1,980, a substantial savings compared to the annual subscription cost of $5,940.

Downloads are the one other additional cost that needs to be considered. With the Professional Edition, every time you pay the $495 fee, you get 250 downloads included with that price. After those downloads are used up, you have the choice of paying another $495 for another 250 downloads (and the ability to edit the contents of the app) or purchasing the next tier of downloads, which is 10,000 downloads for $3,000.

$3,000 sounds like a lot of money in this scenario, but you have to consider that, because you're distributing a digital product, you are theoretically saving the cost of printing. Let's say a small business prints a brochure for $10,000 at the cost of $1.00 per copy. If it distributes that brochure to ten thousand people, it assumes the cost of $1.00 per person who gets the brochure. In the DPS scenario, ten thousand downloads for a total of $3,000 is 30 cents per download. Theoretically, the money the business saves in printing is applied to the cost of the downloads.

The **Single Edition** offers a one-time-only upload of a single publication. For example, let's say you're a graphic designer and an illustrator and you create a children's book titled *My Kid's Book*. You could create a single app in the App Store called My Kid's Book and upload the publication to it. The cost for the Single-Edition subscription is $395. The subscription includes unlimited downloads, but your publication will be available only on the iPad, not other tablets like the Droid. And one-time-only means one-time-only: you can't make any changes or add anything else to the app. If, for example, you write a sequel, you'll need to purchase a new app with a Single Edition subscription for another $395. Since both are free-standing apps, you'll be missing the relationship that you want between the two titles—the relationship you can have if the two are in a single library within the app, like you get with the Professional Edition.

Figure 7 shows a comparison of the three editions as a chart from Adobe.com. Note that the first column—*Included with InDesign CS6*—refers to what we've been doing in Chapters 6 and 7 in this book: using Folio Builder, Folio Overlays, and Adobe Content Viewer to upload and preview layouts on the iPad.

Purchasing a Subscription to the Digital Publishing Suite

You might be wondering exactly what you get when you purchase the Digital Publishing Suite. It's not software. It's not something you download and install; it's not something you open on your computer. Essentially when you purchase a subscription to the DPS, you're purchasing access—access to publishing on the iPad.

Figure 7 *Comparing three subscription editions on Adobe.com*

Compare editions Pricing Resellers	Included with Adobe InDesign® CS6	Single Edition	Professional Edition	Enterprise Edition
Design and create an unlimited number of .folio files	●	●	●	●
Preview interactive content on desktop and iPhone, iPad, iPod Touch, Kindle Fire and other Android devices	●		●	●
Preview Interactive content on desktop and iPad	●	●		
Share content with clients and colleagues	●	●	●	●
Sell single-.folio applications through the Apple App Store		●	●	●
Sell multi-.folio applications through the Apple App Store and Amazon Kindle Fire Newsstand payment system — single-issue or subscription purchase			●	●
Sell multi-.folio applications through the Android Marketplace app payment system — single-issue purchase			●	●
Access prebuilt analytic reports			●	●
Integrate with Adobe Digital Marketing Suite (Adobe SiteCatalyst®)			●	●
Customize the Content Viewer user interface				●
Drive merchandising through a customizable HTML store				●
Accelerate readership by providing content access to existing readers and customers through direct entitlement				●
Target high value content to unique customer segments using restricted distribution				●
Efficiently publish private applications behind a corporate firewall				●
Create customized push notifications				●
Get high-volume discounts				●

Source Adobe®, 2013.

Creating an App and Publishing to the iPad

To purchase a subscription, go to Adobe.com, click Products, then click Digital Publishing Suite. Figure 8 shows the current splash page for the DPS as we go to press. There's a description of each edition in the central part of the page, and on the right is information for ordering the edition that you want: Enterprise Edition, Professional Edition Annual, Professional Edition Monthly, and Single Edition.

Note that the product on the right in the figure is the Professional Edition Annual, and you are offered the option of clicking a button to request a consultation and a phone number for contacting a sales agent. You're not able to purchase the Professional Edition Annual without first going through a sales agent.

Figure 8 *Splash page for subscribing to the DPS on Adobe.com*

What is Digital Publishing Suite?

Adobe® Digital Publishing Suite is a complete solution for individual designers, traditional media publishers, ad agencies, and companies of all sizes that want to create, distribute, monetize, and optimize engaging content and publications for tablet devices.

Adobe Digital Publishing Suite, Enterprise Edition
Enterprise Edition offers a customizable solution for enterprise publishers, global corporations, and worldwide ad agencies that want to transform their digital business through lucrative new revenue streams, deeper customer relationships, and cost-efficient tablet publishing.

Adobe Digital Publishing Suite, Professional Edition
Professional Edition is the off-the-shelf tablet digital publishing software solution for midsize traditional media companies, business publishers, and membership organizations. Rapidly create highly designed, immersive content and publish it across leading marketplaces and devices to drive growth through digital publishing.

Adobe Digital Publishing Suite, Single Edition
Single Edition provides small to midsize design studios and freelance designers an intuitive and affordable way to deliver iPad apps such as brochures, portfolios, and highly visual books without writing code or relying on developers. Use familiar Adobe InDesign® CS6 skills to explore your creativity and develop content that inspires and engages.

The future of digital publishing

Individual designers and leading media publishers worldwide are using Digital Publishing Suite to deliver the next generation of tablet content.

Related products

InDesign CS6
Creative Suite® 6 Design Standard
CS6 Design & Web Premium
Adobe SiteCatalyst®

> ▶ Digital Publishing Suite, Enterprise Edition
>
> ▶ Digital Publishing Suite, Professional Edition Annual
>
> **Digital Publishing Suite, Professional Edition Annual**
> Accelerate tablet publishing with a turnkey offering
>
> **Request a consultation**
>
> **Contact a reseller**
> Sales: 877-792-3623
>
> Digital Publishing Suite, Professional Edition Monthly
>
> Digital Publishing Suite, Single Edition
>
> ▶ Customer login

Buying guide: Compare editions | Pricing | Resellers | Visual overview

Source Adobe®, Digital Publishing Suite®, 2013.

Figure 9 shows ordering options for the Professional Edition Monthly and Figure 10 shows ordering options for the Single Edition. Once you order and pay with your credit card, you'll receive a confirmation email followed by a second email that contains a serial number. Save the serial number; you'll use it as verification when you're creating the app.

Registering with Apple as an iOS Developer

iOS is the operating system for products like the iPad and the iPhone. When you want to create apps for the iPad and the iPhone, you must first register with Apple as an iOS developer. This is the very first step in the Apple component of creating an app for the iPad, and it's free.

The Apple iOS Developer website is the central location for all the work you'll do with

Figure 9 *Ordering options for Professional Edition Monthly*

Source Adobe®, Digital Publishing Suite®, 2013.

Figure 10 *Buy button for the Single Edition*

Source Adobe®, Digital Publishing Suite®, 2013.

Creating an App and Publishing to the iPad

Apple in this process. Go to the following web address: **https://developer.apple.com/devcenter/ios/index.action** This will take you to the login page, shown in Figure 11. Click the Register button, click the Get Started button, then log in with your Apple ID. If you don't have an Apple ID, you'll need to create one. This will take you to the Complete your personal profile page, which assigns a Person ID to you and asks you to provide basic information like your address and phone number. Fill out the profile page, then click Continue.

Figure 11   *iOS Developer website*

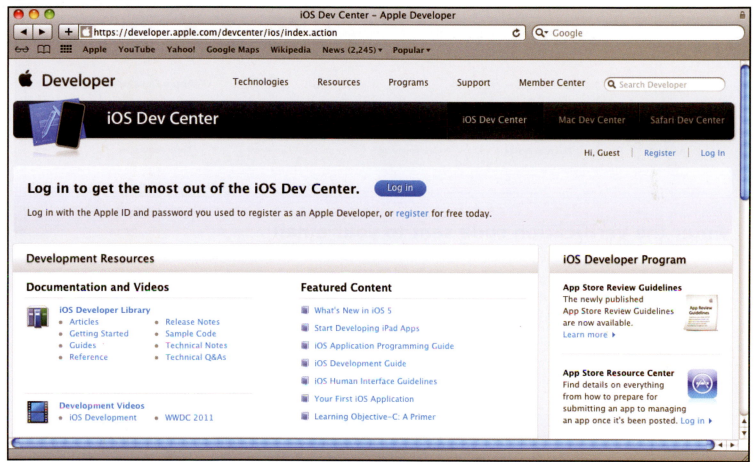

Source Apple®, 2013.

You'll then be asked to complete a short survey about how you use computers. Fill it out, then click Continue. Once you've entered everything, agreed to terms of use, and entered the verification code emailed to you, you'll see the screen shown in Figure 12. This means you've completed the free component required to be an Apple developer. To actually create an app, you have to pay, and we cover that in the next section.

Purchasing an Apple iOS Developer License

Once you've completed your free registration, go to the same web address: **https://developer.apple.com/devcenter/ios/index.action**. Click the

Figure 12 *Confirmation screen*

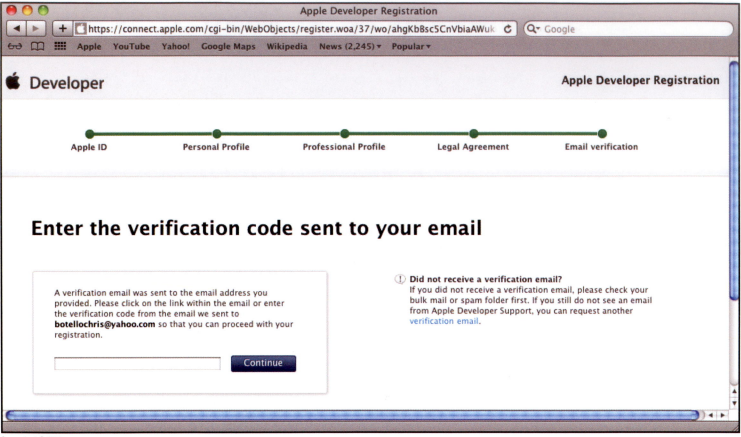

Source Apple®, 2013.

Programs link at the top of the site. This will take you to the Apple Developer Program page. Choose the iOS Developer Program option to go the iOS Developer Program page, shown in Figure 13. Click the Learn more links below the three steps outlined if you'd like to learn more of how Apple describes and packages their iOS development services. When you're ready to pay to purchase a developer license, click the Enroll Now link.

Figure 13 *iOS Developer Program page*

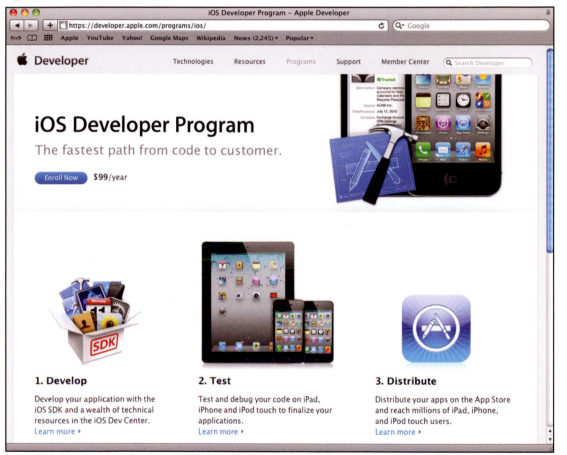

Source Apple®, 2013.

Enrolling involves a series of easy-to-follow steps. When you get to the first screen, choose the option shown in Figure 14, because you have already completed the free registration.

You will be asked to choose to register as an individual or as a company, as shown in

Figure 14 *Identifying your status as an iOS Developer*

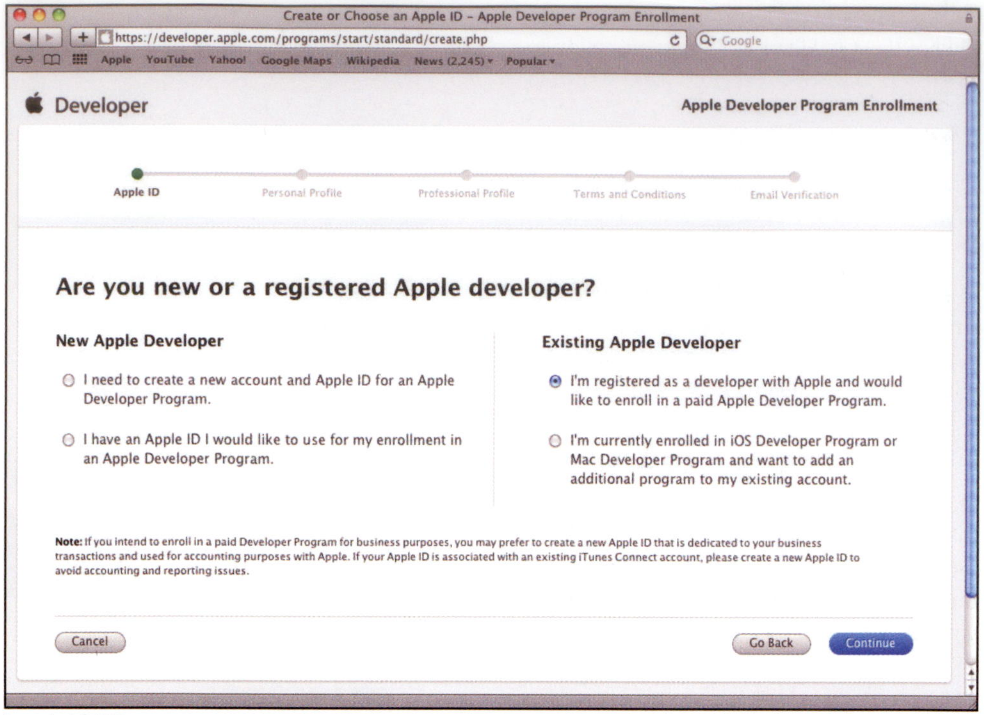

Source Apple®, 2013.

Creating an App and Publishing to the iPad

Figure 15. Note the different terms associated with each choice. For the purposes of this book, we are registering as an individual. When you do so, you'll need to enter your credit card information so that you can be billed the $99 annual fee.

Once you do, you'll be asked to choose which program you want to enroll in; select the iOS Developer Program, as shown in Figure 16.

The actual purchasing of the enrollment is similar to an online retail purchase: you add the $99 subscription to a cart, and this takes you to the checkout page on Apple's online store page. Follow the standard procedure for purchasing online.

Once you've placed your order, you'll need to wait up to 24 hours to receive the login information you will use when logging in to the iOS Development portal and developing your apps.

Figure 15 *Different terms for enrolling as an individual or as a company/organization*

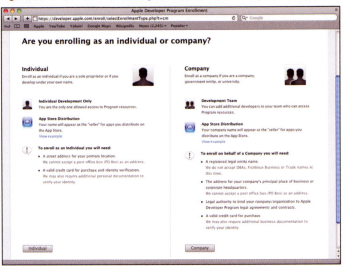

Source Apple®, 2013.

Figure 16 *Choosing the program you're enrolling in*

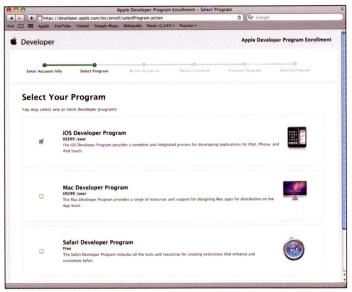

Source Apple®, 2013.

Obtaining Your iOS Development Certificate and Downloading Provisioning Documentation

Before you start creating apps and uploading them to the App Store, Apple wants to know who you are, what app you're creating, and the specific device you're creating it on. When you think about it, this only makes sense: you're putting an app on their distribution network, an app that anyone can access. You can be sure that they want to know who they're doing business with.

It's important to remember that using the Digital Publishing Suite is a new method for creating an app on the App Store. The traditional method developers use is to code in Objective-C within Apple's coding environment, which is called X-Code. Using Adobe's Digital Publishing Suite, you're bypassing many of the traditional steps in the process—in fact, the DPS is creating a "front-end" interface to help you, the non-programmer, get through the process. But the one aspect of the process you can't do through Adobe—the thing you need to do through Apple's iOS Developer website—is obtain your identification documentation.

Before you can upload an app, you must first obtain identifcation documentation known as certificates and provisioning files. The four specific files you need are:

- Distribution P12 certificate
- Distribution mobileprovision file
- Developer P12 certificate
- Developer mobileprovision file

Certificates and provisioning files are electronic documents that you request and download from Apple. They associate your digital identity with the basic information about you and the devices you are creating apps for—like the iPad or the iPhone. You can think of these documents as being an electronic method for verifying your identity.

As an enrolled iOS developer, you have access to the support pages on the iOS Developer website. Figure 17 shows the Provisioning Portal page on the iOS Developer website. Note the Portal Resources and How-To's section in the upper-right corner of the page. These documents will step you through the process of requesting certificates and provisioning files.

Figure 17 *iOS Provisioning Portal page*

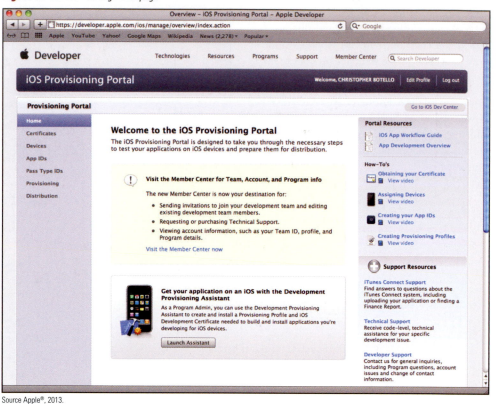

Source Apple®, 2013.

Creating an App and Publishing to the iPad

The process is a bit lengthy and convoluted. See the sidebar, "Using Tech Supports to Create and Convert Apple Certificates."

In addition to these resources, you can click the Launch Assistant button, which is a step-by-step guide for creating and downloading the necessary documentation.

Finally, as a paid iOS developer, you have access to both Apple's and Adobe's crackerjack tech support team to help you if you get stuck in the process or just have questions. Remember, however, that Apple's tech support team does not support anything involving Adobe's DPS, so you're best off using Adobe to help you navigate the process.

Using Tech Support to Create and Convert Apple Certificates

Downloading the required documentation from Apple—certificates and provisioning files—is by far the trickiest sequence in the process. It's a multi-step procedure just to download the files that you need and then the DPS requires that you convert the downloaded documentation to a version of the file that the DPS will work with. We suggest you let the experts do the work. Once you've purchased the Single Edition of the DPS, you have access to Adobe's DPS technical support team. When you call, be sure to ask for the DPS technical support queue specifically.

We suggest you first watch the help videos and try out the Assistant on the Apple iOS Provisioning page. If you feel like you understand the challenge, create your certificate and download your provisioning files. If you don't feel up to the challenge—and it is a challenge—call Adobe tech support and ask for help to get the files that you need. Adobe tech support will help you navigate the Apple iOS Provisioning page.

In any case, once you've downloaded the Apple documentation, you're faced with the challenge of having to convert the Apple documentation to a version the DPS will access. We highly recommend that—even if you downloaded the Apple documentation yourself—let Adobe tech support step you through the process of converting it for the DPS.

Making the Leap from InDesign
TO THE APP STORE

What You'll Do

Source Apple®, 2013.

In this lesson, you will explore the milestones involved in creating an app and injecting your folio into that app.

Exporting a Folio

Once you've created a folio in InDesign, exporting it through the Digital Publishing Suite interface is the first step to publishing it. Before actually exporting it, it's important that you understand what exporting a folio means.

When you're building the folio in the Folio Builder panel—like we did in Chapters 6 and 7—the folio is being created online in your free Adobe account, and when you add articles, those articles are added online as well. So you can think of your folio and its contents as existing not in InDesign and not on your computer, but online in your Adobe account.

When you export your folio online at the Digital Publishing Suite dashboard, all of the elements that make up the folio—the cover images, the articles and the folio itself—are collected and packaged into a .zip file, which you save to your computer. So, in a nutshell, exporting a folio really means taking an online publication, collecting it, and packaging it as a .zip file that is saved locally to your computer.

In this chapter, we're going to export a folio named TA APP Presentation. It is the same folio you created in Chapter 7 with all the folio overlays you applied. It's just been renamed for this chapter and for the app we're creating.

To export the folio, in your web browser, go to **digitalpublishing.acrobat.com**. This takes you to the top page of the Digital Publishing Suite website. Click the Get Started button, sign in with your Adobe ID and password, and this will take you to the Digital Publishing Suite Dashboard page, shown in Figure 18.

You can think of the DPS Dashboard as the control panel for the process of publishing to the iPad.

Note the four publishing tools listed at the top-left corner. (If you've purchased the Single Edition, the top two will be selectable; if you haven't, only the top choice is selectable.) Click Folio Producer to spawn the DPS Folio Producer Organizer page. This page always shows all the folios you've created in the Folio Builder panel in InDesign. Remember, the term *Folio Producer* is just another way of saying "export a folio."

Figure 18 *DPS Dashboard page*

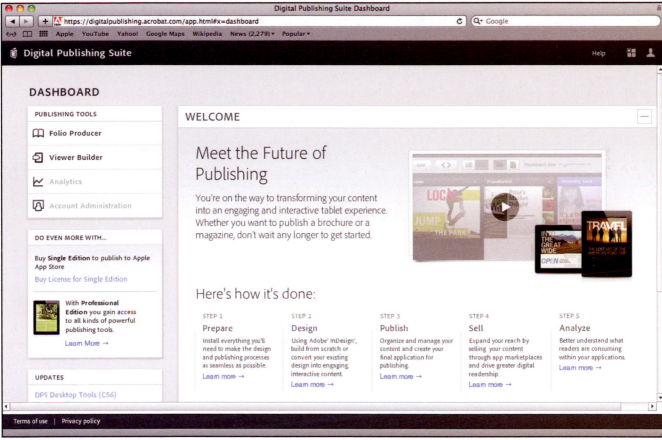

Source Adobe®, Digital Publishing Suite®, 2013.

Figure 19 shows the DPS Folio Producer Organizer page with information we entered to publish the TA APP Presentation folio we created in Chapter 7. We entered TA Waterfront Scenes as the Publication Name.

Every folio you publish must have a number, so we gave this one 100.

Note that in the right column, we have placed both the vertical and horizontal cover images

we created in Chapter 7. All of the fields with an asterisk must have content, so don't forget to enter a description in the field below the cover images.

Figure 19 .DPS Folio Producer Organizer page

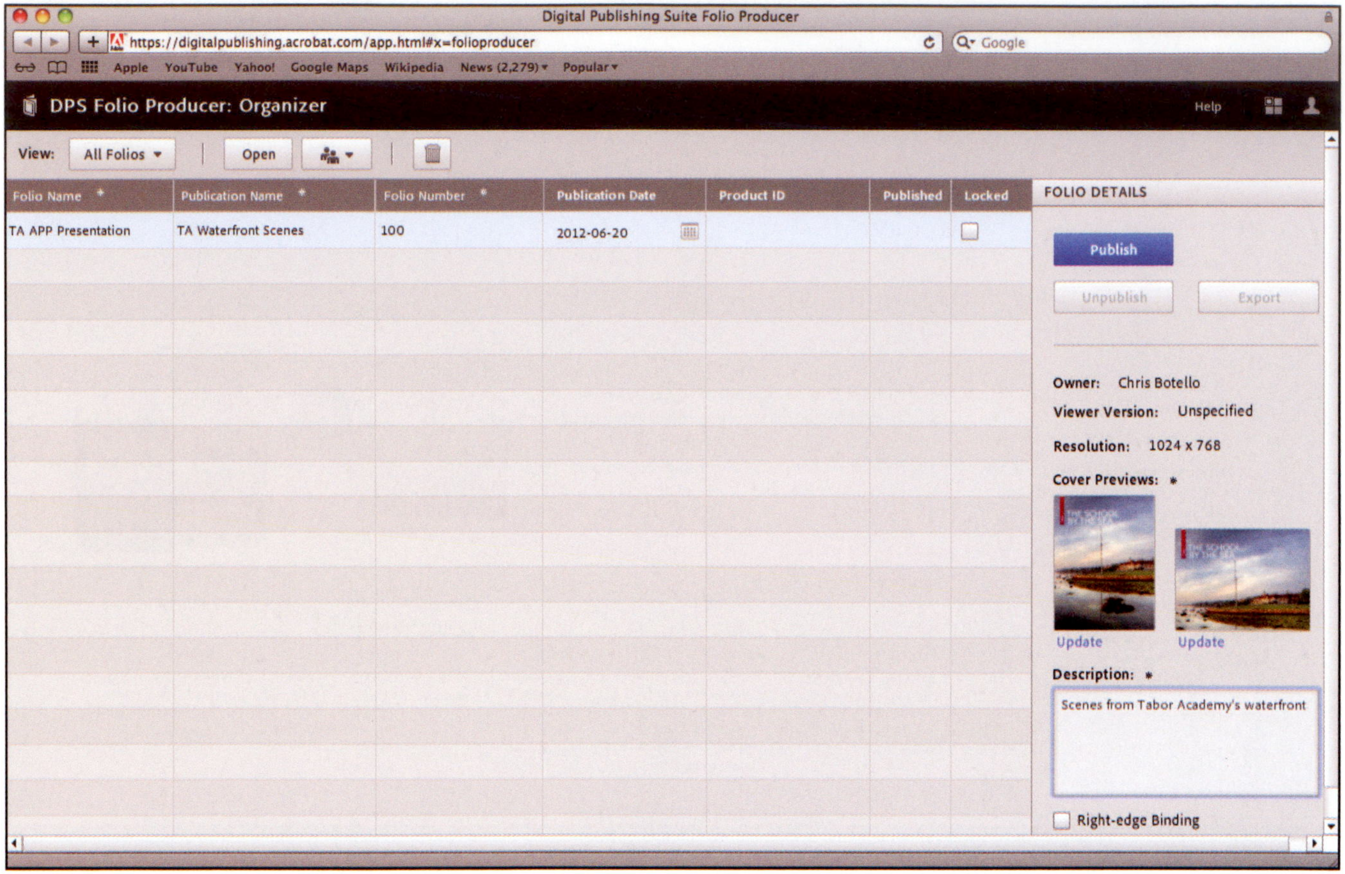

Image courtesy of Tabor Academy. Source Adobe®, Digital Publishing Suite®, 2013.

Once you input your info, click the Publish button at the top of the right column. When you do so, the Publish Folio window appears. Choose Private, Free then enter your product ID as follows: com.yourname. publiction name. For ours we entered com .chrisbotello.tawaterfrontscenes.

When you click the Publish button in the Publish Folio window, all of the elements of the folio are downloaded and collected. This can take a few moments. When the folio is published, a check mark appears in the Published column and the Export button

becomes available, as shown in Figure 20. Click it, and you will be asked to save a .zip file to your computer. This means that the folio and all its elements now exist locally as a .zip file on your computer.

Figure 20 *Exporting the published folio*

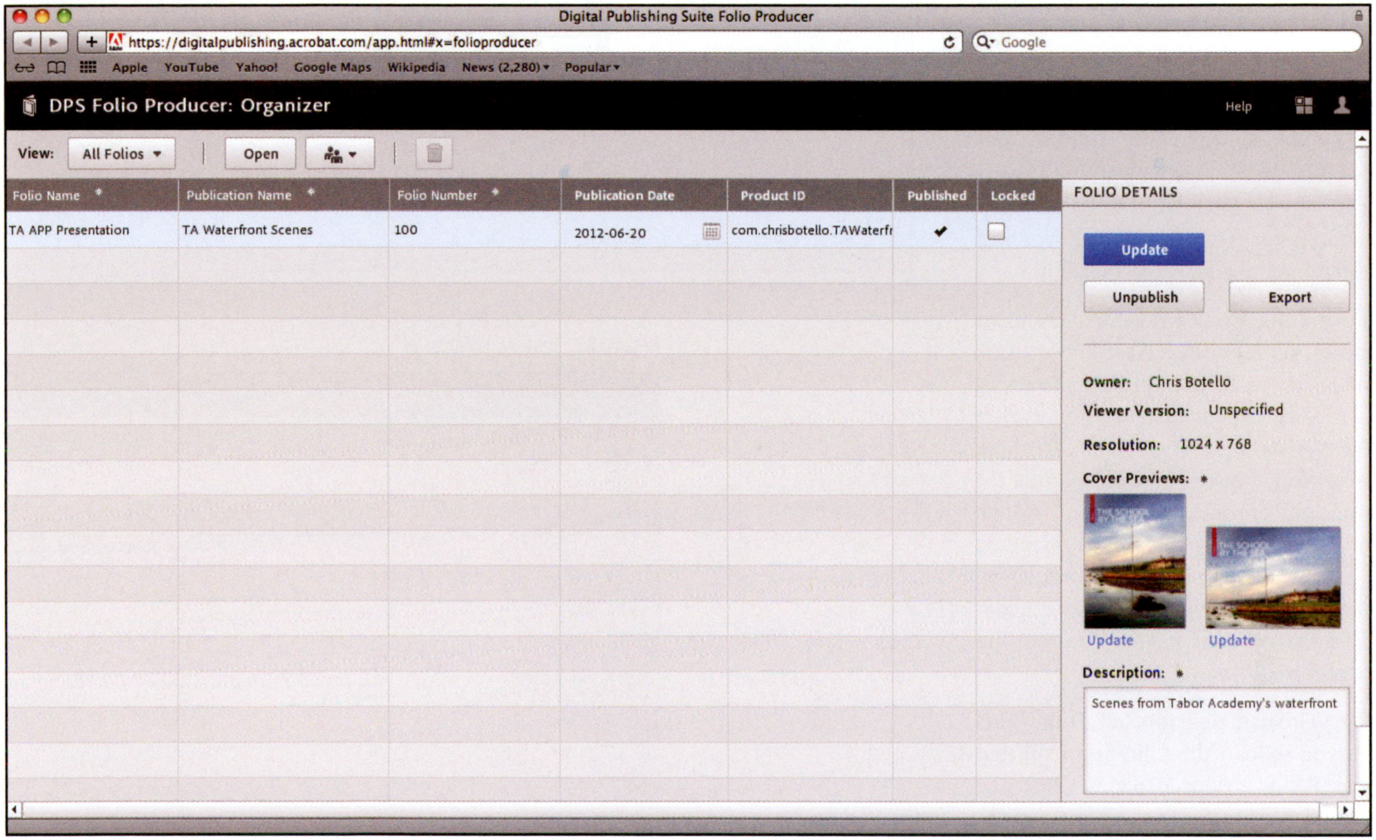

Image courtesy of Tabor Academy. Source Adobe®, Digital Publishing Suite®, 2013.

Using the Viewer Builder Module

After you've published the folio and it exists as a .zip file on your computer, you use the Viewer Builder module on the DPS Dashboard page to package the app. Viewer Builder is the DPS's interface that steps you through this procedure. You can think of this step of the process as creating the actual package for the app into which you'll inject the folio that you published.

Go to the DPS Dashboard page, then click Viewer Builder (note that at press time, Viewer Builder is Mac-only softare—you can't do this on a Windows PC). Viewer Builder is software that needs to be installed on your computer. If it's not installed, you will be prompted to download and install it.

The Viewer Builder welcome screen is shown in Figure 21. Click Create a New Viewer. This opens the Viewer Builder portal, shown in Figure 22. Note the four categories on the left side. The Viewer Builder portal, with these four categories, is a step-by-step module for packaging and producing your app. Adobe has gone to great lengths to make this window as user-friendly as possible. Note that if you position your cursor over an info (i) icon, information is available to you for inputting the data required.

Note the field named Exported Folio. This is where you upload the folio you exported from the Folio Producer page. Click the

Figure 21 *Viewer Builder welcome screen*

Source Adobe®, Digital Publishing Suite®, 2013.

Figure 22 *Viewer Builder portal*

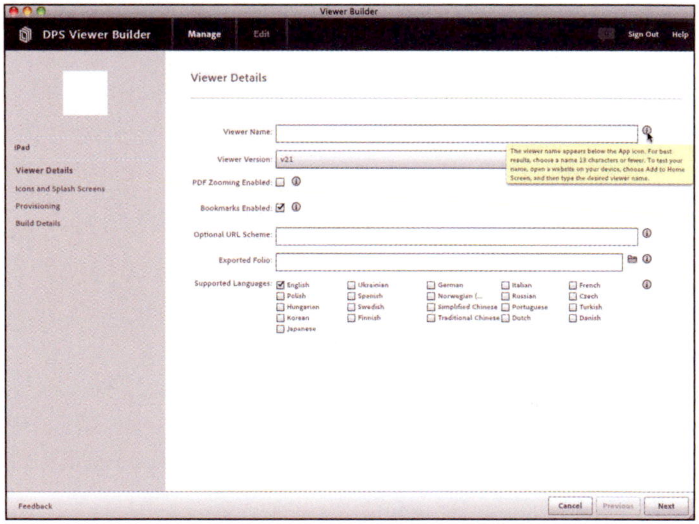

Source Adobe®, Digital Publishing Suite®, 2013.

Creating an App and Publishing to the iPad

folder icon, navigate to where you saved your exported .zip file, then click Select. The path to the file is loaded into the field, as shown in Figure 23.

Click the Next button to go to the Icons and Splash Screens portal, shown in Figure 24. An app in the App Store has many icons associated with it for different screens on which the app may appear. Depending on the screen, the icon will be larger or smaller. Three required sizes and an optional size are listed: 29×29; 50×50; 72×72; and the optional 512×512. All dimensions are in pixels, and the info (i) button beside each lists where the specific icon will be used on the iPad.

Create your icons in Photoshop. The files should be 300ppi in the RGB color mode saved as flattened, high-quality PNG files.

In addition to the icons, you need to create 1024×768 splash screens in both landscape and portrait orientations. This is the same size as the cover images that you created in Chapter 7. Note the difference. The cover images are the thumbnail icons of the app and the full-size cover image when it's launched. When you launch the app, there's a delay during which time the cover image changes to

Figure 23 *Loading the path to the published folio file*

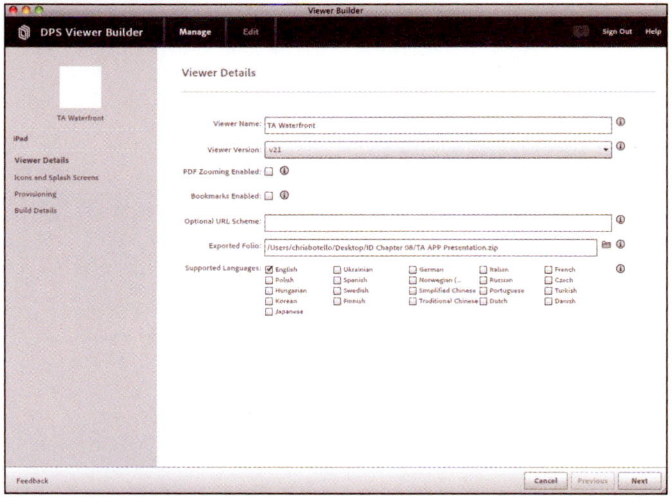

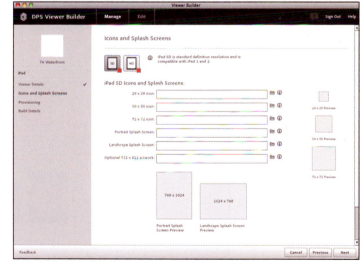

Source Adobe®, Digital Publishing Suite®, 2013.

Figure 24 *Icons and Splash Screens page in the Viewer Builder portal*

Source Adobe®, Digital Publishing Suite®, 2013.

the splash screen image. For that reason, you want the splash screen image to be different from the cover image, so that your user sees the change and knows the app is launching.

All of these images are specified for standard definition resolution on the iPad, and the SD icon should be clicked at the top of the window.

Figure 25 shows the four icons and the two splash screens we created for the TA app. Figure 26 shows those icons loaded into the Viewer Builder window. Note that the color on the SD icon at the top has changed from red to green, indicating that the icons and splash screens for the SD resolution are complete.

Figure 25 *Four icons and two splash screens for the app*

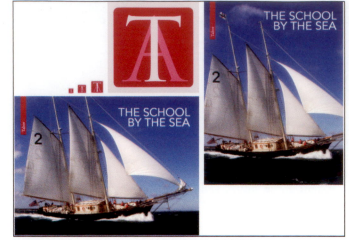

Image courtesy of Tabor Academy. Source Adobe®, Digital Publishing Suite®, 2013.

Figure 26 *Icons and screens loaded into the Viewer Builder portal*

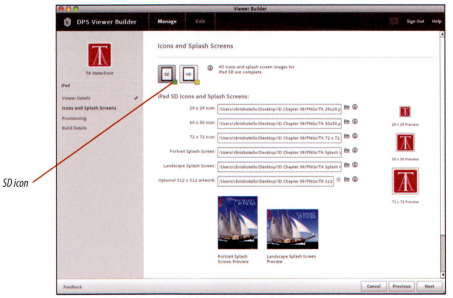

SD icon

Image courtesy of Tabor Academy. Source Adobe®, Digital Publishing Suite®, 2013.

Creating an App and Publishing to the iPad

Click Next to go to the Provisioning page. This is where you load the provisioning documents that you requested and were delivered through the Apple's iOS Provisioning portal page. Figure 27 shows both fields with navigation paths to the documents on the computer.

Click the Next button to go to the last page, Build Details, shown in Figure 28. Click the Submit Build button. It may take a few

Figure 27 *Provisioning page linking to the two provisioning documents*

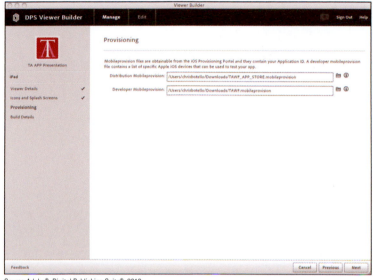

Source Adobe®, Digital Publishing Suite®, 2013.

Figure 28 *Build Details page*

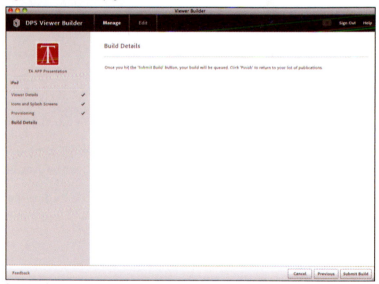

Source Adobe®, Digital Publishing Suite®, 2013.

minutes for the build to queue. When it does, the Submit Build button will change to a Finish button.

Click the Finish button. This will take you to the Viewer Builder app status page, shown in Figure 29. Click the Activate link in the

App Status column. The Activate dialog box appears, as shown in Figure 30. Enter the serial number that you received via

Figure 29 *Viewer Builder App Status page*

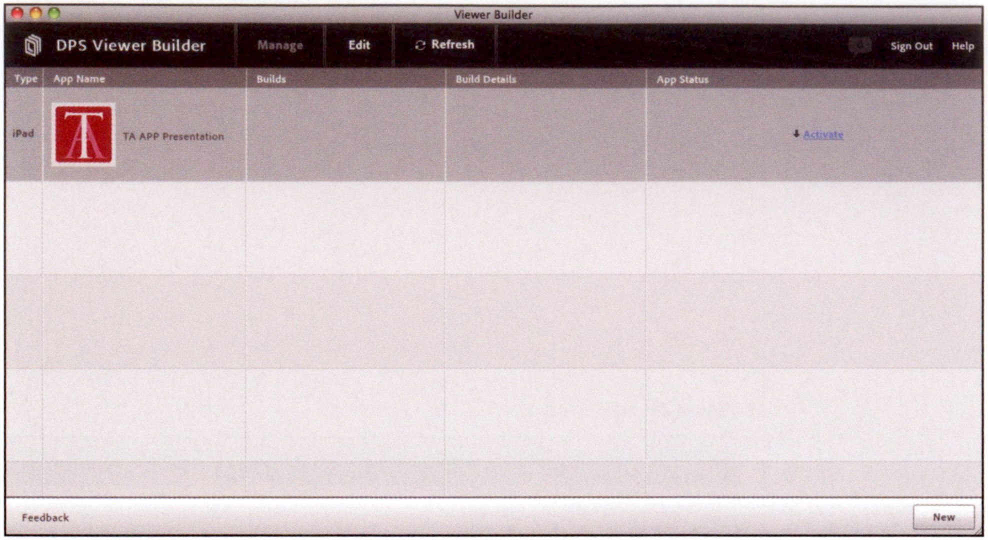

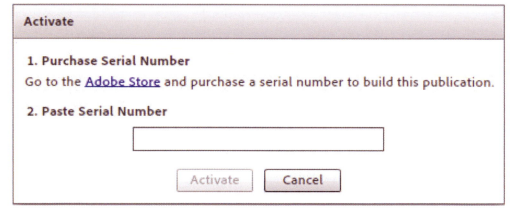

Source Adobe®, Digital Publishing Suite®, 2013.

Figure 30 *Activate dialog box*

Source Adobe®, Digital Publishing Suite®, 2013.

email when you purchased the DPS Single Edition, then click Activate. Once activated, the empty fields will populate as shown in Figure 31.

Testing the App

Before you submit the app to the Apple App Store, test it on your iPad. To do so, you must download the Developer Viewer (.ipa) file from the App Status page to your desktop. Click the Developer Viewer (.ipa) link in the Builds column. This will open the Signing dialog box shown in Figure 32. Link to the

Figure 31 *App Status with fields populated*

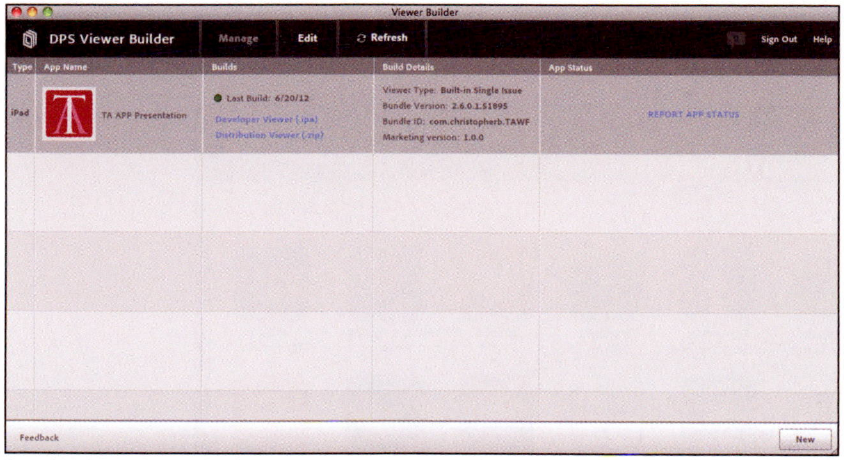

Source Adobe®, Digital Publishing Suite®, 2013.

Figure 32 *Signing dialog box*

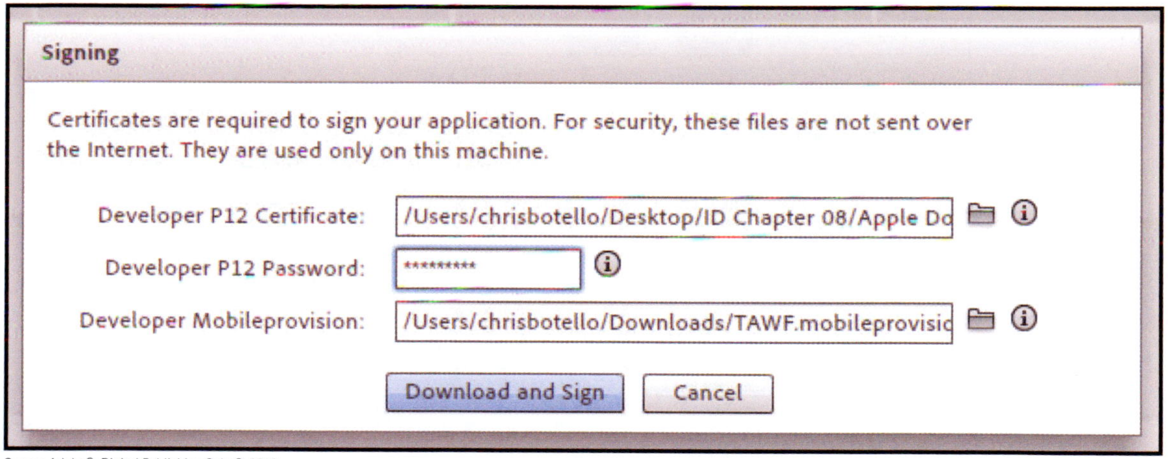

Source Adobe®, Digital Publishing Suite®, 2013.

P12 Developer certificate you downloaded from the Apple iOS Provisioning portal site and converted, enter the password associated with the certificate file, then click Download and Sign. Once downloaded, a file named Developer Viewer.ipa will appear on your desktop. This is the file you will use for testing.

QUICK **TIP**

The P12 Developer file you link to must be the file converted for use by the DPS. You can go to **http://help.adobe.com/en_US/as3/ iphone/WS144092a96ffef7cc-371badff126abc17b1f-7fff. html**, which will take you to the Adobe Help site and specific steps for solving the problem, but we recommend that you contact Adobe DPS tech support to convert the P12 document. See the sidebar in this chapter titled "Using Tech Support to Create and Convert Apple Certificates."

To test the Developer Viewer.ipa file, open iTunes and drag the .ipa file into the Library section of the window. Your app will be added to the Apps section, as shown in Figure 33. Connect your iPad, then sync it. You will see the icon on your iPad, as shown in Figure 34.

Figure 33 *TA app in iTunes*

Source Apple®, 2013.

Figure 34 *TA app on the iPad*

Source Apple®, 2013.

Submitting Your App to
THE APP STORE

What You'll Do

Source Adobe®, Digital Publishing Suite®, 2013.

▶ *In this lesson, you will download your App from Viewer Builder then submit it to the App Store.*

Downloading Your App from Viewer Builder

The Distribution Viewer (.zip) file listed in the Viewer Builder App Status window shown in Figure 35 is your complete and packaged app—the file you'll submit to the App Store. The first step in doing so is to download the .zip file from Viewer Builder to your desktop.

Click Distribution Viewer (.zip) in the App Status window. This opens the Signing dialog box, shown in Figure 36. Enter the Distribution certificate you downloaded and converted, enter your password, then click Download and Sign. A file named Distribution Viewer. zip will appear on your desktop.

Congratulations! You've successfully completed the Digital Publishing Suite process.

Figure 35 *Viewer Builder App Status window*

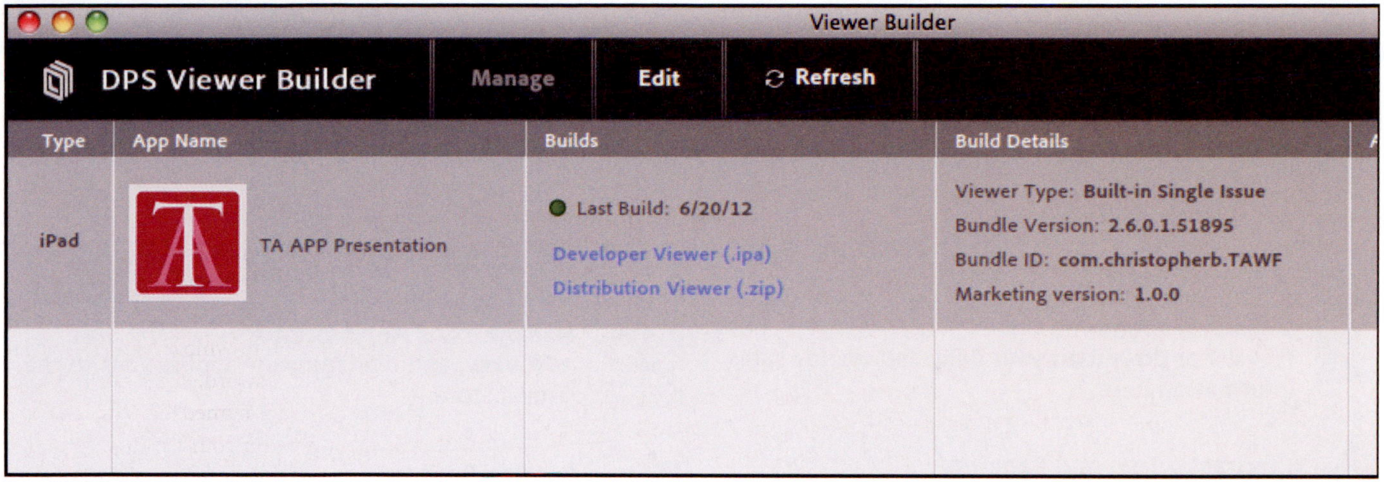

Source Adobe®, Digital Publishing Suite®, 2013.

Figure 36 *Signing dialog box*

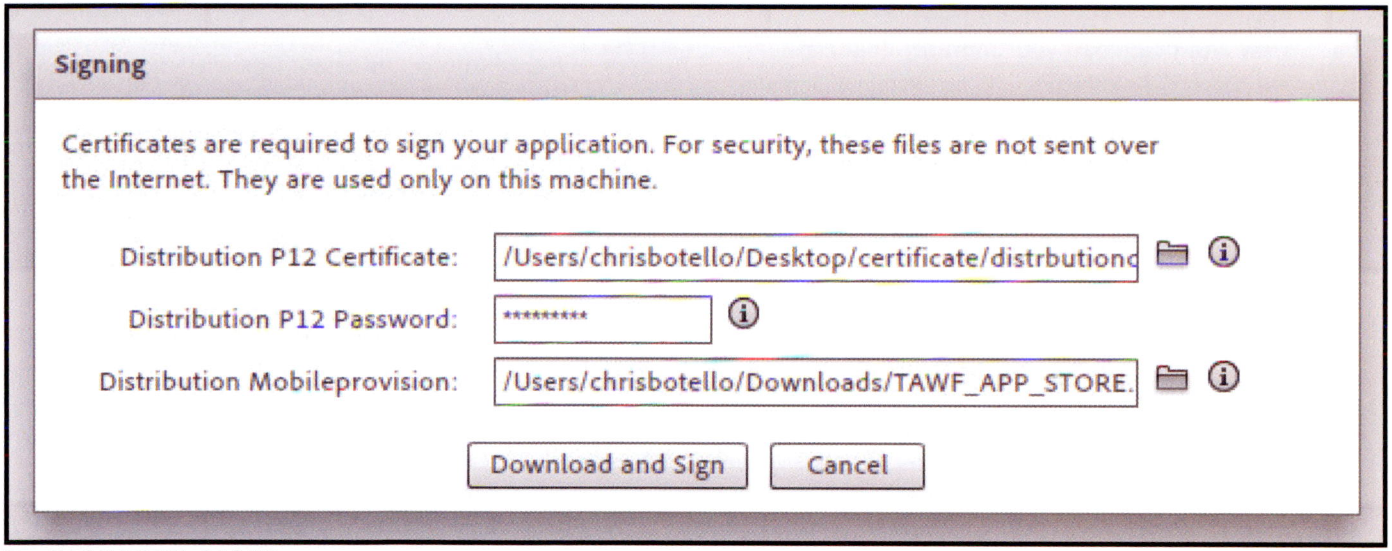

Source Adobe®, Digital Publishing Suite®, 2013.

Uploading Your App to the App Store

Uploading an app to Apple is done using iTunes Connect software. In your browser, go to **https://itunesconnect.apple.com/**. (You can also Google "itunes connect" to get the link.) Once you're there, log in with your Apple ID. The iTunes Connect splash page menu is shown in Figure 37.

Click Manage Your Applications, then click the Add New App button. Enter a name into the Company Name (if you're doing this as an individual, enter your name) then click the Continue button.

Figure 37 *iTunes Connect splash page menu*

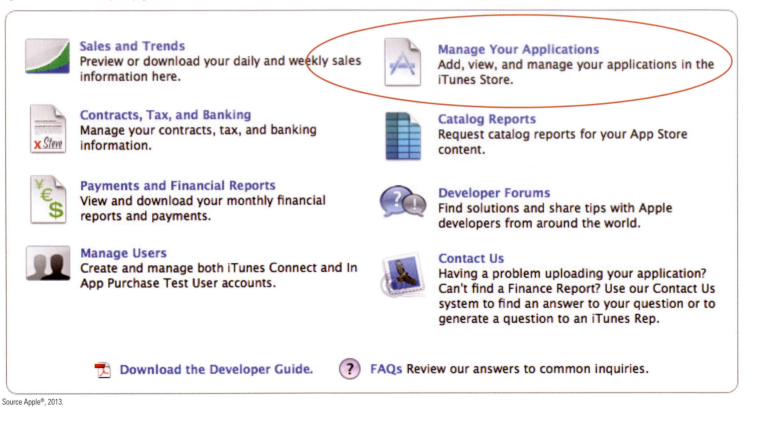

Sales and Trends
Preview or download your daily and weekly sales information here.

Contracts, Tax, and Banking
Manage your contracts, tax, and banking information.

Payments and Financial Reports
View and download your monthly financial reports and payments.

Manage Users
Create and manage both iTunes Connect and In App Purchase Test User accounts.

Manage Your Applications
Add, view, and manage your applications in the iTunes Store.

Catalog Reports
Request catalog reports for your App Store content.

Developer Forums
Find solutions and share tips with Apple developers from around the world.

Contact Us
Having a problem uploading your application? Can't find a Finance Report? Use our Contact Us system to find an answer to your question or to generate a question to an iTunes Rep.

Download the Developer Guide.

? FAQs Review our answers to common inquiries.

Source Apple®, 2013.

Enter your information on the App Information page, then compare your page to Figure 38. Note that the Bundle ID for our app is the same as what was listed in Viewer Builder (see Figure 35).

Click Continue.

In the next screen, enter today's date as the availability date. Enter Free as the Price Tier, then uncheck Discount for Educational Institutions.

Click Continue.

Figure 38 *App information dialog box*

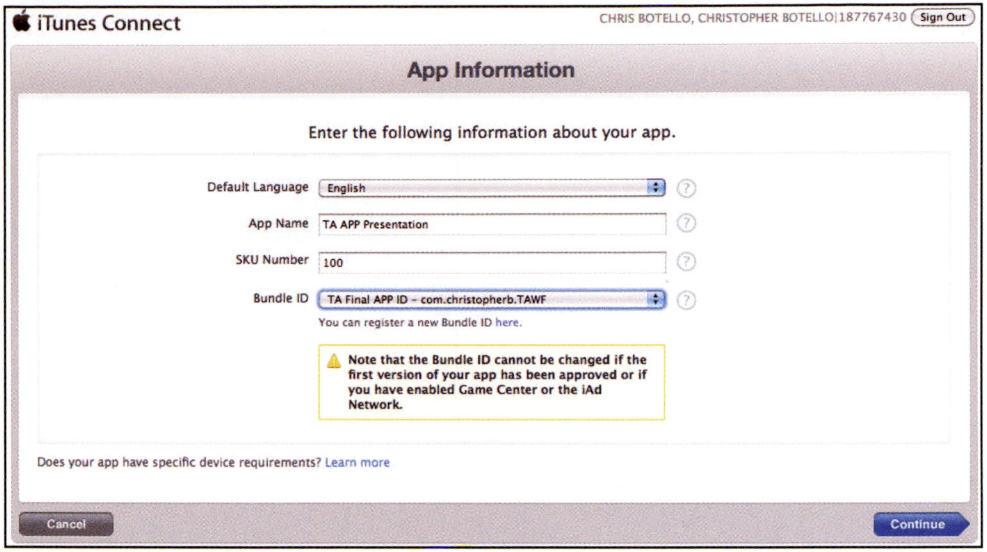

Source Apple®, 2013.

The next screen is very long. Enter your Version information. Figure 39 shows what we entered. Scroll down and fill out the Rating information for your app. Scroll down again, then enter metadata information.

Figure 39 *Our entries for versioning information*

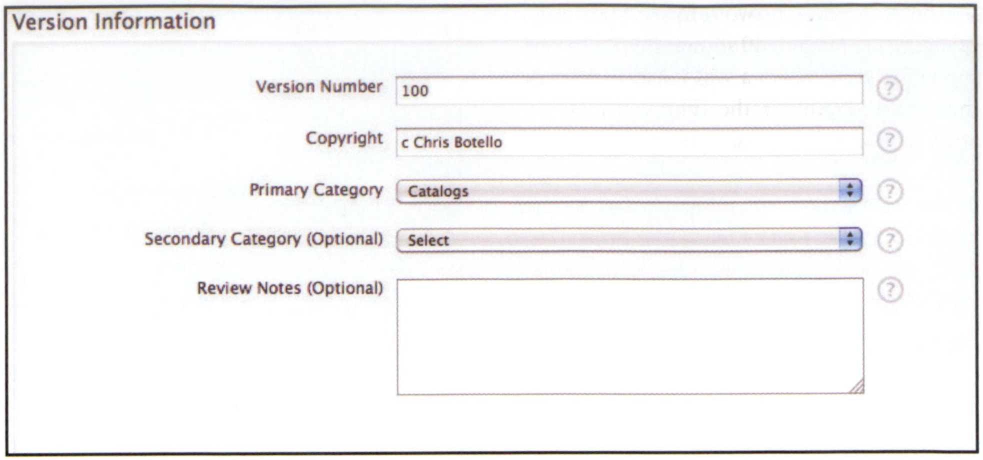

Creating an App and Publishing to the iPad

Scroll down to the Uploads section. Here you will need to link to artwork for an icon and a splash screen. Figure 40 shows that we linked to the 512 × 512 icon, a 960 × 640 version of the splash screen for the iPhone and iPod, and the 1024 × 768 splash screen for the iPad.

Figure 40 *Linking to graphics for the app*

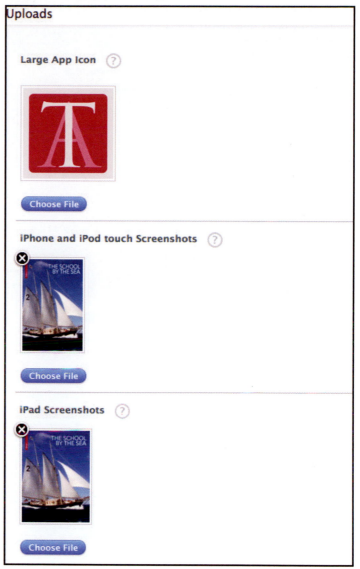

Source Apple®, 2013.

Click the Save button. Doing so takes you to the last page of the module, shown in Figure 41. This summarizes everything you've done in the DPS and Viewer Builder.

Figure 41 *Summary page in iTunes Connect*

Figure 41 *Summary page in iTunes Connect*

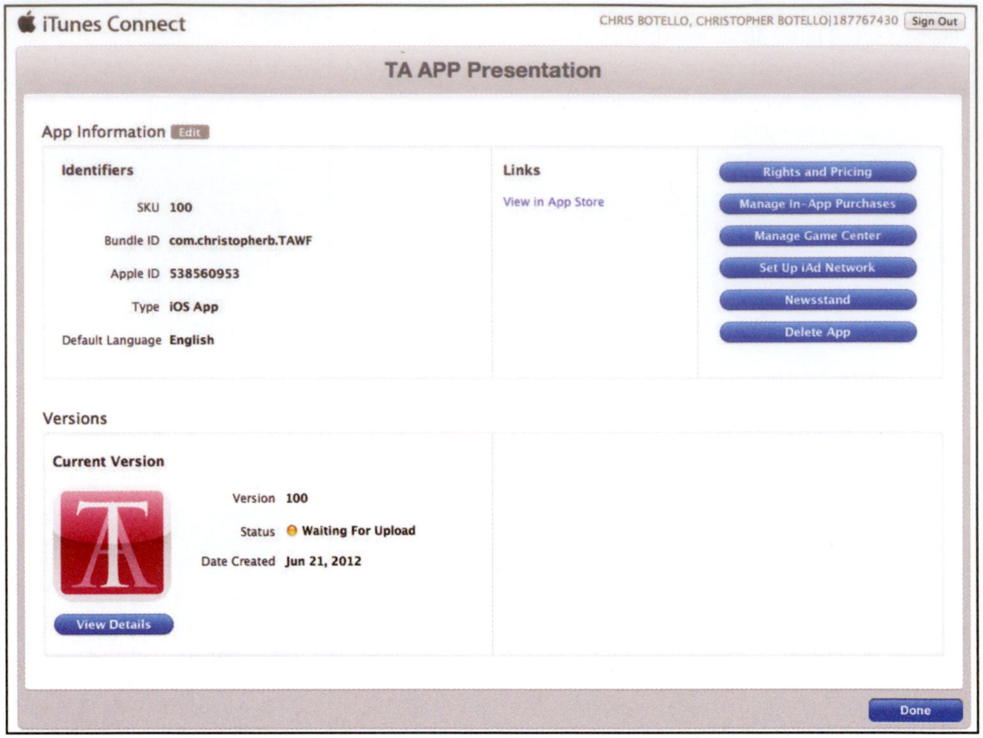

Source Apple®, 2013.

Click the View Details button under the large icon. This takes you to the upload page, shown in Figure 42. Note that the status reads Waiting for Upload.

Click the Ready to Upload Binary button. (The binary being referred to is your .zip file.)

QUICK TIP

If you're asked if your file requires encryption, click No and continue.

Figure 42 *Upload page*

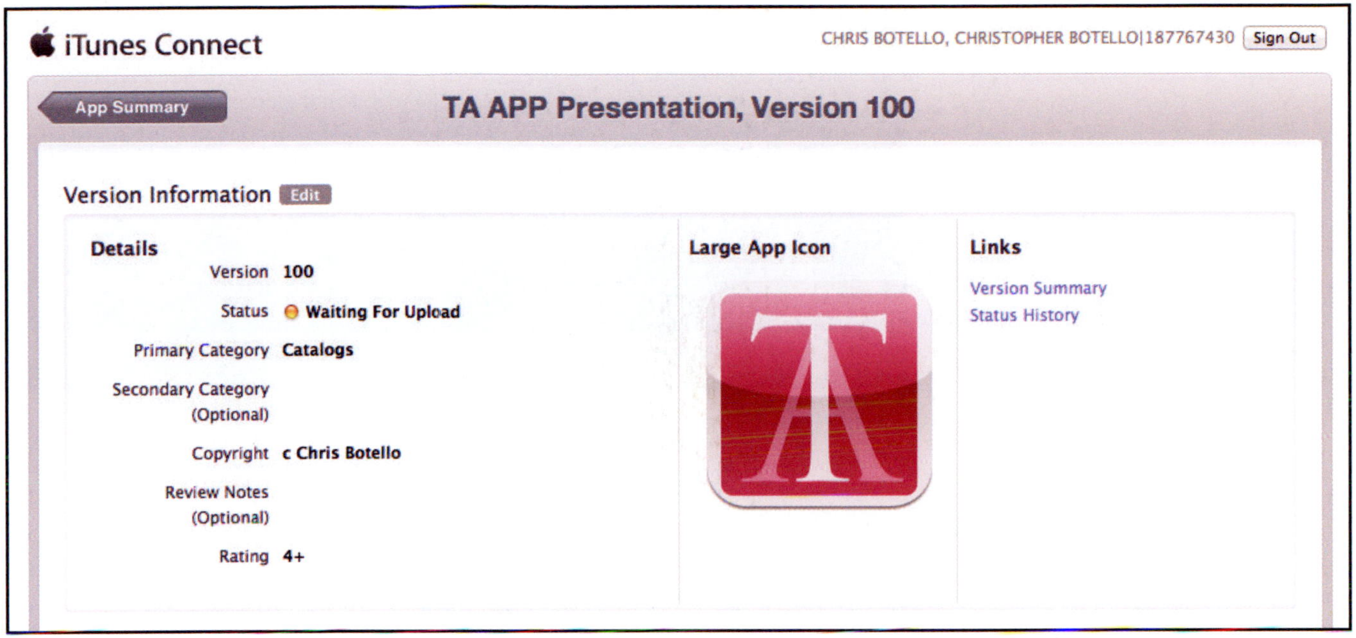

Source Apple®, 2013.

Uploading your .zip file requires a program called Application Loader. If you don't have it installed on your computer, you will see a screen prompting you to download and install Application Loader. Do so, then click Continue.

When Application Loader launches, enter your Apple ID and password. This will take you to the Application Loader welcome page, shown in Figure 43.

Figure 43 *Application Loader welcome page*

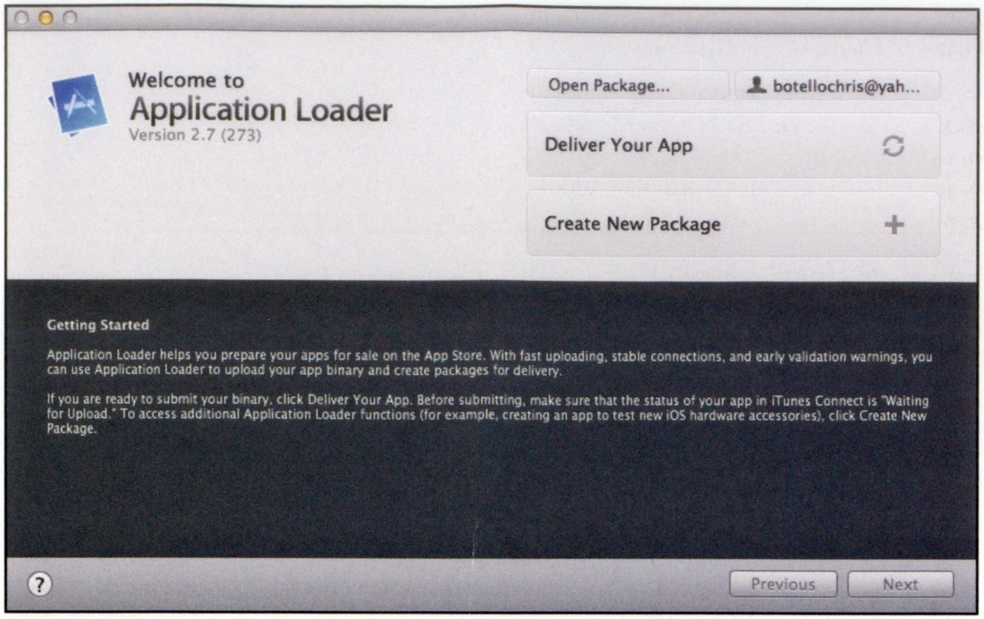

Source Apple®, 2013.

Creating an App and Publishing to the iPad

Click the Deliver Your App button. Load your App into the pull-down menu, as shown in Figure 44, then click the Next button.

In the Application Information window, click the Choose button. Navigate to where you saved the Distribution Viewer.zip file, then click Open. This opens the Adding Application window, shown in Figure 45.

Click the Send button.

Figure 44 *Loading your app into the window*

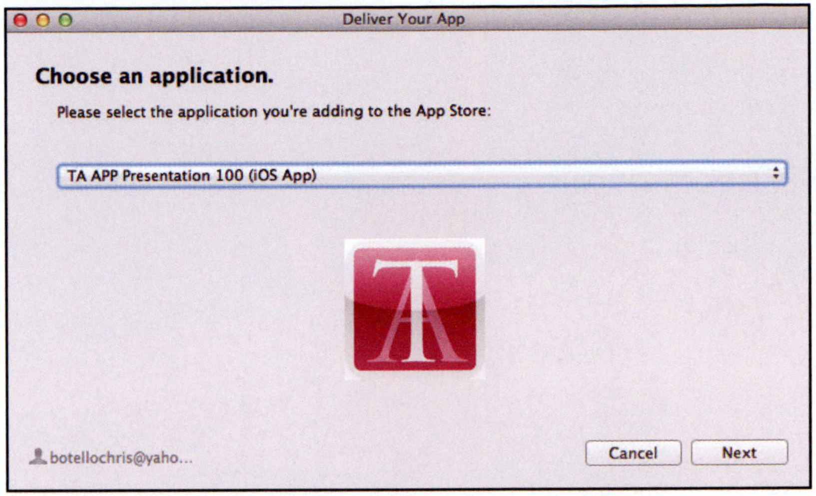

Source Apple®, 2013.

Figure 45 *The Send button becomes available*

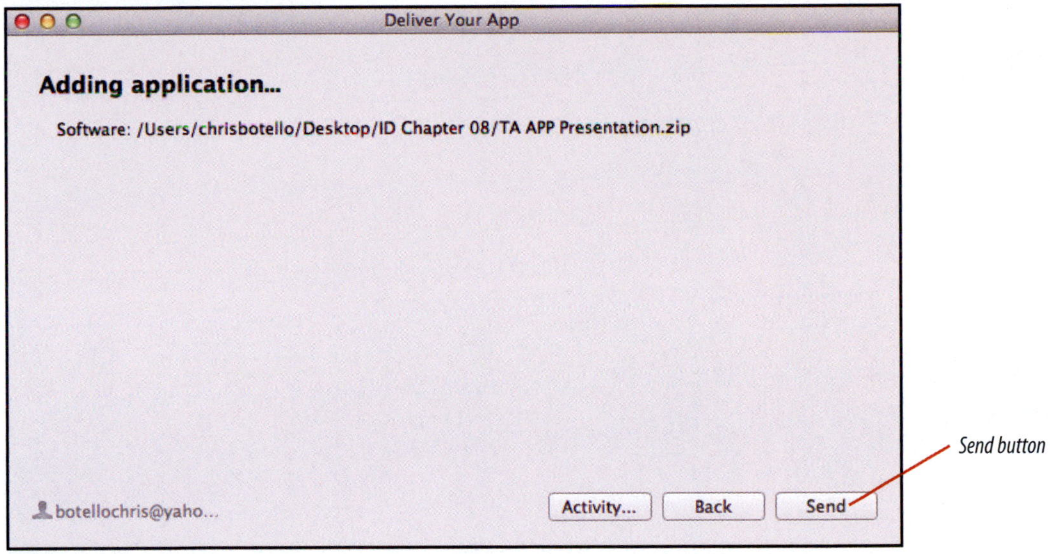

Source Apple®, 2013.

INDESIGN INTERACTIVE			
Chapter	**Data File Supplied**	**Student Creates File**	**Used In**
1	New document	Presentation Document.indd	Lesson 2
	ID 1-1.indd	Italian Presentation.indd	Lessons 3-4
		Italian Presentation.swf	
	New document	Skills Presentation Document.indd	Skills Review
	ID 1-2.indd	Maui Presentation.indd	Skills Review
		Maui.swf	
	ID 1-3.indd	Sample Buttons.indd	Project Builder 1
	Links folder	Sample Buttons.swf	
	Sounds folder		

INDESIGN INTERACTIVE			
Chapter	**Data File Supplied**	**Student Creates File**	**Used In**
2	ID 2-1.indd	Italian Presentation Animated.indd	Lessons 1-4
	ID 2-2.indd	Italian Presentation Animated SR.indd	Skills Review
		Italian Presentation Animated SR.swf	
	ID 2-3.indd	Maui Presentation Animated.indd	Project Builder 1
	Links folder	Maui Presentation Animated.swf	
	Sounds folder		

INDESIGN INTERACTIVE			
Chapter	**Data File Supplied**	**Student Creates File**	**Used In**
3	ID 3-1.indd	Italy Object States.indd	Lessons 1-4
		Italy Object States.html	
		Italy Object States.swf	
	ID 3-2.indd	Interactive Holiday Card	Project Builder 1
	ID 3-3.indd	Retro TV.indd	Project Builder 2
	Links folder	Retro TV.html	
		Retro TV.swf	

INDESIGN INTERACTIVE			
Chapter	**Data File Supplied**	**Student Creates File**	**Used In**
4	ID 4-1.indd	UPLOAD FOLDER	Lesson 3
	Links folder	Document fonts	
		index_Resources folder	
		Links folder	
		ID 4-1 Packaged.indd	
		index.swf	
		index.html	
		Instructions.txt	

INDESIGN INTERACTIVE			
Chapter	**Data File Supplied**	**Student Creates File**	**Used In**
5	ID 5-1.indd	Yearbook Order Form.indd	Lessons 1-6
		Yearbook Order Form.pdf	
		Yearbook Order Form Complete.pdf	
	ID 5-2.indd	Skills Review.indd	Skills Review
	Sunset.jpg	Skills Review.pdf	
		Skills Review Complete.pdf	

INDESIGN INTERACTIVE			
Chapter	**Data File Supplied**	**Student Creates File**	**Used In**
6	ID 6-1.indd	Tabor Lookbook.indd	Lessons 1-4
	Links folder	To iPad folder	
	Cover Images folder		

INDESIGN INTERACTIVE			
Chapter	**Data File Supplied**	**Student Creates File**	**Used In**
7	ID 7-1.indd	Article 01.indd	Lessons 1-6
	ID 7-2.indd	Article 02.indd	
	ID 7-3.indd	Article 03.indd	
	ID 7-4.indd	Article 04.indd	
		Vertical Text.jpg	
		Vertical Text.psd	
	ID 7-5.indd	Article 05.indd	
	ID 7-6.indd	Article 06.indd	Design Project
	Slideshow Images folder	Vertical Transparent BKG Text.psd	
	Links folder		
	Crew Regatta Images folder		
	Crew Mugs folder		
	Cover Images folder		

A

Actions
Applied to buttons, actions indicate what happens in a button event, like clicking on the button or mousing over it.

Alternate layout
A feature in InDesign that allows you to create multiple layouts in a single InDesign document. Alternate layouts are accessed through the Pages panel and are a key feature for creating vertical and horizontal orientation layouts for the iPad.

Animation presets
Predefined animations listed in the Animation panel

App
Software programs that are created for and run on the iPhone and the iPad and usually other non-Apple smart phones and tablet devices

Articles
A single "page" in a folio. Each article in a folio is a single-page InDesign document.

B

Button
Performs actions when an InDesign document is exported to SWF or PDF formats.

Button event
The specific interactive occurrence that triggers the action of a button. Clicking a button is a button event.

Button states
The appearance of a button during various interactions in an exported file; three button states are Normal, Rollover, and Click.

C

Color space
The color model that a software application is using to produce and calculate color. In InDesign, the color space can be CMYK for a printed document and RGB for any onscreen presentation.

Combo box
InDesign button that contains a pull-down list of options that can be chosen in an exported PDF.

D

Digital Publishing Suite (DPS)
Adobe subscription product that you use to upload InDesign folios to the iPad

Digtial Publishing Suite (DPS) Desktop Tools
Adobe software extensions for InDesign; The Folio Builder and Folio Overlays panels in InDesign

Domain Name
A humanly memorable name that people use to identify and access websites. A website and its domain name are the same thing.

Domain name registrars
Ones that administer domain names and sell related domain name services online to the public.

F

Fields
InDesign buttons that can be interacted with as text receptors, check boxes, combo boxes, etc.

File Transfer Protocol (FTP)
Process by which files are transferred from one computer to another. FTP software is used when uploading a website to a web hosting service,

Flash
Adobe's proprietary animation software. All InDesign websites are produced using the Flash file format .SWF. Flash animation is not supported by Apple's iPhone or iPad.

Folio
On the Folio Builder panel, the folio is the complete publication and contains all the articles in the publication.

H

Hyperlink destination
The place to where a hyperlink takes you—in InDesign, the destination can be another InDesign file, an email address, a website, or a page in the same document.

Hyperlink source
The linking element—in InDesign, it can be text, a text frame, or a graphics frame.

I

Image sequence
iPad experience that allows you to place multiple images into a single frame then finger swipe to move forwards and backwards through the images

Internet address suffix
Same thing as a top-level domain (TLD); .com, .net, and .org are all Internet address suffixes

Internet Corporation for Assigned Names and Numbers (ICANN).
Accreditors and managers of domain name registration sites; also oversees a registration database that lists all registrars for all registered domain names.

Internet Protocol (IP) address
A hard-to-remember binary number. An IP address could be anything from a computer that's being used to access the Internet, to a server that's actually hosting a website, to the website itself. In any case, your domain name and your IP address are one in the same.

Internet service provider (ISP)
Vendors that sell web hosting

iOS
Operating system the iPhone and the iPad

iOS Developer program
Subscription-based group that develops apps for the iPhone and iPad

L

Loop
Long-standing video production term referring to when a video repeats automatically, thus creating a never-ending "loop"

M

Monitor resolution
The number of pixels per inch on a monitor screen—standard resolution is 72 pixels per inch

O

Objective-C
Primary computing language iOS developers use to code apps for the iPhone and iPad.

Object States
An InDesign feature that allows you to use a single frame to contain multiple colors and/or multiple images. Object states can work in conjunction with buttons in a scenario that a button triggers a different object state. For iPad presentations, the Object States feature is used in InDesign to create a slideshow of multiple images.

P

Pan and Zoom
Folio overlay that allows you to move an image within a frame to see hidden parts of the image.

PDF
An acronym for Portable Document Format. Allows you to export a single InDesign document as a complete, self-contained file.

Pixels
Smallest component of a computer monitor screen or a digital image. Pixels are also a unit of measurement that can be used in an InDesign layout.

Poster
Like a preview image of a video. In InDesign, the poster is the still frame from a video that shows in a layout when the video is not playing.

R

Radio buttons
Group of buttons in an exported PDF in which only one of the buttons can be chosen.

S

Scrollable text frame
Like a Pan and Zoom for text; iPad experience that allows you to finger swipe as you read so the text scrolls, and you can continue reading.

SWF
An acronym for Shockwave Flash. File format that saves InDesign files—including all animation—and allows it to be viewed through a web browser. Opening an exported SWF file launches Adobe Flash Player, which is free software.

T

Text Fields
InDesign buttons that can be used as receptors for text in an exported PDF.

Top-level domain (TLD)
Same thing as an Internet address suffix: .com, .net, and .org are all TLDs

Transparency blend space
InDesign color setting (RGB or CMYK) that defines the colors of all overlapping transparent areas in an InDesign document when it's output.

U

Uploading
Process by which files are transferred from a computer to the network of computers the ISP is using to host your website

V

Viewer Builder

Adobe software component of the Digital Publishing Suite used to package and produce an app for Apples App Store.

X

X-Code

Apple's proprietary coding environment that iOS developer work within for producing apps for the iPhone and iPad. X-Code works in conjunction with Objective-C

Acrobat Reader, 1–7
actions, adding to buttons, 1–18—19, 1–26—28
Activate dialog box, 8–30
Add New App button, 8–36
Adobe account, creating, 6–6
Adobe Acrobat, 5–34
Adobe Application Manager dialog box, 6–10
Adobe Content Viewer app, 6–4
    installing, 6–7—9
Adobe Reader, 5–34, 5–35
animation(s), 2–1—21
    appear, applying, 2–11
    applying with Animation panel, 2–4—5
    built-in, 1–7
    controlling using Timing panel, 2–14—17
    fade, applying, 2–8—9
    fly-in, applying, 2–6—8
    playing using buttons, 2–18—21
    presets, 2–4—5
    previewing, 2–12—13
    shrink, applying, 2–9—10
Animation panel, 1–7
    applying animations, 2–4—5
app(s)
    Adobe Content Viewer. See Adobe Content Viewer
        app
    App Store. See App Store; exporting folios to
        App Store
    definition, 8–4
    downloading from Viewer Builder, 8–34—35
    exporting folios to App Store. See exporting folios
        to App Store

Objective-C coding language, 8–8
    role, 8–5—7
    submitting to App Store, 8–34—43
    testing, 8–31—33
    uploading to App Store, 8–36—43
App Information dialog box, 8–37
App Store, 8–4, 8–5
    exporting folios to. See exporting folios to App Store
    submitting apps to, 8–34—43
appear animations, applying, 2–11
Apple
    computer, introduction, 1–2
    iOS Developer website, 8–14—16
    iPad. See iPad
    Macintosh computer, 8–9
    purchasing iOS developer license, 8–16—19
    registering as iOS developer, 8–14—16
Application Information window, 8–43
Application Loader, 8–42
Apply to All Spreads button, 1–39
articles
    adding to folios, 6–27—30, 6–32—33
    creating for iPad, 6–12, 6–16—17
Articles Mode, 6–28
    switching between Folios Mode and, 6–30
artwork, converting to buttons, 1–24—25

Background option, Export SWF dialog box, 1–32
buttons
    adding actions, 1–18—19, 1–26—28
    assigning sounds, 1–21, 1–28—29
    assigning to object states, 3–4—6, 3–10—11

converting artwork to, 1–24—25
    creating, 1–15—16
    forms, 5–4—5
    hyperlinks compared, 1–15
    interactive, 7–19—21
    linking to navigation points, 3–25—26,
        3–28—29
    modifying appearances, 1–16—17,
        1–25—26
    playing animations, 2–18—21
    radio buttons. See radio buttons
    Sample Buttons and Forms panel, 1–20
    states, 1–16—17
    Submit Form action, 5–32—33
    video controls, 3–20—23
Buttons and Forms panel, 3–20, 3–21
    adding actions to buttons, 1–18, 1–19
    applying sounds to buttons, 1–29
    changing button appearances, 1–16—17
    check boxes and radio buttons, 5–20—29
    converting artwork to buttons, 1–24
    converting text fields to buttons, 5–5
    creating buttons, 1–15—16

certificates, iOS development, 8–20—21
check boxes, 5–20—21
    formatting fields as, 5–22
Click state, buttons, 1–16, 1–17, 1–26
color(s), fill, button states, 1–16—17
Color Picker, 7–27
color space, 1–5
.com suffix, 4–5

Compression option, Export SWF dialog box, 1–33
covers, Folio Builder panel, 6–32
Create Alternate Layout dialog box, 7–4—6, 7–7—8

data transfer, ISPs, 4–13
Default Format menu, 6–28—29
Deliver Your App button, 8–43
destination, hyperlinks, 1–14
Digital Publishing Suite (DPS), 6–5, 8–8—21
    downloading provisioning information, 8–20—21
    Enterprise Edition, 8–10—11
    obtaining iOS development certificates, 8–20—21
    Professional Edition, 8–11
    purchasing an iOS developer license, 8–16—19
    purchasing subscriptions, 8–12—14
    registering as iOS developer, 8–14—16, 8–20—21
    Single Edition, 8–11
    subscribing, 8–10—12
Digital Publishing Suite (DPS) dashboard
    exporting folios, 8–22—25
    Viewer Builder module, 8–26—31
Digital Publishing Suite Desktop Tools, 6–5
    downloading, 6–9—11
Distribution Viewer (.zip) file, 8–34
DNS (domain name system), 4–5
document(s)
    exported, uploading to web, 4–22—23, 4–28—29
    hyperlinks between pages in, 1–22—23
    interactive. See interactive documents
    packaging, uploading InDesign layouts to web, 4–22, 4–25

setting up for upload to iPad, 6–12—17
traditional, repurposing as InDesign documents, 1–10—11, 1–13
viewing document setup for upload to iPad, 6–14—15
Document Setup dialog box, 1–13, 7–7
document size, repurposing traditional documents as interactive documents, 1–10—11
domain name(s), 4–4—11
    definition, 4–4
    registering, 4–4—5, 4–7—11
domain name registrars, 4–4
domain name system (DNS), 4–5
downloading
    apps from Viewer Builder, 8–34—35
    Digital Publishing Suite Desktop Tools, 6–9—11
DPS. See Digital Publishing Suite (DPS); Digital Publishing Suite (DPS) dashboard
DPS Folio Producer Organizer page, 8–23—24
drawing shapes for buttons, 1–15

e-commerce transactions, 4–5
Ellipse tool, 1–15
email
    ISPs, 4–13
    receiving through websites, 4–5
    website, setting up, 4–17—19
entering data into exported forms, 5–37—41
Export dialog box, 4–26
Export Flash (FLA) dialog box, 1–6
Export option, Export SWF dialog box, 1–31
Export SWF dialog box, 1–7, 1–31—33, 2–17, 4–27
Export to Interactive PDF dialog box, 5–35, 5–37

exported files
    naming, 4–22
    uploading to web, 4–22—23, 4–28—29
exported forms, entering data into, 5–37—41
exporting
    animated documents as SWF files, 2–17
    file size, 1–33
    folios to App Store. See exporting folios to App Store
    image compression, 1–33
    InDesign documents to Flash, 1–6
    InDesign layouts, for upload, 4–26—27
    interactive PDFs, 5–34—35
    "presentation-ready" InDesign documents, 1–6—7
    SWF files, page transitions, 1–31—33, 1–35—36
exporting folios to App Store, 8–22—33
    testing apps, 8–31—33
    Viewer Builder Module, 8–26—31

fade animations, applying, 2–8—9
file formats, saving video, 3–15
file size, exporting documents, 1–33
file transfer protocol (FTP), 4–22
fill colors, button states, 1–16—17
Fill dialog box, Photoshop, 7–27
Fitting commands, 3–13
FLA file format, 1–6
Flash
    exporting InDesign documents to, 1–6
    InDesign related to, 1–5—6
Flatten Transparency option, Export SWF dialog box, 1–33
fly in animations, applying, 2–6—8

folio(s)
    creating folios that will change orientation on
        iPad, 7–10—13
    exporting to App Store. *See* exporting folios to
        App Store
    viewing on iPad, 6–37
Folio Builder panel, 6–11, 6–26–37
    adding articles to folios, 6–27—30,
        6–32—33
    creating covers, 6–32
    creating new folios, 6–26—27, 6–31
    creating thumbnails, 6–30
    exporting folios, 8–22
    naming iPad publications, 6–30, 6–32
    previewing contents, 6–34—36
folio overlays, 6–18—25
    placing sound and video files, 6–18
    playing sound and video files, 6–18—21
    setting up sound files, 6–22—23
    setting up video files, 6–24—25
Folio Overlays panel, 6–18—25
    Pan & Zoom option, 7–14—17
    Scrollable Frame option, 7–25
    Web Content option, 7–36—39
Folio Properties dialog box, 6–32, 7–10—11
Folio Properties panel, 6–30
Folios Mode, 6–27
    switching between Articles Mode and, 6–30
form(s). *See* interactive forms
formatting
    fields as check boxes, 5–22
    pull-down lists, 5–18—19
frame(s)
    placing videos, 3–12—13, 3–16
    playing video from a specific frame, 3–24—26

Frame Rate option, Export SWF dialog box, 1–32—33
frame-within-a-frame trick, 5–7
FTP (file transfer protocol), 4–22

Generate HTML File option, Export SWF dialog box,
    1–32
GoDaddy.com, 4–6, 4–7—11, 4–13

H.264 file format, 3–15
Hide Until triggered option, Buttons and Forms
    panel, 5–21
hiding page transitions icon, 1–31
HTML code, 1–2
HTML files, 4–22—23
hyperlinks, 1–14
    between pages in a document, 1–22—23
    buttons compared, 1–15
    destination, 1–14
    source, 1–14
    viewing in Hyperlinks panel, 1–14
    to a web page, 1–23—24
Hyperlinks panel, 1–14

ICANN (Internet Corporation for Assigned Names and
    Numbers), 4–5
Icons and Splash Screens portal, 8–27
image compression, exporting files, 1–33
image sequences, 7–32—35
Include Interactive Page Curl option, Export SWF
    dialog box, 1–32
InDesign
    documents. *See* document(s)
    evolution, 1–2
    Flash related to, 1–5—6
InDesign Print dialog box, 7–5

index.html files, 4–22
index.swf files, 4–22
installing Adobe Content Viewer app, 6–7—9
interactive buttons, 7–19—21
interactive documents, 1–4—7
    creating, 1–8—9, 1–12
    designing, 5–4—7
    destinations, 1–5
    exporting to Flash, 1–6
    layouts, 5–5, 5–8—11
    "presentation-ready," exporting, 1–6—7
    repurposing traditional documents as,
        1–10—11, 1–13
    traditional documents compared, 1–4
interactive forms, 5–1—43
    buttons, 5–4—5
    check boxes. *See* check boxes
    delivery options, 5–30—33
    designing, 5–4—7
    entering information, 5–37—41
    layout, 5–8—11
    pull-down lists, 5–18—19
    radio buttons. *See* radio buttons
    setting tab order, 5–36
    submitting, 5–42—43
    text input fields, 5–12—17
Interactivity and Media option, Export SWF dialog
    box, 1–32
Internet address suffixes, 4–5
Internet Corporation for Assigned Names and
    Numbers (ICANN), 4–5
Internet Protocol (IP) addresses, 4–4
Internet Service Providers (ISPs), 4–12—13. *See also*
    website hosting
    services provided, 4–13

iOS Developer Program
  obtaining iOS development certificates, 8–20—21
  registering as iOS developer, 8–14—16,
    8–20—21
iOS Provisioning portal page, 8–29, 8–32
IP (Internet Protocol) addresses, 4–4
iPad, 7–1—39
  Adobe Content Viewer app, 6–4, 6–7—9
  alternate layouts, 7–4—6, 7–7—9
  apps. See app(s); exporting folios to App Store
  creating articles for, 6–12, 6–16—17
  creating folios that will change orientation on,
    7–10—13
  folio overlays. See folio overlays
  image sequences, 7–32—35
  incorporating web content, 7–36—39
  object states, 7–18—23
  panning and zooming images, 7–14—17
  publishing to. See publishing to the iPad
  rotating layouts, 7–6
  setting up documents for upload to, 6–12—17
  testing apps, 8–31—33
  uploading to, with Folio Builder. See Folio Builder
    panel
  viewing folios, 6–37
ISPs. See Internet Service Providers (ISPs); website
    hosting
iTunes Connect software, 8–36

Jobs, Steve, 1–2, 8–9
JPEG Quality option, Export SWF dialog box, 1–33

layouts
  alternate, for iPad, 7–4—6, 7–7—9
  for iPad, rotating, 7–6

InDesign, exporting for upload, 4–26—27
interactive documents, 5–5, 5–8—11
scrollable text frames, 7–24—25
uploading to web. See uploading InDesign layouts
    to web
license, iOS developer, purchasing, 8–16—19
Link Stories check box, Create Alternate Layout dialog
    box, 7–4—5
Liquid Page Rule options, Create Alternate Layout
    dialog box, 7–5
loops, video, 3–13
lossy compression, 1–33

mailto: Submit Form action, 5–32
Media panel, 3–13—14, 3–17
  Navigation Points section, 3–24—25, 3–27
monitor resolution, 1–9
.mp4 file format, 3–15

naming
  exported files, 4–22
  iPad publications, 6–30, 6–32
  object states, 3–6
navigation points, 3–24—29
  creating, 3–27—28
  linking buttons, 3–25—26, 3–28—29
  playing video from a specific frame, 3–24—26
New Article dialog box, 6–28, 6–32, 7–6,
    7–7
New dialog box, Photoshop, 7–26
New Document dialog box, 1–8—9, 1–12, 6–12,
    6–13
New Folio dialog box, 6–26—27, 6–31, 7–10
New Hyperlink dialog box, 1–22
Normal state, buttons, 1–16, 1–17

object states, 3–2, 3–4—11, 7–18—23
  assigning buttons, 3–4—6, 3–10—11
  creating, 3–7—9
  creating slideshows, 7–21—23
  descriptive names, 3–6
  iPad, 7–18—23
Object States panel, 3–4, 3–5, 3–7
Objective-C coding language, 8–8
Options menu, 3–20, 3–21

Package Publication dialog box, 6–16
packaging documents, uploading InDesign layouts to
    web, 4–22, 4–25
Page Click event, 2–15
page size, 1–9
Page Size menu, 1–9
page transitions, 1–30—39
  adding, 1–30—31, 1–34
  applying to all pages in a document, 1–39
  applying to selected pages, 1–31
  exporting SWF files, 1–31—33, 1–35—36
  removing, 1–39
  testing interactive settings in SWF files,
    1–37—38
page transitions icon, hiding, 1–31
Page Transitions option, Export SWF dialog box,
    1–32
Page Transitions panel, 1–30, 1–31, 1–34
Pages panel, 1–30
Pan & Zoom option, Folio Overlays panel, 7–14—17
panning images, 7–14—17
PDF. See Portable Document Format (PDF)
Pen tool, 1–15
Photoshop
  creating text files, 7–26—28

Fill dialog box, 7–27
New dialog box, 7–26
pinch/split, 7–14
pixels, 1–9
Place command, 3–12
placing videos, 3–12—13, 3–16
Play from Navigation Point command, 3–26
playing
    animations, buttons, 2–18—21
    audio and video files, Folio Overlays panel,
        6–18—21
Portable Document Format (PDF), 1–6—7
    interactive, exporting, 5–34—35
positioning text, 5–6—7
posters, 3–13—14, 3–17
"presentation-ready" InDesign documents,
        exporting, 1–6—7
preset(s), animations, 2–4—5
preset controls, adding to video, 3–14—15,
        3–18—19
previewing
    animations, 2–12—13
    contents in Folio Builder panel, 6–34—36
provisioning files, iOS development, 8–20—21,
        8–29, 8–32
P12 Developer certificate, 8–32
Publish Folio window, 8–25
publishing to the iPad, 6–1–37, 8–1—43
    apps, 8–4—7
    Digital Publishing Suite. See Digital Publishing
        Suite (DPS)
    Digital Publishing Suite Desktop Tools, 6–5,
        6–9—11
    exporting folios to App Store. See exporting folios
        to App Store

individuals as publishers, 8–7
naming publications, 6–30, 6–32
submitting apps to App Store, 8–34—43
pull-down lists, 5–18—19

radio buttons, 5–21
    creating, 5–23
    using as triggers, 5–21, 5–24—29
Rasterize Pages option, Export SWF dialog box, 1–33
Ready to Upload Binary button, 8–41
Rectangle tool, 1–15
registering domain names, 4–4—5, 4–7—11
removing page transitions, 1–39
Resolution option, Export SWF dialog box, 1–33
Rollover state, buttons, 1–16, 1–17, 1–25
rotating layouts for iPad, 7–6

Sample Buttons and Forms panel, 1–20
saving video, 3–15
Scrollable Frame option, Folio Overlays panel, 7–25
scrollable text frames, 7–24—31
Select Email Client dialog box, 5–43
selecting artwork for buttons, 1–15
Selection tool, 1–15
Shazam, 8–4
Shockwave Flash files. See SWF (Shockwave Flash)
        files
shrink animations, applying, 2–9—10
Signing dialog box, 8–31, 8–35
Size option, Export SWF dialog box, 1–32
slideshow(s), creating using object states,
        7–21—23
Slideshow panel, 7–18
Smooth Scrolling option, Folio Builder panel, 6–29
sound(s), assigning to buttons, 1–21, 1–28—29

sound files
    folio overlays. See folio overlays
    uploading to web, 4–23—24, 4–30—31
source, hyperlinks, 1–14
specifying images, 3–13—14, 3–17
splash screens, 8–27—28
states, buttons, 1–16—17
Submit Build button, 8–29—30
Submit Form action, buttons, 5–32—33
submitting apps to App Store, 8–34—43
    downloading apps from Viewer Builder, 8–34—35
submitting interactive forms, 5–42—43
subscriptions, Digital Publishing Suite, purchasing,
        8–12—14
SWF (Shockwave Flash) files, 1–7, 4–22, 4–23
    exporting animated documents as, 2–17
    exporting interactive documents as, 1–6
    testing interactive settings in, 1–37—38
    uploading, 4–23—24
SWF Output dialog box, 1–35
SWF Preview panel, 2–12—13
swipe, 7–14

tab order, setting for interactive forms, 5–36
Tab Order dialog box, 5–36
tablet readers. See iPad; publishing to the iPad
testing
    apps, 8–31—33
    interactive settings in SWF files, 1–37—38
text, positioning, 5–6—7
text fields, creating, 5–5—6
text files, creating in Photoshop, 7–26—28
text frame(s), scrollable, 7–24—31
Text Frame Options dialog box, 5–10
text input fields, interactive forms, 5–12—17

Text option, Export SWF dialog box, 1–33
thumbnails, Folio Builder panel, 6–30
time code, standard format, 3–13
Timing panel, 2–14—17
top-level domain (TLD), 4–5
traditional documents
    interactive documents compared, 1–4
    repurposing as interactive documents,
        1–10—11, 1–13
transitions. *See* page transitions
transparency blend space, repurposing traditional
        documents as interactive documents, 1–11
triggers, using radio buttons as, 5–21, 5–24—29

Units & Increments dialog box, 1–10—11
uploading
    apps to App Store, 8–36—43
    definition, 4–22
    InDesign layouts to web. *See* uploading InDesign
        layouts to web
uploading InDesign layouts to web, 4–22—31
    exported InDesign documents, 4–22—23,
        4–28—29
    packaging documents, 4–22, 4–25
    sound files, 4–22—24, 4–30—31
    video files, 4–23—24, 4–30—31

video, 3–2
    adding preset controls, 3–14—15, 3–18—19
    folio overlays. *See* folio overlays
    loops, 3–13
    placing, 3–12—13, 3–16
    playing from a specific frame, 3–24—26
    posters, 3–13—14
    saving, 3–15
    specifying images, 3–13—14, 3–17
    uploading to web, 4–23—24, 4–30—31
video controls
    buttons, 3–20—23
    navigation points, 3–24—29
    preset, adding, 3–14—15, 3–18—19
Video menu, 3–20
View SWF after Exporting option, Export SWF dialog
        box, 1–32
Viewer Builder module, 8–26—31
    downloading apps, 8–34—35
Viewer Builder portal, 8–26—28
viewing
    document setup for upload to iPad, 6–14—15
    folios on iPad, 6–37
    hyperlinks in Hyperlinks panel, 1–14
    live websites, 4–31
    websites in frame on iPad, 7–36—39

web, uploading InDesign layouts. *See* uploading
        InDesign layouts to web
Web Content option, Folio Overlays panel,
        7–36—39
web pages, hyperlinks to, 1–23—24
website(s), 4–1—31
    creating, 4–5—6
    delivering forms, 5–30, 5–32—33
    hosting. *See* website hosting
    live, viewing, 4–31
    receiving email through, 4–5
    registering domain names, 4–4—5, 4–7—11
    uploading InDesign layouts. *See* uploading
        InDesign layouts to web
    viewing in frame on iPad, 7–36—39
website hosting, 4–12—21
    purchasing, 4–12—13, 4–14—17
    setting up account, 4–13, 4–20—21
    website email, 4–13, 4–17—19
whois protocol, 4–5
Wozniak, Steve, 1–2

X-Code, 8–20

.zip (Distribution Viewer) file, 8–34
zooming images, 7–14—17